HEMINGWAY

The Writer as Artist

BY CARLOS BAKER

HEMINGWAY

THE WRITER AS ARTIST

PRINCETON, NEW JERSEY

PRINCETON UNIVERSITY PRESS

TO ARTHUR AND EDNA BAKER

Preface to the Fourth Edition

Times change, and one's knowledge changes with them. The first edition of this book came out in 1952, too early to include a chapter on *The Old Man and the Sea*. The second edition in 1956 remedied this omission with a long chapter on this last of Hemingway's books to appear in his lifetime. His death in the summer of 1961 led in 1963 to a third edition, which incorporated yet another chapter on the last years of his life. Since that time two major books have been given posthumous publication: *A Moveable Feast* in 1964 and the novel, *Islands in the Stream*, in 1970. One reason for the present fourth edition is to provide an opportunity for discussion of these books.

Another reason, not less compelling, is my wish to revise the original opening chapters, which have come over the years to need restatement. When the first edition was in preparation, Hemingway was firmly opposed to my including anything biographical. In agreeing to omit most such references in return for his help with information relating to his books, I cleared the first two chapters with him so that he could be assured that I was sticking to my end of the bargain. But in 1951, when most of this work was done, he was far too busy with his own affairs to give these chapters more than cursory attention, and he allowed errors to remain which he, and he alone, was in a position to correct. Although he afterwards apologized for this omission, and remained fairly well disposed toward the bulk of the book during the rest of his life, it was not until I was far into research for his biography that the relative inadequacy of the first two chapters became apparent. They have now been completely revised, incorporating some new material discovered since the publication of my biography in 1969. So, while the content of Chapters III-XIII remains essentially unchanged, except for the correction of errors, the first two and the last two chapters, totalling roughly a quarter of the whole, are new.

My thanks are due to Charles Scribner, Jr., Datus C. Smith, Jr., Herbert S. Bailey, Jr., Mrs. Ernest Hemingway, and my wife, Dorothy S. Baker, as well as to the many hundreds of others who have helped to make both my biographical and critical studies as free from error as I now hope they are. The checklist at the end of the book, revised by Professor William White for the third edition, remains substantially unchanged. It is included for the convenience of the reader who may need it for quick reference, although Audre Hanneman's comprehensive bibliography, published by Princeton University Press in 1967, is now the standard reference work for writings by and about Hemingway.

CARLOS BAKER

Princeton, New Jersey
August 15, 1971

ON THE FOOTNOTES

Full citation, with place and date of publication, is usually given only in the first reference to each book. Further references use the short title. Hemingway's letters to the author are indicated by the abbreviation *EH to CB*, with date. His letters to or from Maxwell Perkins and Fitzgerald are indicated by *EH to MP* and *EH to FSF* or the reverse, with date or approximate date. Other letters are cited and dated for the record.

The following abbreviations have been generally used:

AMF: A Moveable Feast
ARIT: Across the River and Into the Trees
DIA: Death in the Afternoon
FTA: A Farewell to Arms
FWBT: For Whom the Bell Tolls
GHOA: Green Hills of Africa
IITS: Islands in the Stream
OMATS: The Old Man and the Sea
SAR: The Sun Also Rises
THAHN: To Have and Have Not
First 49: The Fifth Column and the First Forty-Nine Stories

The last of these items, the collected short stories, has been preferred to the separate editions of the short stories for purposes of page reference. Other references, unless so indicated, are to the first American editions of Hemingway's books.

Contents

Introduction

"If I desire to pass over a part in silence," wrote Claudian in his account of Stilicho the consul, "whatever I omit will seem the most worthy to have been recorded. Shall I pursue his old exploits and early youth? His recent merits recall the mind to themselves. Shall I dwell on his justice? The glory of the warrior rises before me resplendent. Shall I relate his strength in arms? He performed yet greater things unarmed." [1]

Because this is a book about Hemingway as an artist, it contains relatively little on his old exploits and his early youth. His strong sense of justice, like his pugnaciousness, receives only incidental consideration. There is little about his prowess as hunter or fisherman, as boxer, bullfighter, or soldier. This is not the history of his private battles or his public wars. Taken together and truly related, these would make a proper story, and in some respects a heroic one. But this is not the present purpose.

These pages tell, instead, another story of at least equal interest to any who are seriously concerned about the course of modern literature, or about the relation, in our generation, of the artist to society. This is the story of what Hemingway was able to perform—unarmed but for the good writer's indispensable weapons of brain and heart—during the forty years of his life as an artist, 1921–1961.

The first two chapters offer an account of his expatriate beginnings on the continent of Europe during the period 1921-1925. The emphasis here is on his literary activities, and it is hard to overstate the importance of the European experience in Hemingway's development as an artist. Here in 1918 he had passed through an ordeal by mortar-burst which struck him with the force of revelation. Here he returned in the post-war years to complete the first phases of his adult education. Here he

[1] *De Laud. Stilic.*, i, 13.

taught himself to write, supporting himself by work for newspaper syndicates, exploring the continent as far east as Asia Minor, and joining (partly for economic reasons) that band of serious British and American artists which had then gathered on the Left Bank of the Seine. Within this particular framework his early publications are discussed and evaluated.

The heart of the book is an attempt to examine Hemingway's mature work in detail, as a whole, and outside the critical stereotype of that work which has grown up in the past twenty-five years. Chapter three provides an outline of the practical esthetic assumptions with which Hemingway began and from which, with various additions and modifications, he ever afterwards operated. Chapters four and five analyze the two remarkable novels, *The Sun Also Rises* and *A Farewell to Arms*. By means of these books Hemingway's reputation as a serious writer of fiction was established and consolidated. But their chief importance is other than historical: it is moral and esthetic. They reveal, upon close analysis, a whole side to Hemingway's art which could be called "new" if it had not been there all the time—a substructure of symbolic meanings which has gone unrecorded, and for the most part unobserved, by a majority of those who have written about Hemingway.

The first forty-five stories, representing his parallel achievement in short fiction through the year 1932, provide the substance of chapter six. Although these vary in content and in quality (I dislike, for example, such pieces as "Today Is Friday" and "One Reader Writes"), the best of them provide important additional evidence that Hemingway's contribution to American writing has been unique. They develop a complexity of symbolic action and a structural sturdiness which it is the task of this chapter to demonstrate.

Chapters seven through nine cover the experimental work in fiction and non-fiction from 1932 through 1937. It is a commonplace of Hemingway criticism to say that during these five years Hemingway retrogressed as an artist. This period was ushered in by *Death in the Afternoon,* the somewhat discursive non-fictional bible of the bullfight. Critics who are committed to the notion that Hemingway's descent began after *A Farewell to*

Arms have sometimes cited the bullfight book in evidence. The period in question was brought to a close by *The Fifth Column,* Hemingway's unsuccessful invasion of the dramatic medium. Between these two dates came the *Green Hills of Africa,* a second experiment in non-fiction which is often (and I think erroneously) described as a failure, and *To Have and Have Not,* which Hemingway himself once described with some reservations as a procedural error—an attempt, that is, to make a novel out of what ought to have remained a novelette about a Key West soldier of fortune named Harry Morgan. As none of Hemingway's previous work in fiction had done, this book showed a tendency to split down the middle, and certain of its seams were noticeably ragged. It not only lacked the intricate and emotionated substructure by which *The Sun Also Rises, A Farewell to Arms,* and even the *Green Hills of Africa* were sustained, but it was also written (unlike his other fiction) at disparate intervals over a three- or four-year period.

What these five years prove, however, is that between the times of his greatest achievements the true artist does not die out. Nor does he necessarily retrogress, though at the time, and in the light of the books that have preceded any new effort, there may be an *appearance* of retrogression. Nor does the artist necessarily progress, either, though everything a good artist does experimentally in such times as these is likely to serve him, either positively or negatively (as something, say, that he discovers will or will not work), in coming to his future writing. If the artist neither dies out, nor retrogresses, nor progresses, during such a period, what does he do? The answer might well be that he consolidates his holdings. Or that he seeks to strengthen or enlarge his esthetic grasp. Or that he undertakes to increase his dexterity with the instruments of his trade. Or that he tries new subjects— always experimentally—or tries for new effects to see if now he can bring them off. In such a time he prepares, though not always consciously, for a future time when all his powers, and all that he has learned of pros and cons, will collaborate to some greater end, as happened with Hemingway during the writing of *For Whom the Bell Tolls* in 1939–1940.

The discussion of these interim books, in chapters seven,

eight, and nine, has tacitly assumed that the job of the critic, appraising such work, is first of all to understand, as well as he can, the artist's situation. It is not to hold the artist up to scorn or to accuse him of meretriciousness, unless of course he has been demonstrably guilty of selling out to the writer's perennial foes. The job is rather to separate out the elements of success and the elements of failure, to account as well as possible for the existence of both, and to take note of any technical (or other) experiments which such an interim period may have produced. It is finally to recognize, what is not always immediately apparent, that each individual writer has his individual law of progress, and must be allowed to move in his own way in the performance of whatever wonders it is given him to perform— a point especially applicable to Hemingway.

If he honestly sets himself this kind of job, the student of Hemingway's work during the period 1932–1937 will find much to interest and instruct him, and much on which it is possible to set a high (if not the highest) value. This time was not for Hemingway a *belle époque* in the field of full-length fiction. It may well be significant that in 1932 Hemingway's belief in the short-story form underwent a marked revival. He so wrote Maxwell Perkins, his editor at Scribner's, on February 24 of that year, and the interest was still visible several years later. Until he got far enough into it to see the possibilities for more extended development, the *Green Hills of Africa* took in his mind the shape of a long short story. The Morgan episodes which form the real groundwork (and the only firm part) of *To Have and Have Not* were first conceived and first written as three short stories. If the critic approaches the interim period as preeminently a time when Hemingway was experimenting with the short-story form, he may come to recognize a steady series of excellent works in this genre, culminating in the spring of 1936 with the completion of "The Short Happy Life of Francis Macomber" and "The Snows of Kilimanjaro."

The author of such stories as these can hardly be said to have been in a state of decay. Instead, he had shifted his perspectives from longer to shorter fictional forms, while on two occasions he undertook to explore the possibilities of non-fiction. From

Hemingway's point of view, at any rate, *Death in the Afternoon* was not so much the beginning of his artistic decline as the fulfillment of a plan of seven years' standing. He wished to write a book on the bullfight which might help to "educate" non-aficionados into the intricacies of Spain's national spectacle. The result may well be what Malcolm Cowley calls it: the best book on the subject in any language. Hemingway himself was rather more modest in his claims for the volume. For the student of Hemingway, however, the book has the special value of shedding light down into the deeper reaches of his esthetic theory, and in particular on that conception of tragedy (neither Greek nor Elizabethan) which stands at the center of his art. The book also throws light on his conception of the nature of the hero.

If one looks at his second experiment in non-fiction, it might be argued that the technical brilliance of the *Green Hills of Africa* can not compensate for the fact that its subject-matter— a hunting expedition in Tanganyika—lacks the seriousness and the magnitude which Aristotle prescribes. Yet even if one ignores the difficulty of the technical problems there faced and smoothly overcome, he ought probably to recognize that few writers have been able to match the graphic vitality of Hemingway's presentation of the land, the natives, and the animals. Taken in these terms, and on its own experimental grounds, the *Green Hills* is not a very good example of retrogression, though one may very much prefer to read *The Sun Also Rises* and *A Farewell to Arms*.

Ten years after his completion of *A Farewell to Arms* in January, 1929, Hemingway was ready again for a major effort in the field of long fiction. What he had learned in the interim period of experimentation with short fiction and non-fiction now stood him in good stead. The result of the new effort was *For Whom the Bell Tolls*. The tenth chapter of this present work attempts to make a double explication—of the texture and structure of this novel, and of the situation of mind and heart from which it grew. If it is not a perfect novel, and this point is open to argument, *For Whom the Bell Tolls* is something better, a genuinely great novel. The aim of chapter ten is to show on what grounds this is so.

The eleventh chapter comes round, at the end of a thirty-year revolution, to the mid-century novel, *Across the River and Into the Trees*. Begun, like the *Green Hills of Africa*, as a long short story, the book gradually developed into a short novel. The fact that it was his next published book after *For Whom the Bell Tolls* placed it in the strategically vulnerable position which always results when a lesser novel follows a greater one. Moreover, it was built upon a conception quite different from that which had informed the novel of the Spanish war. It occupied a different genre within the broad range of possibilities which fiction may legitimately invoke. If *For Whom the Bell Tolls* moved in the direction of the epic, *Across the River and Into the Trees* moved in the direction of the lyric. As had happened with Hemingway throughout the 1930's, this book was a new experiment. It was not designed to resemble *For Whom the Bell Tolls* any more than, say, *To Have and Have Not* was designed as a recapitulation in different language of the themes of *A Farewell to Arms*. It was meant to say something new and different from what had been said in any of the preceding books. Also, and the point was worth noticing, it was a kind of preliminary precipitation of materials with which Hemingway would be dealing in various ways in the large novel which he interrupted in order to complete *Across the River*. This had happened once before in his career: *Death in the Afternoon* was a preliminary treatment of some of the materials which would enter into the composition of *For Whom the Bell Tolls*. The translation of Spain and the Spanish into an art form could not come all at once; it needed to pass through several stages of formulation. Similarly, Hemingway could not translate some of the experiences of World War II directly into an art form without certain intermediate steps. *Across the River* was in this sense an interim experiment looking towards the larger work that was still to come. But in another sense it was a backward look through two world wars and thirty years of experience, and an attempt to pull together in the form of a lyrical utterance the spiritual essence of those years.

Although the novel shows serious faults of communication, and although it apparently was unable to overcome by itself the prejudices it evidently aroused, it is nonetheless a more serious, substantial, and complicated piece of work than seems to have been generally recognized. It is a rough and tender fable of an earthly purgatory, and a kind of earthly paradise, with some few inscapes of an earthly inferno along the way. If the idiom is Hemingway's, the mood is Dantesque. So regarding it, and always admitting the book's tentative and preliminary aspect, as well as its reminiscential nature, one may come to think of the Venetian novel as a lesser completing agency in a long cycle of Hemingway's work. The eleventh chapter attempts an exposition of these points.

The twelfth chapter, on the ancient mariner Santiago and his domesday adventure in the Gulf Stream north of Cuba, shows Hemingway once more in masterful action, manipulating, this time, a continuous but unobtrusive parallel between the experiences of his heroic old fisherman and those empirical aspects of the life of Christ which center on the hill of Calvary. "O cunning enemy," cries Angelo in *Measure for Measure*, "that to catch a saint, with saints dost bait thy hook." The shades not only of the Son of Man but also of Christian fathers like Saint Martin and Saint Francis, Saint Peter and Saint James, may be discerned in the background of this remarkable study of stoical endurance. Here also, and more successfully than in *Across the River*, one finds a moving employment of the contrast between youth and age. Once again the technique of the *paysage moralisé*, brought to so high a point of development with the mountain-and-plains imagery of the earlier novels, is used to strengthen the natural striking-power of Santiago's tragic story. Once more, and crowningly now, the novel provides a memorable demonstration of Hemingway's skill in joining nature and art, the truth of things and the poetry of things, a skill of which the present critical study has tried to take the measure.

Between the appearance of *The Old Man and the Sea* in 1952 and the death of Hemingway nine years later, he did not see fit to submit any major work for publication. The airplane accidents in Africa at the beginning of 1954 hurt him so severely that he was unable to go personally to Sweden later that year to receive the Nobel Prize for Literature. Following his recuperation, he busied himself as collaborator and adviser in the preparation of the film version of *The Old Man and the Sea,* made a number of vacation trips to Spain in order to follow the fortunes of the matador Ordoñez, and in the summer of 1960, just before his final visit to Spain, gave up his Cuban establishment at San Francisco de Paula partly because of the steady deterioration of Cuban-American political relations. At the time of his death in July 1961, he had taken up residence in a house on the outskirts of Ketchum, Idaho. A summary of these years from 1952-1961 is the subject of chapter thirteen.

An examination of *A Moveable Feast,* Hemingway's non-fiction memoir of Paris in the 1920s, and of the three-part novel, *Islands in the Stream,* relating to his life at Bimini, in Cuba, and at sea in the period 1936-1943, appears in chapters fourteen and fifteen. Apart from his book-length account of Ordoñez and Dominguin, which he called *The Dangerous Summer, A Moveable Feast* and *Islands in the Stream* were the volumes which Hemingway himself regarded as most deserving of publication in the sense that, with some editing and cutting, they could be brought out virtually as he left them at the time of his death.

HEMINGWAY
The Writer as Artist

I · The Slopes of Montparnasse

"This is to tell you about a young man named Ernest Hemingway, who lives in Paris (an American), writes for the *transatlantic review* and has a brilliant future . . . I'd look him up right away. He's the real thing."—Fitzgerald to Perkins, 1924.[1]

I. EUROPE

Herman Melville called the sea his Harvard and his Yale. Ernest Hemingway's college and *gradus ad Parnassum* was the continent of Europe. His first sight of it was from the deck of a battered old transport called the *Chicago*, which discharged its load of American Red Cross ambulance drivers at Bordeaux early in June, 1918. Within a few days they were all on their way to northern Italy and a barracks in the wool-manufacturing town of Schio under the shadow of the Dolomites. For the remaining weeks in June Hemingway drove a Fiat ambulance, carrying Italian wounded down the hairpin turns of Mount Pasubio. Even this was not enough to satisfy his adventurous spirit, and he volunteered to run a Red Cross canteen in the Piave River Valley. He had hardly established himself in this new post among the mud and the mosquitoes when an Austrian trench mortar and a heavy machine gun wounded him so severely in the legs and feet that his continental education was nearly concluded before it had well begun.

The date of his wounding was the midnight of July 8, and the place a network of trenches and dugouts near the shell-wrecked town of Fossalta-di-Piave. He distinguished himself by carrying a badly wounded Italian comrade to the rear before he collapsed and was taken over by the stretcher bearers. Four days before his nineteenth birthday, he was admitted to the American Red Cross

[1] F. Scott Fitzgerald to Maxwell Perkins, before 10/18/24. Andrew Turnbull, ed., *The Letters of F. Scott Fitzgerald*, New York, 1963, p. 167.

Hospital on the Via Manzoni in Milan. There he idled out the summer and fall, at first holding court from his hospital bed on the fourth floor of the handsome old building, and afterwards limping through the crowded streets on crutches, or sometimes renting an open carriage for a trip to the San Siro racetrack and an afternoon of modest betting.

Apart from his steady recuperation, the chief event of his summer in Milan was that he fell ardently in love with one of his nurses. Agnes von Kurowsky was a dark-haired American girl in her late twenties. She came from Washington, D.C., and seems to have been as deeply devoted to the nursing profession as Hemingway was to her. Despite the gap in their ages, she saw her young lover through a difficult time, corresponded with him during her lengthy absences from Milan on other volunteer nursing assignments, and often urged him to return to useful work in the United States as soon as he was well enough to travel.

Had he but recognized it, the love affair was already on the wane when he took ship for New York in January, 1919. He lived through a restless winter and spring in the house of his parents in Oak Park, Illinois, where everything was the same as it had been before the war, and yet also infinitely changed.[2] Each day he wrote to Agnes, often several times. For the rest, he rose late each morning, renewed friendships with former cronies, wore his uniform proudly around the town, lectured on his war experiences to the students of Oak Park High School, displayed for their benefit the wondrous network of scars on his legs and feet, and longed for the romantic freedom from bourgeois attitudes which he had known for the first time during his months in Italy.[3]

---

[2] Ernest Miller Hemingway was born in Oak Park, July 21, 1899, the second of six children of Dr. Clarence Edmonds Hemingway and Grace Hall Hemingway. His formal education stopped with his graduation from Oak Park High School in 1917.

[3] According to Hemingway (EH to CB, 10/7/51), his conglomerate uniform consisted of a tunic that he had "traded someone out of," a pair of boots and a shirt bought in Gibraltar on the way home, and a black leather Italian coat with sheepskin lining that had belonged to a friend of his who was killed. In fact, however, he had bought the cordovan boots in New York before sailing for France in May, 1918, and the tunic was made for him by Spagnolini, military tailor of Milan. He had also acquired a sweeping Italian officer's cloak with a silver clasp at the

At last, in March, came the blow he had not anticipated: a letter from Agnes with the news that she had fallen in love with someone else. He reacted with rage, scorn, and self-pity, even taking to his bed for a time, writhing with the torments of a rejected lover.

But he assuaged his pain that summer with a joyous return to northern Michigan, where he had lived so happily during the seventeen long vacations of his boyhood. It was a region of woods and trout-streams and sandy soil, dotted with towns and villages such as Boyne City and Petoskey, and strewn with clear lakes like Walloon and Charlevoix. Hemingway divided his time between visits to his friends Bill and Katy Smith at Horton Bay and extended camping and fishing trips to more distant areas of the Michigan wilderness, including one memorable expedition to the Fox River in the Northern Peninsula.[4] The experiences of the summer confirmed his decision to live apart from his parents and to get on with his writing, which he had begun in a small way in high school and continued as a cub reporter with the Kansas City *Star* in 1917-1918.[5] During the fall and early winter he followed out this program, renting a room in a Petoskey boarding house, writing a few short stories, and on one occasion speaking about his war experiences to the Ladies' Aid Society in the town's public library.

Among his auditors at the library was a Mrs. Ralph Connable,

---

throat. This was reserved for dress occasions, but he continued to wear the jacket, breeches, and boots for more than a year after his return.

[4] Dr. Hemingway's summer cottage was built in 1900 on the shore of Bear Lake, later renamed Walloon. Horton Bay, a hamlet on Lake Charlevoix, was the year-round home of the James Dilworth family, who were great friends of the elder Hemingways, and the summer home of the Smith family. The whole region, including the town of Petoskey nine miles from Walloon Lake, was Hemingway's playground in his boyhood, and served as the site for many of the Nick Adams stories. The trip to the Fox River in the Northern Peninsula gave him the substance for the longest of the Nick Adams stories, "Big Two Hearted River," though the actual Big Two-Hearted River lay some miles from the Fox.

[5] Hemingway worked for the Kansas City *Star* from October, 1917 to the end of April 1918 when he left to drive ambulances in Italy. Twelve of his unsigned contributions to the *Star* have been identified and reprinted in Matthew J. Bruccoli, ed., *Ernest Hemingway, Cub Reporter*, 1970.

whose husband was in charge of the Woolworth Stores in Canada. She was so much impressed by the young veteran that he was presently offered and promptly accepted a post as hired companion to her son. In January 1920 he moved to Toronto for the rest of the winter, living in the Connable household and beginning work as a feature writer for the Toronto *Star Weekly*. Although this was only part-time employment, it was a natural sequel to his previous newspaper experience in Kansas City. It served also to revive his interest in journalism as a means of self-support while he continued his work in "serious" fiction.[6]

His final summer in Michigan was marred by quarrels with both his parents but especially with his mother, who believed, as Agnes von Kurowsky had sometimes feared in 1918, that he was in danger of becoming a loafer and a sponger. When he moved to Chicago that fall he was determined to make his way by writing. He rented a room in the apartment of Y. K. Smith, the older brother of Bill and Katy, and began looking for a job. Shortly before Christmas he became a contributing editor of *The Cooperative Commonwealth*, a monthly magazine published for its constituency by the Cooperative Society of America. At the same time he was assiduously paying court to Miss Hadley Richardson of St. Louis, a friend and former schoolmate of Katy Smith's.

The letters they exchanged were filled with dreams of a honeymoon in Europe. Nothing would do for Hemingway but that he get back to the scenes of his triumphs, where he had been a genuine war hero rather than an obscure young midwestern journalist. Although he spoke longingly of northern Italy, the only part of the continent he knew from personal experience, his plans were presently modified during talks with his new friend, Sherwood Anderson, who insisted that France, not Italy, ought to be his primary destination. Anderson had fallen in love with Paris

[6] Hemingway's contributions to the Toronto *Star* between 1920 and 1924 are conveniently listed in Audre Hanneman, *Ernest Hemingway: A Comprehensive Bibliography*, Princeton, 1967, pp. 130-142. Some of these pieces were reprinted in Gene Z. Hanrahan, ed., *Hemingway: The Wild Years*, New York, 1962, and another selection from them appears in William White, ed., *By-Line: Ernest Hemingway*, New York, 1967, pp. 3-131.

during his first visit to Europe. Not only was the monetary exchange rate beneficial to American expatriates, but some of the most interesting people in the world lived in Paris—people like Ezra Pound and Gertrude Stein and James Joyce—as well as many others who could help a young writer up the rungs of his career. Anderson generously offered to write letters of introduction.

The actuality came closer when Hemingway was able to persuade the Toronto *Star* to take him on as a foreign correspondent. He resigned his trade-journal editorship, married Hadley Richardson in the country church at Horton Bay, brought his bride to Chicago for two months in the fall of 1921, and at last set sail for France shortly before Christmas. He was eager to follow the kind of life to which he felt his three postwar years in America had been a more or less unavoidable interruption. There was perhaps as much to be discovered on the slopes of Montparnasse along the Left Bank in Paris as he had learned in Schio and Fossalta and Milan during the last half of 1918.

II. THE CONTINENTAL

The Hemingways soon found a walk-up apartment in the rue du Cardinal Lemoine, a cobblestoned street that climbed the hill overlooking Pont Sully and led into the Place de la Contrescarpe, a small square with leafless trees on an island in the middle and a variety of shops and bistros around the sides.[7] They took a holiday trip to Switzerland and then settled into their cramped Parisian quarters, charmed by the vistas of the winter streets, the smell of roasted chestnuts, and the hearty flavors of *choucroute garni* at Lipp's Brasserie. The flat itself was so crowded that Hemingway rented a room to write in on the top floor of the building where Paul Verlaine had died a quarter-century before. In his introductory letters, Sherwood Anderson had called his young friend a "quite extraordinary newspaper man," although in fact Hemingway was so intent upon writing poetry and fiction that he at first neglected his obligation to the Toronto

---

[7] Hemingway's account of his first Paris apartment appears in *A Moveable Feast*, New York, 1964, pp. 3-7.

Star, and continued to subsist as long as possible on his wife's modest income from her stocks and bonds.[8]

Sometimes in Hadley's company but often alone, he explored the grimy backwaters of the fifth arrondissement and its environs. He was not much impressed by the "strange-acting and strange-looking breed" of pseudo artists and pretenders that crowded the tables of the Left Bank cafés. "They are nearly all loafers," he wrote home to his paper, "expending the energy that an artist puts into his creative work in talking about what they are going to do and condemning the work of all artists who have gained any degree of recognition. By talking about art they obtain the same satisfaction that the real artist does in his work."[9]

During the spring, armed with Anderson's letters of intro-duction, he sought out a few of those whose labors had already gained them fame. One was Ezra Pound, who invited the Hem-ingways to tea at his studio apartment in the rue Notre Dame des Champs beyond the Luxembourg. Hemingway's first reaction was one of dislike for Pound's habit of pontificating in a loqua-cious mixture of slang and polysyllabics. But he soon changed his mind, described him as a "great guy and a wonderful editor," and by March was teaching Pound to box in exchange for lessons in how to write. The *quid pro quo* was plainly more profitable to Hemingway than to Pound, who never excelled with the gloves on. Pound had long since declared himself opposed to all "rhe-torical din and luxurious [verbal] riot," and called for a kind of writing characterized by directness, austerity, and freedom from "emotional slither." This was the kind of counsel that Heming-way most needed and to which he felt himself most strongly and temperamentally drawn.[10]

He later wrote that the mark of Pound in his Paris days, as in

[8] Several of Anderson's letters of introduction for Hemingway are printed in Howard Mumford Jones and Walter B. Rideout, eds., *The Letters of Sherwood Anderson*, Boston, 1953, pp. 82-85.

[9] Hemingway, "American Bohemians in Paris a Weird Lot," Toronto *Star Weekly*, March 25, 1922, magazine section, p. 15.

[10] Hemingway described his meetings with Pound in EH to Sherwood Anderson, 3/9/22. Pound's remarks on the qualities desirable for modern verse were made in 1918.

the early period at Rapallo, was that he devoted only a fifth of his energy to his own work. "With the rest of his time," said Hemingway, "he tries to advance the fortunes, both material and artistic, of his friends. He defends them when they are attacked, he gets them into magazines and out of jail. He loans them money. He sells their pictures. He arranges concerts for them. He writes articles about them. He introduces them to wealthy women. He gets publishers to take their books. He sits up all night with them when they claim to be dying and he witnesses their wills. He advances them hospital expenses and dissuades them from suicide. And in the end a few of them refrain from knifing him at the first opportunity."[11]

It was clearly a tribute to Pound's capacity for recognizing ability that he could admire talents as diverse as those of T. S. Eliot and Ernest Hemingway. When John Peale Bishop reached Paris that summer, he asked Pound who were the ablest American expatriates then in residence. For an answer, Pound took him to see Hemingway. Bishop was impressed. He found a young writer "instinctively intelligent, disinterested, and not given to talking nonsense." He seemed to be humble towards his craft— a good sign in itself. More important, he exuded that "innate and genial honesty which is the very chastity of talent." His integrity could evidently be trusted completely. "He could not be bought," said Bishop.[12]

Another of Hemingway's early conquests was Gertrude Stein who lived with her friend Alice B. Toklas in a sumptuous studio apartment in the rue de Fleurus not far from Pound's studio. Miss Stein thought him an extraordinarily handsome young man, with an aspect more continental than American. She liked the way he sat on the floor of her living room, or in one of the delicate chairs, gazing intently at her magnificent collection of contemporaneous paintings, and listening with seemingly passionate interest to all she chose to say about writing. She agreed to pay

[11] Peter Russell, ed., *An Examination of Ezra Pound*, New York, 1950, p. 74. Hemingway's opinions were set down in 1925.

[12] John Peale Bishop, "Homage to Hemingway," *New Republic* 89 (November 11, 1936), pp. 39-42.

the Hemingways a call at their flat on the Montagne Sainte Geneviève and to offer her opinions on the quality of both his poetry and his prose.[13]

The poems that he brought out when she came were direct and (as she said) somewhat "Kiplingesque"—a kind of barrack-room poetry of statement, but without Kipling's mastery of rhythm and vocabulary. There was also a part of a novel which she did not like, and a new story, "Up in Michigan," evidently written since his arrival in Paris, which she said no one would ever publish because it was too frank about sexual seduction. According to her own report of this encounter, published eleven years later and well after they had had a serious falling-out, her advice to him in the spring of 1922 was to begin over again and concentrate. Like Pound's, the admonition was justified. Nearly any 23-year-old writer could have profited by it. For a horrific example of Hemingway old-style, one could examine the two-page fable called "A Divine Gesture," which appeared in the New Orleans *Double-Dealer* that May. Long before its publication, he was off on a new calendar.[14]

His range of acquaintance among the expatriate literati expanded slowly. One important forward step in his continental education came when he joined the lending library conducted by Sylvia Beach at her bookshop, Shakespeare and Company, in the rue de l'Odéon. There he discovered Dostoievski, Tolstoi, Turgenev, Stendhal, and Flaubert, as well as Henry James and James Joyce. Miss Beach had just published the Paris edition of *Ulysses*, which Hemingway described in March as a "most goddamn wonderful book," though he seems to have had private

---

[13] Gertrude Stein, *The Autobiography of Alice B. Toklas*, New York, 1933, pp. 260-263. Hemingway's posthumous "reply" appeared in *A Moveable Feast*, New York, 1964.

[14] This periodical was the first in America to publish fiction and poetry by Hemingway, apart from high-school juvenilia. "A Divine Gesture" appeared in 3 (May, 1922), pp. 267-268. The June number contained on page 337 a 4-line free verse poem by Hemingway called "Ultimately." Although the fable was not reprinted, the poem was, on the back outside cover of William Faulkner's *Salmagundi*, Milwaukee, 1932. It is possible that Sherwood Anderson, who was in New Orleans during the winter of 1921-1922, helped both Faulkner and Hemingway to be published in *The Double-Dealer*.

reservations. Two years later he praised the characterizations of Leopold and Molly Bloom, but hinted that he could not abide the over-intellectualized Stephen Dedalus. Possibly because he had learned from Miss Beach that Dedalus was a self-portrait of the artist as a young man, he made no attempt to meet the author of *Ulysses* during these early months in Paris, remaining content to gaze at him from a distance when Joyce and his family dined at Michaud's.[15]

Although the Toronto *Star Weekly* printed a few of Hemingway's potboiling articles in February and March, it was not until April, when he covered the international economic conference in Genoa, that he began to act and write like a serious foreign correspondent. He got in with and got on with such veteran journalists as Lincoln Steffens, Guy Hickok, Max Eastman, and George Slocombe, among others, and filed a total of fifteen despatches on the work and personalities of the conference— much the best journalistic work he had done since his arrival in Paris five months earlier.[16]

Most of the rest of the year was given over to travel—in the spring to Switzerland and then to Italy, where the Hemingways revisited the sites of his wartime adventures, and in the summer to the Black Forest and the Rhineland. Among others, he interviewed Benito Mussolini in Milan and Georges Clemenceau at his retreat in the Vendée. In September he went to Constantinople to cover the concluding phases of the war between Greece and Turkey, and in November to Lausanne for the Peace Conference. It was here in December that Hemingway learned of the loss of his entire store of manuscripts. When his wife left Paris to join him in Switzerland shortly before Christmas, she gathered up all the fiction and poetry she could find in the apartment, packed

[15] Hemingway praised *Ulysses* in EH to Sherwood Anderson, 3/9/22. Most of this letter is quoted in Richard Ellmann, *James Joyce*, New York, 1959, p. 543. EH's critique of Joyce's characters occurred in the original conclusion to "Big Two-Hearted River," written in 1924 but deleted before publication. The unpublished portion of the story is quoted in part in Carlos Baker, *Ernest Hemingway: A Life Story*, New York, 1969, pp. 131-132.
[16] Hemingway's contributions to the Toronto *Star* for February-May, 1922, are listed in Audre Hanneman, *Ernest Hemingway: A Comprehensive Bibliography*, Princeton, 1967, pp. 132-135.

the papers into a valise, and left for the Gare de Lyon. During one brief period when it was out of her sight, the bag containing the manuscripts was stolen. Hemingway later said that the loss bulked so blackly in his imagination that he would almost have resorted to surgery in order to forget it.[17]

A few items were saved. Harriet Monroe's *Poetry* had already accepted for publication half a dozen of the "Kiplingesque" poems. Two short stories also survived, both influenced to some degree by Sherwood Anderson. One was the seduction story, "Up in Michigan," which Gertrude Stein had declared unpublishable. The other was "My Old Man," which drew on Hemingway's memories of the San Siro racetrack in Milan and his recent experiences in watching the steeplechase in Paris. Lincoln Steffens had volunteered to send it for consideration to *Cosmopolitan* magazine, and the story was in the mail back to Hemingway with a rejection slip at the time of the thievery. But the survival of these items was little recompense for the loss of so many others, including the partly completed manuscript of what might have become his first published novel.

.Early in 1923, he began to repair his losses, working first in Rapallo and afterwards in Cortina d'Ampezzo. Edward O'Brien encouraged him by taking "My Old Man" for *The Best Short Stories of 1923*, and he began to experiment with a series of hardbitten miniatures, many of them only one paragraph long. Some were based on his wartime experiences in Italy. Two were cameos of the war in Belgium, accomplished in an imitation of a British officer's narrative manner, and in fact based on anecdotes told him by a young Irishman, Captain Eric Edward Dorman-Smith. (*It was a frightfully hot day. We'd jammed an absolutely perfect barricade across the bridge. It was simply priceless.*) The two young men had first met in Milan in 1918 and had enjoyed several recent reunions. Two other miniatures drew on Hemingway's memories of police-court stories from his days in

---

[17] For detailed accounts of EH's trips in 1922, see Baker, *Ernest Hemingway: A Life Story*, New York, 1969, pp. 91-105. On the loss of the manuscripts, EH's best account is in *A Moveable Feast*, New York, 1964, pp. 73-74. See also his preface to Lee Samuels, *A Hemingway Check List*, New York, 1951. He wrote of the same topic in EH to CB, 4/1/51, where his remark on surgery appears.

Kansas City and Chicago. Another was a factual rehearsal of the execution of six Greek cabinet ministers which had been in all the European papers on November 28, 1922. There was an amusing account of someone else's interview with King Constantine in an Athenian garden. (*Like all Greeks he wanted to go to America.*)

Yet another was made over from a despatch that Hemingway had sent back to his paper from Asia Minor in the fall of 1922: "Minarets stuck up in the rain out of Adrianople across the mud flats. The carts were jammed for thirty miles along the Karagatch road. Water buffalo and cattle were hauling carts through the mud. No end and no beginning. Just carts loaded with everything they owned. The old men and women, soaked through, walked along keeping the cattle moving. The Maritza was running yellow almost up to the bridge. Carts were jammed solid on the bridge with camels bobbing along through them. Greek cavalry herded along the procession. Women and kids were in the carts couched with mattresses, mirrors, sewing machines, bundles. There was a woman having a kid with a young girl holding a blanket over her and crying. Scared sick looking at it. It rained all through the evacuation."[18]

This was the despatch that Lincoln Steffens had admired so extravagantly during the Lausanne conference. He thought that it portrayed with memorable force, yet with fitting restraint, "that miserable stream of hungry, frightened, uprooted people"—the vanguard of hundreds of thousands of displaced persons who would stream pitifully across various other landscapes all through the twentieth century. Hemingway was shy of Steffens's praise. He wanted his friend to look at the "cablese" in which the despatch was first presented. "Only the cablese. Isn't it a great

[18] EH to CB, 4/1/51 admits to the hearsay sources of some of these miniatures. The first six appeared in the Exiles number of *The Little Review*, edited by Margaret Anderson, Jane Heap, and Ezra Pound, 9 (Spring, 1923), pp. 3-5. As EH here worked with short paragraphs, he had earlier experimented with single sentences. For examples, under the title of "Paris, 1922," see Baker, *Ernest Hemingway: A Life Story*, New York, 1969, pp. 90-91. The account of Adrianople first appeared in the Toronto *Daily Star*, Nov. 14, 1922, p. 7. The rewritten version quoted above was in *The Little Review*, later collected in the Paris *in our time* and in the New York *In Our Time* (1925).

language?" Later he told Steffens that he had to quit being a journalist and compressing his observations into such economical form: he was becoming too deeply fascinated with the lingo of the transatlantic cable.[19]

The six poems in the January number of *Poetry: A Magazine of Verse* were direct statements in the transitional poetic idiom of the period.[20] The modern reader who looks them up and finds that he does not like them can find many similar examples, both better and worse, in the little magazines of those years. One of Hemingway's, called "Oily Weather," spoke of ships ploughing the sea in what was probably intended as a sexual image. "Roosevelt" pointed up the contrast between Teddy Roosevelt the political fact and TR, the legendary trust-buster. Hemingway's admiration for the toughness of the Arditi, the Italian shock troops, was evidenced in two war-poems, "Riparto d'Assolto" and "Champs d'Honneur"—both of them early excursions into a topic that continued to interest him, the natural history of the dying and the dead. A fifth, "Chapter Heading," said that this generation had danced to devils' tunes and had now come shivering home to pray. And in another, called "Mitrailliatrice," the young poet addressed his typewriter:

> The mills of the gods grind slowly;
> But this mill
> Chatters in mechanical staccato.
> Ugly short infantry of the mind,
> Advancing over difficult terrain
> Make this Corona
> Their mitrailleuse.

The themes in these poems were characteristic of the age: the recent war, a hint of religious feeling, a sexual image, a hatred of sham and posturing, and a conscious acceptance of the roughness of the terrain over which the mind's infantry must advance, with only a Corona that sounded like a machine-gun for support. If the military image was the most arresting of them all, it was

[19] Lincoln Steffens, *Autobiography*, New York, 1931, p. 834.
[20] The six poems were published under the title "Wanderings" in *Poetry*, 21 (January, 1923), pp. 193-195.

doubtless because Hemingway's current concern was to assault those mills of the gods, far off and seemingly impregnable, the publishers of books with hard covers.

Late in March he began another trip for the Toronto *Star*, and before it was over had completed ten articles on the occupation of the Ruhr Valley by French forces, and the desperation and rebelliousness of the German workers in such poverty-stricken cities as Düsseldorf and Essen.[21] On his return to Cortina in mid-April, he wrote a new story called "Out of Season." The first example of a kind that he would soon be experimenting with much more widely, it was a remarkably subtle blend of statement and implication, and by far the best of the short stories he had done so far. His Corona typewriter, a gift from Hadley before their marriage, was now old and battered, but the prose that came out of it was fresh and new.[22]

III. TORONTO AND BACK

Two major developments helped to change the course of Hemingway's life during the early months of 1923. One was the discovery of Hadley's pregnancy, which caused the prospective parents to decide to spend the fall of the year in Toronto, where the baby could be born on American soil, and where the young father would be able to enjoy a steady income as a local reporter for the *Star*. The second development, not less exciting, was the completion of arrangements for the publication of Hemingway's first book. Robert McAlmon, whom he had first met at Rapallo early in the year, had recently formed the Contact Publishing Company, with editorial headquarters in Paris and ready access to a printing plant in Dijon.[23] Another and older friend, William Bird, had bought an ancient handpress in a one-time wine-vault on the Île St. Louis in Paris, and commenced the publication of

[21] For a listing of these articles, see Audre Hanneman, *Ernest Hemingway: A Comprehensive Bibliography*, Princeton, 1967, pp. 138-139.

[22] Hemingway, *A Moveable Feast*, New York, 1964, p. 75. EH to F. Scott Fitzgerald, ca. 12/20/25.

[23] Robert McAlmon, *Being Geniuses Together*, London, 1938, pp. 154-155. See also Robert E. Knoll, *McAlmon and the Lost Generation*, Lincoln, Nebraska, 1962, pp. 11, 88-89, 107-108, 144-148, 184-185.

books in limited editions under the imprint of the Three Mountains Press.[24] Bird's avocation was fine printing and the books were laboriously set by hand. Darantière of Dijon, who did the work for Contact editions, used linotypes in the preparation of McAlmon's books. Before the end of May it was agreed that McAlmon would go ahead with a small collection of Hemingway's poetry and prose.

The eventual title was *Three Stories and Ten Poems*. The stories were "Up in Michigan" and "My Old Man," the sole survivors of the robbery at the Gare de Lyon, together with "Out of Season," recently completed in Cortina d'Ampezzo. The poems included the six that had already appeared in *Poetry*, and four others: "Oklahoma," "Captives," "Montparnasse," and "Along with Youth." Proofsheets finally reached Hemingway early in August on the eve of his departure for Canada. He was beside himself with admiration for the gray-blue wrappers, boldly lettered in square-cut black capitals, and was relieved when Gertrude Stein said that she shared his views.[25] The only flaw in the publishing schedule was that William Bird had fallen far behind with the printing of the second book. Hemingway could not even be certain of having bound copies by Christmas.

A third event, hardly less important to Hemingway than the baby and the books, was his discovery of Spain. His first visit took place in May in the company of McAlmon and Bird.[26] Neither of his companions was greatly impressed by the early-season bullfights they attended, but Hemingway was rapturous over the courage and skills of matadors and bulls alike. Each *corrida* seemed to him a great tragic performance. To be a spectator was as good as having a ringside seat at a war. One visit to Spain was not enough. In July he took Hadley to Pamplona for a first encounter with the annual, wild, drunken, sun-splashed Fiesta of San Fermín. Nothing could exceed his admiration for the country, the people, the food and wine, the

---

[24] William Bird to author, June, 1962.

[25] EH to McAlmon, 8/5/23. See below, p. 409, for order of contents.

[26] Hemingway bawdily memorialized his first introduction to Spain in a six-part poem called "The Soul of Spain with McAlmon and Bird the Publishers," *Querschnitt* 4 (Autumn, 1924), pp. 229-230 and 4 (November, 1924), p. 278.

dancing in the streets, and above all the life-and-death performances each afternoon in the bullring. During May, he had become a convert; by July he was a permanent enthusiast.[27]

After such joys, the staid life of Toronto was a gray anticlimax.
The child was born a month after their arrival, a husky boy who
was given the name of John and (after an interval) the nickname
of Bumby. Hemingway worked faithfully enough as staff reporter
and feature writer for the *Star*. But the experience of having lived
abroad and the prospect of becoming known as a writer of poetry
and fiction had combined to spoil his appetite for journalism.
"The only reason for writing" for newspapers, as he presently
said, was to be well paid. Otherwise the problem was that you
destroyed the valuable material you had accumulated by putting
it into a form as ephemeral as that of day-to-day journalism.[28]

In Canada, he felt, he had a dozen stories that he wanted to
write, but he lacked the time and energy to set them down. He
began to think that Gertrude Stein had been correct in her opinion that newspaper work could be dangerous for the serious
literary aspirant. It did not help his state of mind that he had
conceived a dislike for his city editor that bordered on paranoia.
He was also homesick for Paris and Pamplona. In the end he
resolved that as soon as the baby was old enough to travel he
would resign his post at the *Star*, return to Paris, and take up the
writing he had put aside before sailing for Canada.

He was still in Toronto when his second book was published
in Paris. It was far handsomer than *Three Stories and Ten Poems*.
William Bird had devised a memorable cover—a montage of
newspaper headlines—and the pages were of handmade rag
paper. It was called *in our time*, without benefit of capital letters.
The contents consisted of the six miniature short stories that had
already appeared in *The Little Review*, together with a dozen
others written between March and August, five of them based
on his sharp observations of the Spanish bullfight. This time there
was no verse, as such. But the prose miniatures developed an

---

[27] Hemingway's first accounts of Pamplona appeared in the Toronto
Star Weekly, October 20, 1923, pp. 23 and 33.
[28] Hemingway, "Pamplona Letter," *transatlantic review*, 2 (October,
1924), pp. 300-302.

intensity, economy, and concentration that converted them into
the esthetic equivalent of poetry.

The little book was the sixth and last of a series printed by
Bird and "edited" by Pound as "an inquest into the state of contemporary English prose." From the author's point of view, this
phase of the inquest had been unconscionably slow in bringing
the corpus to light. Bird was properly fussy about the cover design and about the looks of the woodcut, made from a portrait
of Hemingway by his friend Henry Strater, which was being used
as a frontispiece. One cause of the delay was the binder, who
kept the sheets two full months. Another was that, owing to the
inefficiency of a man who was running off the pages on the press,
the frontispiece printed through the page, so that a planned edition of 300 copies was reduced to a mere 170, the ruined copies
being sent out as gifts and for reviewers.[29]

Back in Paris in January, 1924, the Hemingways found an
apartment in the rue Notre Dame des Champs, the street where
Pound lived before his departure for Rapallo. The neighborhood
was somewhat more polite than that of Montagne Saint Geneviève. But it was at least equally picturesque, since their landlord
operated a small sawmill and lumberyard on the ground floor.
The daylight hours were frequently horrendous with the whine
of the circular saw and the racket of the donkey-engine that gave
it power. Hemingway had a small room in the apartment where
he often wrote in the early mornings before the landlord was
astir, but more often than not he began to escape the noise by
visits to cafés. He would take the short cut through the Luxembourg Gardens past the statue of Flaubert which seemed to him
both a symbol and a goal. Breakfast of café-au-lait and a brioche
came to a franc or less at any of the places along the rue Soufflot,

[29] See below, pp. 409-410, for order of contents. The six works in the
series were Pound's *Indiscretions*, Ford's *Women and Men*, B. C. Winde-
ler's *Elimus*, William Carlos Williams's *The Great American Novel*,
B.M.G. Adams's *England*, and Hemingway's *in our time*. On the "inquest"
see D. D. Paige, ed., *Letters of Ezra Pound*, New York, 1950, pp. 183-184.
"It's hell," Pound wrote to Dr. Williams (from Paris, 8/1/22) "the way
I always seem to get sucked into editing something or other." Yet he
threw himself into the work with much good will. Authors in the series
received a fifty-dollar down-payment on delivery of the MS, with an
expectation of another fifty dollars later.

and he could write all morning at a back corner table without fear of prolonged disturbance. Afterwards he could rest strained eyes on the bronze-green of the fountains in the Place de l'Observatoire, where the water flowed thinly over the sculptured manes and shoulders of the horses.[30]

For every serious and determined writer who came to live and work under the benison of twelve francs to the dollar, there were a dozen eccentrics, cut-ups, professional or amateur Bohemians, roisterers, playboys and playgirls. They cluttered the well-known cafés, cadged drinks, fought with bartenders and among themselves, and slept where they fell. The general comportment reflected no great credit on the narrow American main streets from which the gifted and the almost gifted had fled to the new freedom of Montparnasse, which Ford Madox Ford once called "the latest of all Cloud-Cuckoo Lands."[31] They were very numerous, and they came from everywhere, though as often as not from the American midwest. "Young America from the limitless prairies leapt, released, on Paris," said Ford. "They stampeded with the madness of colts when you let down the sliprails between dried pasture and green. The noise of their advancing drowned all sounds. Their innumerable forms hid the very trees on the boulevards. Their perpetual motion made you dizzy."[32]

The serious author, like young Hemingway, could find some of his materials among those who drank and played along the Boulevard Montparnasse and the Boulevard Raspail. But the real importance of Paris in the twenties was quite unconnected, as Douglas Goldring wrote, "with the notoriety it acquired as an international pleasure resort." Few hard-working writers could afford to join the madding crowd, not least Hemingway, who was attempting to get along on the income from his wife's patrimony. In later years, looking back, he was inclined to overstate the degree of their poverty. He mixed work and play by going with T. H. (Mike) Ward to the six-day bicycle races, one of his latest

[30] EH to CB, 4/1/51. See also *GHOA*, New York, 1935, p. 71, and Sisley Huddleston, *Paris Salons, Cafés, Studios*, New York, 1928, pp. 121-123.

[31] F. M. Ford, *A Mirror to France*, New York, 1926, p. 105.

[32] F. M. Ford, Introduction to Hemingway, *FTA*, Modern Library edition, p. xii.

passions. He argued the merits of racehorses with Evan Shipman, a down-at-heel poet whose knowledge of horseflesh made him the ideal racing companion. He used a borrowed press-pass to go to the prizefights with Guy Hickok, Sisley Huddleston, and Bill Bird, his latest publisher. Bird was nostalgic about the brave colored fighters of the immediate past. He liked to quote a punning line made over from François Villon which asked, "Où sont les nègres d'antan?" When the fights were good, like the one between Mascart and Ledoux at the Cirque d'Hiver, Hemingway and his friends yelled themselves hoarse and stopped in at Lipp's for a midnight beer on the way home. With the arrival of warmer weather, he took to playing tennis on the red clay courts just off the Boulevard Arago.[33]

But these afternoons in the sun or evenings in the smoky clamorous dark of the Cirque d'Hiver were interludes of relaxation, now frequent, now widely spaced, between bouts with the old Corona. The stories he wrote were regularly rejected by the American magazine editors to whom they were sent, and he became almost if never quite habituated to watching the familiar envelopes drop with the rest of the mail "through a slit in the sawmill door." To his desperate annoyance, the pencilled notes on the rejection slips would never call them stories, but always anecdotes, sketches, or contes. "They did not want them," as he wrote later on, "and we lived on *poireaux* [boiled leeks] and drank *cahors* and water."[34]

Through all the incidental hubbub of home and street life, he kept "very earnestly at work making himself a writer." So testified Gertrude Stein, who agreed to serve as godmother for Hemingway's son John and once thought she heard the young father murmuring under his breath something about "the career . . . the career."[35] If he was driven by an urge to excel, to storm the citadel of the book and magazine publishers in the United States, he was also determined to write well whatever he wanted to write in the way he thought it must be written. The career would then

<hr />

[33] Huddleston, op. cit., p. 122.

[34] Hemingway, *GHOA*, New York, 1935, p. 70.

[35] Gertrude Stein, *The Autobiography of Alice B. Toklas*, New York, 1933, pp. 260-263.

take care of itself, though it would still take a little longer for the necessary momentum to build up. Fame, the by-product of the real effort, might be "flushed like quail" from the morning thickets if you worked hard enough and were lucky. So Hemingway's new friend Archibald MacLeish summed it up years afterwards:

The lad in the Rue de Notre Dame des Champs
At the carpenter's loft on the left-hand side going down—
The lad with the supple look like a sleepy panther—
And what became of him? Fame became of him.
Veteran out of the wars before he was twenty:
Famous at twenty-five: thirty a master—
Whittled a style for his time from a walnut stick
In a carpenter's loft in a street of that April city.[36]

Although he was now well enough known around the Latin Quarter, and fondly remembered as a young reporter in Toronto, the real secret of his power of survival as a literary force was the time he spent alone, sharpening the English language into a precision instrument, a scalpel for the vivisection of nature and man.

IV. CAPTAIN'S CORVÉE

The beginning of the *transatlantic review* in January 1924 under the editorship of Ford Madox Ford was of further consequence in the continental education of Hemingway, and represented one more rung in his climb up the ladder towards literary eminence. Ford's editorial office was situated on a somewhat rickety platform in the back shop of William Bird's Three Mountains Press on the Quai d'Anjou. Ezra Pound effected an introduction one winter afternoon in his studio, and Ford was at once impressed by Hemingway, who struck him as having "rather the aspect of an Eton-Oxford husky-ish young captain from an English midland regiment"—something after the manner of Captain Dorman-Smith of the Fusiliers.[37] Young Captain Hemingway,

[36] "Years of the Dog," in *Actfive and Other Poems*, New York, 1943, p. 53. Used by kind permission of Archibald MacLeish.
[37] Ford, introduction to Hemingway's *FTA*, Modern Library edition,

going on twenty-five, was shortly a member of that inner circle who listened to General Ford's vast store of literary reminiscences on writers like Joseph Conrad, Thomas Hardy, Henry James, and Sir Edmund Gosse. The Gosse and James anecdotes were among the best. Some of them would appear in Hemingway's *The Torrents of Spring*.

Ford later pretended, jocularly no doubt, that he could not recall Hemingway's exact function on the *transatlantic*. In fact his job was to serve as manuscript scout and unpaid part-time editor. "I used to go down there," Hemingway later wrote, "and take a batch of [manuscripts] out on the Quai and read them. [I] would make an annotation of what Ford was to say in refusal." A typical editorial note might read: "This stinks but he might write a story if he keeps trying." Then Ford, without reading the stories himself, but bringing into play his most diplomatic powers of expression, would write beautiful letters of encouragement to the authors of the rejected stories. For fun and practice Hemingway would sometimes try his hand at rewriting the stories, thus earning intangible profits from his post on the magazine.[38]

His subsequent term for his editorial labors was "a real *corvée*," a piece of drudgery without visible recompense. By means of it, however, he enlarged his literary acquaintance, appearing sometimes at the shop-talk teas that Ford held on Thursday afternoons in the office of the magazine on the Quai d'Anjou. He found Ford personally unattractive—they often quarreled bitterly—and could not abide the pale blue eyes under colorless eyebrows and eyelashes, or the heavy mustache stained with the wine he had consumed at luncheon, or Ford's figure, which at the age of fifty-

---

pp. xiii-xiv. Captain Dorman-Smith, who remained a close friend of Hemingway's as long as he lived, later became a general in the British Army. For a time in the second world war he served as Auchinleck's Chief of Staff in the North African desert fighting. After his retirement from active duty, he resumed his original family name of Dorman-O'Gowan and lived on the family estate in Bellamont Forest, County Cavan, Ireland. His military career is outlined in *Burke's Landed Gentry of Ireland*, London, 1958, p. 538. He died at County Cavan Hospital, May 11, 1969, in his 74th year.

[38] EH to CB, 4/1/51, recalls that the meeting with Ford took place in Pound's studio, and describes his editorial duties. Robert McAlmon, *Being Geniuses Together*, London, 1938, p. 245, offers further comment.

one looked like an "ambulatory, well-clothed, up-ended hogs-head." Nevertheless he continued his editorial work without audible complaint because he knew that the appearance of his stories in the magazine, along with those of Joyce and others already famous, would represent a stepping-stone to an enlarged reputation.[39]

In his capacity as scout, he was able to do Gertrude Stein so good a turn with her unpublished book, *The Making of Americans*, that she continued to feel indebted to him even after a perceptible rift had begun to develop between them. She could seldom forget how Hemingway appeared one day in February, 1924. He seemed to be in a great hurry, and his message was that Ford wanted to publish her book serially in the *transatlantic*. The first installment was needed at once. Miss Stein was "quite overcome" with excitement. Since the only available copy had been sewn and bound, Hemingway helped her to copy out the first fifty pages and hurried off to Ford's office.

His private opinion of the book was that it "began magnifi-cently, went on very well for a long way with great stretches of great brilliance and then went on endlessly in repetitions that a more conscientious and less lazy writer would have put in the waste basket." But he said nothing of this to Miss Stein. He told her instead that he had made it clear to Ford that getting the book was "a remarkable scoop . . . obtained only through my obtain-ing genius. He [Ford] is under the impression that you get big prices when you consent to publish. I did not give him this im-pression but did not discourage it. . . . Treat him high wide and handsome. . . . It is really a scoop for them you know. They are going to have Joyce in the same [April] number."[40]

The April number of the magazine pleased Hemingway by

[39] EH to CB, 4/1/51. EH's later account of Ford appears in *A Moveable Feast*, New York, 1964, pp. 83-84. See also Bernard J. Poli, *Ford Madox Ford and the transatlantic review*, Syracuse, New York, 1967, p. 26.

[40] Gertrude Stein, *The Autobiography of Alice B. Toklas*, New York, 1933, pp. 264-265. EH to Gertrude Stein, 2/17/24, quoted in Donald C. Gallup, "The Making of *The Making of Americans*," *The New Colophon*, New York, 1950, pp. 58-59. See also Hemingway, *A Moveable Feast*, New York, 1964, pp. 17-18.

including the earliest reviews of *Three Stories and Ten Poems* and *in our time*, the latter by Marjorie Reid, who worked as general factotum for Ford. She said that Hemingway had seized upon those "moments when life is condensed and clean-cut and significant, presenting them in minute narratives that eliminate every useless word. Each tale is much longer than the measure of its lines." He had come far since the days of the rejection notes that would not call his stories stories. Here now were the terms "narrative" and "tale"—a clear and notable gain, though his acceptance by American magazines was still well in the future.

This same number was eminently satisfying to him in two other respects. It contained the installment from Gertrude Stein for whose appearance he was primarily responsible. But best of all was the first of his short stories to be published since his two little books had come out in Paris. It was later to be called "Indian Camp," a story about Nick Adams as a young boy, camping with his father and his uncle in the woods of Northern Michigan. But Ford's literary supplement omitted the title in favor of the generic term, *Works in Progress*, and the story had the distinction of appearing cheek by jowl with a piece by Tristan Tzara, the monocled experimentalist who had founded Dada, and (most happily) with an extract from James Joyce's work in progress, later to become world-famous as *Finnegans Wake*.[41]

Meantime he had begun work on a far longer story which he was going to call "Big Two-Hearted River." It was another of the series on Nick Adams, this time not as a small boy but as a young veteran back from the wars, recovering from his wounds, and using a fishing-trip into the wilds of the Northern Peninsula of Michigan for therapeutic purposes. Nick's adventure was based on Hemingway's own trip to the Fox River in the late summer of 1919, when he and two companions had spent a glorious week of fishing, drinking, and eating before their return to Walloon Lake and Horton Bay.

By early summer, the *transatlantic* was nearly out of money. Ford resolved on a trip to the United States to replenish the sup-

---

[41] The review of *Three Stories and Ten Poems* was signed K. J. and that of *in our time* by M. R. [Marjorie Reid]. See *transatlantic review*, 1 (April, 1924), pp. 246-248. The text of "Indian Camp," but without its present title, appeared in the same number, pp. 230-234.

ply with a request to John Quinn, whose munificence had so far sustained the enterprise. The contents of the July number were assembled before he left, and Marjorie Reid and Hemingway undertook to see it through the press. It was also Hemingway's job to put together a series of pieces for the August number in time to hit the deadline of July 1. Since he was eager to be off for Spain and a second encounter with the fiesta of San Fermín in Pamplona, he turned to several of his American friends for contributions. These included fiction by John Dos Passos and Nathan Asch, a long excerpt from Miss Stein's *The Making of Americans*, and a nonfiction piece by Guy Hickok of the Paris office of the *Brooklyn Daily Eagle*. Ford returned from his American tour while Hemingway was in Spain, arriving in Paris in time to insert an editorial note before the August number came off the press. "During our absence on those other pavements," he wrote, "this Review has been ably edited by Mr. Ernest Hemingway, the admirable Young American prose writer. [Except for two pieces] the present number is entirely of Mr. Hemingway's getting together. . . . It provides [the reader] with an unusually large sample of the work of the Young America whose claims we have so insistently—but not with such efficiency —forced upon our readers." This insertion, which he construed as an insult, so much enraged Hemingway that his personal relations with Ford were never quite the same again. Yet his experience as sub-editor of the *transatlantic*, whether or not it was truly a *corvée*, probably helped as much as any of his other serious literary activities to get his name and fame into general circulation around Paris. It offered him a kind of focus, a set of responsibilities, and a magazine outlet for his best work. By means of it, perhaps, his continental education was capped with a master of arts degree. Although he had not yet arrived at the peak of Mount Parnassus, he was plainly far above the motley crowds that milled around on the lower slopes of Montparnasse.[42]

[42] For further details on Ford's trip to New York, see Bernard J. Poli, *Ford Madox Ford and the transatlantic review*, Syracuse, New York, 1967, pp. 98-99, and Carlos Baker, *Ernest Hemingway: A Life Story*, New York, 1969, pp. 128, 131, and 584-585. Ford's critique of Hemingway's editorial practices in developing the August number appeared in *transatlantic review*, 2 (August, 1924), p. 213.

II · The Making of Americans

"Hemingway selected his audience. His rewards will be rich. But thank God he will never be satisfied. He is of the elect. He belongs. It will take time to wear him out. And before that he will be dead."— Ernest Walsh, 1925[1]

I. FOREIGN PARTS

Hemingway's third trip to Spain, accomplished in the early summer of 1924, was an immense success. Before going on to Navarre, he and Hadley visited Madrid and Aranjuez. They were joined in Pamplona by a large group of friends who had been attracted to the fiesta by Hemingway's bubbling enthusiasm for the bullfight, though few of them shared it to a similar degree. The good companions of that year included William and Sally Bird, Robert McAlmon, John Dos Passos, Donald Ogden Stewart, Captain Dorman-Smith, and a young midwesterner named George O'Neil. After the fiesta the group reassembled at the Basque village of Burguete to fish for trout in the rivers and streams of the Pyrenees. It was altogether a golden time, and Hemingway remembered it with nostalgia a year later when he returned to Pamplona once more in far different company and under much less happy circumstances.[2]

Back in Paris he learned from Ford of the recent death of John Quinn, the erstwhile angel for the *transatlantic*, and at once set about finding someone else to serve as financial supporter for the review. The mantle fell upon the slender shoulders of Krebs Friend, whom Hemingway had first known in Chicago in 1920 and who had since contrived to marry an heiress. Friend agreed to advance Ford two hundred dollars a month for the next six

---

[1] Ernest Walsh in *This Quarter*, 1 (Autumn-Winter, 1925-1926), pp. 319-321.

[2] Accounts of this visit to Pamplona appear in Hemingway, Toronto *Star Weekly*, Sept. 13, 1924, p. 18; Robert McAlmon, *Being Geniuses Together*, London, 1938, pp. 212-217; and John Dos Passos, *The Best Times*, New York, 1966, pp. 156-157. See also EH to Gertrude Stein, ca. 7/10/24 and 7/13/24, and EH to Sylvia Beach, 7/24/24.

months and was duly installed as president at an informal directors' meeting in mid-August. With the review once again reasonably solvent, Hemingway finished "Big Two-Hearted River" in a great burst of energy, and began to assemble the other stories that he had been writing since his return from Toronto in January.[3]

It was a remarkable series for a writer in his twenty-fifth year. Besides "Indian Camp" and "Big Two-Hearted River" he had completed "The Doctor and the Doctor's Wife," based on a domestic incident at Walloon Lake in the summer of 1911; "The End of Something" and "The Three-Day Blow," which alluded to one of his temporary romances at Horton Bay in 1919 and included the character and the name of his old friend, Bill Smith. "Cross-Country Snow" was a skiing story dating from his exploits in Switzerland early in 1923 in the company of George O'Neil, called "Gidge." These six were all episodes in the life of Nick Adams from youth to manhood. Two others could easily have used Nick's name, though Hemingway avoided it. One was "Soldier's Home," which was clearly related to his own return from Europe to Oak Park in the winter of 1919; the second, "Cat in the Rain," grew out of his stay with Hadley in Rapallo early in 1923. The ninth was "Mr. and Mrs. Smith," although the title was later changed to "Mr. and Mrs. Elliot" to avoid possible libel action, since it satirized the alleged marital inefficiencies of an American couple, Chard Powers Smith and his wife, for whom Hemingway had conceived a wholly irrational dislike.[4]

Along with the prose pieces from *Three Stories and Ten Poems*, and the miniatures from *in our time*, these nine stories

[3] EH to Gertrude Stein, 8/15/24, printed in Donald Gallup, ed., *The Flowers of Friendship*, New York, 1953, pp. 164-165.

[4] Chard Powers Smith to CB, 5/16/69, indicates that he and his wife (née Olive Cary Macdonald) enjoyed a normal married life rather than the aberrational kind attributed to Mr. and Mrs. Smith in Hemingway's story. Mrs. Smith died in Naples, Italy, in March, 1924, during a pregnancy with twins in which she never recovered from morning sickness, and her husband's first book, *Along the Wind*, Yale, 1925, was mostly about her. Janet Hurter, who is also maligned in Hemingway's story as the presumably Lesbian friend of Mrs. Smith, was not a Lesbian but only Olive's best friend. She lived with the Smiths for a few months in the winter of 1921-1922, and again, at Smith's request, crossed the ocean and went down to Naples in the winter of 1924, when Olive's health was declining, to help care for her.

were more than enough to make a full-length volume. Dos Passos and Stewart both volunteered to help Hemingway find an American publisher. So did a more recent friend, Harold Loeb, whose first novel had just been accepted for publication by Boni and Liveright in New York. And so also, unbeknown to Hemingway, did Sherwood Anderson, who was a much more strongly established author with the same firm. Before the end of September, Hemingway mailed the typescript to Stewart and sat back to await news of its success or failure.[5]

He had not yet decided to abandon poetry. According to George Antheil, a composer from Trenton, New Jersey, who had come to Paris in 1923 and lived with his wife in rooms above Sylvia Beach's bookshop, Hemingway learned through him of a new German periodical, *Der Querschnitt* (*The Cross Section*), published at Frankfurt-am-Main. Antheil persuaded the editors to accept four of Hemingway's poems, together with a new short story, "The Undefeated," begun in September and finished on November 20th. The poems showed the bawdy satirical bent that would emerge strongly in *The Torrents of Spring* a year later, and bore such sardonic titles as "The Soul of Spain with McAlmon and Bird the Publishers," "The Lady Poets with Foot Notes," "The Earnest Liberal's Lament," and (with a bow to Ezra Pound) "The Age Demanded." During the next few months these appeared in *Der Querschnitt* in English; "The Undefeated" was translated into German under the title of "Stierkampf."[6]

The German publishing venture had an amusing epilogue. Years afterwards in East Africa, Hemingway met an Austrian expatriate with literary interests. "Hemingway," the man said, "is a name I have heard. Where? Where have I heard it? Oh, yes. The *Dichter*. You know Hemingway the poet?" It developed that he had formerly subscribed to *Der Querschnitt* for cultural purposes. "This is very strange," he said, as soon as the identity of Hemingway had been established. Hemingway, whose poetic

---

[5] Documentation on Hemingway's preparation of the manuscript of his first full-length book is given in Carlos Baker, *Ernest Hemingway: A Life Story*, New York, 1969, p. 585. Sherwood Anderson also intervened in getting Hemingway's book accepted. See note 14, below.

[6] George Antheil, *Bad Boy of Music*, New York, 1945, p. 147. Hemingway (EH to CB, 4/1/51) denied the veracity of Antheil's claim to have "placed" the poems and the story with *Der Querschnitt*, but offered no alternative explanation.

interests had long since been siphoned off into prose, thought
that the whole episode was fantastic.[7]

Throughout the fall, Hemingway continued his squabbling
with Ford Madox Ford. His satirical impulses were again engaged when Joseph Conrad died and Ford assembled a special
Conrad supplement under the *transatlantic* imprint. Hemingway
admired Conrad, but used the occasion to belittle T. S. Eliot,
whom he regarded as a snob, by observing that if he could revive
Conrad by destroying Eliot, he would not hesitate for a minute.
Ford was caught between his admiration for Eliot and his determination not to interfere with the opinions of contributors to
the magazine. In the end he printed a mild apology for Hemingway's insult to Eliot. It was all the stimulus Hemingway needed
to sever social relations with Ford, although the last two numbers
of the *transatlantic* each contained short stories from his forthcoming collection. In spite of the intercession of Krebs Friend,
the magazine was on the point of expiration. It had served young
Hemingway well as a means of getting his stories before an international public, and he angrily accused Ford of "megalo-
maniac blundering" in bringing about its too-early demise.[8]

Having heard that severe inflation in Austria made living
there advantageous for Americans with dollars to spend, the
Hemingways and their child went down to Schruns in the Vorarlberg shortly before Christmas. They stayed until March, revelling
in the mountain scenery, the clean snow, the excellent food and
beer, and the skiing on the flanks of the high Silvretta range.
They were in the midst of a skiing trip early in February 1925
when Hemingway learned that Boni and Liveright had accepted
his short stories for publication in the fall under the title *In Our
Time*. The publisher, Horace Liveright, had only two objections.
He refused to print the seduction story, "Up in Michigan," thus
bearing out Gertrude Stein's earlier prediction, and he insisted
on the deletion of an allegedly obscene passage in "Mr. and Mrs.
Elliot." Hemingway agreed to tone down the questionable para-

[7] Hemingway, *GHOA*, New York, 1935, p. 7. The Austrian trader there
called Kandisky was actually named Hans Koritschoner.

[8] Hemingway discussed Ford's managerial ineptitudes in EH to Gertrude Stein, 9/14/24 and 10/10/24. His article on Conrad with the quip
about Eliot was in *transatlantic review*, 2 (October, 1924), pp. 341-342.
Ford's apology, intended for Eliot's eyes and those of Eliot's admirers, appeared in the following number, 2 (November, 1924), p. 550.

graph, and at once set to work on a new Nick Adams story to replace "Up in Michigan." He called it "The Battler" and finished it in mid-February, rounding out the content of his first American book. He was still in a state of exultation when he returned to Paris a month later.[9]

Ernest Walsh and Ethel Moorhead were now planning a new "little magazine" to be called *This Quarter*, edited by Walsh and financed by Miss Moorhead. Since it would help to offset the loss of the *transatlantic*, Hemingway volunteered to assist in its launching, and worked long hours with the printer to make certain that the first number would be worthy of Ezra Pound, to whom it was going to be dedicated. He was rewarded for his labors when Walsh accepted and paid for his long fishing story, "Big Two-Hearted River," and his even longer bullfight story, "The Undefeated."[10]

He deferred his cable of acceptance to Boni and Liveright until the end of March only to discover from an unforwarded letter that Maxwell Perkins of Charles Scribner's Sons was interested in seeing some of his work. Since his contract with Boni and Liveright gave them options on his next three books, the possibility of becoming a Scribner author looked remote. But he answered Perkins's letter politely, and promised to notify him immediately if he were ever released from his present contractual obligations.[11]

About the time that the Pound number of *This Quarter* made its appearance, Hemingway ran into F. Scott Fitzgerald at the Dingo Bar. Although they had never met personally until now, Fitzgerald had strongly recommended Hemingway to Perkins, his own editor at Scribner's, after reading one or two of his stories in the *transatlantic review*. This was enough to establish an immediate bond of friendship between the two young midwestern-

[9] Hemingway's two visits to Schruns (1924-1925 and 1925-1926) are memorably described in *A Moveable Feast*, New York, 1964, pp. 198-206. Other details in this paragraph are drawn from EH to Gertrude Stein 12/29/24 and 1/20/25; EH to Harold Loeb, 12/29/24 and 1/5/25; EH to William Smith, 1/27/25; EH to Howell Jenkins, 2/2/25; and EH to Ernest Walsh, 2/13/25.

[10] The first number of *This Quarter* (May, 1925) contained "Big Two-Hearted River," pp. 110-128, and Hemingway's tribute to Pound, "Homage to Ezra," pp. 221-225.

[11] Maxwell Perkins to EH, 2/21/25, and EH to Perkins, 4/15/25. See also EH to Fitzgerald, 12/31/25, and EH to CB, 4/1/51.

ers, despite their differences in manner, temperament, education, and experience. The bond was further cemented when Hemingway read and admired *The Great Gatsby*, Fitzgerald's latest and best novel, which had just been published in April.[12]

Although Fitzgerald had left Princeton University for good in October 1917 (just when Hemingway was beginning his work for the Kansas City *Star*) he was still an ardent Princetonian, and lost no time in introducing Hemingway to Christian Gauss, who had taught French at Princeton since 1905, had befriended and advised Fitzgerald during his undergraduate years, and had just become Dean of the College at the age of forty-seven. One of their conversations turned upon Robert Louis Stevenson's advice to the young writer that he should play the sedulous ape to his elders until, in good time, he develops a matter and manner of his own. Fitzgerald admitted that he owed some parts of his Princeton novel, *This Side of Paradise*, to the fiction of Compton Mackenzie, although some of the scenes also reflected his admiration for Joyce's *Portrait of the Artist as a Young Man*. Hemingway named Sherwood Anderson's *Winesburg, Ohio* as his first pattern. "But both agreed," wrote Gauss, "that you later had to pay for whatever help this sort of imitation gave you in your apprenticeship. It was like consulting a psychiatrist. If you were to go on your own, you soon had to wean yourself of such outside direction."

By this time in 1925, the fiercely competitive Hemingway clearly felt that he was temperamentally an originator rather than an imitator. He had taught himself to write by writing. Both as a newspaper correspondent in the European capitals and as a serious imaginative writer in the privacy of various apartments and small studios, he had trained himself to observe accurately and to express clearly a careful selection of what he saw, heard, and felt. "He was not given," as Dean Gauss remarked, "to picking soft assignments."[13] He was developing a proud prejudice against playing the sedulous ape, yet he was undoubtedly sedulous in his continuing pursuit of excellence. Later in the month of May, he wrote somewhat diffidently from Paris to thank Sherwood Ander-

---

[12] Hemingway somewhat inaccurately described his first meeting with Fitzgerald in *A Moveable Feast*, New York, 1964, pp. 152-155.

[13] Gauss's account of these discussions was given in Christian Gauss to CB, 12/26/50.

son for having helped persuade Horace Liveright to publish *In Our Time*, and to emphasize how much it meant to him to have the short stories accepted and out of the way so that his mind would be clear for future work.[14]

II. FIRST DRAFT

That work, he decided, had to be a first novel. His new friend Fitzgerald was already an established novelist, and Harold Loeb's *Doodab* was on the point of publication. Hemingway later said that all his friends were coming out with novels while he was still wrestling with paragraphs. In June 1925 he began one of his own. It was an attempt to tell the story of his experiences as a Red Cross ambulance driver in 1918, and its title, borrowed from one of his poems, was *Along With Youth*. The locale was the aged transport *Chicago*, on which he himself had crossed the Atlantic for the first time. The book consisted almost entirely of conversations between Nick Adams and several friends. But it failed to satisfy Hemingway as to either tone or content, and he gave it up before Nick had even landed in France.[15]

He had no sooner laid aside his pencil and the blue notebook when it began to dawn on him that he might soon have material for a really successful first novel. It would grow out of his third visit to the San Fermín fiesta in Pamplona that July. Although he could hardly have known it yet, the cast of characters was already assembling around him. They included Bill Smith, who had come to Paris on a visit to Hemingway that spring; Donald Ogden Stewart, a gay member of Hemingway's group at the fiesta of 1924; Harold Loeb, his erstwhile tennis partner, a graduate of Princeton and a practitioner of various arts; and Harold's girl, Kitty Cannell, who knew and liked Hadley but was decidedly wary of Hemingway, whom she did not trust. Finally, there were Lady Duff Twysden, an Englishwoman of thirty-two who had

[14] EH to Sherwood Anderson, 5/23/25. Both Anderson and Dos Passos had written Hemingway of Anderson's part in "putting over" *In Our Time* with Liveright. Anderson elsewhere specifically disclaimed having boasted that Hemingway was one of his imitators. See *The Memoirs of Sherwood Anderson*, New York, 1942, pp. 474-475.

[15] Hemingway's unpublished longhand version of *Along with Youth* is preserved in a blue notebook dated June 15, 1925. It stops on unnumbered page 27.

been married in 1917 to Sir Roger Twysden, a naval officer, from whom she was now bitterly estranged, and Patrick Guthrie, a dissipated Scotsman, who was often seen in Duff's bibulous company. He was said to be living with her when they were both in funds, although Harold Loeb had lately been enjoying a secret liaison with Duff.[16]

This was the ill-assorted group that converged on Pamplona in the second week of July. Hemingway and his wife tried vainly to recapture the same spirit that had prevailed the year before. But the presence of the newcomers, and in particular the triangle formed by Duff and Pat Guthrie and Harold Loeb, did much to destroy the former glow. Hemingway seemed to feel some proprietary interest in Duff, and was angry when he learned that she had spent a week with Loeb at St. Jean-de-Luz. Guthrie was nasty about money and about Loeb. Quarrels and arguments frequently erupted, and at one point Hemingway and Loeb came close to a fist fight. The chief counterforce to all this was a brave young matador from Ronda, Cayetano Ordoñez, whose performances in the ring were so brilliant that his admirers began calling him the "Messiah who had come to save bullfighting," which, as always, was thought to be in a state of decline. Hemingway watched and listened with his customary acuity. If he were able to tell the story of the fiesta of 1925, approximately as it happened, from the preparatory days in Paris to the climax of Ordoñez' best bullfight, inventing where he had to but otherwise following the facts, he would have a first novel of considerable interest. He decided on a first-person narrative, with himself (slightly disguised) as combination observer-participant, somewhat after the manner of Melville's Ishmael in *Moby-Dick*.

He began to set it down almost immediately while the events of Pamplona were still fresh in his memory. For another month he and Hadley stayed on in Spain, following the footsteps of Ordoñez through the bullrings of Madrid and Valencia until the heat drove them north again to San Sebastian and Hendaye on the cool Atlantic coast. Back in Paris towards the end of August

---

[16] For additional details on Duff Twysden (born Mary Duff Stirling Byrom of Richmond, Yorkshire), see *Burke's Peerage*, London, 1959, p. 2269; and Harold Loeb, *The Way It Was*, New York, 1959, pp. 247-257.

he surged past the halfway mark, and by September 21st was able to write "The End" in the seventh of the notebooks in which he had laboriously set down his first draft. He did not really regard the book as finished, but he knew that the task of revision ought not to be rushed, and resolved to take his time about it through the fall and winter. He had already borrowed his title from Ecclesiastes: the book was going to be called *The Sun Also Rises.*[17]

Two weeks later, the American *In Our Time* was published in a two-dollar edition of 1335 copies. Although it made several enterprising publishers and editors, Maxwell Perkins among them, freshly aware of a new literary force, the book caused relatively little public stir. The advertising budget at Boni and Liveright was limited, and review copies were rather parsimoniously distributed. As Malcolm Cowley once remarked, first books by new authors sold poorly in those years, and the market for short stories was not good, even in a time when short fiction was being widely read in magazines. There seems also to have been a creeping prejudice in some quarters against American writers who had "deserted" their native land in order to live abroad. Ernest Boyd, who conducted a book page in *The Independent*, later confessed to some such feeling about Hemingway's first book.[18]

The collection nevertheless got serious consideration from such occasional Montparnassians as Paul Rosenfeld, Anderson's friend and benefactor, and Allen Tate, who did not share in the belief that foreign residence necessarily corrupted American talent. Though Rosenfeld professed to find evidence of the influence of Sherwood Anderson and Gertrude Stein at various points among the stories, his judgment was that the new voice was plainly original. Hemingway had managed to catch the prevalent feeling of that epoch: "a harsh impersonal force in the universe, permanent, not to be changed," at once destructive and constructive.

[17] The first draft of *The Sun Also Rises* is contained in seven small notebooks dated as follows: (1) Valencia, July 23-Aug. 3; (2) Valencia, Aug. 3; Madrid, Aug. 5-6; San Sebastian, Aug. 8-9; Hendaye, Aug. 10-12; (3) [Hendaye], Aug. 12-17; Paris, Aug. 19-20; (4) Paris, Aug. 20-29; (5) "Finished Paris, Sept. 9"; (6) "Sept. 9, Paris"; (7) "The End. Paris—Sept. 21—1925."

[18] Boyd, *The Independent*, 116 (June 12, 1926), p. 694.

Tate was impressed by Hemingway's evident love of nature. Ignoring the implicit symbolism, he praised "Big Two-Hearted River" as the "most completely realized naturalistic fiction of the age." Louis Kronenberger was one of those who discounted the alleged influence of Anderson and Gertrude Stein. What struck him most forcibly was the non-derivative merit, which showed "no important affinity with any other writer." Without knowing anything about Hemingway's boast to Horace Liveright that the book would be widely read by lowbrows and at the same time praised by the highbrows, Kronenberger professed to find intellect, culture, humor, and sophistication between the lines of *In Our Time.* But the real power lay, he asserted, in life, conversation, and action. The right critical term for Hemingway, he felt, was "synthetic observer" rather than psychological or social analyst.[19]

When Ernest Walsh reviewed the book in *This Quarter,* he overstated his case. Yet he managed at the same time to summarize certain of Hemingway's distinguishing talents. All the stories, Walsh thought, gave the impression of having been prepared for by "a growing process as natural as a plant getting ready to bloom." Among the other qualities that set Hemingway apart was his full and willing acceptance of the world. "In these days," wrote Walsh, "when few know where they are going, we get a man who feels what he feels clearly enough to be guided by his convictions into a life that may be said to remember the classical manhood of this age." Hemingway had gone through his dreams like a man, and they now lay well behind him. A process of renunciation of the false and the fantastic had taken place under the discipline of "a Spartan mind and will." What remained was "an uncanny mixture of boy-fresh perception" joined to an understanding and sympathy worthy of a much older artist. Hemingway was therefore "the shyest and proudest and sweetest-smelling story-teller" of Walsh's reading experience. There was no odor of corruption about his work. It would take a long time to wear him out.[20]

---

[19] Rosenfeld, *New Republic,* 45 (November 25, 1925), pp. 22-23; Tate, *Nation,* 122 (February 10, 1926), pp. 160-162; Kronenberger, *Saturday Review of Literature,* 2 (February 13, 1926), p. 555.

[20] Walsh, *This Quarter,* 2 (Autumn-Winter, 1925-1926), pp. 319-321.

Fitzgerald added his own plaudits with an essay in *The Book-man*. *In Our Time* was a bright entry in an otherwise "dismal record of high hope and stale failure" among the younger American writers. Fitzgerald implied, without ever quite saying, that Hemingway's recent aloofness from the United States was one of his strongest defenses against corruption. At this midway point in the twenties, the young writer often felt an insincere compulsion to write "significantly" about something called "the American scene." This was especially lethal when the impulse did not rise naturally within the writer himself. What had been forgotten in the gold rush to exploit native materials was the great truth that a writer's material "is as elusive as the moment in which it has its existence, unless it is purified by an incorruptible style, and by the catharsis of a passionate emotion." In the teeming welter of "American" writing, Fitzgerald could find neither genuine style nor adequate emotional drive, neither sensitivity of response to the given materials nor any firmly grounded ideas about the nature of art itself.

Fitzgerald had chosen two scapegoats to bear the blame for this situation: H. L. Mencken and Sherwood Anderson. Even though Mencken had "done more for American letters than any man alive," he was wedded to invective and had begot upon her a callous tribe of hammer-and-tongs boys who were all "insensitive, suspicious of glamour, preoccupied exclusively with the external, the contemptible, the 'national,' and the drab." The trouble with Sherwood Anderson was not so much his ideas as the absence of them. Reviewers still habitually spoke of him as an "inarticulate fumbling man, bursting with ideas." This was plainly wrong. In fact, Anderson possessed "a brilliant and almost inimitable prose style" and "scarcely any ideas at all."

The capstone of Fitzgerald's essay was *In Our Time*, which he felt offered "something temperamentally new." He had read "Big Two-Hearted River" with the "most breathless unwilling interest" since Joseph Conrad had first compelled him to look at the sea. Even in those other Nick Adams stories that used American backgrounds, the emphasis fell where it lay in the fishing story: on inner experience of a kind that knew no country, yet seemed to know them all. One felt, just below the surface, a snapping of ties, a sharp and nostalgic remembrance of things past, an intensely passionate emotion. With these stories, said Fitzgerald, Hemingway had turned a corner and emerged into a central thoroughfare.[21]

Hemingway chafed at the linkage of his name with that of Anderson. In spite of his laconic letter of thanks for Anderson's having helped to get *In Our Time* accepted, he was not overjoyed to find that Anderson had written the laudatory blurb for the book jacket. To make matters worse, Herschel Brickell's review in the New York *Post* strongly implied that "My Old Man" had been influenced by Anderson's race-track stories.[22] In 1923, Hemingway had specifically denied this allegation in a letter to Edmund Wilson. He also said that Anderson's later work had "gone to hell, perhaps from people in New York telling him too much how good he was."[23] This notion was still brought up frequently wherever two or three of the younger writers were gathered together. Several of Anderson's more recent books read, they pointed out, as if they had been written by Windy McPherson at his windiest. Fitzgerald made no secret of his belief that *Many Marriages* and *Dark Laughter* were "cheap, faked, obscurantic, and awful." He reported that Hemingway shared his own view that Anderson had "let everybody down who believed in him."[24]

Although Hemingway soon explained to Fitzgerald that he had not in any way planned to use *The Torrents of Spring* as a means of breaking his contract with Boni and Liveright, he knew very well that the firm would not and could not publish an attack on Horace Liveright's "present ace and best-seller."[25] The two statements did not, of course, square very well with each other. Whatever his motive, Hemingway put aside *The Sun Also Rises*, which still needed complete revision, and began with almost unseemly haste to write a parody on Anderson. He worked fast, completed the typescript between November 23 and 30 of

[21] "How to Waste Material: A Note on My Generation," *Bookman*, 63 (May, 1926), pp. 262-265.

[22] Brickell, *New York Evening Post*, October 17, 1925, p. 3.

[23] EH to Edmund Wilson, 11/25/23, printed in Wilson, *The Shores of Light*, New York, 1952, pp. 55-57.

[24] Fitzgerald quoted by Arthur Mizener, *The Far Side of Paradise*, Boston, 1951, p. 196.

[25] EH to Fitzgerald, 12/31/25; EH to CB, 4/1/51.

1925, and waited only a week more before sending it off to Liveright with a brash and boastful covering letter.[26]

III. TRAVESTY

The Torrents of Spring turned out to be a satirical *jeu d'esprit* with a serious critical core and a mean streak down the middle. Edmund Wilson had once remarked that Hemingway "was not a propagandist, even for humanity."[27] The new little story went far to prove Wilson's point. Its title came from one of Hemingway's favorite books by Turgenev, and its locale was Petoskey, Michigan, where Turgenev might have felt very much at home. That Hemingway was a satirist of some skill came as no surprise to his friends. The story about Mr. and Mrs. Smith was one example, and there were several other sketches of equal acidity that he had written but chosen not to publish. His letters and poems of the middle twenties showed that he had a lively fancy as well as considerable skill with the difficult art of parody. His hatred for sham literary posturing was profound, and in conversation he had a capacity for rough and bear-like persiflage that reminded at least one reader of Goldsmith's remark about Dr. Samuel Johnson: "When his pistol misses fire, he knocks you down with the butt end of it."[28]

Among the reviewers, Lawrence Morris saw the book as the somewhat ursine shrug with which a young author had thrown off the influence of an older one in a public gesture of proud independence. Hemingway's book stood to Anderson's *Dark Laughter* about as Fielding's *Shamela* did to Richardson's *Pamela*, and with much the same anti-sentimental cast of mind. In the vigor of his youth, Hemingway poked away lustily at Anderson's pretence of naïveté, and accepted as an epigraph Fielding's observation that "life everywhere furnishes an accurate observer with the ridiculous." It is easy to forgive Anderson his opinion that his former disciple had written "a parodistic book

---

[26] EH to Ernest Walsh, 11/30/25; EH to Horace Liveright, 12/7/25.

[27] Edmund Wilson, "Mr. Hemingway's Dry-Points," *Dial*, 77 (October, 1924), p. 34.

[28] James Boswell, *Life of Samuel Johnson*, New York, 1933, Vol. 1, p. 398.

that might have been humorous had Max Beerbohm condensed it to twelve pages."[29]

The torrents of the title are mainly sexual. They flow through the veins of Scripps O'Neil and through the arteries of Yogi Johnson. Scripps is a Harvard esthete who has drifted westward to Petoskey soon after the end of the first world war. Yogi is a war veteran of Swedish descent who works at the local pump factory. When the chinook wind melts the snow along the shores of Lake Michigan, both men begin to feel that vague unrest and sense of frustration so common among the brooding residents of Anderson's Winesburg. Neither of them is able to identify the origin or figure out the meaning of his discomfort. Scripps has been deserted by his first wife and is newly "married" to Diana, the senior waitress at Brown's Beanery. But he is not surprised to find that the strongest tributary to his own torrent is the junior waitress, a girl named Mandy whose chief attraction is that she likes to tell literary anecdotes. Hemingway generously credits Ford Madox Ford with many of these, including a memorable one about the dying words of Henry James. Diana is driven to desperate remedies to save her foundering marriage. In an effort to hold her man, she subscribes to and regularly reads *The Forum, The Mentor, The Literary Digest,* Mencken's *American Mercury, Harper's, The Bookman, The Saturday Review of Literature,* and *The New York Times Book Review.* She also pays close attention to the literary opinions of William Lyon Phelps in *Scribner's Magazine.* As a special temptation to Scripps, she has put aside a new article on chiropractors by H. L. Mencken. But when this fails, she goes softly out into the night, leaving her husband listening to yet another of Mandy's literary anecdotes. Yogi Johnson, a man of sterner stuff, is last seen going back to nature, striding down the G. R. & I. railroad tracks, accompanied by a naked Indian squaw with her papoose, and followed at a little distance by a pair of woods Indians who pick up Yogi's garments as he sheds them one by one.

The slightly sour bouquet of Winesburg is often evident in the atmosphere of Petoskey, and especially when Hemingway parodies the curious internal monologues of Anderson's characters.

---

[29] *The Memoirs of Sherwood Anderson,* New York, 1942, p. 475. See also L. S. Morris, *New Republic* 48 (September 15, 1926) p. 101.

"Scripps strode down the streets . . . to the beanery. He would have liked to ask Yogi to eat with him, but he didn't dare. Not yet. That would come later. All in good time. No need to rush matters with a man like Yogi. Who was Yogi, anyway? Had he really been in the war? What had the war meant to him? Was he really the first man to enlist from Cadillac? Where was Cadillac anyway? Time would tell."

Hemingway is also better than passable in his handling of Anderson's simplistic sentimentalism. "Scripps reached forward," says one paragraph, "to take the elderly waitress's hand, and with quiet dignity she laid it within his own. 'You are my woman,' he said. Tears came into her eyes, too. 'Once again I say: you are my woman.' Scripps pronounced the words solemnly. Something had broken inside him again. He felt he could not keep from crying. 'Let this be our wedding ceremony,' the elderly waitress said. Scripps pressed her hand. 'You are my woman,' he said, simply. 'You are my man and more than my man.' She looked into his eyes. 'You are all of America to me.' 'Let us go,' Scripps said."

Sometimes we are given a glimpse of an Andersonian character dreaming, like Yogi Johnson or Hemingway himself, of escape to regions far away. "Going somewhere now. En route. Huysmans wrote that. It would be interesting to read French. He must try it sometime. There was a street in Paris named after Huysmans. Right around the corner from where Gertrude Stein lived. Ah, there was a woman! Where were her experiments with words leading her? What was at the bottom of it? All that in Paris. Ah, Paris! How far it was to Paris now. Paris in the morning. Paris in the evening. Paris at night. Paris in the morning again. Paris at noon, perhaps. Why not? Yogi Johnson striding on. His mind never still."

Sherwood Anderson was not the only victim of the parody, as this paragraph shows when Hemingway reaches out to include Miss Stein's special forms of echolalia. Part of the second chapter even seems to look askance at Joyce's *Dubliners*. In the geographical catalogues there is sometimes a distant echo of the color-impressionism of John Dos Passos, who was in Paris when the book was written and is introduced into one passage by name. The shade of D. H. Lawrence stalks through the account of the captive bird warmed tenderly in Scripps's shirt-front, the sudden manifestation of the naked Indian squaw in the lunchroom, the "man-woman" talk of the self-married lovers, and the Indians who are made to speak with English accents in the Indian Club. Both in the dedication and occasionally elsewhere, H. L. Mencken comes in for some satirical attention. His irrepressible devotion to the imported word, italicized for emphasis and used to spice up the handsome pages of *The American Mercury*, is amusingly imitated in some of Scripps O'Neil's talk: "No *politzei* for mine. They give me the *katzenjammers*. . . . No more *weltpolitik*. Take Doctor Coolidge away."[30] But Anderson is always kept as the central target of the satire.

Hemingway was wintering for the second time in the Austrian Vorarlberg when Horace Liveright's cable reached him on December 30th: "REJECTING TORRENTS OF SPRING PATIENTLY AWAITING MANUSCRIPT SUN ALSO RISES." If submitting the book to Liveright had indeed been a contract-breaking ruse, as some of Hemingway's friends believed and as he was prompt to deny, it was in any case a ruse that worked. He had carefully laid the groundwork with Maxwell Perkins for just such a contingency. The rejected manuscript soon found its way into Perkins's hands, and the firm of Charles Scribner's Sons accepted it almost immediately, though apparently with some misgivings among Perkins's colleagues. There can be no doubt that Perkins's knowledge of the existence of *The Sun Also Rises* was an important factor in his decision to proceed with *The Torrents*. As such matters go in publishing, the preparation of the letterpress was very swift indeed. Hemingway's satire appeared late

[30] Hemingway sardonically dedicated the book to H. L. Mencken and S. Stanwood Menken. According to Malcolm Cowley (letter to CB, 10/20/51), Menken was a wealthy vice crusader who stood for everything that H. L. Mencken hated. Datus C. Smith, Jr. (letter to CB, 12/18/51) suggested that Hemingway was taking a satirical dig at Menken's leadership in the National Security League, which stood for 100% Americanism. Hemingway carried on his minor engagement with Mencken in *The Sun Also Rises*. "So many young men get their likes and dislikes from Mencken," reflects Jake Barnes, making it plain that he does not belong to that group. *SAR*, New York, 1926, p. 42. As to the intrusion of the shade of D. H. Lawrence into the Anderson parody, it may have been intentional on Hemingway's part. He once wrote Wyndham Lewis: "Lawrence you know was Anderson's God in the old days—and you can trace his effect all through A's stuff after he commenced reading him." EH to Wyndham Lewis, 10/24/27, quoted in part in Lewis's *Rude Assignment*, London, 1950, p. 203.

in May, 1926, a mere five months after Liveright's cable of rejection.

With some exceptions, American reviewers liked the book and agreed with its purpose. Ernest Boyd, who had been doubtful about the merits of *In Our Time*, now found Hemingway's future "immeasurably brighter." Some of the Chicago literary rebels (and, Boyd believed, Sherwood Anderson in particular) had run to verbal seed as a direct result of early success. The old laurels had dried out and needed watering. Hemingway had seized on Anderson's seedier qualities with good humor but also with a sharp eye for the ridiculous. He struck Boyd as "a genuine humorist and a critic so shrewd" that one hoped he might "cure the disease" he so well diagnosed. To Allen Tate, who had hailed the publication of *In Our Time*, *The Torrents* seemed "a small masterpiece." It combined humor, ribaldry, and satire in a manner, Tate thought, that made Hemingway "the best contemporary writer of eighteenth-century prose." But the praise was not universal, as indeed it never is. Harry Hansen much preferred the short stories. Parody, he said, was a gift of the gods, and few were blessed with it. They had plainly not chosen Hemingway as a favorite son.[31]

Hemingway's personal relationship with Anderson was not helped by a letter he wrote shortly before publication date. He explained that in November he had been overcome by a seemingly irresistible urge to push Anderson in the face. *The Torrents of Spring* was the result. It was meant as a joke, though it had a core of absolute sincerity. When Anderson wrote something "rotten," it was Hemingway's obligation to say so, no matter what the consequences. Nothing that was really good could be hurt by satire. Since no personal slight had been intended, it was better to be tough than easy. Hemingway admitted that Anderson might think this a "lousy snotty letter" of explanation about a "lousy snotty book." This, of course, was exactly what Anderson did think. Some years later he called it "possibly the most self-conscious and patronizing" letter ever sent by one literary man to another.[32]

---

[31] Ernest Boyd, *The Independent*, 116 (June 12, 1926), p. 694; Allen Tate, *Nation*, 123 (July 28, 1926), p. 89; Harry Hansen, *New York World* (May 30, 1926), p. 4.

[32] EH to Anderson, May 21, 1926. On Anderson's reaction, see James

More out of simple curiosity than rancor, he sometimes permitted himself to speculate about Hemingway's real motivation. Why had this young dog chosen to bite the very hand that had written such generous letters of introduction for him to the great and near-great expatriates of Paris? Why had he wanted to deliver a "funeral oration" over the grave of a fellow midwesterner who was still very much alive?[33] Anderson did not include among his speculations anything specifically Freudian. Indeed, the concept of himself as "father-figure" would perhaps in itself have seemed to him a kind of travesty. Yet Hemingway seems to have thought, however unjustly, that it was necessary to reject Anderson in order to reach the peak of his own maturity as a writer, well beyond and above the piedmont area which was the habitat of the sedulous apes.

IV. THE MARRING OF AMERICANS

The month when *The Torrents of Spring* appeared marked a turning-point in Hemingway's personal life. He had fallen in love with Pauline Pfeiffer, a wealthy young woman from Arkansas who worked in Paris as a fashion editor for *Vogue* magazine. Hadley learned of the situation during a springtime trip with Pauline through the valley of the Loire. Following the inevitable confrontation between Hadley and Hemingway, he went off alone to Madrid in May to watch the early-season bullfights and to salve his conscience as well as he could by writing short stories.

Hadley, still uncertain of what she ought to do about her marriage, went down to Cap d'Antibes with her son, who was then going on three, and stayed for a time on the estate of Gerald and Sara Murphy. Hemingway joined them there early in June, and took the occasion to confer with Scott Fitzgerald on the opening chapters of *The Sun Also Rises*. Fitzgerald advised certain cuts, which Hemingway considered. But in the end he decided instead to omit the first fifteen pages of his typescript, which

---

Schevill, *Sherwood Anderson*, Denver, 1951, pp. 226-228. As recently as March, 1925, Hemingway had chosen to praise Anderson's autobiography in *Ex Libris*, 2 (March, 1925), p. 176. See Ray Lewis White, ed., *A Story-Teller's Story*, Cleveland, 1968, p. xix.

[33] *The Memoirs of Sherwood Anderson*, New York, 1942, pp. 473-476.

consisted of short biographies of Brett Ashley and Mike Campbell, as well as a quick sketch of Jake Barnes's early career.

This decision had been made and Perkins duly notified by the time that Pauline appeared, determined to pretend that nothing serious was afoot between herself and Hemingway. They waited out the rest of June in a *ménage à trois* that satisfied no one and was in fact a constant source of acute discomfort to Hadley. In July, the Hemingways and Pauline made a trip to Spain in the company of the Murphys, partly to initiate Gerald Murphy into the joys of Pamplona in the time of its annual fiesta. When it was over, Pauline departed with the Murphys, leaving the Hemingways in Spain for the rest of July. When they returned to Paris in August, they had made up their minds to separate. They gave up the flat over the sawmill in the rue Notre Dame des Champs, Hadley and the child took up residence in a small hotel, and Hemingway occupied a studio belonging to Gerald Murphy. It was there, during the latter weeks of August, that he read final proof on *The Sun Also Rises*, the book that was as crucial to his literary career as the break-up with Hadley was for his domestic life.[34]

He had been married to Pauline for six years when his parody of Anderson arose to haunt him once again. The occasion was the publication of a memoir by Gertrude Stein. She had written it in the third person under the pretence that it was in fact what it was called, *The Autobiography of Alice B. Toklas*. For all her air of motherly solicitude with those she liked, including Hemingway in his early Paris years, Miss Stein was capable of feline behavior toward those with whom she had quarreled. Her quarrel with Hemingway took place sometime after the publication of *The Torrents of Spring*. She seems to have felt, though she did not publicly say, that he had parodied her own writing as well as Anderson's.

Her explanation of Hemingway's reasons for writing *The Torrents* was simple professional jealousy. It was obvious, she

[34] For a fuller account of these events, see Carlos Baker, *Ernest Hemingway: A Life Story*, New York, 1969, especially pp. 168-178. Hemingway's marriage to Pauline Pfeiffer occurred in May, 1927, and their two sons, Patrick and Gregory, were born in 1928 and 1931. Pauline divorced Hemingway in 1940, whereupon he took Martha Gellhorn as his third wife. Following his divorce from Martha in 1946, he was married to Mary Welsh, whom he had met in London in 1944.

thought, that he had staked out the field of sport as his own private domain, and he resented the fact that Anderson had also written some sporting stories. She recalled that she had once named Anderson as the only man in America who "could write a clear and passionate sentence." Hemingway, who heard her say it, had disagreed sharply and had also questioned Anderson's taste. What was that if not professional jealousy?

She also mentioned Anderson's visit to Paris in January, 1927. "Hemingway," she said, "naturally was afraid." She and Anderson talked it over and agreed that Hemingway was "yellow"—"just like the flatboat men on the Mississippi as described by Mark Twain." Anderson's own *Memoirs* offered a different and milder version of the story. He remembered that Hemingway had come knocking at his door, suggested that they have a drink at a bistro, and then, after a brief conversation, departed as hurriedly as he had come. Anderson stated, with characteristic charity, that Hemingway's "absorption in his ideas may have affected his capacity for friendship." A third account was Hemingway's own, made on the spot in a letter to Maxwell Perkins: "Sherwood Anderson is in Paris and we had two fine afternoons together. . . . He was not at all sore about *Torrents* and we had a fine time." Since Anderson was in fact still smarting over the book, Hemingway's flat statement ought probably to be taken with a grain of salt. Anderson's story of the meeting reads like something that might have happened. But Miss Stein's opinion that Hemingway was "yellow" and "afraid" of what Anderson might do to him was plainly ridiculous.

So was her further statement that Anderson had taught Hemingway to box, to say nothing of her allegation that Hemingway had learned all about bullfighting from her, although she and Miss Toklas had been to Spain much earlier than he, and it is likely that she was the first to tell him about the fiesta of San Fermín in Pamplona. She also mentioned the assistance Hemingway had given her in securing the serial publication of *The Making of Americans*. For this she was grateful, although she pointed out that he had "learned a great deal" from correcting the proof-sheets of her work, and that he "admired all that he had learned." She went on to say that Hemingway the writer was virtually the creation of herself and Sherwood Anderson, and that "they were both a little proud and a little ashamed of the work of their minds."[35]

All this, of course, was a tissue of lies. *The Autobiography of Alice B. Toklas* was so full of misstatements that many of her former associates felt that the book called for public contradiction. Hemingway's own rejoinder, in a passage of dialogue in *Green Hills of Africa*, indicated his resentment over her having called him a coward, and pointed out that what Miss Stein knew about the writing of dialogue had probably been learned from his own work, instead of the other way round. She was "damned nice before she got ambitious," and it was a shame to see "all that talent gone to malice and nonsense and self-praise." He reserved his strongest attack on Miss Stein for the pages of *A Moveable Feast*, his memoir of his early days in Paris published in 1964, long after both he and Gertrude Stein were dead.[36]

But Gertrude Stein's animadversions and Hemingway's replies still lay well in the future during those latter days of 1926 when he had finished reading proofs and was eagerly awaiting the publication of *The Sun Also Rises*. He was by choice an independent spirit, a sidelong and sardonic observer of the vagaries of the Montparnassians, aggressively critical of all forms of literary pretentiousness, and a declared enemy of poor writing, his own included. It was plainly a strategic error on his part to project himself so fiercely into the literary warfare of that period, whether through stories like "Mr. and Mrs. Elliot," or parodies like *The Torrents*, or through the use of people he closely knew as prototypes for the characters of *The Sun Also Rises*. Literary grudges are among the most lasting, and it was natural enough that the enemies he made at that time should seize the occasions offered by their reminiscences to attack him in turn. Some of this was doubtless in Dorothy Parker's mind when she remarked in *The New Yorker*, shortly after the publication of *A Farewell to Arms*: "Probably of no other living man has so much tripe been penned or spoken."[37]

Those who disliked him were matched at least equally with

[35] Gertrude Stein, *The Autobiography of Alice B. Toklas*, New York, 1933, pp. 265-270.

[36] Hemingway, *GHOA*, New York, 1935, pp. 65-66; and *A Moveable Feast*, New York, 1964, pp. 13-21, and especially 117-119.

[37] Dorothy Parker, *New Yorker*, 5 (November 30, 1929), pp. 28-31. Among books that included attacks on Hemingway were Margaret Anderson, *My Thirty Years' War*, New York, 1930; Aldous Huxley, *Music*

others on whose toes he had not trod. Still in the future were his quarrels with Archibald MacLeish, John Dos Passos, Scott Fitzgerald, William Bird, Donald Ogden Stewart, and Dorothy Parker. These would darkly color the public and private views of Hemingway in the years of his greatest success. But a word-portrait of him by his close associates in 1926 would have read more like that of Elliot Paul, who called him a "shy and diffident man, eager for appreciation and constructive criticism, not at all sure of himself, a gay companion, and a loyal friend."[38] This opinion was shared by Christian Gauss, who had had the opportunity to size him up during a succession of café-table talks in the middle twenties. "His dominant interest," wrote Gauss, "was . . . in learning the craft of the writer. . . . Fitzgerald too was, and remained, an earnest and competent student of the art of writing, and this was one of the bonds between Scott and Hemingway. In other respects they were worlds apart. Hemingway was not interested in the Ritz or playboys. His special interest lay in the more exacting forms of physical proficiency and courage. He himself did some boxing and practiced enough self-control to keep himself in reasonable trim. There was nothing Latin-Quarterish, intellectually or esthetically pretentious about him. He had the clear eye, even temper, and easy bearing of an athlete in condition."[39]

Between 1926 and 1952 Hemingway completed, and Charles Scribner's Sons published, *The Sun Also Rises, Men Without Women, A Farewell to Arms, Death in the Afternoon, Winner Take Nothing, Green Hills of Africa, To Have and Have Not, The Fifth Column, For Whom the Bell Tolls, Across the River and into the Trees,* and *The Old Man and the Sea.* Although not all of them are of equal quality, they served to establish his reputation as one of the leading American writers and to consolidate his international fame. It is to these productions as well as to the posthumous publications, *A Moveable Feast* and *Islands in the Stream,* that the rest of this book is primarily devoted.

---

at *Night,* London, 1932; Alfred Kreymborg, *The Little World: 1914 and After,* New York, 1932; Wyndham Lewis, *Men Without Art,* London, 1934; Max Eastman, *Art and the Life of Action,* New York, 1934; Robert McAlmon, *Being Geniuses Together,* London, 1938; and Harold Acton, *Memoirs of an Aesthete,* London, 1948.

[38] Elliot Paul, *Saturday Review of Literature,* 17 (November 6, 1937), pp. 3-4.

[39] Dean Christian Gauss to CB, 12/26/50.

III · The Way It Was

> "The job of the last twenty-five years was for the writer or artist to get what there was to be got (artistically) out of the world extant."—Ezra Pound [1]

I. PLACE, FACT, SCENE

"A writer's job is to tell the truth," said Hemingway in 1942.[2] He had believed it for twenty years and he would continue to believe it as long as he lived. No other writer of our time had so fiercely asserted, so pugnaciously defended, or so consistently exemplified the writer's obligation to speak truly. His standard of truth-telling remained, moreover, so high and so rigorous that he was ordinarily unwilling to admit secondary evidence, whether literary evidence or evidence picked up from other sources than his own experience. "I only know what I have seen," was a statement which came often to his lips and pen. What he had personally done, or what he knew unforgettably by having gone through one version of it, was what he was interested in telling about. This is not to say that he refused to invent freely. But he always made it a sacrosanct point to invent in terms of what he actually knew from having been there.

The primary intent of his writing, from first to last, was to seize and project for the reader what he often called "the way it was." This is a characteristically simple phrase for a concept of extraordinary complexity, and Hemingway's conception of its meaning subtly changed several times in the course of his career—always in the direction of greater complexity. At the core of the concept, however, one can invariably discern the operation of three esthetic instruments: the sense of place, the sense of fact, and the sense of scene.

The first of these, obviously a strong passion with Hemingway,

[1] Ezra Pound, quoted in Samuel Putnam, *Paris Was Our Mistress,* New York, 1947, p. 154.
[2] *Men at War,* New York, 1942, introduction, p. xv.

is the sense of place. "Unless you have geography, background," he once told George Antheil, "you have nothing." [3] You have, that is to say, a dramatic vacuum. Few writers have been more place-conscious. Few have so carefully charted out the geographical groundwork of their novels while managing to keep background so conspicuously unobtrusive. Few, accordingly, have been able to record more economically and graphically the way it is when you walk through the streets of Paris in search of breakfast at a corner café. Or when your footfalls echo among surrounding walls on the ancient cobblestones of early morning Venice, heading for the market-place beside the Adriatic. Or when, at around six o'clock of a Spanish dawn, you watch the bulls running from the corrals at the Puerta Rochapea through the streets of Pamplona towards the bullring.

"When I woke it was the sound of the rocket exploding that announced the release of the bulls from the corrals at the edge of town. . . . Down below the narrow street was empty. All the balconies were crowded with people. Suddenly a crowd came down the street. They were all running, packed close together. They passed along and up the street toward the bullring and behind them came more men running faster, and then some stragglers who were really running. Behind them was a little bare space, and then the bulls, galloping, tossing their heads up and down. It all went out of sight around the corner. One man fell, rolled to the gutter, and lay quiet. But the bulls went right on and did not notice him. They were all running together." [4]

This scene is as morning-fresh as a design in India ink on clean white paper. First is the bare white street, seen from above, quiet and empty. Then one sees the first packed clot of runners. Behind these are the thinner ranks of those who move faster because closer to the bulls. Then the almost comic stragglers, who are "really running." Brilliantly behind these shines the "little bare space," a desperate margin for error. Then the clot of running bulls—closing the design, except of course for the man in the gutter making himself, like the designer's initials, as inconspicuous as possible.

[3] George Antheil, *Bad Boy of Music*, p. 278.
[4] *SAR*, pp. 165–166.

The continuing freshness of such occasions as this might be associated with Hemingway's lifelong habit of early waking. More likely, the freshness arises because Hemingway loves continental cities, makes it almost a fetish to know them with an artist's eye, and has trained himself rigorously to see and retain those aspects of a place that make it *that place,* even though, with an odd skill, he manages at the same time to render these aspects generically.

As with the cities—and Hemingway's preference is for the Latin cities—so with the marshes, rivers, lakes, troutstreams, gulf-streams, groves, forests, hills, and gullies, from Wyoming to Tanganyika, from the Tagliamento to the Irati, and from Key West to the Golden Horn. "None can care for literature itself," said Stevenson, somewhere, "who do not take a special pleasure in the sound of names." Hemingway's love of names is obvious. It belongs to his sense of place. But like the rest of his language, it is under strict control. One never finds, as so often happens in the novels of Thomas Wolfe or the poetry of Carl Sandburg, the mere riot and revel of place-names, played upon like guitar-strings for the music they contain. Hemingway likes the words *country* and *land.* It is astonishing how often they recur in his work without being obtrusive. He likes to move from place to place, and to be firmly grounded, for the time being, in whatever place he has chosen. It may be the banks of the Big Two-Hearted River of Northern Michigan or its Spanish equivalent above Burguete. It may be the Guadarrama hilltop where El Sordo died, or the Veneto marshes where Colonel Cantwell shot his last mallards from a duckblind. Wherever it is, it is solid and permanent, both in itself and in the books.

The earliest of his published work, descriptively speaking, shows an almost neoclassical restraint. Take a sample passage from *The Sun Also Rises,* not his earliest but fairly representative. This one concerns the Irati Valley fishing-trip of Jake Barnes and Bill Gorton.

"It was a beech wood and the trees were very old. Their roots bulked above the ground and the branches were twisted. We walked on the road between the thick trunks of the old beeches and the sunlight came through the leaves in light patches on the grass. The trees were big, and the foliage was thick but it was not gloomy. There was no undergrowth, only the smooth grass, very green and fresh, and the big gray trees were well spaced as though it were a park. 'This is country,' Bill said." [5]

It is such country as an impressionist might paint almost exactly in the terms, and the subdued colors, which Hemingway employs. More than this, however, is the fact that in such a paragraph Dr. Samuel Johnson's Imlac could find little to criticize. Even the arrangement of the beech trees themselves, like the choice of the words, is clean and classical. The foliage is thick, but there is no gloom. Here is neither teeming undergrowth nor its verbal equivalent. The sage of Johnson's *Rasselas* advises all aspirant poets against numbering the streaks of the tulip or describing in detail the different shades of the verdure of the forest. Young Hemingway, still an aspirant poet, follows the advice. When he has finished, it is possible to say (and we supply our own inflection for Bill Gorton's words): "This is country."

For all the restraint, the avoidance of color-flaunting adjectives, and the plainsong sentences (five compound to one complex), the paragraph is loaded with precisely observed fact: beech wood, old trees, exposed roots, twisted branches, thick trunks, sun-patches, smooth green grass, foliage which casts a shade without excluding light. One cannot say that he has been given a generalized landscape—there are too many exact factual observations. On the other hand, the uniquenesses of the place receive no special emphasis. One recognizes easily the generic type of the clean and orderly grove. where weeds and brush do not flourish because of the shade, and the grass gets only enough light to rise to carpet-level. Undoubtedly, as in the neoclassical esthetic, the intent is to provide a generic frame within which the reader is at liberty to insert his own uniquenesses—as many or as few as his imagination may supply.

Along with the sense of place, and as a part of it, is the sense of fact. Facts march through all his pages in a stream as continuous as the refugee wagons in Thrace or the military camions on the road from the Isonzo. Speculation, whether by the author or by the characters, is ordinarily kept to a minimum. But facts,

[5] *SAR*, p. 120.

visible or audible or tangible facts, facts baldly stated, facts without verbal paraphernalia to inhibit their striking power, are the stuff of Hemingway's prose.

Sometimes, especially in the early work, the facts seem too many for the effect apparently intended, though even here the reader should be on guard against misconstruing the intention of a given passage. It is hard to discover, nevertheless, what purpose beyond the establishment of the sense of place is served by Barnes's complete itinerary of his walk with Bill Gorton through the streets of Paris.[6] The direction is from Madame Lecomte's restaurant on the Île St. Louis across to the left bank of the Seine, and eventually up the Boulevard du Port Royal to the Café Select. The walk fills only two pages. Yet it seems much longer and does not further the action appreciably except to provide Jake and Bill with healthy after-dinner exercise. At Madame Lecomte's (the facts again), they have eaten "a roast chicken, new green beans, mashed potatoes, a salad, and some apple pie and cheese." To the native Parisian, or a foreigner who knows the city, the pleasure in the after-dinner itinerary would consist in the happy shock of recognition. For others, the inclusion of so many of the facts of municipal or gastronomic geography—so many more than are justified by their dramatic purpose—may seem excessive.

Still, this is the way it was that time in Paris. Here lay the bridges and the streets, the squares and the cafés. If you followed them in the prescribed order, you came to the café where Lady Brett Ashley sat on a high stool at the bar, her crossed legs stockingless, her eyes crinkling at the corners.

If an imaginative fusion of the sense of place and the sense of fact is to occur, and if, out of the fusing process, dramatic life is to arise, a third element is required. This may be called the sense of scene. Places are less than geography, facts lie inert and uncoordinated, unless the imagination runs through them like a vitalizing current and the total picture moves and quickens. How was it, for example, that second day of the San Fermin fiesta in the Pamplona bullring after Romero had killed the first bull?

"They had hitched the mules to the dead bull and then the whips cracked, the men ran, and the mules, straining forward,

[6] *SAR*, pp. 79–80.

their legs pushing, broke into a gallop, and the bull, one horn up, his head on its side, swept a swath smoothly across the sand and out the red gate." [7]

Here are a dead bull, men, mules, whips, sand, and a red gate like a closing curtain—the place and the facts. But here also, in this remarkably graphic sentence, are the seven verbs, the two adverbs, and the five adverbial phrases which fuse and coordinate the diverse facts of place and thing and set them in rapid motion. If one feels that the sentence is very satisfying as a scene, and wishes to know why, the answer might well lie where it so often lies in a successful lyric poem—that is, in our sense of difficulty overcome. Between the inertness of the dead bull when he is merely *hitched* (a placid verb) and the smooth speed with which the body finally *sweeps* across the sand and out of sight, come the verbs of sweating effort: *crack, run, strain,* and *break.* It is precisely at the verb *broke* that the sentence stops straining and moves into the smooth glide of its close. The massing, in that section of the sentence, of a half-dozen *s*'s, compounded with the *th* sounds of *swath* and *smoothly,* can hardly have been inadvertent. They ease (or grease) the path of the bull's departure.

The pattern in the quoted passage is that of a task undertaken, striven through, and smoothly completed: order and success. For another graphic sentence, so arranged as to show the precise opposites—total disorder and total failure—one might take the following example from *Death in the Afternoon.* The protagonist is a "phenomenon," a bullfighter who has lost his nerve.

"In your mind you see the phenomenon, sweating, white-faced, and sick with fear, unable to look at the horn or go near it, a couple of swords on the ground, capes all around him, running in at an angle on the bull hoping the sword will strike a vital spot, cushions sailing down into the ring and the steers ready to come in." [8]

In this passage, place has become predicament. The facts, thrown in almost helter-skelter, imply the desperate inward fear which is responsible for the creation of the outward disorder. Verbs are held to a minimum, and their natural naked power is

[7] *SAR,* p. 175.
[8] *DIA,* p. 226.

limited with qualifications. The phenomenon is *unable to look*, and *hoping to strike*, not *looking* and *striking*. He runs, but it is at a bad angle. The disorder of the swords on the ground and the capes all around is increased by the scaling-in of seat-cushions from the benches, the audience's insult to gross cowardice. The author-spectator's crowning insult is the allusion to the steers, who by comparison with the enraged bull are bovine, old-womanly creatures. On being admitted to the ring, they will quiet and lead away the bull the phenomenon could not kill.

The sense of place and the sense of fact are indispensable to Hemingway's art. But the true craft, by which diversities are unified and compelled into graphic collaboration, comes about through the operation of the sense of scene. Often, moving through the Latin language countries, watching the crowd from a café table or a barrera bench, Hemingway seems like a lineal descendant of Browning's observer in *How It Strikes a Contemporary*.

> You saw go up and down Valladolid
> A man of mark, to know next time you saw . . .
> Scenting the world, looking it full in face.

II. WHAT HAPPENED

Although they are clearly fundamental to any consideration of Hemingway's esthetic aims, place, fact, and scene are together no more than one phase of a more complex observational interest. The skillful writer can make them work in harmony, with place and fact like teamed horses under the dominance of the sense of scene. The result is often as striking and satisfactory to watch as a good chariot race. But the event is, after all, mainly an extrinsic matter. These are not Plato's horses of the soul.

The complementary phase is inward: a state of mind causally related to the extrinsic events and accurately presented in direct relation to those events. When Samuel Putnam asked Hemingway in the late twenties for a definition of his aims, the answer was: "Put down what I see and what I feel in the best and simplest way I can tell it." [9] Taken as absolute standards, of course, best-

---

[9] Samuel Putnam, *op.cit.*, pp. 128–129.

ness and simplicity will often be at variance, a fact of which Hemingway at that date was apparently becoming more and more conscious. But his aim from the beginning had been to show, if he could, the precise relationship between what he saw and what he felt.

It is characteristic of Hemingway, with his genuine scorn for overintellectualized criticism, that he has himself refused to employ critical jargon in the presentation of his esthetic ideas. It is also evident, however, that early in his career, probably about 1922, he had evolved an esthetic principle which might be called "the discipline of double perception." The term is not quite exact, since the aim of double perception is ultimately a singleness of vision. This is the kind of vision everyone experiences when his two eyes, though each sees the same set of objects from slightly disparate angles, work together to produce a unified picture with a sense of depth to it. According to Hemingway, he was trying very hard for this double perception about the time of his return from the Near East in the fall of 1922. Aside from knowing "truly" what he "really" felt in the presence of any given piece of action, he found that his greatest difficulty lay in putting down on paper "what really happened in action; what the actual things were which produced the emotion" felt by the observer. No wonder that he was finding it hard to get "the real thing, the sequence of motion and fact which made the emotion." Whatever that real thing was, if you stated it "purely" enough and were likewise lucky, there was a chance that your statement of it would be valid, esthetically and emotionally valid, forever.[10]

Fundamental to the task is the deletion of one's own preconceptions. Such and such was the way it *ought* to be, the way you *assumed* it was. But "oughts" and "assumptions" are dangerous ground for a man to stand on who wishes to take the word of no one else, and to achieve in esthetics what René Descartes thought he had achieved in philosophy, namely, a start at the start. The hope was that the genuinely serious and determined writer-observer might be able in time to penetrate behind the illusions which all our preconceptions play upon the act of clear seeing.

[10] *DIA*, p. 2.

It would then become his task to perfect himself in the discipline of double perception. To make something so humanly true that it will outlast the vagaries of time and change, yet will still speak directly to one's own changing time, he must somehow reach a state of objective awareness between two poles, one inward-outward and the other outward-inward. The first need (though not always first in order of time) is the ability to look within and to describe that complex of mixed emotions which a given set of circumstances has produced in the observer's mind. The other necessity is to locate and to state factually and exactly that outer complex of motion and fact which produced the emotional reaction.

This second class of things and circumstances, considered in their relations to the emotional complexes of the first class, would be precisely what T. S. Eliot called "objective correlatives." [11] His statement calls them variously "a set of objects, a situation, a chain of events which shall be the formula of that particular emotion; such that when the external facts, which must terminate in sensory experience, are given, the emotion is immediately evoked." He states further that the idea of artistic "inevitability" consists in the "complete adequacy of the external to the emotion." Mr. Eliot's generic description fits Hemingway's customary performance. Yet it may be noticed that Eliot's most frequent practice, as distinguished from his theoretical formulation, is to fashion his objective correlatives into a series of complex *literary* symbols. These are designed to elicit a more or less controlled emotional response from the reader (like the Wagnerian passage in *The Waste Land*), depending to some degree on the extent of his cultural holdings. With Hemingway, on the other hand, the objective correlatives are not so much inserted and adapted as observed and encompassed. They are to be traced back, not to anterior literature and art objects, but to things actually seen and known by direct experience of the world.

Hemingway's method has this special advantage over Eliot's —that one's ability to grasp the emotional suggestions embodied in an objective correlative depends almost solely on two factors: the reader's sensitivity to emotional suggestion, and the degree

[11] T. S. Eliot, *The Sacred Wood*, London, 1920, pp. 92–93.

of his imaginative and sympathetic involvement in the story which is being told. With Eliot these two factors are likewise emphatically present, but a third is added. This third, which in a measure controls and delimits the first two, is the factor of "literary" experience. One's emotional response to the Wagnerian passage cannot be really full unless he knows its origin, can see it in both its original and its new and secondary context, and can make certain quick comparisons between the two. Some, though not all, of Eliot's correlatives accordingly show a "twice-removed" quality which in a measure pales and rarefies them. They cannot always achieve the full-bloodedness and immediacy of correlatives taken directly from the actual set of empirical circumstances which produced in the author the emotion which he is seeking to convey to the reader.

The objective correlatives in Hemingway appear to be of two main types, arbitrarily separable though always working together in a variety of ways. The first may be called *things-in-context:* that particular arrangement of facts in their relations to one another which constitutes a static field of perception. The second type may be called *things-in-motion,* since the arrangement of facts in their relations one to another is almost never wholly static. One might call any combination of the two types by the generic term of *what happened,* where the idea of happening implies a sequence of events in a certain order in time, though any event in the sequence can be arrested to form a static field of observation. If you have *what happened* in this special sense, you will have a chance of reproducing, in a perspective with depth, "the way it was."

To write for permanence, therefore, is to find and set down those things-in-context and things-in-motion which evoked a reaction in the writer as observer. Yet even the presence of both of these correlatives will not suffice to produce the total effect unless one also knows and says what he "really felt" in their presence. The important corollary idea of selection, meaning the elimination of the irrelevant and the unimportant at both poles, is clearly implied in Hemingway's phrase, "stated purely enough." During the five years of his early apprenticeship and the next five in which he developed his skills with such remarkable rapidity, the discipline of double perception was for Hemingway the leading esthetic principle. It is hard to imagine a better—or more difficult—task for the young writer to attempt. Although other principles later arose to supplement this first one, it still continued to occupy one whole side of his attention.

III. TRUTH AND FALLACY

The basis of Hemingway's continuing power, and the real backbone of his eminence, is in practical esthetics. "Pure" or theoretical esthetics, of that special bloodless order which can argue to all hours without a glance at concretions, holds little interest for an artist of so pragmatic and empirical a cast of mind. One might even doubt that theoretical esthetics is of real interest to any genuine artist, unless in his alter ego he happens also to be a philosophical critic. If that is true, his artistic life is always in some danger, as Hemingway's is not. In esthetics as in his personal philosophy, he strove very hard to stay free of the wrong kind of illusion, and out from under the control of any cut-and-dried system, always trying instead to keep his eye trained on the thing in itself and the effect of the thing in himself. The actual, he wrote in 1949, is "made of knowledge, experience, wine, bread, oil, salt, vinegar, bed, early mornings, nights, days, the sea, men, women, dogs, beloved motor cars, bicycles, hills and valleys, the appearance and disappearance of trains on straight and curved tracks . . . cock grouse drumming on a basswood log, the smell of sweetgrass and fresh-smoked leather and Sicily." [12] Given the knowledge and experience of these and their unnamed equivalents, the artist can be at home in the world. If he is a practical esthetician whose aim is to "invent truly," he is on firm ground. By experience he knows what will do. By observation he knows what will go—like the eminently practical Aristotle of the *Poetics*.

It was once remarked, though not by Aristotle, that the province of esthetics is the true and the beautiful, the province of morality the good. Of Hemingway as a moral writer there will be much to say. It is clear that the strongest conviction in Heming-

[12] Introd. to Elio Vittorini's novel, *In Sicily*, New York, 1949.

way the esthetician—the principle underlying his sense of place and fact and scene, the principle supporting his "discipline of double perception"—is the importance of telling truth.

To get at the truth of anything is hard enough. For the young artist the task is complicated by the fact that he must steer his way with the utmost care among a set of fallacies, placed like sand-bunkers around a green, or concealed traps around desirable bait. Three of these fallacies stand out: the pathetic, the apathetic, and what may be called the kinetographic.

Ruskin named the first.[13] It is *pathetic* because it comes about through excess of emotion. It is fallacious because, when we are really dominated by an emotion, it is extremely difficult to see things as they are. The curious may read Hemingway's own half-serious opinions on the subject in a disquisition on "erectile writing," which was written to satirize Waldo Frank's *Virgin Spain* in *Death in the Afternoon*.[14] Fundamentally, as that essay makes plain, the pathetic fallacy is an error in perception. But secondarily and by a logical sequence, it is an error of expression, since what has been wrongly seen cannot be rightly described. The intensity of the emotion felt by the writer, if let go on its own, will determine his choice of words. In Charles Kingsley's *Alton Locke,* Ruskin finds an example in which the writing has been made irrational by the author's failure to control the intensity of his emotion. A girl has died in the surf and the seamen bring her body in.

> They rowed her in across the rolling foam—
> The cruel, crawling foam.

"The foam is not cruel," says Ruskin, "neither does it crawl. The state of mind which attributes to it these characters of a living creature is one in which the reason is unhinged by grief. All violent feelings have the same effect. They produce in us a falseness in all our impressions of external things, which I would generally characterize as the pathetic fallacy."

Ruskin goes on to say that the greatest artists do not often admit this kind of falseness of impression and expression. It is only the second or third rankers who much delight in it. It is a

[13] John Ruskin, *Modern Painters*, New York, 1865, Vol. 3, pp. 156–172.
[14] *DIA*, p. 53.

form of self-deception, one of the orders of sentimentality. The good writers are not the creatures of their emotions; theirs is a sanity which helps them to see the world clearly and to see it whole.

Beginning with a standard of performance which rigorously excluded the pathetic fallacy, Hemingway adhered to it with a faith just short of fanatical, all his life. Emotion was of course both permissible and, under proper control, necessary. Excess of emotion, however, was never to be allowed. It would falsify both impression and expression. So many of our habits of seeing and saying take their origin from recollected emotion gone stale. If one could cut loose from these habits, three immediate results might be expected. First, you could see what you really saw rather than what you thought you saw. Second, you could know what you felt rather than "what you were supposed to feel." Third, you could say outright what you really saw and felt instead of setting down a false (and, in the bad sense, a literary) version of it.

Hemingway's earliest plan, therefore, was to start cleanly and all afresh to see what effects could be achieved by straight observation of action, set forth in unadorned prose. The immediate upshot of the effort was the kind of writing presented in the Paris edition of *in our time*. This, for example, on part of Act One at a bullfight:

"They whack-whacked the white horse on the legs and he kneed himself up. The picador twisted the stirrups straight and pulled and hauled up into the saddle. The horse's entrails hung down in a blue bunch and swung backward and forward as he began to canter, the monos whacking him on the back of his legs with the rods. He cantered jerkily along the barrera. He stopped stiff and one of the monos held his bridle and walked him forward. The picador kicked in his spurs, leaned forward and shook his lance at the bull. Blood pumped regularly from between the horse's front legs. He was nervously unsteady. The bull could not make up his mind to charge." [15]

This 120-word miniature is a writer's apprentice-exercise, a minute of a Spanish committee meeting. Without ignoring the be-

[15] *First 49*, p. 262.

ginning (a horse has been gored by a bull) or the end (the horse will be gored again and will die), the young writer is concentrating on the middle of an action. He puts down what he sees, exactly as he sees it. He eliminates from his view the panorama, the weather, the crowd, the waiting matadors, the price of the seats, the hardness of the bench on which he sits, the odor of his neighbor, the color of the sky, the degree of the temperature. Instead he watches the horse, and what takes place immediately around the horse, with a tremendous intensity of concentration. He is not guessing, even when he speaks of the horse's nervous unsteadiness or the bull's indecision. These are immediately visible qualities, shown by the animals through their actions. The prose is as clean as the observation. Nothing is ornamental. None but essential modifiers are called, and only a few are chosen. No similes, no metaphors, no literary allusions, no pathetic illusions, no balanced clauses. There is only one trick, and that is a good one: the three-time use of the word *forward,* which adds to the intensity of the account because "forward" is where the bull stands with one wet horn. Otherwise there is nothing in the least fancy. There is only an ancient horse, in very bad shape, waiting for the *coup de grâce.*

Though he never chose similar subjects himself, Ruskin might well have admired Hemingway's "story." He could have placed it alongside Thackeray's account of Amelia in *Vanity Fair:* that time in Chapter 32 in Brussels when she prays quietly for the well-being of her husband George, in ignorance of the fact that he lies dead at Waterloo. Ruskin's term for the literature of straight statement, without moralizing elaboration or rococo interior decorating, is the "Make-What-You-Will-Of-It" school of fiction—a school diametrically opposed to the school of the pathetic fallacy. Scholars at the Spartan school of "What-You-Will" are content to let well enough alone. Like Hemingway at the Spanish committee-meeting, they say the thing the way it was and let the minutes stand as written.

The passage on the horse also steers clear of the apathetic fallacy, where the reason is so cold and tight that the matter of emotion is squeezed out entirely. At first glance, it is true, one might suppose that Hemingway had ignored both his own and the reader's emotions. The account includes no overt allusion to how the observer felt in the presence of Rosinante Agonistes. There is no evident plucking of the heart-strings, no visible pump inserted into the springs of human sympathy.

Yet the close reader can entertain no real doubt. The passage is neither cold, austere, nor cruel. Pity for the horse (if you are a member of that sector of mankind which pities wounded horses) is revealed by the artist's selection of details: the horse's awkward struggle to a standing position, the swinging of the exposed entrails, the jerkiness of the canter, the bite of the spurs, and the awful regularity of the pumping of the blood. A kind of implicit enmity towards the picador and the ring-servants comes out in verbs like *whack-whacked, pulled and hauled,* the second *whacking,* and the *kicking-in* of the spurs. The pity and the enmity are so firmly in check that at first—to use Aristotle's ethical terms—we suppose a *defect* of sympathy. By the same token, the *extreme* of excessive pathos is carefully avoided. What remains is the *mean,* the province of the writer who seeks to avoid both the apathetic and the pathetic fallacies.

Such an esthetic theory of the "emotive mean" leaves the practitioner open to certain criticisms. What about scope, it is asked, and what about depth? Where is the rest of the act? Who were the parents of the horse that we may establish some sort of sympathetic rapport with him? "Hemingway's art," wrote Wyndham Lewis in 1934, "is an art of the surface—and, as I look at it, none the worse for that." [16] Lewis failed, like many of his contemporaries, to look at this particular art long enough. Had he done so, he might have seen what Hemingway was doing with images and with suggestion far below the surfaces of his better stories —though not too far to be overlooked by the close and sympathetic reader. He also ignored Henry James' observation, which applies to all of Hemingway's miniatures: "an exemplary anecdote" may be also "a little rounded drama." [17] Many of our best critics have consistently underrated Hemingway's esthetic intelligence.

If his chosen approach led to pejorative judgments, or even to

[16] *Men Without Art,* London, 1934, p. 19.
[17] *Works,* New York edition, vol. 13, preface, p. v.

the suggested kind of limitation on depth and scope, Hemingway as an apprentice craftsman was temporarily prepared to accept them. He began, as he knew he must, by centering attention on action, and on what he felt to be the simpler modes of action. "I was trying to learn to write, commencing with the simplest things," he said in 1932, speaking of his program in 1922.[18] As in the laboratory study of biology, one works up only very gradually to more complex organisms. If he were to begin on the human instead of the frog, the young biologist's ignorance might betray him into the most unscientific (which is to say, untrue) conceptions, and he would have the further hazard of getting lost among the ganglia. Hemingway's writing after 1922 was most certainly none the worse for his rigorous self-imposed apprentice training. He advanced well beyond the early state without losing sight of its importance. He continued to employ what he had learned there at the same time that he continued to learn other things.

The most dangerous pitfall for the young Hemingway was what may be called the kinetographic fallacy. This consists in the supposition that we can get the best art by an absolutely true description of what takes place in observed action. It will be kinetic because it must move by definition. It will be graphic because it is a picture. We write down what we see men doing, what they say, what they look like to us. We hold a mirror and a microphone up to life, and report, with absolute though selective precision, the reflections and the noises.

The dangers of such a program, if it is rigorously followed, are clear. The absolutist desire to see and say the truth and nothing but the truth may keep the best-intentioned writer from doing both. No artist who reports the action of men and animals, merely as such, will record things as they are, or really grasp and project "the way it was." He will record actions from the outside, only as they *look* to be. Facts will be distorted in the very attempt to avoid distortion.

The account of the wounded horse cannot be called distortion. But it does nevertheless consist in a concentration so intense that the miniature itself can be appreciated without remembering the larger context of the bullfight, the arena, the town, and the nation

[18] *DIA*, p. 2.

in which the described events took place. The spreading context can, of course, be supplied by the reader's imagination. But one could probably argue that the artist is not justified in overworking his reader's imagination to quite this extent.

Between the "defect" of too little detail and the "excess" of the sand-pile technique (where everything is put in, whether it is relevant or not, until we have a bulk on the horizon too considerable to ignore), there is a mean. By the time Hemingway wrote *The Sun Also Rises,* he was rounding out his writing by allowing the possible to enter his picture of the actual. He was beginning to admit guesses, fictions, motivations, imaginations in far greater profusion than he had done in 1922. He felt justified in doing so because he had so firmly avoided guessing throughout his apprenticeship. Now he had had sufficient experience of the kinetographic reporting of the actual so that he could trust himself to invent, though never to invent except in terms of carefully observed experience. Hemingway, therefore, did not so much avoid as transcend the kinetographic fallacy. His own summary of the "mean position" continued, of course, to stress the importance of truth-telling: "A writer's job is to tell the truth." Then he went on. "His standard of fidelity to the truth must be so high that his invention" which comes always and invariably "out of his experience, should produce a truer account than anything factual can be." [19] This remark, set down in 1942, is the essence of twenty years of experience. It runs very close to a pronouncement by Coleridge, who also based his views on common sense and long experience: "A poet ought not to pick nature's pocket: let him borrow, and so borrow as to repay by the very act of borrowing. Examine nature accurately, but write from recollection; and trust more to your imagination than your memory." [20]

Hemingway's nearly absolute devotion to what is true, coming in an age when absolute devotions are so rare, is not only the dominant drive in his whole esthetic life, but also the firmest guarantee that his works will survive. He continuously entertained a healthy and essentially humble conviction that the truth

[19] *Men at War,* introd., p. xv.
[20] *Table Talk* in *Works,* ed. Shedd, New York, 1853, Vol. 6, pp. 345–346.

is difficult to come by, though sometimes it may drop by chance into a writer's lap. The good parts of a book, as he told Fitzgerald in 1929, may be only something a writer is lucky enough to over-hear, or they may be the wreck of his "whole damned life." [21] But if both partake of the nature of truth, one is as good as the other, though their scope will naturally differ. Any form of truth, however, if it is put into an art form, will help the writing to survive the erosions of time. For the truth is a sturdy core, impervi-ous to the winds of faddist doctrine and the temporary weather of an age.

IV. THE BEAUTIFUL

From truth it is only a step to beauty and *aisthetes*—"one who perceives"—is ordinarily associated with the perception of the beautiful. Although Hemingway the esthetician has spoken much of truth, he has had little to say about what constitutes for him the nature of the beautiful. In the fiction itself there is scarcely any overt emphasis on beauty for its own sake. Remembering Ruskin, one might call Hemingway's the "make-what-you-will-of-it" approach to the perception of the beautiful. It is as if Hem-ingway tacitly agreed with the dictum of Herbert Read: "To live according to natural law, this is also the release of the imagina-tion. In discovering truth, we create beauty." [22]

With respect to the beautiful it appears to be a basic assumption in Hemingway's esthetic that what is true, in the sense of being natural and untinkered-with, is also beautiful. Ugliness in Hem-ingway is almost invariably associated with the abnormal and the unnatural: the unwomanly woman, for example, or the un-manly man. The unclean, the furtive, the cowardly, the enslaved all show an aspect of the sinister. Beauty in Hemingway is the beauty of land, of men and women, of the nobler animals, of the clean, the honest, the well-lighted, the nonconcealing, the brave.

One version of the alliance between the natural and the beau-tiful was very well summarized by the Emperor Marcus Aurelius.

---

[21] EH to FSF, from Madrid, 9/4/29.
[22] Quoted by Kenneth Rexroth in review of Read's *Collected Poems, New York Times Book Review,* June 17, 1951, p. 5.

"The hanging-down of grapes, the brow of the lion, the froth of a foaming wild boar, though by themselves considered they are far from beauty, yet because they happen naturally, they are both comely and beautiful." [23]

The comely is the becoming, the fitting, that which is felt to be naturally right. Whenever in the reading of Hemingway one finds himself arrested by the beauty of a passage, he may discover also that its essential naturalness, in the moral dimension of stoic esthetics, helps to explain its essential beauty.

Following the lead of the Emperor, one might turn to the examples of the rhinoceros and the kudu bull in the *Green Hills of Africa*, one of Hemingway's least appreciated books. [24] About the rhino:

"There he was, long-hulked, heavy-sided, prehistoric-looking, the hide like vulcanized rubber and faintly transparent looking, scarred with a badly healed horn wound that the birds had pecked at, his tail thick, round, and pointed, flat many-legged ticks crawling on him, his ears fringed with hair, tiny pig eyes, moss growing on the base of his horn that grew forward from his nose. M'Cola looked at him and shook his head. I agreed with him. This was the hell of an animal."

Confronted by this passage, the naturalist might well argue that this is the way a dead rhinoceros looks. This is the nature of the beast, and if we follow Marcus Aurelius it would be necessary to conclude that the rhinoceros, since he happens naturally, is a thing of beauty and a joy forever. Yet to argue thus he would have to ignore the very careful accumulation of points in Hemingway's description which suggest the unnatural and the abnormal. The prehistoric look, for example, is not of this present world; the vulcanized-rubber appearance of the skin, though very distinctly of this world, is somehow artificial and ugly on an animal. The horn wound, badly healed and pecked at by the tick birds, has the force of an abnormality. So does the allusion to the verminous ticks, comparable to the horror of flies around a horse's crupper mentioned elsewhere in the same book. The eyes are out of proportion, and the moss at the base of the horn seems an unnatural

---

[23] *Meditations*, Book III, section ii.
[24] *GHOA*, pp. 79 and 231.

growth, like festoons of mildew on a neglected book. This is an offensive animal, disproportioned in its long hulk, abnormal in its appurtenances, a kind of mistaken hybrid, not what you would expect an animal to look like—esthetically wrong, in short, and generally objectionable.

Against such disproportion, abnormality, and unnatural naturalness, one might place the unposed portrait of the kudu bull, killed at long last after many days of unsuccessful hunting.

"It was a huge, beautiful kudu bull, stone-dead, on his side, his horns in great dark spirals, widespread and unbelievable as he lay dead five yards from where we stood. . . . I looked at him, big, long-legged, a smooth gray with the white stripes and the great curling, sweeping horns, brown as walnut meats, and ivory-pointed, at the big ears and the great, lovely, heavy-maned neck, the white chevron between his eyes and the white of his muzzle and I stooped over and touched him to try to believe it. He was lying on the side where the bullet had gone in and there was not a mark on him and he smelled sweet and lovely like the breath of cattle and the odor of thyme after rain."

This is the true hunter's esthetic appreciation. Even the nonhunter, whose conscientious or temperamental objection to killing would not permit him to write in just this way, can share the hunter's admiration for the graceful, strong, handsomely proportioned animal. The size, the clean natural colors, the wholeness ("there was not a mark on him"), and the sweet natural smell which distinguishes the grazing animals from the meat-eaters, are all factors in the kudu's esthetic attractiveness. "Beautiful . . . lovely . . . lovely." Words like these, in the context of the weary hunt now successfully crowned with antlers, are used without apology. Here is the hunter's and the esthetician's dream of an animal, as the rhinoceros was a kind of tickridden nightmare.

The quality of beauty in Hemingway's work seems to come as naturally as the leaves to a tree. Yet the carefully ordered accounts of natural scenery in his pages reveal, on close examination, a deliberate and intelligent artifice. The description is nearly always directly functional within an action. The beauty—or ugliness—of the land is made to belong to the ugliness—or beauty—

of the human events which occur in its midst. Sometimes, as in Frank Norris, natural beauty stands in quiet contrast to whatever it is that men and women are doing in its presence. Hemingway uses this old trick of the naturalistic writers charily and rarely; it is never emphasized in the black-jack manner of, say, Norris in *The Octopus,* or Steinbeck in *The Wayward Bus.* What we tend to get in Hemingway is a subtle interweaving of the natural conditions in the background and the human conditions in the foreground or the middle-distance.

While examining portraits by divers Italian masters, Hemingway always carefully studied the backgrounds, as if to find corroboration in another art for his ideas about the importance of natural settings in prose fiction. As he well knew total effect depends upon placing figures in a context—verbal, schematic. and scenic—and in this respect he is as good a "contextualist" as T. S. Eliot, who adopted if he did not invent this special application of the term. Although Hemingway had rigorously trained himself in the accurate observation of natural objects, his precision of rendering did not prevent these objects from being put to symbolic use. The discipline of double perception requires an ability to penetrate both to the essential qualities of a natural scene and to the essential qualities of a subjective reaction to the scene. These, working together in a dozen ways, produce the total effect.

Hemingway's sense of beauty is stirred, his heart is moved, as much by human beings as by landscapes or the more handsome animals. Here again the normative judgment comes into operation. He scorns perversions of any kind. Whatever is abnormal or unnatural according to his measurement is ugly according to his conclusion. People about their normal business, or people who are able under abnormal circumstances to behave like normal human beings, ordinarily strike him with the impact of the beautiful, though he may not use the word in that connection.

The point may be illustrated by choosing an example of a set of human beings of no extrinsic beauty at all, but modern, unlovely, dirty, urban, and tough. This is a group portrait of the matadors' representatives, the trusted banderilleros who have gathered to appraise the bulls the morning before a *corrida.*

"The representatives, usually short men in caps, not yet shaven for the day, with a great variety of accents, but all with the same hard eyes, argue and discuss." [25]

Goya would have fancied these people; Browning's poet-observer could have met them in Valladolid. Though by themselves considered they are far from beauty, yet because they happen naturally, in the morning chiaroscuro of the plaza corrals, they are both comely and beautiful to the eye of a true esthetician.

Anyone so minded could object to the foregoing position on the grounds that the natural is not by any means always to be equated with the moral. The neohumanists habitually opposed the moral to the natural; they argued that only through the operation of the inner check could the natural be housebroken into conformity with acceptable social standards. Dozens of examples could be assembled to show how anti-social and either amoral or immoral the natural man can be when he really lets himself go.

If such objections were not merely captious, they would be simply irrelevant. The neohumanists, great though their gifts were, could most of them lay no just claim to an understanding of practical esthetics.[26] For the first requirement of esthetics, at least in the area where Hemingway works, is that it shall be based on a moral view of the world. With Anton Chekhov's moral statement that "the aim of fiction is absolute and honest truth," he would agree entirely. He would also agree with Marcus Aurelius that the natural is comely and beautiful, though Hemingway offers evidence throughout his work that the natural must be defined within certain normative and essentially moral limits. Working with the concepts of truth and beauty, it thus becomes possible to see "the way it was" as an idea of empirical truth, taking due account of ugliness and deformity, but warmed and illuminated from within by the strong love of natural beauty.

v. THE SABIDURÍAN

To complete the portrait of Hemingway as esthetician, it is necessary to look at what may be called the underside of the paint-

---

[25] *DIA*, p. 27.

[26] For Hemingway's humorous comment on this group, see *DIA*, p. 139.

ing. The upper side is of course that whole face of his effort as artist which has as its purpose the seeing and saying of truth and "natural" beauty. Truth-telling (whether the "objective" portrayal of things and events in the phenomenal world, or the "subjective" representation of mental-emotional responses to these things and events) is one great criterion by which the worth of writing may be judged. For the upper side of Hemingway's esthetic there is perhaps no better general statement than that of Conrad in his celebrated preface to *The Nigger of the Narcissus*.

"The artist . . . like the thinker or the scientist, seeks the truth. . . . And art itself may be defined as a single-minded attempt to render the highest kind of justice to the visible universe. . . . It is an attempt to find in its forms, in its colours, in its light, in its shadows, in the aspects of matter and in the facts of life what of each is fundamental, what is enduring and essential. . . ."

Although Hemingway's admiration for Conrad later became less intense than formerly, his evident agreement with such statements as the one just quoted gave him, in the years 1923–1924, good reason to defend Conrad against his fashionable detractors, and to refuse to share in the disparagement which was at its height about the time of Conrad's death. When Ford issued the Conrad memorial supplement in the *transatlantic* for September, 1924, Hemingway made his own position clear.[27]

"The second book of Conrad's that I read was *Lord Jim* [said Hemingway]. I was unable to finish it. It is therefore all I have left of him. For I cannot reread them. That may be what my friends mean by saying he is a bad writer. But from nothing else that I have ever read have I gotten what every book of Conrad has given me."

Knowing that he could not reread them, he had saved up four of the novels to be used as a combination anodyne and stimulant whenever his disgust "with writing, writers, and everything written of and to write would be too much." In Toronto the preceding autumn he had used up three, one after the other, borrowing them from a friend who owned a uniform set. When his newspaper sent him to cover the attempt to locate anthracite coal in the Sudbury

[27] *transatlantic review* 2 (October 1924), pp. 341–342. Information in part from W. L. McGeary.

Basin mining district north of Georgian Bay in Ontario, he bought three back numbers of the *Pictorial Review* and read *The Rover,* "sitting up in bed in the Nickle Range Hotel."

"When morning came [he continued] I had used up all my Conrad like a drunkard. I had hoped it would last me the trip, and felt like a young man who has blown his patrimony. But, I thought, he will write more stories. He has lots of time."

The later reviews had all superciliously agreed that *The Rover* was a bad book. But now Conrad was dead, and "I wish to God," said Hemingway, "they would have taken some great acknowledged technician of a literary figure and left [Conrad] to write his bad stories."

The fashionable derogation of Conrad was often accompanied by the praise of T. S. Eliot as a "good writer." As for Hemingway:

"If I knew that by grinding Mr. Eliot into a fine dry powder and sprinkling that powder over Mr. Conrad's grave, Mr. Conrad would shortly reappear, looking very annoyed at the forced return, and commence writing, I would leave for London early tomorrow morning with a sausage-grinder."

Hemingway neither ground in London nor sprinkled in Canterbury. Had he done so, the topic of conversation between exhumed and exhumer might well have been Conrad's preface. In that very eloquent defence of fiction, Conrad makes three other memorable points besides insisting that the artist must seek truth.

The first is on the language of prose. The phrases "like pebbles fresh from a brook" which Ford Madox Ford admired in the early work of Hemingway were not achieved without the most careful attention to the act of verbal selection. Hemingway told Samuel Putnam in 1926 that "easy writing makes hard reading," and that he wished, if he could, to "strip language clean, to lay it bare down to the bone." [28] In practice this meant the studied deletion of all words and phrases which were in any way false. One of the difficulties with language, as many good writers have felt and as Hemingway said, is that "all our words from loose using have lost their edge." [29] Recognizing this fact, Hemingway always wrote slowly and revised carefully, cutting, eliding, substituting, experi-

[28] Samuel Putnam, *op.cit.,* p. 128.
[29] *DIA,* p. 71.

menting with syntax to see what a sentence could most economically carry, and then throwing out all words that could be
spared.

Such an artist would be obliged to agree with Conrad: "It is
only through an unremitting never-discouraged care for the shape
and ring of sentences . . . that the light of magic suggestiveness
may be brought to play for an evanescent instant over the commonplace surface of words: of the old, old words, worn thin, defaced
by ages of careless usage." Magic suggestiveness is a phrase not
to be found anywhere in the published writings of Hemingway;
yet everywhere in his language the magic of suggestion is at work
among the old, old words. If their surfaces are commonplace,
their interiors bear the imaginative supercharging which only the
true artist can bring to them. And this positive charge, which on
being released plays not over but beneath the verbal surfaces, is
one phase of the underside of Hemingway's distinguished achievement in prose.

The second phase is what Conrad calls "communication
through temperament." The Spanish word *sabiduría* comes very
close to the context of this idea. It may be defined as a kind of
natural knowledge, nothing like the "wisdom" of professional
philosophers, but a knowledge available under the surface of their
lives to all responsive human beings. According to Conrad, "the
artist appeals to that part of our being which is not dependent
on wisdom: to that in us which is a gift and not an acquisition—
and therefore more permanently enduring. . . . Fiction, if it
at all aspires to be art, appeals to temperament. And in truth it
must be . . . the appeal of one temperament to all the other
innumerable temperaments whose subtle and resistless power en-
dows passing events with their true meaning, and creates the
moral, the emotional atmosphere of the place and time." One may
remark in passing that the closing phrase, "the emotional atmosphere of the place and time," is a very concise description for a part
of what Hemingway means by "the way it was." Conrad goes on
to say that the artist's appeal must be realized through the senses
—provided of course that it is the artist's high desire to reach
the secret spring of responsive emotions.

This is also the theory and practice of Hemingway. As one

watches the establishment and development of the sabidurian images in his novels or the more ambitious short stories, one comes to see, as Mr. Theodore Bardacke has recently noticed, "this underlying use of associations and emotional suggestion," visible and even audible through the "objectively reported details." It is precisely this power which enabled Mr. Malcolm Cowley to say that "Hemingway's prose at its best gives a sense of depth and of moving forward on different levels that is lacking in even the best of his imitators." Hemingway's own term for it is "the kind of writing that can be done . . . if anyone is serious enough and has luck. There is a fourth and fifth dimension that can be gotten." [30]

In a number of his works, seriously charging and recharging the old, old words and the natural, non-literary temperamental images, Hemingway the sabidurían precisely did such a job. We respond to it as naturally as savages to thunder, or as Dr. Jung's patients to the recurrent opposed symbols of the "Wise Old Man" and "the Shadow." Whether we accept Jung's hypothesis of inherited patterns in the cells of the brain, or try to explain our responses by modern versions of Bentham's psychological hedonism, need not concern us here. However we explain the fact, it operates all through Hemingway's prose.

The total entity we respond to in a work of art is what Conrad's preface calls "the presented vision." It may be a vision of "regret or pity, of terror or mirth." The point is that in its presence no reasonably sensitive human being is an island; he is a part of the mainland. For the presented vision arouses "in the hearts of the beholders that feeling of unavoidable solidarity; of the solidarity in mysterious origin, in toil, in joy, in hope, in uncertain fate, which binds men to each other and all mankind to the visible world."

Hemingway is very clear on this matter of the presented vision. "All good books," he wrote in 1933, "are alike in that they are truer than if they had really happened and after you are finished

---

[30] Theodore Bardacke, "Hemingway's Women," in J. K. M. McCaffery, ed., *Ernest Hemingway: The Man and His Work*, New York, 1950, p. 341; see also Malcolm Cowley, *The Portable Hemingway*, introd., p. xviii. Cf. Hemingway, *GHOA*, pp. 26–27.

reading one you will feel that all that happened to you and afterwards it all belongs to you; the good and the bad, the ecstasy, the remorse and sorrow, the people and the places and how the weather was. If you can get so that you can give that to people, then you are a writer."

No two individualist authors will perfectly agree in generals or in particulars. In every author, esthetically and culturally speaking, one finds a muted echo of Blake's "I must create my own system or be enslaved by another man's." Hemingway would never write the matter of Conrad's preface in the manner of Conrad. Yet he would wholly agree with Conrad in saying to all who demand other things of the artist: "My task which I am trying to achieve is, by the power of the written word to make you hear, to make you feel—it is, before all, to make you *see*. That—and no more, and it is everything." It is everything because it encompasses both the upper- and the underside of all we know as human beings. If the artist achieves his task, it will mean that by all the means at his disposal he has transferred to his reader the true essence of "the way it was."

IV · The Wastelanders

> "It is the mark of the true novelist that in searching the meaning of his own unsought experience, he comes on the moral history of his time."—John Peale Bishop [1]

I. BEAT-UP, NOT LOST

"Hemingway's first novel might rock the country," wrote Alfred Harcourt to Louis Bromfield one day in 1925.[2] The prediction was sound. A year had not gone by before Hemingway awoke one autumn morning in Paris to find that the sun had also risen.

He had labored long and hard to give his first novel (really his third if you counted the one that was stolen and *The Torrents of Spring*) the solid structure and the freshness of texture which have since sustained it. "I started *The Sun Also Rises* on the 21st of July, my [26th] birthday, in Valencia," he wrote. Work on the first draft was continued through the last ten days of July and the month of August in Valencia, Madrid, St. Sebastian, and Hendaye, and the complete run-through was finished in Paris on September 21, 1925.[3]

"There is only one thing to do with a novel," he once told Fitzgerald, "and that is to go straight on through to the end of the damned thing." [4] The remark was perhaps designed as an exhortation to Fitzgerald, whose dilatory habits in the completion of novels occasioned some pain to a friend who wished him well. The first draft of *The Sun Also Rises* was set down in approximately forty-eight writing days, but Hemingway nearly killed himself in the process. "I knew nothing about writing a novel when I started it," he recalled in 1948, "and so wrote too fast and

---

[1] John Peale Bishop, "The Missing All," *Virginia Quarterly Review* 13 (Winter 1937), p. 118. Also in McCaffery, *op.cit.*, pp. 292–307.

[2] Quoted in EH to FSF, 12/31/25.

[3] EH to CB, 4/1/51.

[4] EH to FSF, 9/13/29. Also EH to FSF, 5/4/26.

each day to the point of complete exhaustion. So the first draft was very bad . . . I had to rewrite it completely. But in the re-writing I learned much." [5]

Following a rest period during which he produced *The Torrents of Spring* and gave his first draft a chance to settle and objectify itself, he went down to Schruns in the Vorarlberg in mid-December. Here he spent the period before Christmas in skiing and revising his book. A trip to New York in mid-February provided a brief interlude in the concentrated labors of rewriting. These filled January, part of February, and the month of March. By April first the book was ready for the typist. Heavy cuts in the original opening and elsewhere had now reduced a much longer novel to about 90,000 words. The completed typescript was mailed to Maxwell Perkins on April 24, 1926. The total operation had covered nine months of extremely hard work.[6]

The result justified the effort. If there had been any suspicion that Hemingway's skills were limited to short fiction, the publication of the first novel on October 22, 1926, dispelled it. The book showed, said a pleased reviewer, that he could state a theme dramatically and develop it to book length, a problem not previously attacked except for purposes of travesty in the book on Anderson. Three years later, on September 27, 1929, Hemingway proved with *A Farewell to Arms* that he could do it again. The interim publication of *Men Without Women* (October 14, 1927) indicated that the novelist had not killed the short-story writer. But the books which elevated him to fame, and established him firmly on that eminence, were a pair of remarkable novels.

"Famous at twenty-five; thirty a master" was MacLeish's summary of the record. In their respective ways *The Sun Also Rises* and *A Farewell to Arms* also summarized a record. In reverse chronological order, they represented the essence of that densely packed period in Hemingway's life between 1918 and 1925. They struck a total for the meaning of his own experience, both sought

[5] *FTA*, illustrated edition of 1948, introd., p. viii.

[6] EH to CB, 4/1/51. This paragraph is based on the following additional letters: MP to EH, 2/15/26, 3/15/26; EH to MP, 3/10/26, 4/1/26, 4/19/26, 4/24/26. According to a letter from EH to MP, 11/19/26, he cut 40,000 words from the original first draft.

and unsought, and became in effect two long chapters in the moral history of the nineteen-twenties.

No book is inevitable, though every good book comes out of a strong internal compulsion. Given a man of Hemingway's talents and experience, both books happened naturally. They were done not only for reasons of normal artistic compulsion but also as a means of trying-out the moral essence of seven years. If *The Torrents of Spring* was a declaration of esthetic independence, *The Sun Also Rises* was the means Hemingway chose to declare himself out of the alleged "lostness" of a generation whose vagaries he chronicled. In 1922 he had recorded his humorous scorn for the artistic scum of Montparnasse. Now, through Jake Barnes, he withdrew to the position of a detached observer looking on at aimless revels which at once amused him and left him sick at heart. For it is one view of Jake that he is an imperturbable and damaged Hamlet. By talking thus and thus at the court of the Duchess of the Dôme, he rids himself of a deep-seated disgust for the oppressions of his environment and the people who make it oppressive. In somewhat the same fashion, *A Farewell to Arms* meant the shunting-off of the old war, writing it out, getting rid of it by setting it down in all its true intermixture of humor and horror— until, thirty years after, the rude ceremonial of Colonel Cantwell on a grassed-over Italian battleground could bury it forever.

There was much more to these first two novels, of course, than an act of personal exorcism, however complicated. For to destroy by embodying is also to create by arranging. The artist's special blessing exists in the impulse to destroy an aspect of the thing he creates, and to render permanent what for him, in another and internal dimension, must be permanently destroyed. By 1929, Hemingway had done both tasks. With the attainment, at age thirty, of his majority as a writer, he became what he had not been so completely before—the free man who had served his apprenticeship to an art and fulfilled (in quite another way) his obligations to society. From that date on he moved off on another tack, and one began to catch echoes of one of his favored maxims: "Don't do anything too bloody long."

Of *The Sun Also Rises,* Robert Littell brightly remarked that it "won the *succès de scandale* of a *roman à clef* floated on *vin*

ordinaire." [7] An immediate cause of its success was that if one
knew something about the Montparnassians who frequented the
Dôme, the Rotonde, the Sélect, the Deux Magots, the Napolitain,
the Dingo Bar, or Zelli's during the period 1923–1925, one likewise possessed a key which would admit the bearer to the "real"
identities of the fictional people. As Model-T jokes helped early
Fords to fame, so the international guessing-game of who was
who in *The Sun Also Rises* assisted with the word-of-mouth pro-
motion of the book. The prototypes of Robert Cohn, Lady Brett
Ashley, and Mike Campbell were all familiarly known in the
Latin Quarter. Though Pedro Romero bore the name of an
eighteenth-century matador, he was clearly a projection of Niño
de la Palma in his great period before a series of bad horn-
wounds damaged his nerve. Wielders of the key could, of course,
unlock the identities of Bill Gorton, Mr. and Mrs. Braddocks,
Count Mippipopoulos, Wilson-Harris the Englishman at Burguete, or Robert Prentiss, the American novelist with the cultivated Oxford accent. For a time after the book was published,
Paris gossip asserted that its title should have been *Six Characters in Search of an Author—With a Gun Apiece.* Still, as
Hemingway pointed out to Fitzgerald, "no bullets whistled." [8]
When the *scandale* had run its course, the wise ones turned to
a new topic of absorbing interest: which author had Hemingway
imitated when he wrote *The Sun Also Rises,* Fitzgerald in *This
Side of Paradise* or Michael Arlen in *The Green Hat?* [9]

Littell had observed that many of the people had been "practically kidnapped" into Hemingway's novel. Such kidnapping, if
that was the best descriptive term, was hardly a new experiment.
Sherwood Anderson, starting with the actual residents of his
Chicago boarding-house and allowing his mind to play freely
over their supposed frustrations, had evolved a population for his
Winesburg, Ohio. Lewis's *Main Street,* Fitzgerald's *This Side of*

[7] *New Republic* 51 (August 10, 1927), pp. 303–306.
[8] EH to FSF, 3/31/27. Cf. also *Esquire* 2 (August 1934), pp. 42–43.
[9] Although those who had been members of the group which went to
the fiesta of San Fermin in 1925 all knew that *The Sun Also Rises* had
a base in actuality, they carefully avoided saying so in print. It was not
until Harold Loeb's *The Way It Was* appeared in 1959 that names were
finally named. See further below, footnote 28, at the end of this chapter.

Paradise, or a little later Bravig Imbs' *The Professor's Wife* all had recognizable real-life sources. Among the poets, Frost, Robinson, and Masters invented in terms of people they knew. Yeats in the holy land of Ireland praised Maud Gonne into public property. People knew the background of Douglas' *South Wind,* Huxley's *Antic Hay,* and Joyce's *Portrait of the Artist as a Young Man.* It was, in fact, an age of indirect or direct "transcription," when the perfectly sound esthetic theory was that the author must invent out of his own experience or run the risk of making hollow men of his characters. Hemingway shared in the belief (which has been called behaviorist) that any group of living people, placed under the microscope and candidly watched for typical or idiosyncratic conduct, can be made to provide the groundwork of a novel.

The question with any such novel is always whether it has the power to survive the immediate moment when its possible real-life origins are being gossiped about. Unless the *clef* of a *roman à clef* is finally irrelevant, the novel can have no more just claim on the interest of posterity than the society pages or racing forms from last year's newspaper. The *succès de scandale* of 1926 could not possibly explain the rapidity and assurance with which *The Sun Also Rises* became, as it has remained, one of the genuine classics of modern American fiction.

Hemingway did not at all intend to have his novel construed as a text-book of lost-generationism. But the "Lost Generation" catch-phrase, facing the title page, seemed to sum up for many people an aspect of the social history of the nineteen-twenties. Ernest Boyd said that Hemingway had triumphantly added a new chapter to the story Fitzgerald began in *This Side of Paradise.*[10] The feeling was that both books, though in far different ways, helped to anatomize the desperate gaiety with which the Jazz Age covered its melancholia. And there can be no doubt that, with his brilliant dramatization of the moral predicament of a small group of Jazz Age D. P.'s, Hemingway offered a "myth" whose extension in social space far outreached the novel's na-

---

[10] *Independent* 117 (November 20, 1926), p. 594. About this date Hemingway was writing to Perkins (11/16/26): "It's funny to write a book that seems as tragic as that and have them take it for a jazz superficial story."

tional boundaries of France and Spain. What he had done could be regarded as dramatized social history. But it was not intended to be the social history of a lost generation.

Towards the materials of his book Hemingway's attitude was more complex than has since been generally understood. Because he quite properly refused to explain his position in other than dramatic terms, and because, in his dramatization, he would not consent to oversimplify, he was often taken for the sentimental and mournful singer of an empty day, or, quite as erroneously, as the hardshelled and disillusioned chronicler of social disintegration.

One illustration of the extent of the misunderstanding is the contrast which Hemingway intended to draw by giving the book its two epigraphs, one from Gertrude Stein and the other from Ecclesiastes. The remark there attributed to "Gertrude Stein in conversation" did not represent the position of Hemingway. According to his testimony, she said it in French, and it was supposed to have been said to her by "a garage-keeper in the Midi describing his mechanics, the young ones: *une génération perdue.*" Gertrude Stein sought to extend the application of the remark from the young French mechanics (with their marked ineptitudes in the proper use of screwdrivers) to all the sad young men whom the late war and the high cost of living had cast up on the shores of France.[11]

As Hemingway explained to Perkins on November 19, 1926, he regarded the "lost generation" comment as a piece of "splendid bombast" and was very skeptical of "Gertrude's assumption of prophetic roles." [12] He could not agree with her at all. He himself did not feel lost. His reason for adding the quotation from Ecclesiastes was to indicate his own belief that "there was no such thing as a lost generation."

"I thought [he said in 1951] beat-up, maybe, [deleted] in many ways. But damned if we were lost except for deads, *gueules cassées,* and certified crazies. Lost, no. And Criqui, who was a real *gueule cassée,* won the featherweight championship of the world.

[11] EH to CB, Easter Sunday, 1951.
[12] EH to MP, 11/19/26.

We were a very solid generation though without education (some of us). But you could always get it." [13]

In order to write his book it had been necessary for Hemingway to dissociate himself in a moral sense from the very idea of lostness. He might tell Fitzgerald that *The Sun Also Rises* was "a hell of a sad story" whose only instruction was "how people go to hell." [14] But the point of the book for him, as he wrote Perkins, was "that the earth abideth forever." He had "a great deal of fondness and admiration for the earth, and not a hell of a lot for my generation," and he cared "little about vanities." The book was not meant to be "a hollow or bitter satire, but a damn tragedy with the earth abiding forever as the hero." [15]

The reading public in general did not appear to understand the point or the degree of dissociation between the artist and his characters. One heard that Jake Barnes was a modified self-portrait of Hemingway, dripping with self-pity, when in fact Hemingway was facing the hazards of *la vie humaine* with courage and a reasonably light heart, as, for that matter, was Jake Barnes. "There really is, to me anyway, very great glamour in life—and places and all sorts of things and I would like sometime to get it into the stuff," he wrote to Maxwell Perkins. "I've known some very wonderful people who even though they were going directly to the grave (which is what makes any story a tragedy if carried out until the end) managed to put up a very fine performance en route." [16] It ought to have been plain to discerning readers that Jake Barnes, Bill Gorton, and Pedro Romero were solid—if slightly beat-up—citizens of the republic. They were not lost. They refused to surrender to neuroses like those which beset Robert Cohn, Brett Ashley, and Mike Campbell. And three lost neurotics do not make a lost generation.

It was one of the ironies that Hemingway, having rejected the lost-generation tag both for himself and for his generation, should

[13] EH to CB, Easter Sunday, 1951.
[14] EH to FSF, [probably summer], 1926.
[15] EH to MP, 11/19/26.
[16] EH to MP, 12/7/26. A part of this letter was published by Perkins in a short commentary on Hemingway in *Scribner's Magazine* 81 (March 1927), p. 4.

find his first book widely accepted as Exhibit A of "lost-generation-ism." Another conspicuous irony was that most readers found Brett and her little circle of drinking-companions so fascinating as to overshadow the idea of the abiding earth as the true hero of the book. Hemingway's love and admiration for the natural earth was certainly quite clearly projected. Any beat-up Antaeus who could gain strength and sanity from contact with the earth was a kind of hero in his eyes, as one saw in the portraits of Barnes and Gorton and Romero. Yet all eyes were drawn towards Brett—possibly by the odd mixture of irony and pity, of condemnation and admiration, with which she was treated.

II. COUNTERPOINT

Hemingway had told Perkins that he cared little about the vanities. *The Sun Also Rises* was one of the proofs of that statement. The title comes from the first chapter of Ecclesiastes. It is useful to recognize the strong probability that the moral of the novel is derived from the same book: "All is vanity and vexation of spirit." All is vanity, at any rate, along the Vanity Fair of the Boulevard Montparnasse where the novelist introduces his people and completes his preliminary exposition. "Everybody's sick," says Jake's little *poule* in the Parisian horsecab. The novel goes on to prove that if you concentrate on a certain segment of expatriated society, she is very nearly right. All is vanity at the Pamplona fiesta when Cohn and Campbell, moody and sullen among the empty bottles, bicker over Brett while she makes off with the matador. All is vanity when Jake concludes this little chapter of social history in a taxi on the Gran Via of Madrid. "Oh, Jake," cries Brett, "we could have had such a damned good time together." "Yes," Jake answers, closing the volume. "Isn't it pretty to think so?"

The novel contains, however, enough bright metal to bring out by contrast the special darkness of the sullen ground. We are meant to understand that all is vanity—except the things that are not vain. The moral norm of the book is a healthy and almost boyish innocence of spirit, and it is carried by Jake Barnes, Bill Gorton, and Pedro Romero. Against this norm, in the central antithesis of the novel, is ranged the sick abnormal "vanity" of the Ashley-Campbell-Cohn triangle.

Long before the middle of the book, a reader who is reasonably sensitive to changes in tone may discover that he has been silently forced into a choice between two sets of moral and emotional atmospheres. Something tarnished is opposed to something bright; vanity is challenged by sanity; a world of mean and snarled disorder is set off against a world clear of entangling alliances. The whole mood of the novel brightens, for example, when the men-without-women, Jake Barnes and Bill Gorton, climb to the roof of the bus which will take them to Burguete in the Pyrenees. This bright mood has passed through certain preliminary stages. One is the pleasant dinner which the two friends have shared at Madame Lecomte's in Paris. Another comes when Bill and Jake entrain at the Gare d'Orsay for Bayonne. Almost immediately they are in the well-known eighteenth-century situation where every prospect pleases and only man is vile. Vile is hardly the word, of course, for all the people they meet. Certain fellow-travelers on the train, and later on the bus, admirably sustain their holiday mood. But their delight in "the country" and its quiet beauties, as seen from the train-windows, anticipates the Burguete experience.

If the reader performs the experiment of watching the country over the shoulders of the travelers, he is likely to be struck by the way in which the references to natural beauty are used to document the feeling of holiday (a holiday from the company of Brett and her friends) which Jake and Bill share. An otherwise unforgivable compression of the train-ride chapter will illustrate the point.[17]

"It was a lovely day, not too hot, and the country was beautiful from the start. We went back to the diner and had breakfast. . . . [Later] we ate the sandwiches and drank the Chablis and watched the country out of the window. The grain was just beginning to ripen and the fields were full of poppies. The pastureland was green, and there were fine trees, and sometimes big rivers and chateaux off in the trees. . . . About seven-thirty we had dinner and watched the country through the open window of the

[17] *SAR,* Chapter Nine.

diner. . . . It got dark and we could feel the country hot and
sandy and dark outside of the window, and about nine o'clock we
got into Bayonne. . . . It was a nice hotel, and the people at the
desk were very cheerful, and we each had a good small room. . . .
Bayonne is a nice town. It is like a very clean Spanish town and it
is on a big river. . . ."

The chapter carefully establishes the beauty of the countryside
and the healthy male companionship between Jake and Bill. What
makes them happiest, though they do not say so, is their freedom
from the petty and noxious tribulations of Robert Cohn and company.

Although they meet Cohn in Bayonne and drive with him to
Pamplona, Bill and Jake have already established between them
an unspoken camaraderie into which Cohn and his troubles do
not greatly intrude. Across the Spanish frontier, for example, they
come upon a handsome vista. "The road went on, very white and
straight ahead, and then lifted to a little rise, and off on the left
was a hill with an old castle, with buildings close around it and a
field of grain going right up to the walls and shifting in the wind."
Jake, who is riding in the front seat with the driver, turns around
as if to comment on the scene. "Robert Cohn was asleep, but Bill
looked and nodded his head." No word is spoken, but the friendly
shared reaction of Jake and Bill is silently and strongly affirmed.
Cohn is asleep and out of it.

Being so much involved in his dream of Brett, Robert Cohn,
the man not free of woman, refuses to take the Burguete bus with
the good companions. Instead, by way of preparation for Brett's
imminent arrival, he bathes carefully, gets a shave and haircut,
has a shampoo and an application of pomade, fumes petulantly
over Brett's failure to reach Pamplona on schedule (she has drunk
too much somewhere to the north), and watches Bill and Jake
depart for their fishing-trip without the pleasure of his company.

In Burguete, for five memorable days, all is gold. At that elevation the air is cool and bracing. The good companions walk happily over the uplands among the sturdy beech-trees, fish the clear
brown streams, and recline in the lap of real country. This is what
they were admiring, and silently longing for, during the train-trip
from Paris to Bayonne. Jake digs for worms in the grassy bank;

they catch trout; they eat rustic lunches of wine and sandwiches in the good air. At night they play three-handed bridge with the English sportsman Wilson-Harris. There is much playful and boy-like badinage. The landscape smiles, as healthful and vitalizing as ever the English Lake-district was in Wordsworth. Somewhere in the remote background, out of sight and as far out of mind as possible, is the Ashley-Campbell-Cohn triangle. The comrades are not troubled. For a brief but golden age there is "no word from Robert Cohn nor from Brett and Mike." [18]

Hemingway's careful contrast of emotional and social climates makes the prefatory quotation from Ecclesiastes directly relevant. "One generation passeth away," says the preacher, "and another generation cometh; but the earth abideth for ever." Wherever they go, Brett and her little coterie (the truly "lost" part of that otherwise unlost generation) carry along with them the neuroses of Montparnasse. But the earth fortunately abides. The sun rises and sets over the fields and woods of France and Spain. The fresh winds blow; the rivers run in the valleys; the white roads ascend the mountains. For those who will look at it, all this is available. But the wastelanders pass away and out of the picture, and there is no health in them.

This pleasurable contrapuntal method, with its subtly marked contrast of emotional and moral climates, continues into the climactic phase of the novel. Now, however, there is a new image to take the place of Burguete. When the Pamplona fiesta begins, the light (and the lightheartedness) which the fishermen have known in the Pyrenees grows dim and comes very near to going out. All the sullen jealousies and cross-purposes which Brett's presence causes are released among the vacationers. Outward signs of the venom which works within are Jake's obvious disgust at Cohn's fawning over Brett; Mike's relentless verbal bludgeoning of Cohn; and Cohn's physical bludgeoning of Mike and Jake. As if Brett's own neurosis were somehow communicable, her semi-voluntary victims writhe and snarl. All is vanity at Pamplona as it was in the Montparnasse cafés before the trip was under-taken.

For the Pamplona episodes the contrasting bright metal is not

[18] *SAR*, p. 129.

nature but rather a natural man, the brave matador Romero. He is used as a force of antithesis, manly, incorruptible, healthy, courageous, of complete integrity and self-possession. Beside him Mike seems a poor player indeed, and he conspicuously embodies the qualities which Cohn lacks. His control accents Cohn's emotionalism; his courage, Cohn's essential cowardice; his self-reliance, Cohn's miserable fawning dependence; his dignity, Cohn's self-pity; his natural courtesy, Cohn's basic rudeness and egotism.

The enmity between the bullfighter and the boxer—for the very nature of Romero abhors the moral vacuum in Cohn—reaches its climax when Cohn invades Romero's room and finds Brett there. In a bedroom fist-fight the boxer has every advantage over the bullfighter except in those internal qualities which fists cannot touch. Though he is knocked down fifteen times, Romero will not lose consciousness, give up, shake hands, or stop trying to hit Cohn for as long as he can see him. Afterwards, like a Greek chorus, Bill and Mike close the chronicle-history of Robert Cohn, the pomaded sulker in the tent, and Romero, the manly and unspoiled warrior.[19] "That's quite a kid," says Bill. "He ruined Cohn," says Mike. Cohn presently leaves Pamplona under the cloud of his own ruination. Romero's face may be cut up, but his moral qualities have triumphed, as they do again in the bullring the day following the brawl. He has been "beat-up" like many other members of his generation. But not "lost."

Maxwell Perkins, a good and perceptive editor, understood the intent of the novel perfectly. He admiringly called it "a healthy book, with marked satirical implications upon novels which are not—sentimentalized, subjective novels, marked by sloppy hazy thought." [20] Its morality, like its esthetics, was notably healthy. Against the background of international self-seekers like Cohn, the true moral norm of the book (Bill and Jake at Burguete, Romero at Pamplona) stood out in high and shining relief.

[19] SAR, pp. 210–211.
[20] Quoted in R. Burlingame, Of Making Many Books, p. 87.

III. CIRCE AND COMPANY

Hemingway's first novel provides an important insight into the special "mythological" methods which he was to employ with increasing assurance and success in the rest of his major writing. It is necessary to distinguish Hemingway's method from such "mythologizing" as that of Joyce in *Ulysses*, or Eliot in *The Waste Land*. For Hemingway early devised and subsequently developed a mythologizing tendency of his own which does not depend on antecedent literatures, learned footnotes, or the recognition of spot passages. *The Sun Also Rises* is a first case in point.

It might be jocularly argued, for example, that there is much more to the portrait of Lady Brett Ashley than meets the non-Homeric eye. It is very pleasant to think of the Pallas Athene, sitting among the statuary in one of her temples like Gertrude Stein among the Picassos in the rue de Fleurus, and murmuring to the Achaeans, homeward bound from the battle of Troy: "You are all a lost generation." As for Brett, Robert Cohn calls her Circe. "He claims she turns men into swine," says Mike Campbell. "Damn good. I wish I were one of these literary chaps." [21] If Hemingway had been writing about brilliant literary chaps in the manner, say, of Aldous Huxley in *Chrome Yellow*, he might have undertaken to develop Cohn's parallel. It would not have been farther-fetched than Joyce's use of the Daedalus legend in *A Portrait of the Artist* or Eliot's kidnapping of Homeric Tiresias to watch over the mean little seductions of *The Waste Land*.

Was not Brett Ashley, on her low-lying island in the Seine, just such a fascinating peril as Circe on Aeaea? Did she not open her doors to all the modern Achaean chaps? When they drank her special potion of French applejack or Spanish wine, did they not become as swine, or in the modern idiom, wolves? Did not Jake Barnes, that wily Odysseus, resist the shameful doom which befell certain of his less wary comrades who became snarling beasts?

There are even parallel passages. Says Jake Barnes, thinking of Brett: "I lay awake thinking and my mind jumping around. . . . Then all of a sudden I started to cry. Then after a while it was

[21] *SAR*, p. 149. For *Odyssey* parallels, cf. *SAR*, p. 32 and *Odyssey* x, 490–500; and cf. *SAR*, p. 164 and *Odyssey* x, 552–560.

better . . . and then I went to sleep." Says Ulysses on Aeaea: "My spirit was broken within me and I wept as I sat on the bed. . . . But when I had my fill of weeping and writhing, I made answer." Or what shall be made of Robert Cohn, quietly and classically asleep on the winecasks in the back room of a Pamplona tavern, wreathed with twisted garlics and dead to the world while Brett and the others carouse in the room beyond? "There was one named Elpenor," says the *Odyssey*, "the youngest of all; not very valiant in war nor sound of understanding, who had laid him down apart from his comrades in the sacred house of Circe, seeking the cool air, for he was heavy with wine. He heard the noise and bustle of his comrades as they moved about."

If he had wished to follow the mythological method of Eliot's *Waste Land* or Joyce's *Ulysses*, Hemingway could obviously have done so. But his own esthetic opinions carried him away from the literary kind of myth-adaptation and over into that deeper area of psychological symbol-building which does not require special literary equipment to be interpreted. One needs only sympathy and a few degrees of heightened emotional awareness. The special virtue of this approach to the problem of literary communication is that it can be grasped by all men and women because they are human beings. None of the best writers are without it. It might even be described as the residuum of "natural knowledge" and belief, visible in every artist after the traditional elements have been siphoned off. This is perhaps roughly what Keats meant by saying that Shakespeare led a life of allegory, his works being the comments on it. Thoreau's phrase for the same thing, as R. L. Cook has pointed out, is "dusky knowledge." Pilar, the Cumaean sybil of *For Whom the Bell Tolls*, moves regularly in this half-subliminal area. She inherits her skill and discernment from Hemingway.

Under the matter-of-factness of the account of the feria of San Fermin a sabidurían symbolism is at work. It does not become formally apparent until the party has assembled to prepare for the festival. Then, in several ways, it develops as a dialectical struggle between paganism and Christian orthodoxy—a natural and brilliant use of the fact that the fiesta is both secular and religious, and that the *riau-riau* dancers unabashedly follow the procession which bears the patron saint through the streets of Pamplona.

The contrast is admirably dramatized through Jake and Brett. Without apology or explanation, Jake Barnes is a religious man. As a professing Catholic, he attends masses at the cathedral before and during fiesta week. On the Saturday before the festival opens, Brett accompanies him. "She said she wanted to hear me go to confession," says Jake, "but I told her that not only was it impossible but it was not as interesting as it sounded, and, besides, it would be in a language she did not know." Jake's remark can be taken doubly. The language Brett does not know is Latin; it is also Spanish; but it is especially the language of the Christian religion. When she goes soon afterwards to have her fortune told at a gypsy camp, Brett presumably hears language that she *can* understand.[22]

Her true symbolic colors are broken out on Sunday afternoon. She is in the streets with Jake watching the religious procession in which the image of San Fermin is translated from one church to another. Ahead of the formal procession and behind it are the *riau-riau* dancers. When Jake and Brett try to enter the chapel they are stopped at the door, ostensibly because she has no hat. But for one sufficiently awake to the ulterior meaning of the incident it strikingly resembles the attempt of a witch to gain entry into a Christian sanctum. Brett's witch-hood is immediately underscored. Back in the street she is encircled by the chanting pagan dancers who prevent her from joining their figure: "They wanted her as an image to dance around." When the song ends, she is rushed to a wineshop and seated on an up-ended wine-cask. The shop is dark and full of men singing,—"hard-voiced singing." [23]

The intent of this episode is quite plain. Brett would not understand the language used in Christian confessional. She is forbidden to follow the religious procession into the chapel. The dancers adopt her as a pagan image. She is perfectly at home on the wine-cask amidst the hard-voiced singing of the non-religious celebrants. Later in fiesta week the point is reemphasized. Jake and Brett enter the San Fermin chapel so that Brett can pray for

[22] *SAR*, p. 156.
[23] *SAR*, p. 160.

Romero's success in the final bullfight of the celebration. "After a little," says Jake, "I felt Brett stiffen beside me, and saw she was looking straight ahead." Outside the chapel Brett explains what Jake has already guessed: "I'm damned bad for a religious atmosphere. I've got the wrong type of face." [24]

She has, indeed. Her face belongs in wide-eyed concentration over the Tarot pack of Madame Sosostris, or any equivalent soothsayer in the gypsy camp outside Pamplona. It is perfectly at home in the center of the knot of dancers in the street or in the tavern gloom above the wine-cask. For Brett in her own way is a lamia with a British accent, a Morgan le Fay of Paris and Pamplona, the reigning queen of a paganized wasteland with a wounded fisherking as her half-cynical squire. She is, rolled into one, the *femme fatale de trente ans damnée*. Yet she is always and conspicuously herself. The other designations are purely arbitrary labels which could be multiplied as long as one's list of enchantresses could be made to last. They are not necessary to the full symbolic meaning which Brett has in her own right and by virtue (if that is the word) of what she is made to do in the book.

Although Hemingway carefully skirts the moralistic, as his artistic beliefs require, the moral drift of the symbolic story is unmistakable. Shortly after *The Sun Also Rises* appeared, he remarked, as he had never overtly done in the book, that "people aren't all as bad as some writers find them or as hollowed out and exhausted emotionally as some of the *Sun* generation." [25] The restriction was conspicuous. He did not say, "the lost generation." He said rather, "some of the *Sun* generation." His indictment, put into dramatic terms, was directed against those who allowed themselves to flounder in an emulsion of ennui and alcohol when there was so much else to be done, whether one was a championship-winning *gueule cassée* like Criqui or an ordinary citizen like Jake, engaged in readjusting himself to peace-time living. In contrast to the "hollow men" who went off the stage with something resembling a whimper, Hemingway presented another set of men who kept their mouths shut and took life as it came.

[24] *SAR*, p. 216.
[25] EH to MP, 12/7/26.

The emotional exhaustion of "some of the *Sun* generation" is accentuated by the oppositions Hemingway provides. Obviously no accidental intruder in the book is Romero, standing out in youthful dignity and strength against the background of displaced wastrels among whom Jake moves. The same is true of the interlude at Burguete, with Jake and Bill happily disentangled from the wastelanders, as if in wordless echo of Eliot's line: "In the mountains, there you feel free." However fascinating Brett and Cohn and Mike may be as free-wheeling international adventurers, the book's implicit attitude is one of quizzical condemnation towards these and all their kind.

Despite this fact, one finds in the presentation of Brett Ashley an almost Jamesian ambiguity. It is as if the objective view of Brett were intentionally relieved by that kind of chivalry which is never wholly missing from the work of Hemingway. On the straight narrative plane the book appears to offer a study of a war-frustrated love affair between Brett and Jake. Brett's Circean characteristics are only partly responsible for the sympathy with which she is treated, though all enchantresses from Spenser's Acrasia to Coleridge's Geraldine are literally fascinating and Brett is no exception. Whenever Jake takes a long objective view of Lady Ashley, however, he is too honest not to see her for what she objectively is, an alcoholic nymphomaniac. To Cohn's prying questions about her, early in the book, Jake flatly answers: "She's a drunk." [26]

There is, nevertheless, a short history behind her alcoholism and her constant restless shifting from male to male. During the war she was an assistant nurse; her own true love died; she married a psychotic British baronet who maltreated her; and at the time of the book she is waiting for a divorce decree in order to marry the playboy Mike Campbell. Furthermore—and this fact calls forth whatever chivalry one finds—she is in love with Jake, though both of them realize the hopelessness of the situation. She has not, as her fiancé observes, had an absolutely happy life, and Jake is prepared to take this into account when he judges her character. "Don't you know about Irony and Pity?" asks Bill

[26] *SAR*, p. 39. Cf. also pp. 211–212.

Gordon during a verbal bout at Burguete. Jake knows all about them. They are the combination he uses whenever he thinks about Brett.[27]

One of the ironies in the portrait of Brett is her ability to appreciate quality in the circle of her admirers. After the trip to San Sebastian with Robert Cohn she quickly rejects him. She does not do so sluttishly, merely in order to take up with another man, but rather for what to her is the moral reason that he is unmanly. Towards her fiancé Mike Campbell the attitude is somewhere in the middle ground of amused acceptance. He is Brett's sort, a good drinking companion living on an income nearly sufficient to allow him a perpetual holiday. "He's so damned nice and he's so awful," says Brett. "He's my sort of thing." Even though Brett can be both nice and awful with her special brand of ambiguity, she does save her unambiguous reverence for two men. One is the truly masculine Jake, whose total sexual disability has not destroyed his manhood. The other is Romero, whose sexual ability is obviously a recommendation but is by no means his only claim to admiration. It is finally to Brett's credit, and the measure of her appreciation of quality, that she sends Romero back to the bullring instead of destroying him as she might have done. This is no *belle dame sans merci*. She shows mercy both to her victim and to the remaining shreds of her self-respect.

The Heloisa-Abelard relationship of Brett and Jake is Hemingway's earliest engagement of an ancient formula—the sacrifice of Venus on the altar of Mars. In one way or another, the tragic fact of war or the after-effects of social disruption tend to inhibit and betray the normal course of love, not only in *The Sun Also Rises* but also in *A Farewell to Arms, To Have and Have Not, The Fifth Column, For Whom the Bell Tolls,* and *Across the River and Into the Trees.* Brett, the first of the victims, is a kind of dark Venus. If she had not lost her "true love" in the late war, or if Jake's wound had not permanently destroyed his ability to replace the lost lover, Brett's progressive self-destruction would not have become the inevitable course it now appears to be.

Much of the continuing power of *The Sun Also Rises* comes from its sturdy moral backbone. The portraits of Brett Ashley and

[27] *SAR*, p. 117.

Robert Cohn, like that of their antithesis Romero, are fully and memorably drawn. A further and deep-lying cause of the novel's solidity is the subtle operative contrast between vanity and sanity, between paganism and orthodoxy, between the health and humor of Burguete and the sick neuroses of the Montparnassian ne'er-do-wells. Other readers can value the book for the still-fresh representation of "the way it was" in Paris and Pamplona, Bayonne and Burguete, during the now nostalgically remembered middle Twenties. Yet much of the final strength of *The Sun Also Rises* may be attributed to the complicated interplay between the two points of view which it embodies. According to one of them, the novel is a romantic study in sexual and ultimately in spiritual frustration. Beside this more or less orthodox view, however, must be placed the idea that it is a qualitative study of varying degrees of physical and spiritual manhood, projected against a background of ennui and emotional exhaustion which is everywhere implicitly condemned.[28]

[28] Harold Loeb's version of the events on which Hemingway drew for the story in *The Sun Also Rises* does not specifically identify any actual person with the fictional characters. Yet it is clear from his narrative that he associates Lady Duff Twysden with Brett Ashley, Pat Swazey with Mike Campbell, Hemingway with Jake Barnes, himself (remotely) with Robert Cohn, and either Donald Ogden Stewart or Bill Smith with Bill Gorton. While Hemingway followed the broad outlines of what happened, he freely invented fictional episodes. Duff, for example, had no affair with Niño de la Palma, nor was there any fist-fight between the matador and Harold Loeb. Further details on the actual events which Hemingway made over into fiction appear in Carlos Baker, *Ernest Hemingway: A Life Story*, New York, 1969, pp. 144-154.

V · The Mountain and the Plain

> "Learn about the human heart and the
> human mind in war from this book."—
> Hemingway, in another connection.[1]

I. LANDSCAPE IN GORIZIA

The opening chapter of Hemingway's second novel, *A Farewell to Arms*, is a generically rendered landscape with thousands of moving figures. It does much more than start the book. It helps to establish the dominant mood (which is one of doom), plants a series of important images for future symbolic cultivation, and subtly compels the reader into the position of detached observer.

"In the late summer of that year we lived in a house in a village that looked across the river and the plain to the mountains. In the bed of the river there were pebbles and boulders, dry and white in the sun, and the water was clear and swiftly moving and blue in the channels. Troops went by the house and down the road and the dust they raised powdered the leaves of the trees. The trunks of the trees too were dusty and the leaves fell early that year and we saw the troops marching along the road and the dust rising and leaves, stirred by the breeze, falling and the soldiers marching and afterward the road bare and white, except for the leaves."

The first sentence here fixes the reader in a house in the village where he can take a long view across the river and the plain to the distant mountains. Although he does not realize it yet, the plain and the mountains (not to mention the river and the trees, the dust and the leaves) have a fundamental value as symbols. The autumnal tone of the language is important in establishing the autumnal mood of the chapter. The landscape itself has the further importance of serving as a general setting for the whole first part of the novel. Under these values, and of basic structural importance, are the elemental images which compose this remarkable introductory chapter.

The second sentence, which draws attention from the moun-

[1] Hemingway, *Men at War*, introd., p. xx.

tainous background to the bed of the river in the middle distance, produces a sense of clearness, dryness, whiteness, and sunniness which is to grow very subtly under the artist's hands until it merges with one of the novel's two dominant symbols, the mountain-image. The other major symbol is the plain. Throughout the sub-structure of the book it is opposed to the mountain-image. Down this plain the river flows. Across it, on the dusty road among the trees, pass the men-at-war, faceless and voiceless and unidentified against the background of the spreading plain.

In the third and fourth sentences of this beautifully managed paragraph the march-past of troops and vehicles begins. From the reader's elevated vantage-point, looking down on the plain, the river, and the road, the continuously parading men are reduced in size and scale—made to seem smaller, more pitiful, more pathetic, more like wraiths blown down the wind, than would be true if the reader were brought close enough to overhear their conversation or see them as individualized personalities.

Between the first and fourth sentences, moreover, Hemingway accomplishes the transition from late summer to autumn—an in-exorability of seasonal change which prepares the way for the study in doom on which he is embarked. Here again the natural elements take on a symbolic function. In the late summer we have the dust; in the early autumn the dust and the leaves falling; and through them both the marching troops impersonally seen. The reminder, through the dust, of the words of the funeral service in the prayer-book is fortified by the second natural symbol, the falling leaves. They dry out, fall, decay, and become part of the dust. Into the dust is where the troops are going—some of them soon, all of them eventually.

The short first chapter closes with winter, and the establish-ment of rain as a symbol of disaster. "At the start of the winter came the permanent rain and with the rain came the cholera. But it was checked and in the end only seven thousand died of it in the army." Already, now in the winter, seven thousand of the wraiths have vanished underground. The permanent rain lays the dust and rots the leaves as if they had never existed. There is no excellent beauty, even in the country around Gorizia, that has not some sadness to it. And there is hardly a natural beauty in the whole first chapter of *A Farewell to Arms* which has not some symbolic function in Hemingway's first study in doom.

II. NOT IN OUR STARS

To call *A Farewell to Arms* a "first" study in doom might seem unfair to *The Sun Also Rises*. But the total effect of the first novel, whatever its author's intention, is closer to that of tragicomedy than of tragedy. The tragic sense of life exists in the undertones of *The Sun Also Rises*. Its surface tone is, however, somewhere within the broad range of the comic. Reading it, one is oftener reminded of the tragi-comic irony of a work like Chaucer's *Troilus and Criseyde* than, say, the tragic irony of the Greeks and the Elizabethans. The operation of pity—again as in Chaucer— is carefully equivocal, somehow in itself a phase of irony, and under a restraint so nearly complete that it can scarcely move. Possibly because of the nature of the material, possibly because of the cultivated habit of understatement, one does not find in *The Sun Also Rises* the degree of emotional commitment which becomes visible in *A Farewell to Arms*.

After the experience of writing and revising his first novel, Hemingway worked more wisely and more slowly on his second. The preparation of the first draft took six months instead of six weeks. It was begun in Paris about the first of March, 1928. Through the spring and summer the work went on in Key West, where Hemingway made himself relax by deep-sea fishing while writing some 40,000 words. He continued the draft in Piggott, Arkansas, and Kansas City, Missouri, where he ran the total number of words to something like 87,000. The book was completed in preliminary form near Big Horn, in Sheridan County, Wyoming, about the end of August, 1928.

Following a brief interlude, he began revision, an extremely painstaking job of cutting and rewriting which filled another five months. On January 22, 1929, he wrote Perkins that the final draft stood complete in typescript, and by mid-February it had been decided to serialize the book in *Scribner's Magazine*, beginning with the number of May, 1929. Still Hemingway was dissatisfied. In Paris during the spring he continued to labor over

the galley-proofs of the magazine version, rewriting some por-
tions and keeping them by him until the last possible moment.
Book-proof reached him in Paris on June 5, 1929.[2] By the twenty-
fourth, when he had finally satisfied himself that everything possible had been done, he was able to report to Perkins that he had
at last achieved a "new and much better ending" for his novel.
There is a persistent tradition that the present ending was rewritten seventeen times before Hemingway got the corrected galley-
proof aboard the boat-train.

In the midst of life, runs the Book of Common Prayer, we are
in death. "During the time I was writing the first draft," said
Hemingway in 1948, "my second son Patrick was delivered in
Kansas City by Caesarean section, and while I was rewriting
my father killed himself in Oak Park, Illinois. . . . I remember
all these things happening and all the places we lived in and the
fine times and the bad times we had in that year. But much more
vividly I remember living in the book and making up what happened in it every day. Making the country and the people and
the things that happened I was happier than I had ever been. Each
day I read the book through from the beginning to the point
where I went on writing and each day I stopped when I was still
going good and when I knew what would happen next. The fact
that the book was a tragic one did not make me unhappy since I
believed that life was a tragedy and knew it could only have one
end. But finding you were able to make something up; to create
truly enough so that it made you happy to read it; and to do this
every day you worked was something that gave a greater pleasure

---

[2] Details on the composition are drawn from the following letters: *EH
to MP*, 3/17/28, 3/21/28, 6/7/28, *ca.* 9/5/28, 9/28/28, 1/8/29,
1/10/29, 1/22/29, 6/7/29, 6/24/29. Also EH to Bridges, 5/18/29; and
MP to EH, 5/24/29, and 7/12/29. At the time he began *FTA*, Hemingway had been for some time at work on another novel—"a sort of modern
Tom Jones," which was up to nearly 60,000 words when he dropped it in
favor of the story of Frederick Henry and Catherine Barkley. On Thanksgiving Day, 1927, he told Perkins that he had completed 17 chapters of the
Tom Jones work and was only a third through. He had decided to change
the narrative method to the third person, having "got tired of the limitations" imposed by first-person narrative. But *FTA*, like *SAR*, used the
first-person method. Hemingway did not begin to employ the third person
consistently until the middle 1930's.

than any I had ever known. Beside it nothing else mattered." [3]

The appearance of *A Farewell to Arms* in book form on September 27, 1929, marked the inception of Hemingway's still lengthening career as one of the very few great tragic writers in twentieth-century fiction. His next book, *Death in the Afternoon,* furthered his exploration into the esthetics of tragedy. Through the 1930's he continued at intervals to wrestle with the problem. *To Have and Have Not* (though with limited success) examined the tragic implications of social and political decay. *For Whom the Bell Tolls* attacked a similar problem on an epic and international scale. Ten years after that, at the age of fifty, Hemingway rounded out a full twenty years of work in tragedy with his character-study of Colonel Richard Cantwell.

The position occupied by *A Farewell to Arms* among Hemingway's tragic writings may be suggested by the fact that he once referred to the story of Lieutenant Frederick Henry and Catherine Barkley as his *Romeo and Juliet.*[4] The most obvious parallel is

[3] See Hemingway's introduction, dated June 30, 1948, to the illustrated edition of *FTA,* New York, Scribner's, 1948, pp. vii–viii. Hemingway seems to be in error when he gives the impression that the original publication date was "the day the stock market crashed"—that is, October 30, 1929. The book had been published September 27th. For an excellent review of *FTA* following publication, see Malcolm Cowley, *New York Herald Tribune Books,* October 6, 1929, pp. 1 and 6.

[4] The *Romeo and Juliet* comment is quoted by Edmund Wilson in "Ernest Hemingway: Bourdon Gauge of Morale," which first appeared in the *Atlantic Monthly* 164 (July 1939), pp. 36–46. The essay was collected in *The Wound and the Bow,* New York, 1941, and reprinted by J. K. M. McCaffery, ed., *Ernest Hemingway, The Man and His Work,* New York, 1950, pp. 236–257. Further page-references to this essay will be to the McCaffery reprint only.

In *A Farewell to Arms* Hemingway was dealing imaginatively but also retrospectively with his own first adult love affair, which had taken place in Milan at the base hospital during his recuperation there in the late summer and autumn of 1918. Harold Loeb alludes to it in *The Way It Was,* New York, 1959, pp. 219–220, stating erroneously that the girl was English. She was in fact Agnes von Kurowsky, an American of Polish ancestry working as a Red Cross nurse. It was she who voluntarily ended the association by letter after Hemingway's return to the United States early in 1919. I am indebted for materials documenting this episode to Mr. J. C. Buck. The portrait of Cathèrine Barkley appears to have been influenced by Hemingway's recollection of his

that Henry and Catherine, like their Elizabethan prototypes, might be seen as star-crossed lovers. Hemingway might also have been thinking of how rapidly Romeo and Juliet, whose affair has begun as a mere flirtation, pass over into the status of relatively mature lovers. In the third place, he may have meant to imply that his own lovers, caught in the tragic pattern of the war on the Austrian-Italian front, are not far different from the young victims of the Montague-Capulet family feud.

Neither in *Romeo and Juliet* nor in *A Farewell to Arms* is the catastrophe a direct and logical result of the immoral social situation. Catherine's bodily structure, which precludes a normal delivery for her baby, is an unfortunate biological accident. The death of Shakespeare's lovers is also precipitated by an accident—the detention of the message-bearing friar. The student of esthetics, recognizing another kind of logic in art than that of mathematical cause-and-effect, may however conclude that Catherine's death, like that of Juliet, shows a kind of artistic inevitability. Except by a large indirection, the war does not kill Catherine any more than the Veronese feud kills Juliet. But in the emotional experience of the novel, Catherine's dying is directly associated and interwoven with the whole tragic pattern of fatigue and suffering, loneliness, defeat and doom, of which the war is itself the broad social manifestation. And one might make a similar argument about *Romeo and Juliet*.

In application to Frederick and Catherine, the phrase "star-

---

first wife, Hadley Richardson. His second wife, Pauline Pfeiffer, was delivered of a son by Caesarean section in Kansas City in 1928 while Hemingway was at work on the novel. See his introduction to the illustrated edition of *FTA* (New York, Scribner's, 1948), p. vii. The manner of Catherine's death was perhaps suggested to Hemingway by this experience. But the portrait of Catherine seems to have been founded chiefly on his remembrance of the Red Cross nurse in Milan. Ten years later, when he was readying *The Fifth Column and the First Forty-Nine Stories* for publication, Hemingway directed Maxwell Perkins to change the name of the nurse in "A Very Short Story" from Ag (for Agnes) to Luz—on the grounds that the name Ag was libellous. EH to MP, 7/12/38. Perkins complied. It is therefore quite clear, as many have surmised, that the central episode of "A Very Short Story" is connected with the love affair in *A Farewell to Arms*.

crossed lovers" needs some qualification. It does not mean that they are the victims of an actual malevolent metaphysical power. All their crises are caused by forces which human beings have set in motion. During Frederick's understandably bitter ruminations while Catherine lies dying in the Lausanne hospital, fatalistic thoughts do, quite naturally, cross his mind. But he does not, in the end, blame anything called "Fate" for Catherine's death. The pain of her labor reminds him that her pregnancy has been comfortable and apparently normal; the present biological struggle is perhaps a way of evening things up. "So now they got her in the end. You never got away with anything." But he immediately rejects his own inference: that is, that her sufferings in labor are a punishment for sinful pleasures. Scientifically considered, the child is simply a by-product of good nights in Milan —and there is never a pretence that they were not good. The parents do not happen to be formally married; still, the pain of the child-bearing would have been just as it is even if they had been married fifty times. In short, the pain is natural, inevitable, and without either moral or metaphysical significance. The anonymous "they" is nothing but a name for the way things are.

A little later Frederick Henry bitterly compares the human predicament first to a game and then to a swarm of ants on a log in a campfire. Both are homely and unbookish metaphors such as would naturally occur to any young American male at a comparable time. Living now seems to be a war-like game, played "for keeps," where to be tagged out is to die. Here again, there is a moral implication in the idea of being caught off base— trying to steal third, say, when the infield situation and the number of outs make it wiser to stay on second. "They threw you in and told you the rules and the first time they caught you off base they killed you." One trouble, of course, is that the player rarely has time enough to learn by long experience; his fatal error may come in the second half of the first inning, which is about as far as Catherine seems likely to go. Even those who survive long enough to learn the rules may be killed through the operation of chance or the accidents of the game. Death may, in short, come "gratuitously" without the slightest reference to "the rules."

It is plainly a gratuitous death which comes to the ants on the

burning log in Frederick's remembered campfire. Some immediately die in flame, as Catherine is now dying. Others, like Lieutenant Henry, who has survived a trench-mortar explosion, will
manage to get away, their bodies permanently scarred, their future
course uncertain—except that they will die in the end. Still others,
unharmed, will swarm on the still cool end of the log until the
fire at last reaches them. If a Hardyan President of the Immortals
takes any notice of them, He does little enough for their relief.
He is like Frederick Henry pouring water on the burning campfire log—not to save the ants but only to empty a cup.

Catherine's suffering and death prove nothing except that she
should not have become pregnant. But she had to become pregnant in order to find out that becoming pregnant was unwise.
Death is a penalty for ignorance of "the rules": it is also a fact
which has nothing to do with rule or reason. Death is the fire
which, in conclusion, burns us all, and it may singe us along the
way. Frederick Henry's ruminations simply go to show that if
he and Catherine seem star-crossed, it is only because Catherine
is biologically double-crossed, Europe is war-crossed, and life is
death-crossed.[5]

III. HOME AND NOT-HOME

As its first chapter suggests, the natural-mythological structure
which informs *A Farewell to Arms* is in some ways comparable
to the Burguete-Montparnasse, Catholic-Pagan, and Romero-
Cohn contrasts of *The Sun Also Rises.* One has the impression,
however, of greater assurance, subtlety, and complexity in the
second novel, as if the writing of the first had strengthened and
consolidated Hemingway's powers and given him new insights
into this method for controlling materials from below.

Despite the insistent, denotative matter-of-factness at the surface of the presentation, the subsurface activity of *A Farewell to
Arms* is organized connotatively around two poles. By a process
of accrual and coagulation, the images tend to build round the
opposed concepts of Home and Not-Home. Neither, of course, is
truly conceptualistic; each is a kind of poetic intuition, charged

---

[5] On Catherine's bad luck, see *FTA*, pp. 342, 350.

with emotional values and woven, like a cable, of many strands. The Home-concept, for example, is associated with the mountains; with dry-cold weather; with peace and quiet; with love, dignity, health, happiness, and the good life; and with worship or at least the consciousness of God. The Not-Home concept is associated with low-lying plains; with rain and fog; with obscenity, indignity, disease, suffering, nervousness, war and death; and with irreligion.

The motto of William Bird's Three Mountains Press in Paris, which printed Hemingway's *in our time,* was "Levavi oculos meos in montes." The line might also have served as an epigraph for *A Farewell to Arms.* Merely introduced in the first sentence of the first chapter, the mountain-image begins to develop important associations as early as Chapter Two. Learning that Frederick Henry is to go on leave, the young priest urges him to visit Capracotta in the Abruzzi. "There," he says, "is good hunting. You would like the people and though it is cold, it is clear and dry. You could stay with my family. My father is a famous hunter." But the lowlander infantry captain interrupts: "Come on," he says in pidgin Italian to Frederick Henry. "We go whorehouse before it shuts." [6]

After Henry's return from the leave, during which he has been almost everywhere else on the Italian peninsula *except* Abruzzi, the mountain-image gets further backing from another low-land contrast. "I had wanted," says he, "to go to Abruzzi. I had gone to no place where the roads were frozen and hard as iron, where it was clear cold and dry and the snow was dry and powdery and haretracks in the snow and the peasants took off their hats and called you Lord and there was good hunting. I had gone to no such place but to the smoke of cafés and nights when the room whirled and you needed to look at the wall to make it stop, nights in bed, drunk, when you knew that that was all there was."

Throughout Book I, Hemingway quietly consolidates the mountain-image. On the way up towards the Isonzo from Gorizia, Frederick looks across the river and the plain to the Julian and Carnic Alps. "I looked to the north at the two ranges of moun-

[6] *FTA,* pp. 9, 13.

tains, green and dark to the snow-line and then white and lovely in the sun. Then, as the road mounted along the ridge, I saw a third range of mountains, higher snow mountains, that looked chalky white and furrowed, with strange planes, and then there were mountains far beyond all these that you could hardly tell if you really saw." [7] Like Pope in the celebrated "Alps on Alps arise" passage, Hemingway is using the mountains symbolically. Years later, in "The Snows of Kilimanjaro," he would use the mighty peak of East Africa as a natural image of immortality, just as in the *Green Hills of Africa* he would build his narrative in part upon a contrast between the hill-country and the Serengeti Plain. When Frederick Henry lowers his eyes from the far-off ranges, he sees the plain and the river, the war-making equipment, and "the broken houses of the little town" which is to be occupied, if anything is left of it to occupy, during the coming attack. Already now, a few dozen pages into the book, the mountain-image has developed associations; with the man of God and his homeland, with clear dry cold and snow, with polite and kindly people, with hospitality, and with natural beauty. Already it has its oppositions: the lowland obscenities of the priest-baiting captain, cheap cafés, one-night prostitutes, drunkenness, destruction, and the war.

When the trench-mortar explosion nearly kills Henry, the priest comes to visit him in the field-hospital, and the Abruzzi homeland acquires a religious association. "There in my country," says the priest, "it is understood that a man may love God. It is not a dirty joke." Repeating, for emphasis, the effect of the priest's first account of the highland country, Hemingway allows Frederick to develop in his mind's eye an idyllic picture of the priest's home-ground.

"At Capracotta, he had told me, there were trout in the stream below the town. It was forbidden to play the flute at night . . . because it was bad for the girls to hear. . . . Aquila was a fine town. It was cool in the summer at night and the spring in Abruzzi was the most beautiful in Italy. But what was lovely was the fall to go hunting through the chestnut woods. The birds were all good

[7] *FTA*, p. 48.

because they fed on grapes, and you never took a lunch because the peasants were always honored if you would eat with them in their houses. . . ." [8]

By the close of Book I, largely through the agency of the priest, a complex connection has come clear between the idea of Home and the combination of high ground, cold weather, love, and the love of God. Throughout, Hemingway has worked solely by suggestion, implication, and quiet repetition, putting the reader into potential awareness, readying him for what is to come.

The next step is to bring Catherine Barkley by degrees into the center of the image. Her love affair with Henry begins as a "rotten game" of war-time seduction. Still emotionally unstable and at loose nervous ends from her fiancé's death, Catherine is a comparatively easy conquest. But in the American hospital at Milan, following Henry's ordeal by fire at the front not far from the Isonzo, the casual affair becomes an honorable though unpriested marriage. Because she can make a "home" of any room she occupies—and Henry several times alludes to this power of hers—Catherine naturally moves into association with ideas of home, love, and happiness. She does not really reach the center of the mountain-image until, on the heels of Frederick's harrowing lowland experiences during the retreat from Caporetto, the lovers move to Switzerland. Catherine is the first to go, and Henry follows her there as if she were the genius of the mountains, beckoning him on. Soon they are settled into a supremely happy life in the winterland on the mountainside above Montreux. Catherine's death occurs at Lausanne, after the March rains and the approaching need for a good lying-in hospital have driven the young couple down from their magic mountain—the closest approximation to the priest's fair homeland in the Abruzzi that they are ever to know.

The total structure of the novel is developed, in fact, around the series of contrasting situations already outlined. To Gorizia, the Not-Home of war, succeeds the Home which Catherine and Frederick make together in the Milan Hospital. The Not-Home of the grim retreat from the Isonzo is followed by the quiet and happy retreat which the lovers share above Montreux. Home ends

[8] *FTA*, p. 78.

for Frederick Henry when he leaves Catherine dead in the Lausanne Hospital.

Developed for an esthetic purpose, Hemingway's contrasting images have also a moral value. Although he has nothing to say about the images themselves, Mr. Ludwig Lewisohn is undoubtedly correct in saying that *A Farewell to Arms* "proves once again the ultimate identity of the moral and the esthetic." In this critic's view, Hemingway "transcended the moral nihilism of the school he had himself helped to form" by the very intensity of his feelings for the contrast of love and war. "The simply wrought fable," Lewisohn continues, ignoring all the symbolic complexities yet still making a just appraisal, "has two culminations—the laconic and terrible one in which the activity of the battle police brings to an end the epically delineated retreat of the Italian army with its classically curbed rage and pity . . . and that other and final culmination in Switzerland with its blending in so simple and moving a fashion of the eternal notes of love and death." The operation of the underlying imagery, once its purposes are understood, doubly underscores Mr. Lewisohn's point that there is no moral nihilism in the central story of *A Farewell to Arms.*[9]

The use of rain as a kind of symbolic obligato in the novel has been widely and properly admired. Less apparent to the cursory reader is the way in which the whole idea of climate is related to the natural-mythological structure. (Hemingway's clusters of associated images produce emotional "climates" also, but they are better experienced than reduced by critical descriptions.) The rains begin in Italy during October, just before Henry's return to Gorizia after his recovery from his wounds. The rains continue, at first steadily, then intermittently, throughout the disastrous retreat, Henry's flight to Stresa, and the time of his reunion with Catherine. When they awaken the morning after their reunion night, the rain has stopped, light floods the window, and Henry, looking out in the fresh early morning, can see Lake Maggiore in the sun "with the mountains beyond." Towards these mountains the lovers now depart.

Not until they are settled in idyllic hibernation in their rented chalet above Montreux are they really out of the rain. As if to

---

[9] *Expression in America*, New York, 1932, p. 519.

emphasize by climatic accompaniment their "confused alarums of struggle and flight," the rain has swept over them during their escape up the lake in an open boat. Once in the mountains, however, they are out of the lowlands, out of danger, out of the huge, tired debacle of the war. Above Montreux, as in the priest's homeland of Abruzzi, the ridges are "iron-hard with the frost." The deep snow isolates them, and gives them a feeling of domestic safety, tranquillity, and invulnerability.

For several months the rainless idyll continues. "We lived through the months of January and February and the winter was very fine and we were very happy. There had been short thaws when the wind blew warm and the snow softened and the air felt like spring, but always the clear, hard cold had come again and the winter had returned. In March came the first break in the winter. In the night it started raining."

The reader has been prepared to recognize some kind of disaster-symbol in the return of the rains. Much as in *Romeo and Juliet,* several earlier premonitions of doom have been inserted at intervals. "I'm afraid of the rain," says Catherine in the Milan Hospital one summer night, "because sometimes I see me dead in it." In the fall, just before Henry returns to the front, they are in a Milan hotel. During a break in the conversation the sound of falling rain comes in. A motor car klaxons, and Henry quotes Marvell: "At my back I always hear Time's wingèd chariot hurrying near." He must soon take a cab to catch the train that will project him, though he does not know it yet, into the disaster of the great retreat. Months later, in Lausanne, the Marvell lines echo hollowly: "We knew the baby was very close now and it gave us both a feeling *as though something were hurrying us and we could not lose any time together.*" (Italics added.) The sound of the rain continues like an undersong until, with Catherine dead in the hospital room (not unlike that other happy one where their child was conceived), Henry walks back to the hotel in the rain.[10]

---

[10] *FTA,* pp. 135, 165, 267, 326, and 332 show, in order, the various premonitions and the obligato use of rain. Malcolm Cowley was one of the first of Hemingway's critics to point to his symbolic use of weather. See *The Portable Hemingway,* New York, 1944, introd., p. xvi.

One further reinforcement of the central symbolic structure is provided by the contrast between the priest and the doctor, the man of God and the man without God. In line with the reminiscence of *Romeo and Juliet,* it may not be fantastic to see them respectively as the Friar Lawrence and the Mercutio of Hemingway's novel. The marked contrast between the two men becomes especially apparent when Henry returns to the Gorizia area following his discharge from the hospital.

The return to Gorizia is a sharp come-down. After the "home-feeling" of the hospital and the hotel in Milan, the old army post seems less like home than ever. The tenor of life there has noticeably changed. A kind of damp-rot afflicts morale. The major, bringing Henry up to date on the state of affairs, plays dismally on the word *bad.* It has been a "bad summer." It was "very bad" on the Bainsizza plateau: "We lost three cars. . . . You wouldn't believe how bad it's been. . . . You were lucky to be hit when you were. . . . Next year will be worse. . . ." As if he were not fully convinced by the Major's despair, Henry picks up the word: "Is it so bad?" The answer is yes. "It is so bad and worse. Go get cleaned up and find your friend Rinaldi."

With Rinaldi the doctor, things also are bad, a fact which has been borne in upon the major so strongly that he thinks of Rinaldi when he mentions the word *bad.* Things are not bad for Rinaldi from a professional point of view, for he has operated on so many casualties that he has become "a lovely surgeon." Still, he is not the old Mercutio-like and mercurial Rinaldi. If mercury enters into his picture at all it is because he has syphilis, or thinks he has. He is treating himself for it and is beginning to entertain certain delusions of persecution. Except for his work, and the temporary opiates of drink and prostitutes, both of which interfere with his work, Rinaldi, the man of the plain, the man without God, is a man without resources.

With the priest, the man from the Abruzzi highlands, tacitly reintroduced as a contrast for Rinaldi, things are not so bad. "He was the same as ever," says Henry at their meeting, "small and brown and compact-looking." He is much more sure of himself than formerly, though in a modest way. When Rinaldi, in the absence of the foul-mouthed captain, takes up the former indoor game of priest-baiting, the priest is not perturbed. "I could see," says Henry, "that the baiting did not touch him now."

Out of the evils of the past summer the priest has even contrived to gather a nascent hope. Officers and men, he thinks, are gentling down because they "realize the war" as never before. When this happens, the fighting cannot continue for very much longer. Henry, playing half-heartedly the *advocatus diaboli*, argues that what the priest calls "gentling down" is really nothing but the feeling of defeat: "It is in defeat that we become Christian . . . like Our Lord." Henry is maintaining that after the fearless courage of His ministry, Our Lord's gentleness and His refusal to fight against the full brunt of the experience on Calvary became the ideal of Christian meekness. If Peter had rescued Christ Jesus from the Garden, suggests Henry, Christian ethics might be something different. But the priest, who is as compact as he looks, knows otherwise. Our Lord would not have changed in any way. From that knowledge and belief comes the priest's own strength. He has resources which Dr. Rinaldi, the man without God, does not possess.[11]

The priest-doctor contrast is carried out in the sacred-versus-profane-love antithesis which is quietly emphasized in the novel. Through the agency of Rinaldi the love affair begins at a fairly low level. The doctor introduces Frederick to Catherine, and takes a jocularly profane view of the early infatuation, seeming to doubt that it can ever be anything but an unvarnished war-time seduction. On the other hand, the background symbols of home and true love and high ground suggest that the lovers' idyllic life in Switzerland is carried on under the spiritual aegis of the priest. Neither Rinaldi nor the priest appears in the latter part of the book. But when, having been driven to the lowlands by the rains of spring, Catherine enters the hospital, it is naturally enough a doctor who takes over. And though this doctor does all he can to save her life, Catherine dies.

Projected in actualistic terms and a matter-of-fact tone, telling the truth about the effects of war in human life, *A Farewell to Arms* is entirely and even exclusively acceptable as a naturalistic

.

---

[11] On the low morale among the Italian troops, see *FTA*, pp. 174–175. On Rinaldi's affliction, see p. 181. On the priest's firmness, see pp. 183–184.

narrative of what happened. To read it only as such, however, is to miss the controlling symbolism: the deep central antithesis between the image of life and home (the mountain) and the image of war and death (the plain).

IV. THE FEMALE OF THE SPECIES

Coleridge once made the questionable remark that in Shakespeare "it is the perfection of woman to be characterless. Every one wishes a Desdemona or Ophelia for a wife—creatures who, though they may not always understand you, do always feel [for] you and feel with you." [12] To make so inordinate a generalization, Coleridge was obliged to ignore the better than half of Shakespeare's "perfect" women who are anything but characterless.

The modern reader, brought up on similar generalizations about the heroines of Hemingway, may wish to reconsider the problem. The most frequent adverse comment on Hemingway's fictional heroines is that they tend to embody two extremes, ignoring the middle ground. This fact is taken to be a kind of sin of omission, the belief being that most of their real-life sisters congregate and operate precisely in the area which Hemingway chooses not to invade at all.

The strictures of Mr. Edmund Wilson may be taken as typical of a recurrent critical position. He puts the argument in terms of a still-to-be-written chapter on the resemblances between Hemingway and Kipling. The two writers seem to him to share in "certain assumptions about society" with particular reference to the position of women. Kipling and Hemingway show, says Mr. Wilson, "much the same split attitude toward women. Kipling anticipates Hemingway in his beliefs that 'he travels fastest who travels alone' and that 'the female of the species is more deadly than the male'; and Hemingway seems to reflect Kipling in the submissive infra-Anglo-Saxon women that make his heroines such perfect mistresses. The most striking example of this is the amoeba-like little Spanish girl, Maria, in *For Whom the Bell Tolls*. Like the docile native 'wives' of English officials in the early stories of

[12] Coleridge, *Table Talk,* in *Works,* ed. Shedd, vol. 6, p. 349.

Kipling, she lives only to serve her lord and to merge her identity with his; and this love affair with a woman in a sleeping-bag, lacking completely the kind of give and take that goes on between real men and women, has the all-too-perfect felicity of a youthful erotic dream." [13]

The relevance of this commentary is that it underscores the idea of the two extremes in Hemingway's fictional treatment of women. In one group are the "deadly" females. Their best-realized (because most sympathetically presented and most roundly characterized) representative is Brett Ashley. The horrible example would presumably be someone like Margot Macomber, who is really and literally deadly. In varying degrees—and the fact that it is a matter of degree ought to be noticed—these women are selfish, corrupt, and predatory. They are "bad" for the men with whom they are involved. At the other extreme would stand the allegedly docile and submissive mistress-types, of whom Catherine Barkley and Maria are the conspicuous examples. These, for Mr. Wilson, are incredible wish-projections, youthfully erotic dream-girls, or impossibly romantic ideals of wife-hood. They bear, it seems, little resemblance to the women with whom one is acquainted. Where now, Mr. Wilson seems to be asking, are the day-by-day vagaries, the captious bickerings, the charming or enraging anfractuosities which combine to produce the "normal" or "real" married state? The greater number of the female kind obviously occupy some realm intermediate between the Becky Sharps and the Amelia Sedleys, between the pole of Goneril and Regan and the pole of Ophelia and Desdemona. By his failure, or his tacit refusal, to depict realistically the occupants of this realm and to use them as the heroines of his fiction, Hemingway has somehow failed in his obligation to present things as they are.

This point of view naturally affects Mr. Wilson's judgment of *A Farewell to Arms*. On the whole he finds the novel to be "a less serious affair" than Hemingway's previous work. Catherine Barkley and Frederick Henry, at least during the period of their Swiss idyll, strike him as "not in themselves convincing as human personalities." For him their relationship is merely an

[13] McCaffery, *op.cit.*, p. 254, note.

idealization, "the abstraction of a lyric emotion." [14] Mr. Cowley evidently shares this view. "To me," writes Mr. Cowley, "[Catherine] is only a woman at the beginning of the book, in her near madness"—as if, perhaps, some degree of emotional instability were a criterion of credibility in the portrait of a fictional heroine.[15]

For those who find it hard to accept Mr. Wilson's view of Catherine as an abstraction and of Maria as an amoeba, four practical points might well be made. The first has to do with the relation of Brett Ashley and Catherine Barkley to what Mr. Wilson might call the Great Infra-Anglo-Saxon tradition of fictional heroines. It is of some interest to observe that Mr. Wilson's strictures on the heroines of Hemingway could be applied with equal justice, not only to the heroines of Kipling but also to a considerable number of other heroines throughout the history of English and American fiction. Hemingway shares with many predecessors an outlook indubitably masculine, a certain chivalric attitude not without ironic overtones, and a disinclination to interest himself in what may be called the prosaisms of the female world.

The second point is that through a method of comparative portraiture, Hemingway carefully establishes a moral norm of womanly behavior. Then, whether by ethical intent or by temperamental attitude, he uses the established norm as a means of computing various degrees of departure from it. Depending on their own views in this area, readers may find Hemingway's "norm-women" less interesting and less credible than their "abnormal" cousins. For the inveterate reader of fiction and narrative poetry it is perhaps a psychological truism that the *femme fatale,* the general type of the temptress, seems more "interesting" than the stable heroine.

In the early work of Hemingway the point is well illustrated by the contrast between Brett and Catherine. There are, to begin with, certain resemblances. Like Brett, Catherine is an Englishwoman; like Brett, she is beautiful, tall, and blonde. She talks as Brett does, stressing certain words which in print are italicized.

[14] *ibid.,* p. 242.
[15] Malcolm Cowley to CB, 10/20/51.

Like Brett, she has lost her own true love early in the war, and her emotions, like her way of life, have become confused as a result of the bereavement. But here the resemblances stop.

Brett's neurosis drives her from bar to bar, from man to man, and from city to city. None of it is any good: her polygamy, with or without benefit of justices of the peace, leads only to more of the same, as one drink leads to another in the endless round. Brett is not "good" for the men she knows. Romero wants her to let her hair grow out, to become more feminine, to marry and live with him. The basic abnormality at work in Brett opposes such feminization. She is the short-haired companion of men, wearing a man's felt hat, calling herself a "chap." She does not really like other women, and neither has nor wishes to have any real friends among them. She is never happier than in the Pamplona wineshop, the center of raucous masculine singing, as if she were a half-woman half in love with damnation.

Catherine Barkley, on the other hand, is all woman. At once dependent and independent, she half-mothers, half-mistresses Frederick Henry. She wants no other life than with him, no other man than he. She drinks little and displays none of Brett's geographical restlessness. She is temperamentally monogamous. Where she is, home is. Even the red-plush hotel room in Milan (which for several minutes makes her feel like a whore) is changed by her presence until she herself can feel at home in it. "In a little while," says her lover, "the room felt like our own home. My room at the hospital had been our own home and this room was our home too in the same way." Trying at first to help her out of the harlot-feeling, Henry kisses her and assures her, "You're my good girl." "I'm certainly yours," says Catherine, wryly. But she is also, and preeminently, a "good girl"—even more so, for example, than Hardy's Tess, who was so designated on the title page.[16] As if Hemingway were looking back for contrast to the Circean figure of his first novel, Rinaldi refers to Catherine as "your lovely cool . . . English goddess." But she is a woman, not a goddess. She rescues, pities, comforts, companions, and sustains, just as she in turn is rescued from the "craziness" induced

---

[16] On Catherine's connection with the "home-feeling," see *FTA*, p. 163. Rinaldi's remark on her goddess-like qualities is on p. 71.

by her lover's death when she has finally involved herself sufficiently in Henry's growing love. Her hair is long; she dresses like a woman and gets on well with other women like her friend Ferguson. Yet she is evidently happiest alone with her husband. She would be unhappy and possibly frightened on the wine-cask in Pamplona. She is at ease in Milan in the midst of a war because she is a young woman in the midst of love. Like Maria, she is a completing agent for the hero, and is in turn completed by her association with him. But Brett, on the other hand, is an agent of depletion, as she herself realizes, and as her unselfish renunciation of Romero is presumably meant to show.[17]

The third point to be made about Hemingway's heroines is that they are, on the whole, an aspect of the poetry of things. It is perhaps a sign of an attitude innately chivalric that they are never written off, as sometimes happened in Kipling, as mere bundles of rags, bones, and hanks of hair. Even Margot Macomber, in the bottomless slough of her bitch-hood, is seen to be "damned beautiful." The treatment of Catherine, like that of Brett, shows in Hemingway a fundamental indisposition to render his heroines "reductively." And if one argues that he nowhere seems to commit himself to the emancipation of women, or to become in the usual sense of the term an ardent feminist, the answer would be, perhaps, that his women are truly emancipated only through an idea or ideal of service. His heroines, to make the statement exactly, are meant to show a symbolic or ritualistic function in the service of the artist and the service of man.

The final point grows naturally out of the preceding ones. It is, in brief, that all of Hemingway's heroines, like all of his heroes, are placed in a special kind of accelerated world. We do not see them puttering in their kitchens, but only dreaming of that as a desirable possibility. They are never presented as harassed mothers; their entire orientation tends to be, in this connection,

---

[17] Mr. Theodore Bardacke has an interesting essay on "Hemingway's Women" in McCaffery, *op.cit.,* pp. 340–351. Among its contributions is a discussion of Hemingway's "symbolic" use of long and short hair as a mark of femininity or the relative lack of it. The point is of special interest in connection with Maria, who has been raped and shorn by the fascists. The growing-out of her hair is a reminder of her gradual return to mental and physical health under the double tutelage of Pilar and Roberto.

premarital. Wars and revolutions, the inevitable enemies of peace and domesticity, set them adrift or destroy their lives. Yet they contrive to embody the image of home, the idea if not the actuality of the married state, and where they are, whatever the outward threats, home is.

Mr. Wilson's feeling that Catherine is not convincing as a human personality, his belief that her love affair with Frederick Henry is an "abstraction of lyric emotion," may be partly explained by the fact that a majority of the characters in the first two novels are oddly rootless. With a few notable exceptions like Robert Cohn, Brett Ashley, or the priest from Abruzzi, they seem on the whole to possess no genealogies or previous biographies. We know nothing about Henry's background, and next to nothing about Catherine Barkley's. Like Jake Barnes, Bill Gorton, and Dr. Rinaldi, they seem to come from nowhere, move into the now and here, and depart again for nowhere after the elapsed time of the novels. They have substance and cast shadows, but they lack the full perspective and chiaroscuro that one finds among most of the people in *For Whom the Bell Tolls.* We are seldom permitted to know them in depth. The inclination is to accept them for what they do more than for what they are. They are the men and women of action, the meaning of whose lives must be sought in the kind of actions in which they are involved, very much, again, as in *Romeo and Juliet.*

This feeling about the characters can be accounted for in two different ways. One has to do with Hemingway's esthetic assumptions as of 1928–1929; the other is a natural consequence of the kind of stories he chose to tell. His working assumption that character is revealed through action will, if rigorously adhered to, produce the kind of fiction in which characterization-in-depth is in a measure sacrificed to the exigencies of narrative movement. Even there, however, it is advisable to notice that a close reading of any of the early books reveals far more in the way of nuances of light and shade, or in subtle shifts of motivation, than one at first imagined was there. This half-concealed power is easily explained by what is now acknowledged in all quarters: Hemingway's carefully controlled habit of understatement. As for the second explanation, it might be pointed out that nearly all the im-

portant characters in the first two novels are "displaced persons"
—either men fighting a war far from their former home-environ-
ments, or aliens in foreign lands whose ties with nearly everything
they have known before are now severed—for better or for worse,
but severed.

These two explanations, the esthetic and the "geographical,"
may throw some further light into the reasons behind Mr. Wilson's
strictures. If Hemingway had not yet met head-on the problem
of characterization-in-depth, perhaps it was unfair to ask a writer
who had done so much so brilliantly that he should do so much
more. He had developed a memorably individualized style—
whittled it, as MacLeish said, from the hard wood of a walnut
stick. He showed an unerring ability to keep his narratives in motion. Finally, he had achieved mastery of that special combination of naturalistic and symbolic truth-telling which was the despair of those who could (and so frequently did) imitate his style
and his narrative manner.

In the absence of other evidence, it is probably wisest to assume that Hemingway knew what he was doing. That he could
draw a character fully, roundedly, and quickly is proved by a
dozen minor portraits in the first two books—Cohn's acidulous
mistress, for example, or Brett's friend Mippipopoulos, or the
wonderful old Count Greffi, with whom Henry plays at billiards
and philosophy in the hotel at Stresa, or the Milanese surgeon who
does the operation on Henry's leg after the affair of the trench
mortar, a surgeon who seems, and is, four times as good as the
three old-maiden doctors who have wisely wagged their heads
an hour before and advised Henry to wait six months for the
operation. These are only four examples, but they are enough to
show that the ability to draw character was by no means lacking
in the Hemingway of 1929. If he went no deeper into the backgrounds of his displaced persons, he went as deeply as he needed
to do for the purposes of his narrative. And the paring-out of the
superfluous had always been one of his special addictions.

There is, finally, a *tendenz* in *A Farewell to Arms* which helps
to account for the opinion that Hemingway has somehow failed
in his attempt to present Catherine as a credible characterization. In a large and general way, the whole movement of the novel

is from concretion towards abstraction. This became apparent in our consideration of the wonderfully complex opening chapter, and the importance of the observation is enhanced by what happens in the closing chapters of the book. The fact that the whole story is projected in actualistic terms ought not finally to obscure the symbolic mythos on which it is built and from which a great part of its emotional power derives. Catherine may be taken as an English girl who has a Juliet-like liaison with a young American officer. Similarly, one may read the novel as a naturalistic narrative of what happened to a small group of people on the Italian front during the years 1917–1918.

In the central antithesis between the image of life, love, and home (the mountain), and the image of war and death (the plain), Catherine however has a symbolic part to play. It is indeed required of her that she should become, as the novel moves on towards its dénouement, more of an abstraction of love than a down-to-earth portrait of an actual woman in love and in pain. The truly sympathetic reader may feel that she is a woman, too. But if she does move in the direction of abstraction, one might argue that the *tendenz* of the novel is in this respect symbolically and emotionally justified. For when Frederick Henry has closed the door of the hospital room in order to be alone with his dead wife Catherine, he learns at once, as if by that act, the finality and totality of his loss. It is the loss of a life, of a love, of a home. Saying good bye is "like saying good bye to a statue." The loved woman has become in death an abstract unvital image of her living self, a marble memorial to all that has gone without hope of recovery. Her death exactly completes the symbolic structure, the edifice of tragedy so carefully erected. This structure is essentially poetic in conception and execution. It is achieved without obvious insistence or belaboring of the point, but it is indubitably achieved for any reader who has found his way into the true heart of the book. And it is this achievement which enables Hemingway's first study in doom to succeed as something far more than an exercise in romantic naturalism. Next to *For Whom the Bell Tolls*, it is his best novel.

VI · The First Forty-five Stories

"A man should find things he cannot lose."—A major in Milan [1]

I. UNDER THE ICEBERG

"The dignity of movement of an iceberg," Hemingway once said, "is due to only one-eighth of it being above water." His short stories are deceptive somewhat in the manner of an iceberg. The visible areas glint with the hard factual lights of the naturalist. The supporting structure, submerged and mostly invisible except to the patient explorer, is built with a different kind of precision—that of the poet-symbolist. Once the reader has become aware of what Hemingway is doing in those parts of his work which lie below the surface, he is likely to find symbols operating everywhere, and in a series of beautiful crystallizations, compact and buoyant enough to carry considerable weight.

Hemingway entered serious fiction by way of the short story. It was a natural way to begin. His esthetic aims called for a rigorous self-discipline in the presentation of episodes drawn, though always made over, from life. Because he believed, firmly as his own Abruzzian priest, that "you cannot know about it unless you have it," [2] a number of the stories were based on personal experience, though here again invention of a symbolic kind nearly always entered into the act of composition.

The early discipline in the short story, and it was rarely anything but the hardest kind of discipline, taught Hemingway his craft. He learned how to get the most from the least, how to prune language and avoid waste motion, how to multiply intensities, and how to tell nothing but the truth in a way that always allowed for telling more than the truth. From the short story he learned wonderfully precise lessons in the use of dialogue for the purposes of exposition. Even the simpler stories showed this power. In the struggle with his materials he learned to keep the poker face of

[1] *First 49*, p. 369.
[2] *FTA*, p. 77.

the true artist. Or, if you changed the image to another game, he learned the art of relaying important hints to his partner the reader without revealing all at once the full content of his holdings. From the short story he gained a skill in the economical transfer of impressions—without special rhetoric or apparent trickery. His deepest trust was placed in the cumulative effect of ostensibly simple, carefully selective statement, with occasional reiteration of key phrases for thematic emphasis.

Like James, he has been rightly called an architect rather than a manipulator, and he himself has said that prose is architecture rather than interior decoration—an esthetic fact which the short story taught him.[3] The writing and rewriting of the stories gave him invaluable experience in the "hows" of fiction, and suggested almost endless possibilities for future development. When he was ready to launch out into the novel, he might have said, as Henry James did about *Roderick Hudson:* "I had but hugged the shore on sundry previous small occasions; bumping about, to acquire skill, in the shallow waters and sandy coves of the short story." [4] The difference was that on occasion, though not invariably, Hemingway's cove dropped off quickly into waters that were deep enough to float an iceberg.

Through the year 1939, he had published fifty-five short stories.[5] This count does not include all the sixteen short miniatures of *In Our Time* or several others which appear as interludes among the technical expositions of *Death in the Afternoon.* Most of the fifty-five were collected in 1938 in *The Fifth Column and the First Forty-nine Stories.* There omitted was "The Man with the Tyrolese Hat" from *Der Querschnitt* (1936). Also still unreprinted in 1951 were three stories, first printed in *Esquire Magazine,* about Chicote's Madrid bar during the Spanish Civil War, as well as two others first published in *Cosmopolitan* in 1939. The volume of 1938 contained four stories not previously brought together: "Old Man at the Bridge," cabled from Barcelona in April,

[3] *DIA,* p. 191.

[4] Henry James, *Works,* New York edition, Vol. 1, preface, p. vi.

[5] Four of the stories relating to the Spanish Civil War were posthumously collected and published: *The Fifth Column and Four Stories of the Spanish Civil War,* New York, 1969.

1938; "The Capital of the World," a fine story on the "athlete-dying-young" theme, with a setting in Madrid and, as leading character, a boy from Estremadura; and the two long stories which grew out of Hemingway's hunting-trip in Africa, "The Short Happy Life of Francis Macomber" and "The Snows of Kiliman-jaro." But the first forty-five stories may be conveniently taken as a kind of unit, since they were all written within ten years, and since they represent what Hemingway thought worthy of includ-ing in his first three collections: *In Our Time* (1925), *Men With-out Women* (1927), and *Winner Take Nothing* (1933). Taken together or separately, they are among the great short stories of modern literature.

Their range of symbolic effects is even greater than the variety of subjects and themes employed. The subjects and themes, in turn, are far more various than has been commonly supposed. Like any writer with a passion for craftsmanship, Hemingway not only accepts but also sets himself the most difficult experimental problems. Few writers of the past fifty years, and no American writers of the same period except James and Faulkner, have grap-pled so manfully with extremely difficult problems in communi-cation. One cannot be aware of the real extent of this experimenta-tion (much of it highly successful, though there are some lapses) until he has read through the first three collections attempting to watch both the surfaces and the real inward content. Even that task, though pleasurable as a voyage of discovery, is harder than it sounds. For it is much the same with the short stories as with *The Sun Also Rises* and *A Farewell to Arms:* they are so readable as straight narratives that one is prepared to accept them at face-value—to admire the sharp lines and clean curves of the eighth of the iceberg above the surface, and to ignore the real causes of the dignity or worth of the movement.

With perhaps half a dozen exceptions, each of the short stories doubly repays the closest reading. The point could be illustrated as many times as there are stories to serve as illustrations. As one example, there is the Chekhov-like "Alpine Idyll," an apparently simple tale in which two American sportsmen have gone skiing in Switzerland. On the way to a village inn in a Swiss valley, the Americans pass a cemetery where a burial has just taken place.

When they reach the inn, they drink at one table; at another table, the village sexton splits a bottle of wine with a Swiss peasant from the lonely mountain-country up above. When the peasant leaves to go to another tavern down the street, the Americans hear the story behind the burial.

In the winter the peasant's wife died. Since he could not bury her, he placed the body in his woodshed. There it froze stiff in the intense mountain cold. Whenever the peasant went to get wood to keep himself warm, he found that the body was in his way. So he stood it up against the wall. Later, since he often went for wood at night, carrying a lantern, and since the open jaws of the corpse provided a convenient high place, he took to hanging his lantern in his dead wife's mouth. Evidently he thought nothing of it at the time. By spring, when he was able to bring the body to the valley for burial, the mouth had become noticeably ragged. This is the shocking anecdote under which the story is built.

Actually, however, the story is not "about" the peasant. Its subject, several times emphasized early in the narrative, is "not ever doing anything too long." The Americans have been trying some spring skiing high in the Silvretta. Much as they love the sport, they have found it a queerly unpleasant experience. May is too late in the season to be up there. "I was a little tired of skiing," says one. "We had stayed too long. . . . I was glad to be down, away from the unnatural high mountain spring, into this May morning in the valley." When the story of the peasant and his wife is told, the idea of the "unnatural" and the idea of "not ever doing anything too long" are both driven home with a special twist of the knife. For the peasant has lived too long in an unnatural situation; his sense of human dignity and decency has temporarily atrophied. When he gets down into the valley, where it is spring and people are living naturally and wholesomely, he sees how far he has strayed from the natural and the wholesome, and he is then deeply ashamed of himself. For spring in the valley has been established by the skier's internal monologue as the "natural" place. In the carefully wrought terms of the story, the valley stands in opposition to the unnatural high mountain spring. The arrival of this season in the area near his lonely hut has activated the peasant to bring his wife's body down to the valley for burial.

But for him the descent has been especially meaningful—nothing less, in short, than a coming to judgment before the priest and the sexton. Here again, the point is made possible by careful previous preparation. One of the skiers has commented on the oppressiveness of the spring sun in the high Silvretta. "You could not get away from the sun." It is a factual and true statement of the skier's feeling of acute discomfort when the open staring eye of the sun overheated him and spoiled the snow he wished to ski on. But it is also a crafty symbolic statement which can later be brought to bear on the unspoken shame of the peasant, who could not get away from the open staring eye of the "natural" people who in a sense brought him to judgment. Like "Alpine Idyll," many of the stories deserve to be read with as much awareness, and as closely, as one would read a good modern poem.

The consideration of "Alpine Idyll" makes another point relevant: the frequent implication that Hemingway is a sports-writer. In some of the hop-skip-and-jump critiques of Hemingway, the reader is likely to find "Alpine Idyll" classified as a skiing story. But to say that Hemingway sometimes deals with sports like horse-racing, boxing, bullfighting, fishing, and skiing really tells very little even about the "sports-stories." None of them is primarily "about" a sport; and only ten of the first forty-five make special or incidental use of any sport at all. The point of "Cross-Country Snow," which opens with a breathlessly described skiing episode, is something quite different from the statement that skiing is fun. The true function of the opening is to summarize, dramatize, and establish firmly a phase of masculine living (men-without-women) which is being justly challenged by another phase of living—and in such a way that a state of tension is set up between the two. When a choice is compelled, Nick Adams, one of the skiers, readily accepts the second phase. Similarly, although one might classify "Out of Season" as a fishing story, the point of the story is that nothing (including fishing) is done. The strength of the story is the portrayal of the officious guide Peduzzi, a fine characterization. He serves to focus sharply the "out-of-season" theme, which relates both to the young man's relations with his wife Tiny, and to the proposal (by Peduzzi) that the young man fish out of season in evasion of the local game laws.

If one turns from these to the two long stories, "Fifty Grand" and "The Undefeated," both of which devote considerable space to the close descriptions of athletic events, it might be argued that here, anyhow, Hemingway's real interest is in the athletic events.[6] Not so. His interest is in the athletes, and not so much because they are athletes as because they are people. The two stories may be seen as complementary studies in superannuation. Jack Brennan, the aging welterweight fighting his last fight in Madison Square Garden, is a rough American equivalent to the veteran Manolo Garcia, meeting his last bull under the arclights of the bullring in Madrid.

Both men show, in crucial situations, the courage which has sustained them through their earlier careers. Both are finished. Jack earns his fifty thousand both by standing up under the intentional low blow of his opponent and by thinking fast enough under conditions of extreme pain to return the low blow, lose the fight, and win the money he has bet on his opponent. Manolo earns the right to keep his *coleta,* the badge of the professional matador, by a courage that is much greater than his aging skill, or, for that matter, his luck. The stories are as different in conception and execution as the Spanish temperament is from the Irish-American, or the bullfight from the prizefight. The sign at the center of the Brennan story is a certified check for fifty thousand dollars; a bullfighter's pigtail is the sign at the center of the other. One could almost believe that the stories were meant to point up some kind of international contrast.

Yet the atmosphere in which both stories transpire is one of admirable courage. The aging athletes Brennan and Garcia stand in marked opposition to another pair who are united by their too early acceptance of defeat. These are the half-symbolic Ole Andreson, the intended victim of Al and Max in "The Killers"—

[6] Hemingway grouped these two stories with "My Old Man" as belonging to another category than stories like "Out of Season." These three were "the kind that are easy for me to write." His own preferences among the early stories were for "Big Two-Hearted River," "Indian Camp," "Soldier's Home," and the first and last paragraphs of "Out of Season." EH to FSF, from the Vorarlberg, *ca.* 12/20/25.

the only real classic to emerge from the American gangwars of the prohibition era except W. R. Burnett's *Little Caesar*—and the half-symbolic figure of William Campbell, the man under the half-symbolic sheet in the story half-symbolically called "A Pursuit Race."

"Half-symbolic" is an awkward term. What makes it necessary in talking about stories like "A Pursuit Race" and "The Killers" is that both Andreson and Campbell are real enough to be accepted in non-symbolic terms. They are dressed in the sharp vocabulary of the naturalistic writer. We are given (almost coldly) the place, the facts, the scene, out of which grows, however, an awful climate of hopelessness and despair. It is impossible to escape the conviction that the function of these two is to stand for something much larger than themselves—a whole, widespread human predicament, deep in the grain of human affairs—with Andreson and Campbell as the indexes.

The Chesterfield-coated killers, Al and Max, are likewise the indexes of a wider horror than their cheap and ugly hoodlumism could ever be in itself. Nowadays the generic term for that horror is fascism, and it may not be stretching a point to suggest that, with "The Killers," Hemingway solidly dramatized the point of view towards human life which makes fascism possible. If that is so, then the figures of Andreson and even Campbell take on a meaning wide as all the modern world. They are the victims, the men who have given up the fight for life and liberty. Nothing can rouse them any more.

Whatever it is that William Campbell seeks to escape by remaining in bed, the ultimate horror gets its most searching treatment in "A Clean Well-Lighted Place," a superb story and quite properly one of Hemingway's favorites. It shows once again that remarkable union of the naturalistic and the symbolic which is possibly his central triumph in the realm of practical esthetics. The "place" of the title is a Spanish café. Before the story is over, this place has come to stand as an image of light, cleanness, and order against the dark chaos of its counter-symbol in the story: the idea of *nada,* or nothingness. The *nada*-concept is located and pinned to the map by a kind of triangulation-process. The three elements consist in the respective relationships of an old waiter and a young waiter to an elderly man who sits drinking brandy every night in their clean, well-lighted café.

The old waiter and the young waiter are in opposition. They stand (by knowledge, temperament, experience, and insight) on either side of one of the great fences which exist in the world for the purpose of dividing sheep from goats. The young waiter would like to go home to bed, and is impatient with the old drinker of brandy. The old waiter, on the other hand, knows very well why the old patron comes often, gets drunk, stays late, and leaves only when he must. For the old waiter, like the old patron, belongs to the great brotherhood: all those "who like to stay late at the café . . . all those who do not want to go to bed . . . all those who need a light for the night." He is reluctant to see his own café close—both because he can sympathize with all the benighted brethren, and for the very personal reason that he, too, needs the cleanness, the light, and the order of the place as an insulation against the dark.

The unspoken brotherly relationship between the old waiter and the old patron is dramatized in the opening dialogue, where the two waiters discuss the drinker of brandy as he sits quietly at one of the tables. The key notion here is that the young and rather stupid waiter has not the slightest conception of the special significance which the old waiter attaches to his young confrère's careless and unspecialized use of the word *nothing*.

Young Waiter: Last week he tried to commit suicide.
Old Waiter: Why?
Young Waiter: He was in despair.
Old Waiter: What about?
Young Waiter: Nothing.
Old Waiter: How do you know it was nothing?
Young Waiter: He has plenty of money.

They are speaking in Spanish. For the old waiter, the word *nothing* (or *nada*) contains huge actuality. The great skill displayed in the story is the development, through the most carefully controlled understatement, of the young waiter's mere *nothing* into the old waiter's Something—a Something called Nothing which is so huge, terrible, overbearing, inevitable, and omnipresent that, once experienced, it can never be forgotten. Sometimes in the day, or for a time at night in a clean, well-lighted place, it can be held temporarily at bay. What links the old waiter and the old patron most profoundly is their brotherhood in arms against this beast in the jungle.

Several other stories among the first forty-five—perhaps most notably the one called "A Way You'll Never Be"—engage the *nada*-concept. And whoever tries the experiment of reading "Big Two-Hearted River" immediately after "A Clean Well-Lighted Place" may discover, perhaps to his astonishment, that the *nada*-concept really serves as a frame for what is ostensibly one of Hemingway's happiest stories.

If we read the river-story singly, looking merely at what it says, there is probably no more effective account of euphoria in the language, even when one takes comparative account of *The Compleat Angler*, Hazlitt on the pleasures of hiking, Keats on the autumn harvest, Thoreau on the Merrimack, Belloc on "The Mowing of a Field," or Frost on "Hyla Brook." It tells with great simplicity of a lone fisherman's expedition after trout. He gets a sandwich and coffee in the railway station at St. Ignace, Michigan, and then rides the train northwest to the town of Seney, which has been destroyed by fire. From there he hikes under a heavy pack over the burned ground until he reaches a rolling pine-plain. After a nap in a grove of trees, he moves on to his campsite near the Two-Hearted River. There he makes camp, eats, and sleeps. Finally, as sum and crown of the expedition, there is the detailed story of a morning's fishing downstream from the camp. At the surface of the story one finds an absolute and very satisfying reportorial accuracy.

During one of the colloquies of Dean Gauss, Fitzgerald, and Hemingway in the summer of 1925, "Big Two-Hearted River" came up for consideration. Both of Hemingway's friends had read it in the spring number of Ernest Walsh's little magazine, *This Quarter*. Half in fun, half in seriousness, they now accused him of "having written a story in which nothing happened," with the result that it was "lacking in human interest." Hemingway, Dean Gauss continued, "countered by insisting that we were just ordinary book reviewers and hadn't even taken the trouble to find out what he had been trying to do." This anecdote is a typical instance of the unfortunately widespread assumption that Hemingway's hand can be read at a glance. Dean Gauss found that his own return to the story was profitable. There was much more there than had first met his eye.[7]

For here, as elsewhere in Hemingway, something is going on down under. One might echo Hamlet's words to the ghost of his father: "Well said, old mole, canst work i' the earth so fast?"— and with just Hamlet's mixture of admiration and excitement. Malcolm Cowley, one of the few genuinely sympathetic critics of Hemingway, has suggested that "the whole fishing expedition . . . might be regarded as an incantation, a spell to banish evil spirits." [8] The story is full of rituals. There is, for example, the long hike across the country—a ritual of endurance, for Nick does not stop to eat until he has made camp and can feel that he has earned the right to supper. There is the ritual of homemaking, the raising-up of a wall against the dark; the ritual of food-preparation and thoughtful, grateful eating; of bedmaking and deep untroubled sleep. Next morning comes the ritual of bait-catching, intelligently done and timed rightly before the sun has warmed and dried the grasshoppers. When Nick threads one on his hook, the grasshopper holds the hook with his front feet and spits tobacco-juice on it—as if for fisherman's luck. "The grasshopper," as Mr. Cowley says, "is playing its own part in a ritual." The whole of the fishing is conducted according to the ritualistic codes of fair play. When Nick catches a trout too small to keep, he carefully wets his hands before touching the fish so as not to disturb the mucous coating on the scales and thus destroy the fish he is trying to save. Down under, in short, the close reader finds a carefully determined order of virtue and simplicity which goes far towards explaining from below the oddly satisfying effect of the surface story.

Still, there is more to the symbolism of the story than a ritual of self-disciplined moral conduct. Two very carefully prepared atmospheric symbols begin and end the account. One is the burned ground near the town of Seney. The other is the swamp which lies farther down the Big Two-Hearted River than Nick yet wishes

[7] Christian Gauss to CB, 12/26/50.
[8] Malcolm Cowley, introd., *The Portable Hemingway*, p. xix.

to go. Both are somehow sinister. One probably legitimate guess on the background of the first is that Nick, who is said to have been away for a long time, is in fact a returned war-veteran, going fishing both for fun and for therapeutic purposes. In some special way, the destroyed town of Seney and the scorched earth around it carry the hint of war—the area of destruction Nick must pass through in order to reach the high rolling pine plain where the exorcism is to take place. In much the same way, the swamp symbolizes an area of the sinister which Nick wishes to avoid, at least for the time being.

The pine plain, the quiet grove where he naps, the security of the camp, the pleasures of the open river are, all together, Nick's "clean, well-lighted place." In the afternoon grove, carefully described as an "island" of pine trees, Nick does not have to turn on any light or exert any vigilance while he peacefully slumbers. The same kind of feeling returns that night at the camp after he has rigged his shelter-half and crawled inside. "It smelled pleasantly of canvas. Already there was something mysterious and home-like. . . . He was settled. Nothing could touch him. . . . He was there, in the good place. He was in his home where he had made it." Back in the low country around Seney, even the grasshoppers had turned dark from living in the burned-over ground. Up ahead in the swamp "the big cedars came together overhead, the sun did not come through, except in patches; in the fast deep water, in the half light, the fishing would be tragic. . . . Nick did not want it." For now, on his island between sinister and sinister, Nick wants to keep his fishing tender and if possible comic.

II. THE EDUCATION OF NICHOLAS ADAMS

"Big Two-Hearted River" was based on an expedition which Hemingway once made to Michigan's northern peninsula. His determination to write only those aspects of experience with which he was personally acquainted gave a number of the first forty-five stories the flavor of fictionalized personal history. He was always prepared to invent people and circumstances, to choose backgrounds which would throw his people into three-dimensional relief, and to employ as symbols those elements of the physical setting which could be psychologically justified by the time and place he was writing about. But during the decade when the first forty-five stories were written, he was unwilling to stray very far from the life he knew by direct personal contact, or to do any more guessing than was absolutely necessary.

The recurrent figure of Nicholas Adams is not of course Hemingway, though the places Nick goes and the events he watches are ordinarily places Hemingway had visited or events about which he had heard on good authority and could assimilate to his own experience of comparable ones. Future biographers will have to proceed warily to separate autobiographical elements from the nexus of invented circumstances in which they may be lodged. For present purposes it is enough to notice that well over half of the first forty-five stories center on Nick Adams, or other young men who could easily be mistaken for him.

They might be arranged under some such title as "The Education of Nicholas Adams." It could even be said that when placed end to end they do for the twentieth century roughly what Henry Adams did for the nineteenth, though with obvious differences in formality of approach. The education of Henry Adams in Boston, Quincy, Berlin, London, and Washington presented an informative contrast with the education of Nicholas Adams in Chicago, northern Michigan, Italy, and Switzerland. Nick's life in the twentieth century was on the whole considerably more spectacular than Henry's in the nineteenth; it was franker, less polite, less diplomatic. Chicago, where Nick was born just before the turn of the century, was a rougher climate than Henry's mid-Victorian Boston, just as Nick's Ojibway Indians were far more primitive than Henry's Boston Irish. Partly because of the times he lived in and partly, no doubt, because he was of a more adventurous temperament, Nick came more easily on examples of barbarism than Henry was to know until his visit to the South Seas. In place of the Great Exposition of 1900 which so stimulated Henry's imagination, Nick was involved in the World's Fair of 1914–1918. But in retrospect one parallelism stood out momentously: both Henry and Nicholas had occasion to marvel bitterly at how badly their respective worlds were governed.

Nick's father, Dr. Henry Adams, played a notable part in Nick's early education. He was a busy and kindly physician whose chief avocations were hunting and fishing. There was opportunity for both in the Michigan wood and lake country where the Adams family regularly summered. Mrs. Adams was a Christian Scientist; her temperament was as artistic as that of her husband was scientific. After the death of Nick's grandfather she designed a new house for the family. But Nick was his father's son, loving his father "very much and for a long time." From the son's fictional reminiscences a memorable portrait of Dr. Henry Adams is made to emerge. He was a large-framed man with a full dark beard, a hawklike nose, striking deepset eyes, and an almost telescopic power of far-sightedness. Though they gradually grew apart, they were the best of companions during Nick's boyhood. In middle life Dr. Adams died by his own hand for reasons that Nick sorrowfully hints at but does not reveal.

Ten of the stories record Nick's growing-up. He recalls the move from one house to another and the accidental burning of Dr. Adams's collection of Indian arrowheads and preserved snakes. One Fourth of July, he remembers (and it is one of the century's best stories of the growing-up of puppy-love) there was a ride in a neighbor's wagon back from town past nine drunken Indians, while bad news of his girl, Indian number ten in the story called "Ten Indians," was relayed to him by his father on his return home. Nick had already had his adolescent sex-initiation with the same girl, a half-breed named Trudy. He watched a very humiliating argument between his father and a crew of sawyers, and a terrifying Caesarean birth and suicide (addition and subtraction simultaneously achieved) at the Indian settlement. Nick's best friend in Michigan was a boy named Bill who could talk baseball, fishing, and reading with equal ease. Both in Michigan and in Illinois Nick encountered the underworld. It was part of his informal education to be manhandled by two gangsters in a Chicago lunchroom, and to share supper with two tramps, one of them a dangerously punch-drunk ex-prizefighter, in the woods near Mancelona, Michigan.

Like Hemingway, Nick Adams went to war. The earliest glimpses of his career as soldier come in the sixth and seventh miniatures of *In Our Time*. One shows Nick fiercely praying while Austrian artillery pounds the Italian trenches near Fossalta di Piave. In the other, he has been hit in the spine by an Austrian bullet and is leaning back with paralyzed legs against the wall of an Italian church. "Now I Lay Me," one of the longer stories, shows Nick as twice-wounded Tenente Adams, troubled by insomnia and talking out the night with his Italian orderly, a fellow-Chicagoan. "In Another Country" does not name its narrator, but it could well be the same young Tenente in conversation with an Italian major, a fellow-patient in the base hospital at Milan. In "A Way You'll Never Be," Nick is reporting back to battalion headquarters in American uniform. Though he is still recuperating from a severe wound and battle-shock, he is supposed to help build morale among Italian troops by means of the uniform. It is meant as a sign that the A. E. F. will shortly come to their support.

There are no Nick Adams stories of the homecoming, the process which Henry Adams found so instructive after his service abroad. The fate of the male character in "A Very Short Story" might, however, be thought of as one episode in the postwar adventures of Nick Adams. In a base-hospital at Padua, he falls in love with a nurse named Luz—an idea much expanded and altered in *A Farewell to Arms*. But when the young man returns to Chicago to get a good job so that he can marry Luz, he soon receives a letter saying that she has fallen in love with a major in the Arditi. The protagonist in "Soldier's Home" is called Harold Krebs, and he is a native of Oklahoma rather than Illinois. But once again the story might have had Nick Adams as its central character. Like Nick's mother, Mrs. Krebs is a sentimental woman who shows an indisposition to face reality and is unable to understand what has happened to her boy in the war.

Nick Adams returned to Europe not long after the armistice. "Cross-Country Snow" reveals that he is married to a girl named Helen who is expecting a baby. "Out of Season" and "Alpine Idyll" could easily be associated with Nick's life on the continent, while the very moving "Fathers and Sons," which stands as the concluding story in Hemingway's collected short fiction, shows Nick on one of his return trips to the United States, driving his own son through familiar country and thinking back to the life and the too early death of the boy's grandfather, Dr. Henry Adams.

The story of Nick's education, so far as we have it, differs in no essential way from that of almost any middleclass American male who started life at the beginning of the present century or even with the generation of 1920. After the comparatively happy boyhood and the experimental adolescence, the young males went off to war; and after the war, in a time of parlous peace, they set out to marry and build themselves families and get their work done. The story of Adams is a presented vision of our time. There is every reason why it should arouse in us, to use the phrase of Conrad, "that feeling of unavoidable solidarity" which "binds men to each other and all mankind to the visible world."

Future biographers, able to examine the Nick Adams stories against the full and detailed background of Hemingway's life from his birth on July 21, 1899, until, say, his thirty-first birthday in 1930, should uncover some valuable data on the methods by which he refashioned reality into the shape of a short story. What they may fail to see—and what a contemporary evaluator is justified in pointing out—is that Hemingway's aim in the Nick Adams stories is always the aim of an artist. He is deeply interested in the communication of an effect, or several effects together, in such a way as to evoke the deep response of shared human experience. To record for posterity another chapter in his own fictional autobiography does not interest him at all.

III. MANY CIRCLES

"Really, universally, relations stop nowhere," said Henry James in one of his prefaces, "and the exquisite problem of the artist is externally but to draw, by a geometry of his own, the circle within which they shall happily *appear* to do so." [9] The first forty-five stories of Hemingway draw many such circles—concentric, tangential, or overlapping—in which to contain the great variety of human relations which interest him. Two of the circles, and they might be seen as tangential, are those called Home and Not-Home.

[9] *Works,* New York edition, Vol. 1, p. vii.

Nick Adams is perfectly at home in his tent in the Michigan wilderness, but the institution that is supposed to be home for the returned veteran Krebs merely causes him acute discomfort. Bed is home to William Campbell. The sheet drawn up over his face is a protection against the Not-Home of the active world, though it is also, in movies and in morgues, the accepted ritualistic sign that the person underneath is dead. The clean, well-lighted café is much more home than his actual home to the old Spaniard who comes there nightly to stay until the place closes.

The Not-Home is another of the names of *nada,* which Carlyle once rhetorically defined as the vast circumambient realm of nothingness and night. It was perhaps never more sharply drawn than by Goya in the horrific etching which he calls "Nada." An arc of the *nada*-circle runs all the way through Hemingway's work from the night-fears of Jake Barnes to the "horrorous" of Philip Rawlings and the ingrowing remorse of Richard Cantwell. Malcolm Cowley has well described him as one of "the haunted and nocturnal writers," akin, in his deeper reaches, to Melville and Hawthorne.[10] Another way of defining *nada* might be to say, indeed, that it falls about midway between the "Black Man" of Hawthorne and the "White Whale" of Melville. In the first forty-five stories, this besieging horror of the limitless, the hallucinatory, the heartland of darkness, bulks like a Jungian Shadow behind the lives of many of the protagonists. Outside the circle which Hemingway has drawn by the special magic of his geometry, man's relations to the shadow stop nowhere.

But the Home-circle has another alternate than that of *nada.* This is the idea of male companionship, rough and friendly camaraderie, an informal brotherhood with by-laws which are not written down but are perfectly understood and rigidly adhered to by the contracting parties. Hemingway summed up the matter in his title *Men Without Women.* For woman, closely associated with the Home-symbol, stands in opposition, perhaps even in a kind of enmity, to that wholly happy and normal condition which two men, hiking or drinking or talking together, can build like a world of their own. One sees this world in the Burguete of Jake Barnes and Bill Gorton, in the Gorizia of Lieutenant Henry and

[10] *The Portable Hemingway,* introd., p. vii.

Doctor Rinaldi, in the Guadarrama hide-out of Robert Jordan and Anselmo, and in the Gritti Palace Hotel dining-room where Colonel Cantwell and the Gran Maestro (with their unspoken loyalties, their completely shared ethical code, and their rough and friendly badinage) discuss together the latest affairs of *El Ordine Militar, Nobile y Espirituoso de los Caballeros de Brusadelli.*

"Dramatize it, dramatize it," cried Henry James. "Then, and not sooner, would one see." [11] The most direct dramatization of the men-without-women theme occurs in "Cross-Country Snow." Here Nick Adams and his friend George, between whom there is something of a father-and-son relationship, are skiing near Montreux. When they stop for wine at the inn, the obvious pregnancy of their waitress reminds George that Nick's wife Helen is expecting a child. Both men know that the birth of the child will certainly interrupt and probably destroy their comradeship. "Maybe we'll never go skiing again," says George. "We've got to," Nick answers. "It isn't worth while if you can't." George wishes, boy-like, that they could make some kind of promise about it. "There isn't any good in promising," says young Nick Adams. "It's hell, isn't it?" says George. "No, not exactly," says Nick.

Nick and George are as free and happy as Jake and Bill at Burguete. On the other side, for Nick, is all that involvement with woman, all the approaching domestication, all that half-ruefully, uncomplainingly accepted responsibility which will arrive at the moment Nick's fatherhood begins. It is not exactly hell. That is the province of *nada.* Nick recognizes, without complaint, that domestic responsibility presents a powerful case. It could, conceivably, cancel out those things in his life that are symbolized by the skiing with a good companion. And really, universally, the opposed relations of men-without-women and men-with-women stop nowhere. The conversational episode in the inn near Montreux is simply the little circle in which they *appear* to do so.

Closely related to the men-without-women theme is that of fathers and sons. In the early Nick Adams stories Nick is seen as the son of a father; in the latest, he is the father of a son. Some half-dozen of the first forty-five stories draw circles around the

[11] Henry James, *Works,* New York edition, Vol. 17, p. xxvii.

father-son relationship. It is movingly dramatized, for example, through Nick's sympathy with his father's shame and anger after the encounter with the sawyers, in which Dr. Adams has been insultingly bested. The following conversation closes "The Doctor and the Doctor's Wife":

"Your mother wants you to come and see her," the doctor said.

"I want to go with you," Nick said.

"All right. Come on, then," his father said. . . .

"I know where there's black squirrels, Daddy," Nick said.

"All right," said his father. "Let's go there."

At the other end of the line there is Nick's unspoken sympathy for his own son "Schatz" in the little story called "A Day's Wait." Not knowing the difference between Fahrenheit and centigrade thermometers, the boy (who had gone to school in France) naturally supposes that with a temperature of 102 degrees he will certainly die. It was common talk among his French schoolmates that you could not live with a temperature of 44 degrees, normal being 37 degrees. During the day's wait, he manages to keep a firm and stoical grip on himself. When he learns the truth, which is also the time when Nick first understands what is troubling the boy, the hold gradually relaxes. "The next day," says Nick, with a laconic quality that nearly conceals his own emotion, the boy's hold on himself "was very slack and he cried very easily at little things that were of no importance."

A third aspect of the father-and-son theme is the inevitable and paradoxical gulf between generations. It shows very clearly in the early story, "My Old Man," with its contrast between Joe's adoring innocence and his father's vicious world of thrown horse-races. But the paradox of togetherness and separateness is nowhere more poignantly dramatized than in the Nick Adams story called "Fathers and Sons." One great skill of the story is its compression of the generations of men, until the whole Adams clan of grandfather, father, son, and son's son are seen in a line, each visible over his son's shoulder. Each father is near his son, each son near his father. Yet between each generation comes the wall which neither side can fully cross—or would want to if it were possible.

IV. MANY MARRIAGES

Paradox is also at work in what may be called Hemingway's "marriage-group," that very considerable number of the first forty-five stories where the subject is some form of male-female relationship. Like Chaucer or Shakespeare or Keats or Browning, he watches with fascination the odd wave-like operation of attraction and repulsion between the two sexes. In his poems "Meeting at Night" and "Parting at Morning," Browning dramatizes the magnetic attraction of a tryst, and the "need for a world of men" which afterwards draws the lover away as rapidly as he came. Hemingway's stories often engage this paradox.

The women in Hemingway nearly always fail to understand fully the strength and extent of the attraction-repulsion phenomenon. Often, however, they are compelled—and it is on the whole an unhappy experience for them—to recognize its existence. One example will serve. "Up in Michigan," the earliest story in the collection, written in Paris in December, 1921, is one of the very few which Hemingway chooses to tell from the woman's point of view. Here a fine, neat country girl named Liz Coates worships a fine handsome blacksmith named Jim Gilmore from a respectful distance. One foggy evening, after a hunting trip, a good dinner, some whiskey, and exposure to the heat of an open fire, Jim rudely, painfully, and crudely seduces Liz on a cold boat-dock. Afterwards, being unable to talk to or even to wake her importunate lover, Liz covers him with her coat and walks home. This story is the first in a long line of similar instances where male virility, though often rough and wayward in its manifestations, seems to be the axis on which the world of womankind revolves.

"Cat in the Rain," another story taken in part from the woman's point of view, presents a corner of the female world in which the male is only tangentially involved. It was based on Rapallo early in 1923. From the window of a hotel room where her husband is reading and she is fidgeting, a young wife sees a cat outside in the rain. When she goes to get it, the animal (which somehow stands in her mind for comfortable bourgeois domesticity) has disappeared. This fact is very close to tragic because of the cat's association in her mind with many other things she longs for:

long hair that she can do in a knot at the back of her neck; a candle-lighted dining-table where her own silver gleams; the season of spring and nice weather; and, of course, some new clothes. But when she puts these wishes into words, her husband mildly advises her to shut up and find something to read. "Anyway," says the young wife, "I want a cat. I want a cat. I want a cat now. If I can't have long hair or any fun, I can have a cat." The poor girl is the referee in a face-off between the actual and the possible. The actual is made of rain, boredom, a preoccupied husband, and irrational yearnings. The possible is made of silver, spring, fun, a new coiffure, and new dresses. Between actual and possible stands the cat. It is finally sent up to her by the kindly old inn-keeper, whose sympathetic deference is greater than that of the young husband.

In "The Kreutzer Sonata," Tolstoi presents an extreme example of the mild schizophrenia where a desired involvement and a desired freedom co-exist in the mind of the male. Two of Hemingway's stories approach the same problem in a comic spirit. In "The End of Something," Nick bluntly concludes his serious love affair with Marjorie, evidently by previous agreement with his friend Bill. In "The Three-Day Blow," while the wind of autumn rises in background accompaniment, Nick and Bill converse on the mature wisdom they showed in having stopped the love affair before it went too far. Despite this wisdom, Nick cannot help feeling uncomfortable about the finality of the termination. Thus when Bill rather cynically guesses that it might not be so final after all, Nick is wonderfully relieved. He can always go into town where Marjorie lives on the coming Saturday night. It is "a good thing to have in reserve."

Despite the need for detachment after involvement, Hemingway's work always stresses the essential normality and rightness of the male-female relationship.[12] Anything which distorts it, any-

---

[12] A passage of dialogue between Hemingway and the Old Lady (*DIA*, 179–180) bears on this point. "Do you know any true stories about those unfortunate people?" says the Old Lady, meaning by unfortunate the sexually abnormal. "A few," answers Hemingway, "but in general they lack drama, as do all tales of abnormality, since no one can predict what will happen in the normal while all tales of the abnormal end much the same."

thing which brings it to an unhappy conclusion, is basically a kind of tragedy. In 1918, for example, there was a major in a Milan hospital whose wounded right hand had shrunk until it was no bigger than a baby's. Before the war he had been the best fencer in Italy. He was now using an exercise machine which was supposed to strengthen and enlarge the withered hand. Beside him at these sessions was a young American, taking similar treatments for a wounded leg, but more hopeful of its restoration. One day the major asked the American if he were married, and the American replied that he would like to be.

"The more of a fool you are," the major said. He seemed very angry. "A man must not marry."

"Why, Signor Maggiore?"

"Don't call me 'Signor Maggiore.' "

"Why must not a man marry?"

"He cannot marry. He cannot marry," he said angrily. "If he is to lose everything, he should not place himself in a position to lose that. He should not place himself in a position to lose. He should find things he cannot lose."

The major's wife had just died of pneumonia. Death is the absolute distortion, the unequivocal conclusion. The story, and there is much more to it, is called "In Another Country." The country is Italy; but it is also another country still, a country (it is just possible) where a man can find things he cannot lose.

Divorce or separation is a form of death in Hemingway's marriage-group. In the ironic story called "A Canary for One," the narrative turns upon a point of information not revealed until the final sentence: "We were returning to Paris to set up separate residences." Hemingway's strategy here is to establish through dialogue a parallel between the about-to-separate husband and wife and an enforced separation about which they hear on the train-ride between Cannes and the Gare de Lyon in Paris. They

It might be added that Hemingway everywhere celebrates the normal values of sexual intercourse between a man and a woman who are in love. It is probable that he agrees with the opinion of Remy de Gourmont: "Il y aurait peut-être une certaine corrélation entre la copulation complète et profonde et le développement cérébral." See Ezra Pound's postscript to his translation of de Gourmont's *Natural Philosophy of Love*, published by Boni and Liveright, New York, 1922.

share a compartment with a deaf American lady who is taking home to her daughter a canary which she has picked up during a Cook's Tour. The lady's conviction that "American men make the best husbands" embroils the reader in a double irony. Two years before, she has broken up a match between her daughter and a Swiss engineering student on the grounds that "I couldn't have her marrying a foreigner." The daughter's reaction has not been favorable. "She doesn't seem to take an interest in anything. She doesn't care about things." The canary is a consolation prize, a substitute interest which will obviously fail. But the lady will not give up her belief that Americans make the best husbands, even though she is in the same compartment with an American couple whose marriage has failed.

The canary (if the lady would face it) and the couple (if the lady knew about them) might together penetrate the lady's rook-ribbed assurance that she is in the right. Both the married people must henceforth content themselves with those forlorn substitutes for each other of which, in another domestic situation, the canary is the epitome. But the lady's deafness is itself a symbol of her impenetrability to suggestion; and she will never know how much the canary will mean to the about-to-separate American couple as a symbol of distortion.

Other stories explore the predicament of divorce. Mr. Johnson, a writer waiting for his train in the station café at Vevey, desperately supposes that he can blunt the edge of the shame he feels by talking over his imminent divorce with three dignified Swiss porters. Though he buys them wine, and curiously raises what for him is the central question, he is met by that sympathetic but somewhat enigmatic politeness which was to be expected.

"You say you have never been divorced?"

"No," says one porter. "It would be too expensive. Besides, I have never married."

"Ah," says Johnson. "And these other gentlemen?"

"They are married."

"You like the married state?" says Johnson to one of them.

"Oui. C'est normal."

"Exactly," says Johnson. "Et vous, monsieur?"

"Ça va," says the third porter.

"Pour moi," says Johnson, "ça ne va pas."

Seeing then, after a futile attempt to change the subject, that his bull-blundering investigation has come to nothing, Johnson excuses himself and goes outside. "It had only made him feel nasty"—because he has possibly embarrassed the porters while certainly embarrassing himself, but mainly because he has recognized, with more shame and discomfort than ever, the normality of the married state, the "abnormality" of his own, and, finally and acutely, that whole nexus of half-humorous shrugging acceptance which is summed up in the second porter's "Ça va." Pour Monsieur Johnson, ça ne va pas.

If the healthy married state, or its approximate equivalent, is strongly recommended in these stories as the normal situation for men and women, one finds also the occasional recognition of other forms of abnormality than divorce. There is, for example, the extreme travesty of the relationship between "Mr. and Mrs. Elliot," who at last settle into an old-maid marriage, all calm and acceptable superficially, all in jagged remnants underneath. Another story, "The Sea Change," examines at its crux the problem of an otherwise satisfactory liaison. The girl faces the pull of an unnatural attraction, and the lover sees that he has no choice but to let her go. Except for one pronoun, and a noun which the girl rejects as too ugly to apply to her own situation, the story might be that of an ordinary lovers' triangle, with the girl leaving one man for another. The pronoun appears in the man's fierce threat towards the third corner of the triangle: "I'll kill her," he cries.

V. MANY MUST HAVE IT

To say that Hemingway is preoccupied with such subjects would be wrong. His preoccupation is rather with the healthy norm of ordinary sexual behavior. He merely sees that the normality of the norm is sometimes most effectively measured in terms of departures from it. Furthermore, a writer dedicated, like Hemingway, to the rendering of things as they are soon recognizes that departures from the usual are numerous enough to make ignoring them a fault of seeing. His personal views, which can be determined inductively, seem to range from the artist's simple acceptance of the fact that abnormality exists up to an outright scorn full of moral echoes of disgust and disapproval, or over into an amused raillery at the expense of the afflicted. Somewhere near the area of simple acceptance would be the story called "A Simple Enquiry," in which an Italian major asks his youthful orderly certain guarded but leading questions. These are familiar enough in an amusing way to all who have ever been through the stock interview with the army psychiatrist at an induction center. Before this particular interview is over, the reader is aware that the major's interests are not, on the whole, scientific.

Among the humorous stories is one called "The Light of the World." Hemingway included it among the six or seven which he liked best, though he said that "nobody else ever liked" it.[13] One need not like the substance of the story, or the people, or the language. But even with these reservations, one can still enjoy the story's triumph, which is that it adds up to a very complicated defense of the normal against the abnormal. The scene is a provincial railroad depot in northern Michigan at an autumn nightfall. Two tough youngsters, coming in, find themselves in the midst of ten men and five women. The group conversation, conducted in roaring comic terms, establishes the homosexuality of one of the men to serve as contrast to the loudmouthed lying sentimentality of one of the five prostitutes. She says that she was once the true love of Steve Ketchel, a prizefighter. Her forthright contradicter, an even fatter professional tart named Alice, stands (at least in context) for the normal, the honest, and the sound. The raucous play of human emotion, bald as a turkey-egg, loud as a brawl, sets up an effective contrast to the furtive yearnings of the homosexual cook. In an odd way, and not without some strain on the moral judgment, the huge Alice in her iridescent silk dress comes to be the true heroine of the comedy. Love may be, as the sentimental blonde asserts, the light of the world. But an even stronger light may be cast by the honest common sense of people like Alice, the Michigan Wife of Bath.

Hemingway's skills as a comic writer are probably not enough

[13] One of Hemingway's letters to Perkins suggests that this story has some points in common with Maupassant's *La Maison Tellier*. EH to MP, 7/31/33.

appreciated. "The Gambler, the Nun, and the Radio," for example, is a fine and subtle study, depending to a great degree on the humor of character, and setting up a memorable contrast among three levels of the apprehension of reality.[14] So is the portrait of the old French couple in "Wine of Wyoming." Here as elsewhere in the first forty-five stories, it is his championship of the normal and the natural which runs like a backbone down through the substance of the tales he elects to tell.[15] His devotion to the honest and the actual is a moral decision which also happens to coincide with his esthetic views.

The record, if it is examined justly and with detachment, simply does not bear out the frequent critical implication that he invokes the spectacular or leans on the unusual to carry the burden of his stories. If "Hills Like White Elephants" throws light into the nether regions of selfish human abnormality—which is one way of looking at the matter of abortion—one can balance it with such insights into the normal married state as "Cat in the Rain." The raving sentimentality of the peroxide blonde in "The Light of the World" is neatly deflated by the solid honesty of Alice, who has long since left (if she was ever inside) her friend's cheap and banal wonderland. Even the nightly excursions of the old Spanish waiter into that vast *nada* which lies outside the normal world of everyday affairs are wrenched back by a final twist into the realm of the recognizable. "After all," he says to himself, "it is probably only insomnia. Many must have it." The world of Hemingway's short stories is above all the world we know. Many of us have it—or at least enough of it so that we easily recognize its outlines in his pages.

His oddly continuing reputation as an "archpriest of violence" really finds little support in the first forty-five stories. The overwhelming majority are extremely non-athletic. Their points are carried by talk far more often than by action. Outwardly, at least, nothing much happens, even though several kinds of burning

[14] This story evidently grew out of Hemingway's hospitalization in Billings, Montana, following an automobile accident in November 1930. The story was finished early in February 1933.

[15] "Wine of Wyoming" is apparently related to Hemingway's sojourn in the Sheridan area during the summer of 1928. The story contains topical allusions to the presidential candidacy of Governor Alfred E. Smith.

emotion are implied and at intervals may erupt into the briefest violence of language. Otherwise there is seldom more movement than such as is necessary to raise a glass to the lips, row a boat across an inlet, cast a fly into a troutstream, or ski down a snowy slope into the true center of a story.

At café tables, in quiet rooms, or in the compartments of trains, men and women talk together with a concentrated diffidence which almost conceals the intensity of their feelings. Upon examination, it turns out to be this very intensity, this intensity very close to the intensity of poetry, which has deceived some of his critics into supposing that Hemingway is an exponent of violence for its own sake. Even in the relatively rare athletic stories, this is never so. He is after intensity, and his brand of intensity is to be achieved not by physical exercise but only through the exercise of the utmost restraint.[16]

[16] The origin of the titles *Men Without Women* and *Winner Take Nothing* may be noted for the record. The first was evidently a twist on the title of a novel by Ford, *Women and Men*. Hemingway's title was given in turn a twist by Wyndham Lewis for his critical book, *Men Without Art*. Hemingway's jocular explanation of his choice of the title was that he hoped the book would have a big sale among graduates of Vassar and homosexuals. EH to FSF, *ca*. late September 1927. But he had already given Perkins a serious explanation: "In all of these [stories], almost, the softening feminine influence [is] absent," whether as a result of "training, discipline, death, or other causes." EH to MP, 2/14/27. Hemingway had decided on the *Winner Take Nothing* title by 6/11/33. The title derives from the epigraph of the book. This epigraph, ostensibly drawn from an antique book of rules for gaming, was actually written by Hemingway himself. EH to CB, 11/22/51.

VII · The Spanish Earth

> "Like a bistro to which you can take your
> own food on condition that you wash it
> down with a bottle of the host's unpre-
> dictable wine, Spain is the traditional
> ruminating ground."—Geoffrey Brere-
> ton [1]

I. TAUROMAQUIA

After the land of his birth and boyhood, Italy was Hemingway's first love, and France his second. But of all the nations
of Europe, Spain in the period before Franco stood out most
strongly in his affections. There was even a time, in Burguete in
1925, when he told his new friend Fitzgerald that his idea of
heaven would be a big bullring in which he owned two barrera
seats, with a troutstream outside that no one else was allowed to
fish.[2] Almost from the beginning of his career he had been writing about Spain and the people of Spain. There were, however,
two more or less distinct periods of interest. The first, 1922–1932,
used Spanish backgrounds for six of the miniatures of *In Our
Time,* as well as for five of the longer stories. All but the introductory section of *The Sun Also Rises* was laid in Spanish towns
(Burguete, Pamplona, and Madrid). The terminal book for this
period was *Death in the Afternoon,* completed in 1931–1932,
though begun much earlier and sporadically worked on through
most of the time between the fall of 1929 and its publication in
the fall of 1932. It was primarily a Baedeker of the bullfight, and
it sought to do in graphic prose something like what Goya's
"Tauromaquia" had achieved on canvas. But it was undertaken
also as a preliminary summing up of ten years of intermittent
experience with the Spanish earth and the people who lived on it.

The second period, culminating in *For Whom the Bell Tolls,*
ran from 1936 to 1940. The Spanish Civil War—a tragedy

---

[1] *New Statesman and Nation* 39 (June 24, 1950), p. 716.
[2] EH to FSF, from Burguete, July 1, 1925.

enacted on a far greater scale and with far greater suffering and bloodshed than the weekly tragedies of the *corridas de toros*— was a strong catalyst to Hemingway's imagination. His interest in war as a subject, and his love of first-hand experience as an object, made it almost obligatory that he should watch over the Spanish tragedy until the final curtain fell. In 1937 he worked with Joris Ivens on a war-documentary film, *The Spanish Earth*, in which his friends MacLeish and Dos Passos had an equal interest. Hemingway not only accompanied Ivens and his cameraman, John Ferno, but also provided the commentary and the sound-track narration. In the fall of the same year he drafted his only full-length play, *The Fifth Column*. It showed that Hemingway's capabilities as playwright were strictly limited. Its subject was that of espionage and counter-espionage in the besieged city of Madrid.

Seventeen months after Madrid fell to the fascists on March 28, 1939, he completed *For Whom the Bell Tolls*. It is still, and may well continue to be, the one indubitable classic among the accounts, both fictional and non-fictional, which took Spain's civil tragedy as subject matter. Although the author's sympathies are clearly on the people's side, the book is in no sense a propagandist tract. Its depth and its lucidity arise from its summing up of Hemingway's long and devoted (but also artistically detached) affection for the land and the people—including his sensitive appreciation of the way these were changed, and yet not changed, by the tragic fact of civil war.

The end-product of the first ten years in Spain, *Death in the Afternoon*, has been called the best work on bullfighting in English. It is quite likely the best of its kind in any language and Hemingway worked long and hard to make it so. It is a serious attempt to write a technical handbook of *toreros*, memorable (and not so memorable) *corridas*, and the noble animals, in such a way as to interest and instruct the lay reader. For his amusement, it is diversified with narratives and sketches, often prejudiced commentaries on the arts, satire of *The Torrents of Spring* variety, characterizations, word-pictures, and observations of a social and ethnological nature. It also contains a glossary of Spanish terms; several appendices including an estimate of the author's good friend,

Sidney Franklin, the bullfighter from Brooklyn, New York; and a careful selection of photographs which Hemingway gathered and winnowed during a stay in Spain in May, June, and July, 1931.

Some such book as *Death in the Afternoon* had been on Hemingway's mind for more than seven years before the final version appeared. His first letter to Maxwell Perkins on April 15, 1925, said that he hoped sometime to write a sort of Doughty's *Arabia Deserta* of the bullring, a large book full of wonderful pictures.[3] But the project was sidetracked while Hemingway prepared *In Our Time* for publication by Liveright, composed *The Torrents of Spring*, and finally established his reputation as an artist with *The Sun Also Rises, Men Without Women*, and *A Farewell to Arms*.

He continued his studies of the bullfight in Spain during the summer of 1926, and in December of that year indicated once more to Perkins how close to his heart the bullfight book still was. It must be not merely a textbook history or an apologia for bullfighting, but, if possible, "the bullfight itself." Except for church ritual, it was the one thing that had come down intact from the old days in Spain. It was of great tragic interest, being literally a matter of life and death. Few people outside Spain knew much about the real art of the *torero*. Finally, bullfighting was a profession in which a young peasant or bootblack could make eighty thousand a year before the age of twenty-three. Such a combination of interests, said Hemingway, must inevitably "do something" to people. But his book would take a long time to finish.[4]

It did. He returned to Spain in the summer of 1929 and made further notes on the status of the sport. But it was not until the fall of 1930 that he was able to report to Maxwell Perkins that the still untitled bullfight book was nearly finished. Two chapters, four appendices, and the glossary then remained to be done. But the work was again interrupted, this time by a serious automobile

[3] EH to MP, 4/15/25. Hemingway once denied the recurrent rumor that *Death in the Afternoon* was originally planned in collaboration with Picasso about 1925, with Hemingway doing the text and Picasso the pictures, the whole to be published in a deluxe German edition. EH to CB, 4/1/51.

[4] EH to MP, 12/6/26.

accident and a long period of recuperation. Further observations were added in Spain in the summer of 1931. The glossary was completed in Paris during August. During the last two weeks of November the final chapter was written. After six weeks of revision, the manuscript was completed on January 13, 1932. It was at last published on the 26th of September.[5]

It was the large handsome book with wonderful pictures which Hemingway had looked forward to writing seven years earlier. It was a history, a guide, a report, and a descriptive analysis bound into one. Yet it cannot be too strongly emphasized that the initial impulse behind the book was esthetic. Hemingway was drawn to the bullfight in the early twenties because it seemed to promise an opportunity to study a simple, cruel, and barbaric sport, showing a definite three-act pattern ending in death. Of all the legitimate "subjects that a man may write of," death was one of the simplest, apparently, and one of the most fundamental.[6] By watching it enacted, thought Hemingway, he might get the "feeling of life and death"—the deep contiguity—which he always wanted in his writing. *Death in the Afternoon* shows how the idea grew.

As he watched, time after time, the killing of bulls and the goring of horses and men, he learned more than he had first bargained for about the nature of tragedy, tragic catharsis, the tragic sense of life, and the feeling of doom. Having come only to observe, he remained as an *aficionado*. His presence during the destruction of 1500 bulls, over a ten-year period, convinced him that the bullfight was neither simple, barbaric, cruel, nor really a sport. It was complex in the extreme, ritualized and stylized nearly to the point of decadence.

Though ostensibly an athletic contest between a wild animal and a dismounted man, it differed from other sports in being played "for keeps" at the highest possible stakes. Very early he came to believe that it was "not a sport but a tragedy." [7] He developed the true *aficionado*'s appreciation of bravery, dignity, passion, and *pundonor*, as well as the opposites and the sundry shad-

[5] EH to MP, 10/28/30, 8/1/31, 12/9/31, 1/14/32.

[6] *DIA*, pp. 2–3.

[7] *DIA*, p. 16. Hemingway had said the same thing much earlier in one of his despatches to the *Toronto Star Weekly*.

ings of these qualities. He learned many lessons in how to tell the false from the real, the pose from the risk, the decadent from the healthy. Also useful to a foreigner (who was likewise a novelist) was what one learned about the inside of the Spanish temperament. The initial esthetic impulse grew outwards, without losing its esthetic significance, to suggest the outlines of a whole culture.

A very careful and sometimes labored distillation of all the years during and after his nominal residence in Paris, when Hemingway was nearly as often in Spain as out of it, *Death in the Afternoon* was not to be confused with the "one-visit books." [8] These impressionistic tours, written by observant travelers who saw the sights by day and kept diaries by night, required quick publication before the complications set in. According to Hemingway, two good examples of the "one-visit" books would be Julius Meier-Graefe's *The Spanish Journey* and Waldo Frank's *Virgin Spain*. He wished his own book, like that of Professor Robert Jordan, to contain "what he had discovered about Spain in ten years of travelling in it, on foot, in third-class carriages, by bus, on horse- and mule-back, and in trucks." [9] Hemingway could hardly have written a one-visit book even if he had wanted to do so. He had been in Spain so often that the country was a part of him.

Because *Death in the Afternoon* is primarily a handbook of tauromaquia, other aspects of Spanish life gain only incidental admittance. Yet Hemingway's account (in the novel) of Jordan's knowledge of Spain is a sincerely modest understatement of his own: "He knew the Basque country, Navarre, Aragon, Galicia, the two Castiles, and Estremadura well." An attentive and sympathetic reader should be able to gain from the bullfight handbook a vicarious knowledge of "the way it was" for the devoted traveler in Spain in the last years of the monarchy and the first of the People's Republic. Hemingway is invariably trustworthy, for example, on the atmosphere of the cities and towns; the raw ugliness of Bilbao, the tawdry cheapness of Santander, the green oasis of Aranjuez on the brown plain among dirt-colored and stone-green hills. Or the precipitous picturesqueness of Ronda where, if your

[8] *DIA*, p. 52.
[9] *FWBT*, p. 248.

honeymoon or elopement could not succeed in such an environment, "it would be as well to start for Paris and both commence
making your own friends." He recalls the Senegal heat of Cordoba
in summer, the semi-tropical freshness of Valencia (so well remembered by Pilar), the swimming by night off the beach there,
the high cloudless Spanish sky arching over the handsome city
of Madrid, Hemingway's favorite of them all. The sense of place is
strong in the book.

For the sense of the past, so important in *For Whom the Bell
Tolls,* there were the villages with bells, the squares with standing
horses—"the small, careful stepping horses"—the ancient, eroded,
baked-clay hills, or the powdery, hub-deep dust of the dipping
country roads. One got the sense of the past from the crowding,
various smells: leather, road-dust, olive-oil, tarry wineskins, loops
of twisted garlics. Or from the rope-soled shoes, the natural
wooden pitchforks with branches for tines, or the fine old castle
at the head of the valley near Aoiz.

If one comes fresh to a reading of *For Whom the Bell Tolls*
after having laid down *Death in the Afternoon,* he will see how
much of the old Spain has been transferred out of the manual
and into the novel, always with a noticeable gain in dramatic intensity. For, in the novel, what was formerly only a piece of direct
personal observation has very often taken on a functional significance. One of the uses of *Death in the Afternoon,* both for Hemingway and for the serious student of his work, is that it serves as
a kind of sourcebook for *For Whom the Bell Tolls.* In the mob-
murder of the fascists by Pablo and his associates, for example,
the wooden pitchforks are put to a use for which they were never
meant by their rural manufacturers. The welcome sense of abun-
dance in that semi-arid land is not lost on the guerrillas in their
necessarily somewhat austere mountain fastness. They can recall
such delicacies as the fresh strawberries packed on damp green
leaves in wicker baskets, asparagus as thick as thumbs, Valencia
melons, the cider of Bombilla, prawns sprinkled with lime juice,
and the delectable sea-food *paellas.* The sense of place and fact
and scene are strong in the novel not only because Hemingway
knows the country, but also because, in a preliminary way, he had
seized on and arranged them in the earlier book.

Despite romantic overtones (the natural consequence of writing about a country one loves and has been happy in), *Death in the Afternoon* is about an actual Spain. It is honest and realistic. It is even, in certain respects, straightforwardly reportorial, a fact which tells somewhat against it when it is compared with works of fictional art. *For Whom the Bell Tolls* combines a similar tough-minded sense of the actual with similar romantic overtones. Unlike *Death in the Afternoon,* however, the novel has completely assimilated the reportorial element to the needs of art. In the novel, that is to say, we are not told: we learn by experience so sharp that it hardly seems vicarious.

To attempt to compare *Death in the Afternoon* with *For Whom the Bell Tolls* is of course to understand that no genuine comparison is possible. One is intended, as Hemingway reminds us in his "Bibliographical Note" at the end of the book, "as an introduction to the modern Spanish bullfight," where the attempt has been to "explain that spectacle both emotionally and practically." It was written for that purpose because there was no other book in Spanish or English which did precisely that kind of job. The novel, on the other hand, is not a handbook of anything, but an art work of a very high imaginative order. The motivations of the two books are accordingly quite different.

For the student of Hemingway who is seriously interested in the developmental aspects of his fiction, a reading of *Death in the Afternoon* is indispensable. In the same way, one's appreciation of the imaginative stature of *Huckleberry Finn* as a work of art is considerably enhanced by a reading of *Life on the Mississippi.* *Life on the Mississippi* is obviously not in the same class with *Huckleberry Finn.* The laws which govern the composition of such diverse books cannot be the same. But this is hardly to say that the study of *Death in the Afternoon* will not, in various ways, illuminate the study of *For Whom the Bell Tolls.* One of the values of the bullfight book is the light it throws on the esthetics of tragedy in Hemingway.

II. THE ESTHETICS OF TRAGEDY

Nowhere in either of Hemingway's Spanish books could one find the "bedside mysticism" of Waldo Frank's *Virgin Spain*. A comparison between *Death in the Afternoon* and Frank's travelogue emphasizes the great differences between the two men in point of esthetic view. Frank was sometimes excellent as when, describing a dance, he heard "the castanets click their dry commentary," or when he caught some Aragonese peasants as "small weazened men, with heads like nuts and eyes like iron." But Frank loved pseudo-poetry. The girls of Cordoba struck him as "sinuous walking lilies," promising a "snare of momentary passion." [10] When he really set forth in pursuit of an *O Altitudo,* he was capable of flights like the following, on Saragossa's cathedral, *Nuestra Senora del Pilar:*

"From its mournful mass rise suddenly, inappositely, the huge *azulejo* domes, their hypertrophic rhetoric gleaming of Andalusia and Morocco."

In something like the railing manner of *The Torrents of Spring,* Hemingway called this "erectile writing," or the unavoidable mysticism of one who "writes a language so badly he cannot make a clear statement." [11] To account for the unrelieved turgidness of the prose in *Virgin Spain,* he developed a bawdy hypothesis like one of Swift's in *A Tale of a Tub.* Hemingway's own problem in *Death in the Afternoon* was of a different kind. "Madame," he asks the old lady who winningly serves as his tuning fork, "does all this writing of the bullfights bore you?" The old lady says that her patience is a little limited. "I understand," says the author. "A technical explanation is hard reading. It is like the simple directions which accompany any mechanical toy and which are incomprehensible." [12] Whatever the limitations of his own expository writing might be, and they might be many, Hemingway did not take refuge in pseudo-poetry. His prose contained nothing

[10] *Virgin Spain:* Castanets (p. 84), peasants (p. 92), Cordoban girls (p. 60). With Frank's picture of Spanish women contrast Hemingway's (*DIA*, pp. 41–42).

[11] On *erectile writing* see *DIA*, pp. 53–54. See Dos Passos's review of *Virgin Spain* in *New Masses* 1 (July 1926), p. 27, for a similar position.

[12] *DIA*, p. 179.

turgid or intentionally obscure. The reader found no hypertrophic rhetoric gleaming through the pages of *Death in the Afternoon.* Its essential down-to-Spanish-earthness was one of its values.

Frank and Hemingway are in agreement on the larger three-act outline of the typical Spanish bullfight. "The horse," says Frank, "is the comedian of the drama." What happens to the horse is farce, though it involves also a "sense of the imminence of danger." For what has happened to the horse may happen to a man. Hemingway likewise observes that "in the tragedy of the bullfight the horse is the comic character." Frank's account of the second act shows the banderilleros enraging and sobering the bull to make him realize "that the holiday of the horse is no more." By the end of the act the bull is chastened, "cleansed for the tragedy." For Hemingway, the bull in Act Two has lost the free wild quality he began with, gone on the defensive and become more dangerous in that now, sobered and serious, "he aims every horn stroke," concentrating his hatred on an individual object. One finds nothing in Hemingway about the bull's being cleansed for the tragedy, however, and it is apparent that he has kept his writer's eye more steadily fixed on the animal than has Frank.

At the climactic moment of the killing in Act Three, both writers agree that a profundity of feeling is transferred to the spectator. Frank says that the torero is enacting "the ultimate rite of life" by assuming proprietorship of "the ultimate gift of the gods," which is death. Hemingway's view is again similar: "When a man is still in rebellion against death he has pleasure in taking to himself one of the Godlike attributes, that of giving it." This gift is given in pride—"a Christian sin and a pagan virtue. But it is pride which makes the bullfight, and true enjoyment of killing which makes the great matador." [13]

So far Hemingway will go in Frank's company. But in his down-to-earthness he is never tricked into the pseudo-poetic erotic symbolism of a passage like this of Frank's: "And now another change in the beauty of their locked encounter. The man becomes the woman. This dance of human will and brutish power is the

---

[13] Cf. *Virgin Spain*, pp. 232–233 and *DIA*, p. 6. On the sobered bull see *DIA*, p. 98. On the killing of Act III, compare *Virgin Spain*, p. 234, and *DIA*, p. 233.

dance of death no longer. It is the dance of life. It is a searching symbol of the sexual act. The bull is male; the exquisite torero, stirring and unstirred, with hidden ecstasy controlling the plunges of the bull, is female." This is erectile writing with a vengeance. Frank, says Hemingway, discovered some "wonderful stuff about Spain during his short stay there preparatory to writing of the soul of the country, but it is often nonsense." At least it is the kind of writing against which Hemingway had been in very open rebellion since the beginning of his career. *Death in the Afternoon* proceeds sensitively but also with sanity. "The beauty of the moment of killing is that flash when man and bull form one figure as the sword goes all the way in, the man leaning after it, death uniting the two figures in the emotional, esthetic, and artistic climax of the fight. That flash never comes in the skillful administering of half a blade to the bull." The reader will see how simple it would have been to write these sentences in the erotic manner. Knowing truth from falsehood, however, Hemingway does not confuse the torero with a woman, the uniting of the two figures with the sexual act, or the thrust of the blade with the thrust of anything else. His habitual devotion to the truth of the matter may not always save him from self-deception. But he is never guilty of Freudian fiddle-faddle.[14]

He well knows, nevertheless, what emotional and spiritual intensity a genuine fight can produce. The effect can be "as profound as any religious ecstasy"—an experience ordered, formalized, passionate, and with a mounting disregard for death which leaves the spectator "as empty, as changed, and as sad" as any other tragic catharsis.[15]

Death is for Hemingway somewhere near the center of life. Some of his critics have not seen that after the tragi-comedy of *The Sun Also Rises,* all of Hemingway's novels have been tragedies. Nor have they usually understood that such a tragedian must employ his interest in death at the center of the art form he uses. As soon as Hemingway abandoned his early misconception of the bullfight, he immediately saw it as an art form of great com-

[14] Cf. *Virgin Spain,* p. 235, and *DIA,* pp. 53 and 247.
[15] *DIA,* pp. 206–207.

plexity, always producing, when it was well done, tragic emotions and effects. If falsified or weakly performed, it could of course fall as flat as an amateur production of *Hamlet*. Without death at the end of it, further, it would be anticlimactic and unfulfilled, as if one were to tack a happy ending to *King Lear*. The proximity of death gave meaning to all parts of the *corrida*. But the torero alone performed a special work of art in bringing death extremely close, by enthralling it in an art form in such a way as to transmit to the observer the feeling of his own immortality. When the feeling stretched between spectator and actor, the torero cut it with his sword, as a taut wire is cut, relieving the tension and allowing the spectator to relax back into the ultimate emotional situation which Aristotle called catharsis.[16]

The Castilian attitude towards death is evidently very close to Hemingway's own. Unlike the Galicians and the Catalans, who have very little feeling for death, the Castilians "have great common sense. . . . They know death is the unescapable reality, the one thing any man may be sure of. . . . They think a great deal about death and when they have a religion they have one which believes that life is much shorter than death." Since by going to the bullring they have a chance of seeing death "given, avoided, refused, and accepted," they pay their money and go.[17] Such a healthy attitude towards death is one way of overcoming the usual sentimental taboos. To face the fact of death is as necessary to the writer of tragedy as a healthy facing of the other facts of life. If it is a general attribute of the English, the French, and the Americans to "live for life" and to avoid discussion or thought of death, their chances of writing good tragedy are so much the worse.

Hemingway's first visits to the bullfights were made for "the feeling of life and death" which he thought might be gained there. *Death in the Afternoon* shows what happened when Hemingway had learned his way into the esthetics of tragedy which govern the bullfight. It also helps to explain his sense of belonging among the people of the two Castiles, his special love for the people of

[16] *DIA*, pp. 213.
[17] *DIA*, pp. 265–266.

Madrid and the country round it. This locale, this people, and this sense of belonging were important factors in the development of *For Whom the Bell Tolls.*

III. THE HERO AS PRAGMATIST

If Spain taught Hemingway something about the tragic facts of life, it likewise contributed to his conception of the nature of heroism. His earliest and most revealing statements on the qualities of the hero come in *Death in the Afternoon.* Evidently his standard of selection falls somewhere between the hero as man of action and the hero as artist. For the first of these one need look no further than the indomitable figure of Manuel Garcia, called Maera.

"Era muy hombre," says Hemingway of Maera, who for a number of seasons served Belmonte as banderillero and then went on to be a brilliant matador. "Tall, dark, thin-hipped, gaunt-eyed, his face blue-black even after a close shave, arrogant, slouching, and sombre," Maera became one of the "best and most satisfying" fighters in Hemingway's lengthy experience as a spectator. The story of his encounter with the cement-shouldered bull at the close of the eighth chapter of *Death in the Afternoon* documents Hemingway's admiration, with reasons. As his qualities are summed up there, Maera was "generous, humorous, proud, bitter, foul-mouthed, and a great drinker. He neither sucked after intellectuals nor married money. He loved to kill bulls and lived with much passion and enjoyment although the last six months of his life he was very bitter. He knew he had tuberculosis and took absolutely no care of himself; having no fear of death, he preferred to burn out, not as an act of bravado, but from choice." [18] The reader of *Across the River and Into the Trees* will find a number of these qualities translated to fictional form in the person of the professional soldier, Colonel Cantwell.

Goya, the hero as artist, had certain characteristics in common with the hero as man of action. These showed most graphically in the kind of painting he chose to do. According to Hemingway, who contrasts Goya with Velásquez and especially with El Greco,

[18] *DIA,* pp. 77, 80–83.

Goya's painting was the direct outcome of his hard-won empirical convictions. He believed in "blacks and grays, in dust and in light, in high places rising from plains, in the country around Madrid, in movement, in his own cojones, in painting, in etching, and in what he had seen, felt, touched, handled, smelled, enjoyed, drunk, mounted, suffered, spewed-up, lain-with, suspected, observed, loved, hated, lusted, feared, detested, admired, loathed, and destroyed. Naturally no painter has been able to paint all that but he tried." [19] No student of Hemingway can fail to see how exactly this description of Goya's beliefs summarizes the attitudes of all the fictional heroes from Lieutenant Henry to Colonel Cantwell.

The realm in which these heroes move is extraordinary in two important particulars. First, it is a world in a state of flux, like Goya's revolutionary Spain or like the tense microcosm of the various bullrings in which Maera so brilliantly fought his battles. This world requires constant activity of its inhabitants. Second, it is a world screened, as it were, at both ends. One finds that the hero's experiential heritage from the past has little direct bearing on his decisions, though occasionally, as in the case of Robert Jordan's warrior-grandfather, a heroic action in the past may serve as a model for the hero in a present-day predicament. With this kind of exception, however, the Hemingway hero must work out his values for himself almost, if not quite, on the spot. Nor does he incline to take count of the future, the long future after death. He finds his way of life through action, and he acts in the way of the world.

"Perhaps as you went along," Jake Barnes once ruminated, "you did learn something. I did not care what it was all about. All I wanted to know was how to live in it. Maybe if you found out how to live in it you learned from that what it was all about." [20] How to live in it. How to live. The Hemingway hero is always a pragmatist. The function of his thought is, in the end, to serve as a guide for action. The abstraction has little meaning for him until it is particularized in a specific situation. Like Keats, to be convinced of the truth of a thing, he must have tried it on his own pulses. Indeed, much that Hemingway wrote of Goya could also

[19] *DIA*, p. 205.
[20] *SAR*, p. 153.

apply to Keats. The hero tests "truth" by observing the practical consequences of belief. His cast of mind is towards the integration of what is workable. But his vision is usually narrowed to the problems of immediate need. He is at some pains to keep his values from hardening into a final scheme. By preference and predetermination they are held in a more or less fluid state.

One naturally thinks of William James's formulation: pragmatism is "the attitude of looking away from first things, principles, 'categories,' supposed necessities, and of looking towards last things, fruits, consequences, facts." Although the statement summarizes with some precision the attitude of Hemingway's heroes, it is only partly applicable to Hemingway himself. For, as artist and esthetician, he must be and indubitably is concerned with first things and principles as well as the last things—consequences and facts.

His abnegation of his inheritance from the past means that the Hemingway hero must learn his own way to a great extent independently of every other man. In one way this fits the facts of living as we know them. The full significance of a piece of inherited folk-wisdom, say a proverb, never comes really home to us until we have the experience that proves it true. At another and higher point, however, the process of independent discovery, if insisted on exclusively, is a kind of willful evasion of a great part of what we need to know. It is probably fair to say that Hemingway's heroes are anti-intellectuals and even behaviorist anarchists to the extent that each of them must work out his code for himself, without taking full cognizance of the accumulated experience of other men. Yet this is true, to a more limited extent, of most people. At their own dramatic level of working matters out in action, Hemingway's heroes belong among the normal males of our time.

"I did not care what it was all about" is Jake Barnes's way of saying that he has not found any world view which will entirely account for and contain the facts of the world as he has garnered them through youth, war, demobilization, frustrated love, and work for the newspapers. In one of Albert Schweitzer's studies of Goethe, the position is admirably expanded. "Because he knows this one thing," says Schweitzer, "that he belongs to nature and to God, Goethe needs no artistically constructed world view complete to the last detail, but is satisfied to live with a world view which is not complete and cannot be completed. He does not want to be richer than he can be through the absolutely honest acquisition of truth. With that he is confident that he can live." [21] One might not entirely agree with Schweitzer on the question of Goethe's attitude towards a *Weltanschauung*. But Jake Barnes almost takes the words out of Schweitzer's typewriter. "It seemed like a fine philosophy," says Jake about one of his attempts to account for the human predicament. "In five years, I thought, it will seem just as silly as all the other fine philosophies I've had." No ethical or metaphysical speculation can adequately represent the world as it is, unless, of course, it is a scheme to avoid the schematic.

Although the Hemingway hero is not a reasoner in the abstract, and therefore not a builder of world-views, he is an extraordinarily careful planner on the practical plane. It is presumed to be the intelligent man's duty and responsibility to use his powers of planning to the utmost. Leaving as few unknowns as can be, he must organize the known, predict possible variables, estimate the probabilities, decide on a mode of action, and act. If his advance preparation has been good, his results have a chance of being good—up to a point. Beyond that point luck takes over, luck being the unpredictable contingency, present in the unknowns and the possible variables, which may go for or against the best of planners.

Even luck, however, may be controlled in a negative way if one takes the further commonsense precaution of following the rules. Knowledge of the rules of living is perhaps the hardest of the lessons man must learn because there is really no short cut to it. Yet one measure of man's ability to live successfully in the world is clearly his ability to assimilate and then to follow the rules. Matthew Arnold's generic term for this ability was the "sense for conduct." But whatever Arnold may have believed, the sense for conduct is not an innate characteristic. It must be learned empirically. As for the rules, when one gets to know them they are seen to conform rather closely to what would result if the Decalogue were intelligently revamped to present-day usage with-

[21] Albert Schweitzer, *Goethe: Four Studies*, Boston, 1949, p. 49.

out recourse to any form of legalism. One does not commit adultery, bear false witness, steal, or covet—at least not often. He honors his father and mother if they are worth admiration. If not, he can always go back to his grandfather or grandmother, or adopt someone to honor. The matter of conduct demands concentration. "We are mathematicians only by chance," said Dr. Johnson, "but we are perpetual moralists." Simple, unthinking loyalty to another man's code of behavior will not suffice. One must sensibly and consciously choose an ethical pattern whose virtues have been pragmatically proved by one's own experience, including one's experience of watching the conduct of his living companions.

If varying degrees of rationalism, pragmatism, and empiricism meet and merge in the working philosophy of the Hemingway hero, one finds also a suggestion of psychological hedonism. Man's natural tendency, according to the formula promulgated by Benthamist ethics and adapted into a new context by Freudian psychology, is to seek pleasure and avoid pain. Jake Barnes and Brett Ashley, evaluating their past actions and seeking moral guidance for future conduct by discovering which make them feel good and which bad, are perfectly practical Benthamites, whatever their Freudian frustrations. In the world of action, of Lockean empiricism, Jamesian pragmatism, and perhaps even Deweyan instrumentalism, it is hardly surprising to find a Benthamist idea. The falsehood, of course, is to insist that these heroes are merely psychological or ethical hedonists. The rules in Hemingway are far more extensive and complex than that.

The sturdiness of Hemingway's position from an empirical point of view is that the meaning of conceptions must be sought in their practical consequences. This hardly makes him the atavistic man over whom some critics have crowed. (Wyndham Lewis refers, for example, to his "penetrating quality, like an animal speaking.") [22] But it does raise the question, so often raised and answered in the affirmative, of whether or not Hemingway is a "primitivist." To an extent he seems to be. His truth and his beauty are generally to be found in the natural rather than the artificial. In further support of the idea, one could point to his evident admiration of active virtues like courage or what the Spanish call

[22] Wyndham Lewis, *Men Without Art*, London, 1934, p. 17.

pundonor, which "means honor, probity, courage, self-respect and pride in one word." [23] Or his praise of man's ability to handle the instruments of sport or warfare or love-making—the clubs, rods, guns, swords, or other equipment with which he works. If, like the historical primitivist, he seems often to portray a state of society in which such active virtues and skills are necessary for survival, he does not follow the historical primitivist in idealizing that state of society. Unlike the nineteenth-century romantic primitivists, he does not lose himself in a golden age of the remote past or in a future and roseate Utopia. He finds the skills and virtues here and now on the battlefronts and in the bullrings of the world. And there are many bullrings besides those ordinarily so designated, just as there are many battlefronts. The manly virtues, at any rate, are as whole and real now as they were in Sparta, and as useful to man at play or at work. All of this would suggest that the loose term primitivist is a misnomer for Hemingway. Call him a utilitarian, one who realizes that (especially in the present state of the world) such skills and virtues are indispensable, and indeed are constantly in use whether or not a war is on.

If he agrees with Tolstoy that western society is decadent and immoral (and there is plenty of evidence in Hemingway to support the view), he would not, like Tolstoy, seek to impose a primitivistic social idea on the modern world. For he is the pragmatist rather than the idealist. By definition and temperament, he does not in his fiction go beyond a series of individual performances which are too limited in actual scope, even when placed end to end, to constitute a complete social ideal or form the basis for an ideal society. At the same time, no social ideal or ideal society would succeed unless it took account of such virtues and skills as Hemingway celebrates.

This is not to say, of course, that some of the individual performances (for example, Robert Jordan's) will not serve to suggest symbolically a larger social ideal out of which might grow, in the course of time and with luck, a better society. There is an ethical content in Hemingway which transcends the pleasure-pain strategy, a content not less useful because of the author's refusal to state it in other than dramatic terms, worked out in action.

[23] *DIA,* p. 91.

But here again, his perennial distrust of the abstract blue-print, as well as the whole slant of his esthetic conviction, gives him pause and makes him stop short of using his fiction for the purposes of social programming.

One conspicuous virtue of *Death in the Afternoon,* and it is always a virtue in an artist or an art, is the temperamental rejection of the bloodless abstraction. The heroes Hemingway chooses, Goya on canvas and Maera on the bloody sand, are *aficionados* of the actual, believing in what they empirically know, facing the facts of life, one of which is the fact of death, in full consciousness of the inter-relations and the psychological interdependence of the two. The same sturdy quality of belief runs like a thick red line through the whole gallery of Hemingway heroes, and evidently through the consciousness of the artist to whom they owe their origin.

Death in the Afternoon has not yet converted the Anglo-Saxon world to a love of the bullfight, nor is it likely to do so. The author of such a book must expect to find a considerable degree of resistance among those who do not wholly share his interests and his experience. Hemingway admits in the course of the book that some of the technical descriptions may be incomprehensible, which is another way of saying that to the uninitiated or the unsympathetic or the uninterested, parts of the book will seem dull. Other readers, for sundry reasons, may be disgruntled by the tabulation, in one of the appendixes, of "Some Reactions of A Few Individuals to the Integral Spanish Bullfight." Some of Hemingway's critics have even professed to find evidence of a kind of hectic hysteria within the book itself, a point for which the objective reader is likely to discover little support.

Whatever its limitations—and one may doubt that Hemingway finally achieved his aim of writing an *Arabia Deserta* of the bullfight—much of the book remains sound and true. Reviewing a British reissue of *Death in the Afternoon* some twenty years after its original appearance, Geoffrey Brereton attributed the book's staying qualities to "the author's obstinate devotion to the fact and its accompanying sensation." The devotion was evidently intense enough to save Hemingway from "gross errors of observation" and to minimize his "errors of judgment." [24] If one wishes to state the case somewhat more positively, there can be little doubt that Hemingway's enviable ability to stand at once inside and outside of history brings his account of bullfighting—at certain points in the handbook—close to the realm of art.

[24] Same reference as for headnote to this chapter. See above, note 1.

VIII · The Green Hills of Africa

> "I was always discovering places where I
> would like to spend my whole life."—
> W. B. Yeats, *Autobiographies* [1]

I. SAFARI

Hemingway's earliest book review, published in 1922 soon
after he reached Paris, was in praise of *Batouala,* a novel about the
life and death of a native African chieftain which had won its
Negro author, René Maran, the Goncourt Academy prize of
5000 francs for the best fiction by a young writer in 1921. What
made the book newsworthy was Maran's straightforward indictment of French colonial policy in the heart of Africa. For the
young artist Hemingway, however, it was chiefly remarkable for
its unimpassioned presentation of the way it was in an African
village from the native's point of view. "You smell the smells of
the village," wrote the reviewer, "you eat its food, you see the
white man as the black man sees him, and after you have lived
in the village you die there. That is all there is to the story, but
when you have read it, you have been Batouala [the native chief],
and that means that it is a great novel." [2]

Though it has long been forgotten, this review may well mark
the beginning of Hemingway's interest in Africa. Still, he had enjoyed shooting since boyhood, and the plains and hills of East
Africa were a logical destination for one who wanted to hunt on
a bigger scale than was common in Europe or the United States.
He wrote Maxwell Perkins from Wyoming in the fall of 1930
to say that though he had shot much game on the high slopes of
the western mountains, he was still dreaming of a trip to Africa.[3]
If he had another motive than the wish to hunt the green hills of
Tanganyika, it was that of the artist—the aim of seeing for him-

---

[1] Yeats, *Autobiographies* (new edition, New York, 1927), p. 73. Hemingway was an avowed admirer of this book.
[2] *Toronto Star Weekly*, March 25, 1922, p. 3.
[3] EH to MP, 9/28/30.

THE GREEN HILLS OF AFRICA   163

self, perhaps, just how close to the actual René Maran's *Batouala* really was.

"What do you want?" asked a man named Kandisky not long after Hemingway reached the game country of East Africa in the winter of 1933–1934. Kandisky was an expatriate Austrian who worked as employment agent for an Indian sisal-grower in Tanganyika. He had a consuming interest in literature, and none whatsoever in big-game shooting. "To write," answered Hemingway, "as well as I can and learn as I go along. At the same time I have my life which I enjoy and which is a damned good life." Was the hunting of kudu an important part of life, Kandisky wanted to know: "You really like to do this, what you do now, this silliness of kudu?" Hemingway replied that he would as soon hunt kudu as explore the Prado. Both were necessary to a writer.[4] He did not feel apologetic for doing as he liked to do with his life, particularly if he kept his eyes and ears open.

The four-month trip had begun with embarkation from Marseilles in November, 1933, and would end April 3, 1934, when the Hemingways returned to New York on the *Paris*. By the middle of December, 1933, the motorized outfit had moved west from Mombasa, and from the first hunting headquarters at M'utu-Umbo, to an encampment on a low hillside at the edge of the Serengeti Plain. The hunters arrived in time to watch the migration of huge herds of wildebeeste and other grazing creatures, "a plainfull of moving animals" whose numbers were officially estimated at nearly three million. Here also were the very numerous beasts of prey which followed and fed on the grazing-stock. By January the party's bag already included several kinds of gazelles, antelope, waterbuck, and impalla rams, as well as leopard and cheetah. In something over two weeks along the fringes of the plain, they saw eighty-four lions and took their quota of four. Happily also, and to the vast amusement of the gun-bearer M'Cola, they had destroyed some thirty-five hyenas.

Along with the good luck went some that was bad. Whatever happens to a writer, as Hemingway told Fitzgerald later on that spring, ought to be of some use to him. If one is hurt, the thing is not to complain about it but to find some way of putting the hurt

[4] *GHOA*, p. 25.

to work. Hemingway was speaking, as usual, from experience. Early in January he fell ill of an amoebic dysentery, probably contracted on the dirty French ship coming down through the Red Sea and the Indian Ocean. Though he continued to hunt on every day but two, his condition presently became so serious that he was advised to leave the expedition for medical treatment. In an occurrence of which he would later make fictional capital, employing it as the closing incident (much altered, of course) in "The Snows of Kilimanjaro," he was flown out from the Serengeti on January 16 in a small two-seater plane. The 200-mile dogleg route went by way of the Ngorongoro Crater and the Rift Escarpment to the pleasant town of Arusha. From there they flew past the huge elongated bulk of Mount Kilimanjaro (with the dramatically sudden rise of its main peak) and to Nairobi in Kenya.

Following a period of medical care, Hemingway grew strong enough to rejoin the expedition. It had now moved cross-country to the area south of Ngorongoro in the vicinity of the Rift Valley and Lake Manyara. As his strength slowly returned, Hemingway's delight in the country began once more to rise. Sometimes the sweep and roll of the brown land—as well as the shy herds of antelope—reminded him of the western plains of Wyoming; again, in the uplands, he thought of abandoned New England apple orchards, with ancient gnarled trees well spaced out among the flourishing grass. At other times they would come on terrain that looked for all the world like a remembered part of Aragon or Galicia. Now they shot buffalo and rhinoceros, and hunted kudu and sable until the arrival of the rains in February sent them back to the Kenya coast for a round of sailfishing. In a decrepit launch called the *Xanadu,* Ancient Mariner Hemingway and his white hunter proved to themselves that all the big game was not on shore.[5]

The Tanganyika safari could have been just another hunting-

---

[5] See Hemingway's articles in *Esquire,* as follows:
"a.d. in Africa," 1 (April 1934), pp. 19, 146.
"Shootism versus Sport," 2 (June 1934), pp. 19, 150.
"Notes on Dangerous Game," 2 (July 1934), pp. 19, 94.
"Sailfish off Mombasa," 3 (March 1935), pp. 21, 156.
Also EH to FSF, 5/28/34.

adventure in the life of the world-traveling Hemingway. But this hunter was also an artist. "You ought to always write it," he remarked to his white hunter one February night in the hills above Lake Manyara, "to try to get it stated. No matter what you do with it." [6] Back in Key West during the summer and fall he decided what to do with it. He would write a true account, changing some of the names but not the situations, of that last month in Africa before the seasonal rains had worked north from Rhodesia and the shooting was over.

After this had been set down, to be serialized first in *Scribner's Magazine* and afterwards published (on October 25, 1935) as *The Green Hills of Africa,* there would be time to invent people and situations against the background of the Serengeti Plain and the country just south of Mount Kilimanjaro. This he did in the form of two remarkable short stories, both finished in the spring of 1936: "The Snows of Kilimanjaro," published in *Esquire* for August, 1936, and "The Short Happy Life of Francis Macomber," published in *Cosmopolitan* that September.

II. THE ESTHETICS OF PURSUIT

The *Green Hills of Africa* was frankly an experiment. "The writer," says the foreword, "has attempted to write an absolutely true book to see whether the shape of a country and the pattern of a month's action can, if truly presented, compete with a work of the imagination." Telling the truth was nothing new with Hemingway, though he had normally woven truth together with care-

---

[6] *GHOA,* p. 193. The composition of *GHOA* began mid-April 1934, soon after Hemingway's return to Key West. By June 20, he had reached p. 141 of the MS (*ca.* 20,000 words). By October 3, the word-length was 50,000, and on November 16 Hemingway wrote Perkins that he had finished the first draft (73,000 words) that morning. He had already been over the first half of it three times, rewriting and cutting. The completed MS was finally sent to Scribner's on February 7, 1935. It was serialized, with excellent decorations by Edward Shenton, in *Scribner's Magazine,* May to October 1935. It is of interest that the book began as a short story, growing to book-length as Hemingway's sense of the value of his subject grew; and that Hemingway compared it in his mind to "Big Two-Hearted River." The working title through 1934 was *The Highlands of Africa.* Hemingway decided on the present title sometime in January 1935.

fully controlled invention. What was new here, what constituted the experiment proper, was the determination to stay absolutely with the facts as they happened in Africa—Hemingway would spare no one, including most of all himself, in the attempt to provide a straight record.

The two major aspects of the experiment are the attempt at verisimilitude ("the shape of a country") and architectonics ("the pattern of a month's action"). The first of these had the importance it had always had in Hemingway's work. Here it meant specifically the attempt to transfer to the unsafaried reader a sense of the way it was to move cross-country through the hills and plains of Tanganyika. He wished to project accurately and sharply his own apprehensions of the lie of the land, the habits of the animals, the living personalities of the natives he met, the state of the.weather, the quality of the food, the methods of the camp, the procedures of the hunt, and—running through it all like elastic threads in a pattern—the emotional tensions and re-laxations which gave the events of each day their tone and mean-ing.

From this point of view, the *Green Hills of Africa* is clearly successful. "Nothing that I have ever read," said Hemingway, "has given any idea of the country or the still remaining quantity of game." The reader of Hemingway's book can have no such complaint. There is the lion, a few feet off, "looking yellow and heavy-headed and enormous against a scrubby-looking tree in a patch of orchard bush." Frightened by the explosion of the Mann-licher, he moves off "to the left on a run, a strange, heavy-shouldered, foot-swinging cat run." Or there is the hyena, "com-ing suddenly wedge-headed and stinking out of the high grass by a *donga*," or dry watercourse, to lope away across "the brown plain, looking back, mongrel-dog-smart in the face." One sees the cloud of flamingoes rising into the sun across Lake Manyara, "making the whole horizon of the lake pink." Again, an entire "sky full of locusts" passes westward, with daylight flickering through their massed moving wings "like an old cinema film." [7]

The way it was to see the animals; to sit in a twig-and-branch blind by a salt-lick at dawn; to watch the quarry, long-waited-for

[7] Lions and others: *GHOA*, pp. 40, 37–38, 133, 184.

but now scared away by some small noise or slight odor, trotting nervously out of range; to follow the "starry splatter" of blood-spoor across the rocky hills in the hot afternoon—such experiences as these are available to any reader who would like to have them. There is also much more—the look of various sections of that country, the feel of the air in sundry weathers, the manners and character of the natives, and the conduct of daily life on safari. These the author manages to transmit without recourse either to the Rider Haggard romanticizing of many travel-books or the "it-is-important-to-note" pose of the amateur ethnologist.

It is probable that this communication of the sense of place, and the sense of the immediacy and palpability of the experience in that place, is what gives the *Green Hills of Africa* its special distinction. "I loved this country," says Hemingway on one occasion, "and I felt at home, and where a man feels at home, outside of where he's born, is where he's meant to go." He had got the home-feeling also among the happy hunting-grounds of Montana and Wyoming in 1928 and 1930. One of the canyons opening into the Rift Valley reminded him strongly of the south slopes of Timber Creek in the Clark's Fork country of northwest Wyoming near the wild eastern boundary of the Yellowstone. Some of the timbered mountains he now saw might well be the American peaks, Pilot and Index, transplanted to African settings without loss of face. One who had trailed deer, moose, elk, and bighorn sheep among the American Rockies could scarcely avoid feeling at home in the mountain-terrain of Tanganyika.[8]

The necessity of achieving verisimilitude is common to both fiction and non-fiction. So is the challenge of working out a reasonably tight architectural structure. In these two respects, at any rate, the *Green Hills of Africa* rises above the status of a "noble experiment" and becomes in its own right a work of art. Yet if one compares the book with such novels as *A Farewell to Arms* and *For Whom the Bell Tolls*, the lower stature of *The Green Hills* is evident enough. For even in the hands of a skilled writer, the unvarnished truth can rarely equal in emotional intensity a

[8] *GHOA*, pp., 283–284 and 92. See also Hemingway's essay, "The Clark's Fork Valley, Wyoming," in *Vogue* 93 (February 1939), pp. 68, 157.

fictional projection of that truth. To accept in any "absolute" sense the obligation of portraying non-fictional events precisely as they happened is to fetter the imagination, to limit, perhaps fatally, the novelist's comparative freedom of movement in and through his materials. Because of these fetters and limits, however cheerfully Hemingway assumes them for experimental purposes, the non-fiction book about Africa cannot fairly stand comparison with the novel of Italy and the novel of Spain.

The other side of Hemingway's undertaking is an architectonic experiment of great interest. What he had to work with, as the foreword indicates, was a "month's action." The period to be covered was that which lay between the author's return from medical treatment at Nairobi and the party's final retreat to the coast in the face of seasonal rains—roughly January 21 to February 20, 1934. To complicate the structural problem further, Hemingway wished to deal with certain incidents from the Serengeti period of December and early January—notably the shooting of the first lion, and M'Cola's amusement over the self-eating hyena. Such incidents as these were to be inserted as flashbacks, for the purpose of the dramatic contrast, in the main course of the action.

Given that month of unprocessed raw material, the basic technical problem was to discern the action-pattern, and to select out those events which would best dramatize it. Another immediate necessity was to rearrange, not the actual order of events, but the order in which the events were to be presented to the reader. The author was not content with a simple play-by-play description of the events as they happened, in the manner of a sports reporter broadcasting a football game. Such a procedure, obviously the easiest, would not satisfy his formal architectonic requirements.

Still another aspect of the experiment was Hemingway's attempt to use the mountain-plain contrast which had informed *The Sun Also Rises* and *A Farewell to Arms*. The book makes it quite clear that he preferred the timbered hills to the plains of Tanganyika. On the Serengeti they had ridden too much in cars. Though it teemed with game, the country there stretched out flat, hot, brown, dusty, and unbroken. At that time also, Hemingway was seriously ill with one of man's most miserable and dispiriting diseases. Part of the experiment, therefore, was to project several degrees of that misery to the reader.

Among the green hills of the final month, the party could move on foot and at will over rugged, broken terrain. The recuperating patient now "had that pleasant feeling of getting stronger each day." Once, on the way east from Kandoa-Irangi and Kibaya across the flatlands and desert-country, he asked his white hunter what the continent was like further south. It was nothing, said Pop, but "a million miles of bloody Africa." [9] The phrase summed up Hemingway's own emotional attitude towards the lowlands of Tanganyika and a great part of his hunting-experience there. Up in the forested mountains again, he felt much better. This was the kind of hunting, and the rugged kind of country, to which he had always felt emotionally drawn.

The task which Hemingway undertook in writing the *Green Hills of Africa* was therefore a difficult one. He had not only assumed the obligation of verisimilitude, both as to the country and to the residents of that country whether human or animal. He had also faced up to a fairly complicated structural problem, and rendered even this more difficult by his attempt to deal with contrasting emotional atmospheres.

As this was a hunting expedition its fundamental form was obviously pursuit. The book is accordingly divided into four parts: "Pursuit and Conversation" (two chapters); "Pursuit Remembered" (chapters iii–ix inclusive); "Pursuit and Failure" (two chapters); and, with a serious pun on the Declaration of Independence, "Pursuit as Happiness" (the closing chapters xii–xiii). The form of the book is so devised as always to point to the climactic account of the kudu-hunt in the twelfth chapter. To achieve this pointing, the opening chapters deal with the early phases of the kudu sequence. They have been after kudu ten days and the oncoming rains will allow them only three days more. The seven intervening chapters—"Pursuit Remembered"—double back in time to the relatively unsatisfactory rhinoceros and buffalo hunting before the party went after the kudu. From this

[9] *GHOA*, p. 159.

beginning the reader is gradually returned to the then present until, in the tenth chapter, the splicework is completed and one finds himself back in the time of the book's opening.

The formal advantages of such a procedure are clear. Much less obvious is the author's careful preparation of the reader for an appreciation of the natural beauties of the ultimate kudu bull. He leads up very deftly to the high-tension emotional excitements which surround that event. The whole "Pursuit Remembered" section is geared into the marked contrast which is to come. As part of the total plan of attack, Hemingway places various disappointments, dissatisfactions, and emotional confusions under the surface of the prose in the "buildup" sections of his book.

The bagging of the first lion, for example, took place back on the edge of the Serengeti Plain. Hemingway carefully reduces it to an emotionally unsatisfactory event. The party had been "prepared for a charge, for heroics, and for drama." But the lion succumbed with disappointing ease. Even while the natives shouted their victory song, with its imitation of the deep, asthmatic cough of the lion as an iterative chorus, Hemingway was feeling "more let down than pleased." This was not what they had paid to see. Of course it *was* what they had paid for, like everything else recorded in the book. But Hemingway is writing that way as a part of his plan of attack. Similarly, he tells us that he admired and respected the heavy power of the buffalo, yet felt that this truck-like, scaly-hided creature was slow and ponderous. "All the while we shot I felt it was fixed and that we had him." The buffalo had neither the speed, the grace, nor the elusiveness of the kudu.[10]

The kudu is clean and beautiful. Through the early parts of the book Hemingway subtly introduces, at strategic intervals, various images of physical disgust and loathing to point up his later contrast. The hyenas skulking along the plain are seen as foul, hermaphroditical, belly-dragging beasts. The rhinoceros, described in a detailed set-piece still pointing towards the kudu-bull, is "the hell of an animal"—hulking, malformed, anachro-

---

[10] One suspects that Mr. Wilson's misunderstanding of Hemingway's plan underlies his belief that *GHOA* is "one of the only books ever written which make *Africa and its animals* seem dull." (Italics mine.)

nistic, and tick-ridden. One allusion to the ever-possible snakes in the underbrush has the force of a minor horror. Even more loathsome is the incident of the baboons. While the party was in search of buffalo, they came to a part of the forest which had just been traversed by a tribe of baboons. Hemingway uses an obviously effective concentration of disgust-words when he says that the whole area was filled with "a nasty stink like the mess cats make."

From the ninth chapter onwards, through the frustrations of "Pursuit and Failure," the reader is led upwards to the quarry of the twelfth, the crown of the expedition and the artfully-prepared-for crown of the book. For "Pursuit as Happiness" is handsomely embodied in the very opposite of all preceding disgusts and disappointments: "the huge beautiful kudu bull," sweetsmelling, wholesome, perfectly formed and marked, with the walnut-meat-colored horns sweeping back from the proud head. The thirteenth chapter, closing the book, is by intent a structural anti-climax— the uncrowned (or cow-crowned) pursuit of the wounded bull-sable—bringing the reader back to solid ground after the glories he has known. The form of the book has in fact been conditioned throughout by Hemingway's "emotionated" recollection of the best and worst parts of the safari. But it is planned, and worked out as an entity, with very thoughtful attention to the esthetic principles of big-game hunting in Africa.

Other formal, and semi-formal, aspects of the book show the same kind of careful planning, designed to enable "the truth" to compete with fiction. What the trade knows as *love-interest* enters in a subdued form, and the foreword (Mark-Twain-like) directs any dissatisfied reader "to insert whatever love interest he or she may have at the time." *Suspense* is always present in the formula of pursuit as well as in the sense of urgency at the approach of the seasonal rains. Hemingway, indeed, once comments on "that most exciting perversion of life: the necessity of accomplishing something in less time than should truly be allowed for its doing." *Conflict* is established in the undeclared war between the author and his colleague Karl, a lucky hunter who consistently manages to bring in better trophies, though as a pursuer of game he is much less experienced than his grumpily loyal opposition. And for an *idyllic interlude* we have the wing-shooting on the flats of Lake Manyara, with teal, black duck, and snipe enough to satisfy the greediest consumer.

As always with Hemingway, however, form is inseparable from substance, and it is to the packed substance of the book that one can always return with profit. There are the night birds rising "in soft panic" from the sandy edges of the tracklike road as the car-lights shine into their eyes; the red-clay-colored rhino, seen clear and small through binoculars, "moving with a quick, water-bug-like motion" across the far flank of a hill; the cough of a leopard hunting baboons in the night-time forest; the "shiny dark splatter" of dried buffalo-blood on a stone, and later the sad dying bellow of the same buffalo, "like hearing a horn in the woods." [11]

There is no neglect of humankind: the ebullient Kandisky; the brave and laconic white hunter Pop; the tensely generous Karl, least obtrusive of shooting companions. Among the most substantial parts of the book are the portraits of the natives. Hemingway's fine old gun-bearer, M'Cola, plays a very winning Nigger Jim to the author's over-explosive Huckleberry Finn. An association between them which began in shared suspicion develops into one of mutual respect and genuine friendship. In the manner of true comrades, for example, they share many private jokes. One only partly shared is M'Cola's amusement over religious belief. Charo, the other gun-bearer, is a highly devout Mohammedan. "All Ramadan he never swallowed his saliva until sunset." When the sun is nearly down one evening, Hemingway sees him watching it nervously.

"Charo was deadly thirsty and truly devout and the sun set very slowly. I looked at it red over the trees, nudged him and he grinned. M'Cola offered me the water bottle solemnly. I shook my head and Charo grinned again. M'Cola looked blank. Then the sun was down and Charo had the bottle tilted up, his Adam's apple rising and falling greedily and M'Cola looking at him and then looking away."

This is close to high comedy, done without words in complete pantomime.[12]

[11] Night birds and others: *GHOA*, pp. 5, 50, 58, 114, 119.
[12] *GHOA*, pp. 38–39.

The relationship with M'Cola produces several other degrees of the comic. Often the joke is on Hemingway. From M'Cola's position, bird-shooting, whiskey-drinking, beer-bibbing, and failure to hit a large target through excitement or bull-headedness, were all good jokes. Hyenas were a farcical, low-comedy dirty joke. Between Hemingway and his wiry old companion the humor of character is tossed back and forth like a medicine ball. For the out-and-out comic, nothing could be better than the self-complacent theatrical posing of one of the native guides, an efficiently unendurable "sportsman" for whom Hemingway conceived an instant dislike. Though he is nicknamed David Garrick, out of compliment to his studied stage-presence, he is obviously the Malvolio of the piece. He is just as obviously in need of the deflation he finally gets—to M'Cola's deep amusement—at the hands of the author.

Besides these full-length portraits, there are other quick line-drawings of a variety of people. One is the matchless tracker Droopy, wearing a red fez and little else but courage and enthusiasm. Another, Droopy's antithesis, is the evil-smelling Wanderobo, solemn as a stork, "useless as a bluejay." Still another is Kamau, the Kikuyu driver, who "with an old brown tweed coat some shooter had discarded, trousers heavily patched on the knees and then ripped open again, and a very ragged shirt, managed always to give an impression of great elegance." [13] But it was an elegance backed up with a modesty, a skill, and a pleasantness of demeanor which Hemingway very much admired. One of the happiest sections of the book is the group-portrait of the merry Masai, joyously racing the car, delighting in the noise of the klaxon, and eating with relish the cold tinned mincemeat and plum pudding which the visitors hand out as largesse to good humor.

There is much more. There is the sense of home as the firelight gleams through the trees to guide the returning, dogtired hunters; the oncoming file of porters bringing back "quarters of tommy, Grant, and wildebeeste, dusty, the meat seared dry by the sun"; the smiling, bulldozing insistence of the native boys that one's canvas *bathi* of warm muddy water is ready to be entered. There

[13] *GHOA*, p. 177.

are the meals, happily detailed, like the midday dinner in the shade of a big tree under the green fly of the dining-tent: "Grant's gazelle chops, mashed potatoes, green corn, and then mixed fruit for dessert"; or the picnic lunch of cold sliced tenderloin, bread, mustard, and canned plums, eaten, with one's back against a tall tree, at the edge of shadowy woodland; or the banquet of roast teal, shot at Lake Manyara, and eaten with red wine and Pan-Yan pickles in the cold house high in the hills.[14]

There is much meat in the *Green Hills of Africa,* both the kind that walks on four hooves to be shot as food or trophy, and the less tangible kind which one is glad to have because of what it reveals about the complexities of the narrator's character, his prejudices, judgments, and reminiscences, and his ideas on life and art. René Maran, as well as some of his successors to the Goncourt Academy prize, might be glad to have written thus richly of the pursuit of the kudu in the Tanganyika bush.

III. WHAT DO YOU THINK OF RINGELNATZ?

"I knew a good country when I saw one," said Hemingway of his latest love, Africa. "Here there was game, plenty of birds, and I liked the natives. Here I could shoot and fish. That, and writing, and reading, and seeing pictures, was all I cared about doing. And I could remember all the pictures. Other things I liked to watch but they were what I liked to do."

The implications of such a statement were distressing to Herr Kandisky, the little bandy-legged, culture-hungry man in leather shorts and Tyroler hat. He could not find his way comfortably into a mind where kudu and Prado ruled as approximate co-equals. Africa's big game meant less than nothing to him; it was too familiar. But the big game of literary Europe and America—there was another matter. How could it be that this literary man, this *Dichter,* this former contributor to *Der Querschnitt,* should attach any significance to the pursuit of the kudu when it was so clearly within his power to pursue the things of the mind? Kandisky pushed down hard on the other scale in Hemingway's

---

[14] Wildebeeste and others: *GHOA,* pp. 74, 60, 29, 111, 134.

balance. The honor of the Prado, the world of art as opposed to the world of nature and the kudu, must somehow be upheld. What about Hemingway's reading?

Under Kandisky's persistent questioning the Prado aspect emerged. Hemingway gladly set forth his definition of good literature, and with a show of geniality allowed himself to be trapped into certain judgments of individual writers.

"Tell me," asked Kandisky, "what do you think of Ringelnatz?"

"He is splendid."

"So. You like Ringelnatz. Good. What do you think of Heinrich Mann?"

"He is no good."

"You believe it?"

"All I know is that I cannot read him?"

"He is no good at all. I see we have things in common." [15]

What Hemingway had in common with his interlocutor was a love of those books which can be read, above all, with a sense of personal participation. About a year after the interview with Kandisky, he prepared a list of the sixteen titles in fiction which he "would rather read again for the first time" than be assured of a million-dollar annual income. The million-dollar list was, one observed, predominantly continental. Only two English and two American works were included: *Wuthering Heights* and *Far Away and Long Ago, Huckleberry Finn* and *Winesburg, Ohio.* George Moore's *Hail and Farewell* and Joyce's *Dubliners* (along with Yeats's *Autobiographies*) represented the Irish. Mann's *Buddenbrooks* was the sole German entry. All of the others were French and Russian. Stendhal's *The Red and the Black* and *The Charterhouse of Parma*, Tolstoi's *Anna Karenina* and *War and Peace* were major items. But one also found Dumas' *Queen Margot*, Flaubert's *Madame Bovary*, Dostoievski's *Brothers Karamazov, The Sportsman's Sketches* of Turgenev, and Maupassant's bucolic comedy on *The House of Madame Tellier*.[16]

Later in 1935, for the benefit of an apprentice writer who asked for a reading-list, Hemingway repeated most of these titles and

---

[15] *GHOA*, pp. 7 and 285. The excellent humorous poet Hans Bötticher (pseud.-Joachim Ringelnatz) died the year this conversation took place.

[16] *Esquire* 3 (February 1935), p. 21.

added five more authors: two novels by his old master Henry
Fielding, three by Captain Marryat, and the short stories of Kip-
ling, Stephen Crane, and Henry James. This time also he added
Joyce's *Portrait of the Artist* and *Ulysses*, Flaubert's *Sentimental
Education*, "any other two" novels by Dostoievski, and "all of
Turgenev." The total roster came to perhaps twenty-five titles.
But the list, said Hemingway, could easily be quadrupled.[17]

Neither to Kandisky nor to the young apprentice did Hemingway explain the reasons for his preferences. Nor did he ever isolate any "hundred best novels." But as a writer who had always
read the works of others both hungrily and seriously, his primary
aim had been to establish standards and norms for his own performance. Writing is competitive, he had said. The writer must
therefore discover, by selective reading, what he has to beat or to
equal.

Aside from its help in the establishment of standards, writing
succeeds or fails for Hemingway according to whether or not
it conveys to the reader a sense of "the way it was" at the time
and place the novelist has chosen to write about. Reading Tolstoi's *Sebastopol Sketches* one February noon as he lay in the
shadow of trees on a Tanganyika hillside, he found himself imaginatively sharing in the military life of Czarist Russia. This sense
of participation was the standard he had used in judging René
Maran's *Batouala* in 1922 and Conrad's *The Rover* in 1923.
Something similar happened when he moved among the rural
scenes of Turgenev, or shared the second breakfasts of the burgh-
ers in Mann's family Buddenbrooks. One walked delightedly at
Sorel's side through the domestic and ecclesiastical complications
of *The Red and the Black*. Because all great writers appear to
share in the ability to involve the reader's imagination, "we have
been there," said Hemingway, "in the books." He was thinking
of his African safari, but also of his boyhood in Michigan, his
education in Paris, his experiences in Madrid and Key West and
Wyoming, when he added, speaking for himself and all writers,
"Where we go, if we are any good, there you can go as we have
been." [18] For the practical esthetician, no other standard of judg-

[17] *Esquire* 4 (October 1935), pp. 21, 174A, 174B.
[18] *GHOA*, p. 108.

ment is qualitatively preferable to this principle of the "participation index."

There are other practical standards, and it is not difficult to see them operating between the lines of Hemingway's pseudo-diffident lecture to Kandisky on the nature of literature. One is a standard of vital verisimilitude. The writing must be true to our sense of the way things happen, but also vital in the sense that nothing that is in life, whether language as it is spoken or thought as it is thought or action as it is acted, can be wholly excluded without some loss to the vital principle. In one of the letters to Maxwell Perkins, written about the time when the serialization of *A Farewell to Arms* had stirred up the censors in Boston, Hemingway says that he feels, however modest the effects may be, that he is fighting "for the return to the full use of the language." [19] This determination helps to account for his general disagreement with and opposition to the genteel tradition in American letters.

Towards writers who flourished before 1880 Hemingway was evidently little drawn. His attitude, for example, to the giants of the New England renaissance resembles the view a frequenter of orchards in apple time might later take to the fruit after it had been cut into strips, strung on strings, and hung in the rafters to dry out. For the benefit of Kandisky, Emerson is grouped with Hawthorne and Whittier, and they are characterized as "very good men with the small, dried, and excellent wisdom of Unitarians; men of letters; Quakers with a sense of humor. . . . They were all very respectable. They did not use the words that people have always used in speech, the words that survive in language. Nor would you gather that they had bodies. They had minds, yes. Nice, dry, clean minds." [20]

This is admittedly a safari's eye view of the flowering of New England, suggesting that the flower lies pressed in a book instead of nectareously blooming on the vine. And it is no more than Whitman, to take a single instance, felt about transcendentalism and certain of its habits of abstract thought. In fact Hemingway's position was at least adumbrated in some of Father Taylor's wry

[19] EH to MP, 6/7/29.
[20] *GHOA*, p. 21.

pronouncements on the course of Unitarianism in New England. Hemingway's humorous statement is obviously open to all kinds of objections. But on the score of the limitations which the genteel tradition placed upon the use of language, it is clearly justified. Even Emerson admitted to similar opinions, though he had a temperamental bias against acting on them.

Two other practical standards emerge in what Hemingway told Kandisky about Thoreau and Melville. The first is his opposition to the intrusion of the "literary" quality in "naturalistic" writing; the other is his dislike of "rhetoric." One might expect that Hemingway would be more sympathetic than he is towards Thoreau, the man of the woods, and Melville, the man of the sea. The late F. O. Matthiessen once pointed out, for example, that many of "Thoreau's convictions about the nature of art look forward to Hemingway's." Among the resemblances is Thoreau's well-developed admiration for the writer who is "satisfied with giving an exact description of things" *as they appear to him* and as they exert "their effect upon him." Thoreau liked Homer's wonderful skill in conveying the physical sensation of action: "If his messengers repair but to the tent of Achilles, we do not wonder how they got there but accompany them step by step along the shore of the resounding sea." [21]

Under the surface of both Thoreau and Hemingway one finds an operative consciousness of what Thoreau himself called "dusky knowledge," a sense of the connotations of things existing in and below their denoted shapes and colors. But Hemingway draws back from the intrusion of the "literary quality" in Thoreau. It tends to stand between his powers of apprehension and the capacity to transcribe directly "from the life." Matthiessen observes, tongue in cheek, that "Thoreau's product was ordinarily somewhat less full-bodied" than one finds in D. H. Lawrence or Hemingway.[22] And Hemingway's comment sums up the matter: "I cannot read other naturalists unless they are being extremely accurate and not literary." [23]

It is once again the intrusion of a "literary" drapery between

[21] *American Renaissance*, New York, 1941, p. 85 and note.
[22] *ibid.*, p. 165.
[23] *GHOA*, p. 21.

the artist and the actual which limits Hemingway's admiration for Melville. Considering how much he might have liked Melville if they had met, or comparing their respective obsessions, or seeing their shared respect for the man who can do things "properly," one regrets the brevity of Hemingway's characterization of Melville:

"We have had writers of rhetoric who had the good fortune to find a little, in a chronicle of another man and from voyaging, of how things, actual things can be, whales for instance, and this knowledge is wrapped in the rhetoric like plums in a pudding. Occasionally it is there, alone, unwrapped in pudding, and it is good. This is Melville." [24]

This is not Melville, of course. But it is a single point made against Melville by another writer who had sought from the first to rid his own writing of all forms of padding, all ornamental literary language, and who told Maxwell Perkins in 1926 that one of his great aims was "trying to write books without any extra words" in them.[25] Hemingway's own Ahabs and Starbucks and Billy Budds speak a stylized dialogue. Yet they talk more like people than like the devils of Milton or the supermen of Kit Marlowe. It is in great part his refusal to puddingize his plums that gives Hemingway's work its special quality of direct, undraped transcription from the life around him.

If we look, on the other hand, to American writers for whom Hemingway expressed admiration, three may be singled out: James, Stephen Crane, and Twain. This is not a preferential order. These are "the good writers" but that is "not the order they're good in. There is no order for good writers." He liked the short stories of James, giving special mention to *Madame de Mauves* and *The Turn of the Screw*, and (among the longer works) *The American* and *The Portrait of A Lady*. From Crane he selected out *The Red Badge of Courage* as "one of the finest books of our literature," a "boy's dream of war" that is "truer to how war is than any war the boy who wrote it would ever live to see." Of the shorter pieces, Hemingway liked both *The Open Boat* and *The Blue Hotel*, with the second the better of the two. As for

[24] *GHOA*, p. 20.
[25] EH to MP, 8/26/26.

Twain, whom Kandisky recalled only as a "humorist," Hemingway was unequivocal:

"All modern American literature comes from one book by Mark Twain called *Huckleberry Finn.* If you read it you must stop where the Nigger Jim is stolen from the boys. That is the real end. The rest is just cheating. But it's the best book we've had. All American writing comes from that. There was nothing before. There has been nothing as good since." [26]

The dogmatic tone invites rejoinder. Yet in terms of the practical esthetician, scanning the field for evidence of an indubitably "modern" note in American writing, the choice of *Huckleberry Finn* is hardly astonishing. Rereading the book with Hemingway's own work in mind one is constantly arrested by events and passages where the tone and strategy are (by anticipation) Hemingwayesque.

"It was a monstrous big river down there—sometimes a mile and a half wide; we run nights and laid up and hid daytimes; soon as night was most gone we stopped navigating and tied up— nearly always in the dead water under a towhead; and then cut young cottonwoods and willows, and hid the raft with them. Then we set out the lines. Next we slid into the river and had a swim . . . then we set down on the sandy bottom where the river was about knee-deep, and watched the daylight come. . . . The first thing to see, looking away over the water, was a kind of dull line—that was the woods on t'other side; you couldn't make nothing else out; then a pale place in the sky; then more paleness spreading around; then the river softened up away off and warn't black any more, but gray. . . ."

"You do not know how long you are in a river when the current moves swiftly. It seems a long time and it may be very short. The water was cold and in flood and many things passed that had been floated off the banks when the river rose. I was lucky to have a heavy timber to hold on to, and I lay in the icy water with my chin on the wood, holding as easily as I could with both hands. I was afraid of cramps and I hoped we would move toward the shore. We went down the river in a long curve. It

[26] *GHOA,* p. 22. See also *Esquire* 4 (October 1935), p. 21 and *Men at War,* introd., p. xvii.

was beginning to be light enough so I could see the bushes along the shoreline. There was a brush island ahead and the current moved toward the shore." [27]

Huck's native idiom betrays the first passage as Twain's; the grammatical usage shows that the second is from Hemingway. Otherwise Frederick Henry's river might be the Mississippi in early spring, and Huck's (by deleting the cottonwoods) the Tagliamento in June. The shared quality—and one comes on it dozens of times in the course of Huck's journey downstream— is one of direct and "simple" transcription of things as they are, without literary interpositions, and with many similarities in the general drift of the syntax.

No influence is alleged. What Hemingway found effective in Twain was whatever corroborated his own point of view about the writer's obligation to truth. A whole chapter of comparable passages could be assembled: Huck's description of the interior of the Grangerford household, for example, with Hemingway's picture of the interior of Harry Morgan's living-room in *To Have and Have Not;* or Hemingway's characterization of the native guide Garrick (the theatrical one) with Huck's descriptions of the King and the Duke. But the chapter would merely underscore the point already made, which is that Twain's notable ability to project in ostensibly "simple" language the essence of active experience is the quality that endears *Huckleberry Finn* to Hemingway. "Simplicity," wrote Lytton Strachey, "is often the surest test of an artist's power. A bad artist must fail when he is simple; but whoever is simple and succeeds must be great." [28]

Their common interest in war, the sea, the American west, and the men-without-women situation would sufficiently explain Hemingway's neighborly feeling for Crane. But there is also in Crane what Mr. John Berryman describes as "the immense power of the tacit"—a quality which "gives his work kinship . . . with Chekhov and Maupassant." [29] A similar operative grasp on this power, and a similar kinship may be noted in the best of Hemingway's short stories. The vivid impressionism of Crane, in some

[27] *Huckleberry Finn,* opening of Ch. XIX; *FTA,* opening of Ch. XXXI.
[28] *Spectator* 101 (October 3, 1908), pp. 502–503.
[29] *Stephen Crane,* New York, 1950, pp. 291–292.

ways his most spectacular poetic skill, is present, though relatively
rare, in Hemingway. Take, for example, the portrait of André
Marty in *For Whom the Bell Tolls:*

"The tall, heavy old man looked at Gomez with his outthrust
head and considered him carefully with his watery eyes. Even
here at the front in the light of a bare electric bulb, he having just
come in from driving in an open car on a brisk night, his gray face
had a look of decay. His face looked as though it were modelled
from the waste material you find under the claws of a very old
lion." [30]

The last touch seems Cranesque without being precisely dupli-
cable anywhere in Crane. The image is used focally because the
completed portrait of Marty will fill out the thematic suggestion
of senile decadence. Hemingway's usual practice is far closer to
that of such post-impressionists as Cézanne, just as on the whole
his imagery (like his irony) is cooler, less explosive, less tricky
than Crane's. He is a neighbor rather than an occupant of Crane's
house.

At first glance the connection is not apparent between the
world of Henry James, society-centered, ghoul-haunted, politely
agonistic, externally inactive, and that of Hemingway, sharp in
definition, quick in movement, and (at least comparatively) brash
in manner. The difference in idiom is also striking, though no
greater than one would expect to find between a late Victorian
and a leader in the twentieth-century revolt against the bourgeois
norms of *politesse*. But it is a matter of at least preliminary interest
that Hemingway has written on three of the topics which most
engaged James's imagination: the American in Europe, the artist
in society, and the buried life which rises up to obsess its unwilling
recollector. The reader of James also gets a fairly constant illusion
of being directly in touch with human life at an essentially non-
literary level, and without the intrusion of a "literary" personality
between reader and experience.

As Hemingway moved through the experimental period of the
nineteen thirties, he independently faced, on a number of occasions, certain technical problems which had earlier engaged the
attention of James. One noticed his deepening interest, for ex-

[30] *FWBT*, p. 417.

ample, in the establishment of various centers of revelation. Like James, however, he tended to concentrate on the individual mind as the instrument of revelation, and to project his stories as from one engaged on a journey of discovery, finding out more and more about the central situation and its implications while he progressed through it.

There is also the matter of dialogue. No one engaged in a systematic examination of resemblances between James and Hemingway could afford to ignore similarities in the conduct of the conversations. One need not be put off by the far greater elaborateness of James's framing phrases. Hemingway tends to eliminate stage directions as far as possible, though as his career developed he became more willing than formerly to make some concessions in this matter. What we remember chiefly is "Rinaldi said" or "she said," the bareness being with Hemingway a matter of principle, looking to the elimination of all that is not necessary. In James the phrases range from "I gaily confessed" through "she rather inscrutably added" and on to "I attempted the grimace of suggesting." Like his use of italicized words, these phrases are meant to mark the tone and emphasis, the special ring, of a particular speech. James is in effect gesturing silently from the prompt-box. Hemingway, on the other hand, expects the reader to supply or discover the interpretation, always seeking to reduce his directives to the least obtrusive of available mechanisms.

Yet if one tries the experiment of lifting a Jamesian conversation *verbatim* from its framework, substituting "he saids" and "she saids" for James's more complicated directives, the dialogue proceeds in a manner scarcely distinguishable from Hemingway's.

"I'm afraid you don't approve of them," he said.

"They are very common," she said. "They are the sort of American that one does one's duty by not—not accepting."

"Ah, you don't accept them?"

"I can't . . . I would if I could but I can't."

"The young girl is very pretty."

"Of course she's pretty but she is very common." [31]

This is a conversation about Daisy Miller and her family—the early James. Miles Winterbourne and his aunt Mrs. Costello are

[31] *Daisy Miller*, Part I.

the speakers. It is laconic, often stichomythic. It uses a technique familiar to readers of Hemingway in the repetition of key words and phrases. Here, for example, the key word is *common*. M s. Costello uses it in her opening remark about the Miller family, and in her final characterization of Daisy. This gives the quoted segment a stanzaic roundness of its own, so that one might say the colloquy transpires between *common* and *common*. Winterbourne uses the word *approve* in his first statement. In her reply, the aunt nearly echoes it. Then, catching herself, she takes refuge in the weaker word *accepting*. *Accept* is a word used of fine society, with many overtones. *Approve* implies individual character judgment. Mrs. Costello is staying carefully on the social plane, knowing quite well that what Winterbourne really has in mind is the true character of Daisy herself—not a social but an individual matter. The little conversation thus embodies the major theme of the book—the conflict between individual rights or freedoms and the arbitrary norms of society. It is also a tightly knit conversation, each sentence linked to its successor by an echoed word. Thus Winterbourne echoes his aunt's *accept*. She repeats *I can't*. He takes the new tack of Daisy's *prettiness*. She echoes the word *pretty* and returns to the opening word *common*.

In a comparable passage from *A Farewell to Arms*, the key word is *love*. Frederick and the priest are talking of the Abruzzi.

"You love the Abruzzi!"

"Yes, I love it very much."

"You ought to go there then."

"I would be too happy. If I could live there and love God and serve Him."

"And be respected," I said.

"Yes and be respected. Why not?"

"No reason not. You should be respected."

"It does not matter. But there in my country it is understood that a man may love God. It is not a dirty joke."

"I understand."

He looked at me and smiled. "You understand but you do not love God."

"No."

"You do not love Him at all?" he asked.

"I am afraid of Him in the night sometimes."

"You should love Him."

"I don't love much." [32]

Like the passage from *Daisy Miller,* this segment of dialogue embodies the theme of the novel in so far as the priest and his homeland and his love of God are the spiritual goals towards which Frederick is moving through the deepening of his love for Catherine. A linkage is carefully established between ideas of love, respect, and happiness in such a way that when these key tones are struck again at intervals throughout the book, one half-consciously recognizes them as something entered on the score of memory and now played back in a different context.

What Hemingway thinks of Ringelnatz or of the holdings of the Prado are matters of importance to any who would see his art against the background of European and American art and literature. Future investigators of Hemingway's literary background are likely to find many resemblances, both profound and superficial, between his work and that of the European masters he used to borrow from Sylvia Beach's bookshop in the rue de l'Odéon during his expatriate years. One recalls that he got the title of *The Torrents of Spring* from Turgenev; or that he often thought of his short story, "The Light of the World," in connection with Maupassant's "Maison Tellier"; or that Bridges re-

---

[32] *FTA,* pp. 76–77. Another remarkable similarity in the conduct of dialogue by James and Hemingway is what may be called the hovering subject. James often establishes the subject of a conversation by hint and allusion rather than overt statement. At other times he introduces the subject briefly (often it is a single word at the end of a sentence), and then conducts the dialogue by reference to it, while it hovers, helicopter-like, over the surface of the conversation. In either instance the neuter pronoun *it,* or its unuttered equivalent, is the index to what is being talked about. *It* is the apex of a pyramid whose base is the dialogue, and the real subject is the star at which the apex points. Of many instances, one might cite the interchange between Mrs. Bread and Newman in *The American,* Chapter XIV. Of many instances in Hemingway, see the talk on food between Gino and Frederick in *FTA,* Chapter XXVII. For a discussion of the differences between Hemingway and James, the reader may consult George Hemphill's essay in McCaffery, *op.cit.,* pp. 329–339. A number of further allusions to James in later chapters of this present work will make it plain that I am unable to share Mr. Hemphill's belief: "There is a broad rift in the possibilities of fiction today. . . . Hemingway and James are representative of the factions."

jected the "Alpine Idyll" story, refusing to print it in *Scribner's Magazine* because it was "too terrible"—like something by Chekhov or Gorky.[33] But the future investigators are almost certain to discover, before they have gone very far, that Hemingway's doctrine of "imitation" is of a special kind. What he imitates is nature, the world around him, expansed before his eyes. Dante, like his renaissance audience, is dead. The modern writer writes for his own and future time. It is proper that he should know Dante, indeed that he should have a close reading acquaintance with the best that has been said, thought, and painted from Dante to Shakespeare, from Cervantes to Goya, and from Tintoretto's *Crucifixion* to Picasso's *Guernica*. But what he seeks to imitate is not the texture, it is the stature of the great books he reads and the great pictures he admires. These show what can be done with words and paint, with intellect and emotion; they also show what can be equalled if the modern writer has the time, the gifts, the devotion, and the luck: and if, chiefly, he chooses to derive his own work from the life of his time rather than from the art of former times.

IV. DANGEROUS GAME

In the other two stories which grew out of his African adventure, Hemingway abandoned his experimental attempt to see whether an "absolutely true book" like the *Green Hills of Africa* could compete on terms of equality with a work of the imagination. In "The Short Happy Life of Francis Macomber" and "The Snows of Kilimanjaro" he was still determined to tell "the truth"; but now he was ready to invent the characters, and to imagine the circumstances in which they were to be entangled. The circumstances in these two stories differ markedly. At the same time they share certain inward thematic stresses. Both deal, for example, though in varying ways, with the achievement and loss of moral manhood. Both look further into the now familiar men-without-women theme. The focal point in each is the corrupting power of women and money, two of the forces aggressively men-

[33] MP to EH, 6/14/26.

tioned in the *Green Hills of Africa* as impediments to American writing men.

Francis Macomber does not write. He is a wealthy American sportsman hunting the Tanganyika plains with his wife. But he must nevertheless wrestle with problems relating to women, money, and moral manhood. Easily the most unscrupulous of Hemingway's fictional females, Margot Macomber covets her husband's money but values even more her power over him. To Wilson, the Macombers' paid white hunter, who is drawn very reluctantly into the emotional mess of a wrecked marriage, Margot exemplifies most of the American wives he has met in the course of his professional life. Although his perspectives are limited to the international sporting set, the indictment is severe. These women, he reflects, are "the hardest in the world; the hardest, the cruelest, the most predatory, and the most attractive, and their men have softened or gone to pieces nervously as they have hardened." [34] With Margot in mind, this story might well have carried the title which Hemingway attached to one of his despatches from Tanganyika to *Esquire:* "Notes on Dangerous Game." The lion and the buffalo are vanquishable in a way that Margot is not.

Too much money and a woman also underlie the predicament of Harry, the dying author in "The Snows of Kilimanjaro." Having given up to a luxurious way of life by marrying wealth and then growing into complete dependence on it, he has died artistically long before his physical death. What harrows him more than the knowledge of approaching dissolution is the consciousness of all the literary riches, none of them committed to paper, which will go with him underground. Worst of all are the sharply etched memories of his former life—Liberty, Integrity, Opportunity—qualities which were all once joyously owned and now are all irrecoverably lost.

So both stories are moral tragedies tipped with irony. Macomber dies at the very moment he is commencing to live. Harry's death by gangrene symbolizes all spiritual suicides among American writers. "We destroy them in many ways," said Hemingway

[34] *First 49,* p. 107.

sardonically in the *Green Hills of Africa.* "First, economically, They make money . . . increase their standard of living and . . . are caught. They have to write to keep up their establishment, their wives, and so on, and they write slop . . . not on purpose, but because it is hurried. . . . Then, once they have betrayed themselves, they justify it and you get more slop." [35] Whether through women or the desire for money, self-betrayal is what kills a man before he has lived out his time. Women and money are nothing but instruments and agents: they exist, sometimes passively, sometimes aggressively, to help the individual writer in his moral self-destruction. If he surrenders, the fault is his own. The emphasis on the value of integrity in these short stories suggests that they may be thought of as two more chapters in the history of Hemingway's artistic obsessions.

The happy life of Francis Macomber begins on the plains of East Africa and lasts about thirty minutes. The tall young man has previously disgraced himself before his wife, his British white hunter, and his gun-bearers, by ignominious flight from a wounded and charging lion. Besides the loss of his own self-respect, such as it was, the extreme mental tortures of the experience include the barbed and vicious scorn of his wife, the lifted eyebrows and unspoken insults of the white hunter Wilson, and the visible disapproval of the native boys in his entourage. After a night of torment, during which he is obliged to watch his wife sleepily returning from the Englishman's tent, the party goes after buffalo. Since the wife knows her husband for a coward, she seems to have him where she wants him, which is under her thumb.

Suddenly, in the midst of the second day's shooting and with the white hunter as an aid, Macomber loses his fear. His wife at once senses and hates this change because it undermines her power. But Wilson silently welcomes Macomber into manhood, and together they enter the tall grass after one of the wounded buffalo, leaving the wife behind them in the open car.

Almost immediately the buffalo charges. Fearless and happy in its path stands Macomber, a coward no longer, reveling in his new-found self-trust, firing repeatedly until the buffalo is practically upon him. Then a bullet from his wife's Mannlicher plows

[35] *GHOA,* p. 23.

through his skull from back to front and the short happy life is over.

The great technical virtue of this story—and it is one of Hemingway's favorites possibly for this reason—is the development of an emotional intensity to a degree seldom approached in modern literature. The ragged feelings generated by the lion-incident and verbalized in a kind of noonday nightmare during the conversations in the dining-tent, are just short of unendurable to any who have entered into the spirit of the situation. Yet the tension actually mounts when, during the next day's shooting, we watch the Macombers in their contest for the possession of a soul.

Hemingway silently points up this contest by the varying positions of the central trio in their boxlike open car. On the way to the lion, Macomber sits in front, with Margot and Wilson in the back. After that day's débâcle, Macomber slumps in the back seat beside his frozen wife, Wilson staring straight ahead in the front. When Macomber has proved himself with the three buffalo, it is Margot who retreats into the far corner of the back seat, while the two men happily converse vis-à-vis before her. And finally, as Macomber kneels in the path of the buffalo, it is his wife from her commanding position in the back seat of the car who closes the contest.

Of equal interest is the skill with which Hemingway balances off the two days of hunting against each other. Part of the balance is achieved by the repetition of first effect: the buffalo, like the lion of the preceding day, is wounded, takes cover, and charges without warning. This time, however, the charge moves into a reversed moral situation. Between times, by various devices, the reader has been fully awakened to the degree of physical courage needed in facing wounded and dangerous animals. But where the lion was an instrument for the establishment and build-up of emotional tension, the oncoming horns of the buffalo are the pronged forceps for Macomber's moral birth. Two different worlds fill the two adjacent days.

The yardstick figure, Wilson, a fine characterization, is the man free of woman and of fear. He is the standard of manhood towards which Macomber rises, the cynical referee in the nasty war of man and wife, and the judge who presides, after the murder, over the further fortunes of Margot Macomber. His dominance over the lady is apparent from the moment she sees him blast the lion from which Macomber ran. But he accepts that dominance only because it is thrust upon him. The kind of dominance he really believes in, and would gladly transfer to the suffering husband, is well summarized in a passage from Shakespeare's *Henry IV* which he quotes as a kind of tribute to Macomber's own loss of fear on the second day: "By my troth, I care not; a man can die but once; we owe God a death . . . and let it go which way it will, he that dies this year is quit for the next. . . ." [36] Having brought out, almost by accident, this attitude he has lived by, Wilson is much embarrassed. "But he had seen men come of age before and it always moved him. It was not a matter of their twenty-first birthday."

Those who object that true manhood is not necessarily proved by one's ability to face a charging beast may be doing Hemingway an injustice. Dramatically speaking, physical courage is often a convenient and economical way of symbolizing moral courage. We are glad, for example, at Hamlet's skill and bravery with the foils. In this African story Hemingway is obviously dealing with both kinds of courage, though, as the situation naturally requires, it is the physical aspect which is stressed.

It would be possible to argue that Francis and Margot Macomber are more nearly caricatures than people. The probability is that the line-drawing in their portraits is the natural consequence of an approach to material chosen for its intrinsic emotional intensity rather than to provide opportunity for depth of characterization. One rightly concludes that they are as fully developed as they need to be for the purposes of the narrative. Further development might well impede the quick march of the short, happy life.

Still it is true that Hemingway's satirical steam, never far below the surface, tends to erupt whenever he deals with leisure-class wastrels. The tendency is visible, for example, in the accounts of Cohn and Campbell in *The Sun Also Rises*. In *Death in the Afternoon*, the author scornfully watches the bored, sport-shod,

[36] *First 49*, p. 131. The speech is made by one of the country soldiers, Feeble, in *II Henry IV*, III, ii, 253–258.

ex-collegians who leave the *corrida* early. The same reaction appears in his sketches of the wealthy yachtsmen in Key West harbor in *To Have and Have Not,* part of which was written at the same time as the Francis Macomber story. It is almost as if, throughout the Depression, Hemingway had resolutely set himself to oppose F. Scott Fitzgerald's temperamental conviction that the rich are glamorous. As Hemingway's scorn rises, the satirical steam-pressure rises with it, and the result is often close to caricature.

If the story of the Macombers is judged, as it probably should be judged, in terms of an experiment in the development of emotional intensity, it is hard to match. As an instance of tragic irony, exemplified in overt action, it has its faults. But dullness is not one of them, and formally speaking the story is very nearly perfect.[37]

V. LESSON FROM THE MASTER

"The Snows of Kilimanjaro" is a tragedy of a different order.[38] Its setting is the final afternoon and evening in the second life of a writer named Harry, dying of gangrene in a camp near the edge of the Tanganyika plains country. "Francis Macomber" proceeds through and by action; "The Snows of Kilimanjaro" is an experiment in the psychology of a dying man. Like *Across the River and Into the Trees,* it contains almost no overt physical activity, though much is implied. Judged in terms of its intention, it is a triumphant piece of writing.

Hemingway's own experiences on safari help to account for the origin of the story. The undeveloped germ of "Francis Macomber" may have been the occasion when Hemingway and M'Cola entered a bush-covered area in pursuit of a lion they heard but never saw. The general outline of "The Snows" was

[37] This story was Hemingway's choice for *This Is My Best,* ed. Whit Burnett, New York, 1942. He so wrote Mr. Burnett 5/12/42.

[38] Hemingway once told Roger Linscott that he regarded "The Snows" as "about as good as any" of his work in short fiction. "On the Books," *New York Herald Tribune Book Review,* December 29, 1946. The story was finished April 7, 1936. EH to MP, 4/9/36.

almost certainly suggested by Hemingway's own grave illness, the flight out of the plains country, and the distant view of the enormous, snow-capped mountain of Kilimanjaro. During the flight east, and no doubt also during the period of treatment in Nairobi—his head aching and his ears ringing from the effects of emetine [39]—Hemingway had ample time to reflect on a topic which would naturally occur to him in such a situation: the death of a writer before his work is done. As in "Francis Macomber," however, most of the other circumstances of the story were invented or overheard.

Like Hemingway, the writer Harry in the story has been "obsessed" for years with curiosity about the idea of death. Now that it is close he has lost all curiosity about it, feeling only a "great tiredness and anger" over its inexorable approach. "The hardest thing," Hemingway had written in the *Green Hills of Africa*, is for the writer "to survive and get his work done." [40] This is mainly because the time available is so short and the temptations not to work are so strong. Harry has succumbed to the temptation *not* to work at his hard trade. Now his time is over, and possessive death moves in.

The story gains further point and poignancy from another obsession of Harry's, the deep sense of his loss of artistic integrity. Despite the difference between London and Tanganyika and the lapse of time between the rule of Edward VII and that of Edward VIII, Hemingway's position is that of Henry James in "The Lesson of the Master." Harry's dying self-accusations are well summarized in the words of Henry St. George, the sold-out novelist in James's novelette. "Don't become in your old age what I have in mine," he tells his young admirer, "—the depressing, the deplorable illustration of the worship of false gods . . . the idols of the market; money and luxury . . . everything that drives one to the short and easy way." [41] The dying writer in Hemingway's story has followed that route, and his creeping gangrene is the mark he bears. He knows that he has traded his

[39] The principal alkaloid of ipecac, used as a specific in the treatment of amoebic dysentery.

[40] *GHOA*, p. 27.

[41] James, *Works*, New York edition, vol. 15, p. 36.

former integrity for "security and comfort," destroying his talent by "betrayals of himself and what he believed in." Henry or Harry, England or Africa, the lesson of the master is the same: Thou shalt not worship the graven images of false gods, or acquiesce in the "life of pleasant surrender." [42]

Although the setting of "The Snows of Kilimanjaro" is as completely un-Jamesian as one could possibly imagine, the themes which the story engages are, on the contrary, very close to those regularly employed by James. "I wonder," Hemingway once ruminated, "what Henry James would have done with the materials of our time." One answer might be that a modern James would simply have altered the costume, the idiom, and certain of the social customs which appear in his novels. The themes, which were matters of greatest interest to him, would scarcely need to be changed at all. The close reader of "The Snows of Kilimanjaro" easily recognizes and responds to its theme of confrontation. The dying writer is far different from the ghost of his former self, the young, free, unsold writer who took all Europe as his oyster and was seriously devoted to his craft. As he listens to the self-accusations with which Harry tortures himself, the reader acquainted with James may be reminded of "The Jolly Corner." In this long story, an American expatriate, returning to his old and empty house at the corner of the American city street, finds himself beleaguered by the ghost of his other self, the ravaged man he might have been had he not followed his esthetic ambitions to Europe. Although the situation is obviously quite the opposite of the one detailed by Hemingway, the strategy is exactly the same: the face-to-face confrontation of an ego by an alter ego. The corner of the tent in which Harry finally dies might well be called, in an echo of Jamesian irony, the jolly corner.

The story is technically distinguished by the operation of several natural symbols. These are non-literary images, as always in Hemingway, and they have been very carefully selected so as to be in complete psychological conformity with the locale and the dramatic situation. How would the ideas of death and of immortality present themselves in the disordered imagination of a writer dying of gangrene as he waits for the plane which is sup-

[42] *First 49*, pp. 158, 160, 162.

posed to carry him out of the wilderness to the Nairobi hospital? The death-symbols were relatively easy. Every night beasts of prey killed grazing animals and left the pickings to those scavengers of carrion, the vultures and the hyenas.

It is entirely natural that Harry, whose flesh is rotting and noisome—is, in fact, carrion already—should associate these creatures with the idea of dying. As he lies near death in the mimosa shade at the opening of the story, he watches the birds obscenely squatting in the glare of the plain. As night falls and the voice of the hyena is heard in the land, the death-image transfers itself from the vultures to this other foul devourer of the dead. With the arrival of his first strong premonition of death, which has no other form than "a sudden, evil-smelling emptiness," Harry finds without astonishment that the image of the hyena is slipping lightly along the edge of the emptiness. "Never believe any of that," he tells his wife, "about a scythe and a skull." His mind has been far away in the days of his former life in Paris, and now it has come back to Africa. "It can be two bicycle policemen as easily, or be a bird. Or it can have a wide snout like a hyena." Death has just come as if to rest its head on the foot of the cot, the direction from which the infection will rise up towards the vital center. Presently it moves in on him, crouching on his chest so that he cannot breathe.

Harry's dying directive, "Never believe any of that about a scythe and a skull," is an important commentary on Hemingway's own habitual approach to the development of natural symbols. He is prepared to use, where they conform to the requirements of an imaginary situation, any of the more ancient symbols—whether the threes and nines of numerology, or the weight of the Cross in Christian legend. But the scythe and the skull, though ancient enough, simply do not fit the pattern of Harry's death and are therefore rejected in favor of the foul and obscene creatures which have now come to dominate Harry's imagination.

Like the death-symbol, the image for immortality arises "naturally" out of the geography and psychology of the situation. When the weight leaves his chest, Harry finds that morning has brought the rescue plane to carry him to Nairobi. Helping him aboard,

Old Compton says that they will have to refuel at Arusha. Everything happens as if it were actually happening—the take-off, the long view of the plain and its moving animals, the hills and forests to the east passing in slow majesty under the belly of the plane—until it dawns on Harry that for some reason they have by-passed Arusha. At first he does not know why. But as the plane emerges from a rain-squall, he suddenly sees ahead of them the square top of Kilimanjaro, "wide as all the world," incredibly white in the sun. "Then he knew that there was where he was going."

While he was in Africa Hemingway learned that the Masai name for the western summit of Kilimanjaro is Ngàje Ngài, which means "House of God." The association between mountainous terrain and the idea of home was, however, already an old one in his mind. He had used it symbolically in the Burguete section of *The Sun Also Rises* and also, far more extensively, in the Abruzzi and the Montreux locale-images of *A Farewell to Arms*. "I will lift up mine eyes to the hills," runs the Psalm, "from whence cometh my help." But there is no psalm-quoting in the back-to-earth dénouement of Hemingway's story. There is only Harry's wife Helen, waking in the middle of the night down in the flat plains-country, far from Kilimanjaro, and calling to a husband who does not answer.[43]

[43] Psalm 121 might do as a motto for Hemingway's collected works. In this connection one might suggest the relevance of the leopard whose enigmatic history is given in the epigraph of "The Snows." "Close to the Western summit of Kilimanjaro there is the dried and frozen carcass of a leopard. No one has explained what the leopard was seeking at that altitude." Professor C. C. Walcutt (*Explicator* 7, April 1949, item 43) sees that the conflict in Harry's life is between a "fundamental moral idealism" and an "aimless materialism." When Harry looks at Kilimanjaro, he sees it as a symbol of Truth, the "undefined ideal for which he has struggled." The leopard is then a symbol for Harry's moral nature. It is not logical that Harry "should continue to believe in man and search for meanings and values"; neither is it logical that "a purely predatory leopard" should have reached that snowy height. What drove the leopard there "is the same sort of mystery as the force that keeps idealism alive in Harry. All reason, in a predatory world, is against it, but there it is." Following this line, Professor E. W. Tedlock, Jr. finds that both leopard and mountain symbolize the preservation of integrity for Harry. "In contrast to the leopard's dried and frozen carcass," writes Tedlock, "Harry lies dying of a gangrenous leg amid heat and glare." The physical infection is the re-

Anyone interested in the methods by which the patterns of experience are translated to the purposes of art should find abundant materials for study in the three stories—non-fiction and fiction—which grew out of Hemingway's African expedition. The foreword to the *Green Hills of Africa* contains an implicit question. Given a country as interesting as Africa, and given the shape of a month's hunting-action there, and given the author's determination to tell only the truth, the question then becomes this: Can such a book possibly compete on equal terms with a work of the imagination? The answer is that it certainly can *compete,* provided always that the narrative is managed by a very skilled writer who takes both truth (the truth of "the way it was") and beauty (the extremely careful formal construction) as his watchwords. Yet the experiment proved also that the narrator who takes no liberties with the actual events of his experience, who tells things exactly as they were, who invents nothing and suppresses nothing important, will place himself at a real disadvantage in the competition. He gives the opposition too large a handicap. Good as the *Green Hills of Africa* is in two respects (verisimilitude and architectonics), it lacks the intensities which Hemingway was able to pack into "The Short Happy Life of Francis Macomber," and it cannot possibly achieve anything like the genuine pathos of "The Snows of Kilimanjaro." The experience of wrestling with the African book, followed as it was with the writing of the two short stories, undoubtedly established one esthetic principle very firmly in Hemingway's mind. The highest art must take liberties, not with the truth but with the modes by which the truth is projected. This was no new discovery for Hemingway. But for any serious writer it is a useful maxim.

---

sult of carelessness—"the typical analogue of a spiritual infection also resulting from carelessness." Thus we have both physical and spiritual decay, while leopard and mountain represent those things which do not decay. Professor Tedlock calls attention to how often Harry's thoughts "revert . . . to experiences in high altitudes and snow." Physically, this can be explained as the "feverish man's desire for coolness and relief"; spiritually the reversions represent a longing for "the good life" of the past. (See *Explicator* 8, October 1949, item 7). For full information on the actual leopard and its discoverer, see John M. Howell, editor, *Hemingway's African Stories*, New York, 1969.

IX · Depression at Key West

> *"Having* is not an absolute, but a gradated power; and consists not only in the quantity or nature of the thing possessed but also (and in a greater degree) in its suitableness to the person possessing it and in his vital power to use it."—John Ruskin [1]

I. THE FASHION OF THE TIMES

Hemingway set down his convictions on the writer in politics in the fall of 1934. "A writer can make himself a nice career while he is alive," said he, "by espousing a political cause, working for it, making a profession of believing in it, and if it wins he will be very well placed. . . . A man can be a Fascist or a Communist and if his outfit gets in he can get to be an ambassador, or have a million copies of his books printed by the government, or any of the other rewards the boys dream about. . . . But none of this will help him as a writer unless he finds something new to add to human knowledge while he is writing." [2]

As for making one's latest piece of fiction into an amateur textbook of economics, Hemingway's position was clear. "Books should be about the people you know, that you love and hate, not about the people you study up about. If you write them truly they will have all the economic implications a book can hold." Once again, the artist was speaking. Those who wished to and could were welcome to write the histories, the economic treatises, the political expositions, the interpretations of current trends. The serious artist, whose task it was to write fiction that would survive, must take a different course. "A country, finally, erodes and the dust blows away," said Hemingway, "the people all die and none of them were of any importance permanently, except those

---

[1] *Unto This Last,* Essay IV, "Ad Valorem." Cf. Ruskin's definition of wealth: "The possession of the Valuable by the Valiant."
[2] "Old Newsman Writes," *Esquire* 2 (December 1934), pp. 25–26.

who practised the arts. . . . A thousand years makes economics silly and a work of art endures forever, but it is very difficult to do and now it is not fashionable." [8]

Hemingway's views on man in society were determined, in the 1930's, by three major considerations. First, he was a veteran of World War I, and he knew what war was really like. Second, he was a veteran newspaper correspondent who had watched, with increasing disgust and hatred, the postwar machinations of European diplomats and dictators in their struggles for power. "It is not enough," said he, "to have a big heart, a pretty good head, a charm of personality, baggy pants, and a facility with a typewriter to know how the world is run; and who is making the assists, the put-outs, and the errors; and who are merely the players and who are the owners." As an old newsman, he was prepared to defend the position that "no history is written honestly. You have to keep in touch with it at the time, and you can depend on just as much as you have actually seen and followed." Nor could he agree with the earnest liberals who were invoking *Das Kapital* as a political and economic bible or were beginning to write in the overblown style of the *Communist Manifesto*. "It isn't all in Marx nor in Engels," said Hemingway. "A lot of things have happened since then." [4]

Much, indeed, had happened, and in the course of his coverage of the European newsfronts or in his clinical observations of the Machado regime in Cuba, he had become familiar with the two ends of the scale: the behind-the-scenes operations of the planners and the power-mongers, and the ultimate blood-spilling among those who fought out the issues in the streets. When Clemenceau's Garde Républicaine broke up the parade of war-mutilated poilus, the results were not greatly different from those which ensued upon Hoover's dispersal of the bonus army at Anacostia Flats, whether in their effect on human relations, or in the amount of blood that flowed. Seen in the flesh and in conflict, the Cuban revolutionists were much like the Italian revolutionists he had watched in the streets of Genoa in 1922. Whether it formed

[8] *GHOA*, p. 109.
[4] "Old Newsman Writes," *loc.cit.*

a pool among the peanut shells on a Havana sidewalk or stained the front of a dirty shirt somewhere in Illinois, the blood of people looked about the same everywhere. To show that this was a fact was one prerogative of the artist.

The third factor in the development of Hemingway's views on the writer in politics was the most important. This was his belief that the novelist who pontificated on the course of contemporary history would always tend to betray his real artistic purposes. Even Tolstoi, great as he could be at his best, allowed himself ponderous commentaries which exposed the limits of his historical knowledge. "I love *War and Peace*," said Hemingway, "for the wonderful, penetrating, and true descriptions of war and of people but I have never believed in the great Count's thinking. I wish there could have been someone in his confidence with authority to remove his heaviest and worst thinking and keep him simply inventing truly. He could invent more with more insight and truth than anyone who ever lived. But his ponderous and Messianic thinking was no better than [that of] many another evangelical professor of history, and I learned from him to distrust my Thinking with a capital T and to try to write as truly, as straightly, as objectively and as humbly as possible." [5]

Thinking with a capital T (which does not rule out another hard kind of thinking which the artist must do) may be vainglory in a writer of fiction. It may well, in the end, be the greatest enemy a writer can have, though he has many, all the time, of both the inner and the outer kind. To pass off amateur "history" or political propaganda as real writing seemed to Hemingway to be an evasion of the serious writer's fundamental obligation. It went without saying that those who played the market of current public interest in a particular political or economic fad or fashion of the age were heading for a crash as writers, no matter how much money they might make in the process. "The hardest thing in the world to do," said Hemingway, "is to write straight honest prose on human beings. First you have to know the subject; then you have to know how to write. Both take a lifetime to learn, and anybody is cheating who takes politics as a

---

[5] *Men At War*, New York, 1942, introd., p. xviii.

way out. It is too easy. All the outs are too easy, and the thing itself is too hard to do." [6]

When the Great American Depression, which made many things possible that had not been possible before, assisted in promoting a marriage between literature and politics, Hemingway was not a member of the wedding. The vows had been spoken often enough in the literary history of the United States, though usually, one noticed, in times of moral rather than merely political crises. What made the depression marriage memorable was that the contracting parties had so recently been living in widely separated areas. Jazz Age literature, with some few exceptions, had flirted most noticeably and openly with Sigmund Freud and Tristan Tzara. In Greenwich Village and its purlieus after the war the loudest talk was likely to be about dreams and sex and psychoanalysis, or about the latest esthetic experiments of Dada. It is true that if one listened closely at a prohibition beer-party in 1925 or 1926, a persistent Marxist mutter was audible among the intelligentsia—something like bridesmaids whispering over the qualities of the groom. But the engagement was not announced or the bans called until the crash of 1929, and the real wedding had to wait for the Depression.

The hard glitter of the new European political ideologies did not cause Hemingway to mistake them for gold. As a working newspaper correspondent on the continent, he had been too intimately in touch with the political actualities for a number of years. By 1923 he was on record as anti-Mussolini, and at a time when many of his fellow Americans were still saying that Mussolini's regime was doing those lazy and shiftless Italians a lot of good. He personally dated his anti-fascism from the murder of Giacomo Matteotti in June, 1924.[7] The socialist Matteotti was virtually the only prominent outspoken Italian critic of Mussolini's *fascisti* between their seizure of power and his death. Many an earnest liberal dated his own change of heart from the kidnapping and murder of Matteotti by Mussolini's henchmen.

Throughout the Jazz Age, Hemingway continued his opposition to the spread of fascism. His short story called "Che Ti Dice

[6] "Old Newsman Writes," *loc.cit.*
[7] EH to CB, 4/1/51.

La Patria" is a true account of a motor-trip he made through Fascist Italy with his friend Guy Hickok.[8] It left no doubt in the minds of *New Republic* readers, when it first appeared there in 1927, as to where Hemingway stood on Il Duce and the political philosophy (if that was the name for it) by which he continued in power. Nor did one gather, though the evidence was sparser, that Hemingway was an avid supporter of Lenin or Trotsky or Stalin. The young and starry-eyed revolutionist is a recurrent and often a pitiable figure in his fiction. The short story called "The Revolutionist" can hardly be said to blaze with the message of the *Communist Manifesto*. As a young artist developing his art, and as a veteran who had fought and been badly wounded in the most wasteful butcher-shop of all wars, he had a right to feel sick at the mention of capitalized Great Causes. He was too busy with his serious writing, and his work for the news-services among the political entanglements of the European continent, to follow Mike Gold in anti-capitalist or anti-republican war-whoops. Though he once sent them the story "Alpine Idyll" when the editors asked him for a contribution, and twice wired them memorials on the dead, at their request, his considered opinion of *The New Masses* was that it was a puerile house-organ.[9]

As an artist, he would not have been at all surprised in the winter of 1929–1930 to hear a critic say that his first two novels showed no special political bias. Had he cared to do so, he might have pointed out that his attitude towards the wastrels of *The Sun*

[8] The new title may be translated, "What do you hear from home?" or "What is the news of the fatherland?"

[9] "Alpine Idyll" was not printed by the magazine; EH to FSF from Paris, [*ca.* September] 1926. At the time of the scandalous, and needless, drowning of the work camp veterans in September 1935, Hemingway's party went at once to visit Camp Five on Matecumbe Key. He was horrified and angry at the failure of those in charge to rescue the veterans in time, and saw more dead in one place than he had seen since the lower Piave in June 1918. On September 14, 1935, he wired a 2800-word despatch on the hurricane disaster to *The New Masses* at their request. He would take no pay, since, as he told Perkins (9/14/35), he did not believe in making money out of murder. But, as he also told Perkins, he had less respect than ever for the magazine and its policy. For the story, see *New Masses* 16 (September 17, 1935), p. 9. A somewhat similar despatch on "The American Dead in Spain" was wired to this magazine three years later. See *New Masses* 30 (February 14, 1939), p. 3.

Also Rises, though tinged with compassion, could likewise be seen as a viewing-with-alarm of one phase of capitalism's drunken hayride through the Jazz Age. Or he could have said that *A Farewell to Arms* was an anti-war novel, while the execution scene beside the Tagliamento, being an example of force exerted by legally constituted bullies, was a condemnation of what would later be known as the fascist temperament. It is clear enough that in the 1920's he read at least some of the signs of the times. Without adopting the political jargon of the period, he was sufficiently aware of the implications inherent in the growing political decadence of European society. But he had preferred to work at his art rather than to confuse his job of work with that of the propagandist.

When the Depression reaffirmed for American society the connection between literature on the one hand and politics and economics on the other, the minority fashion of the late twenties became the majority fashion of the early thirties. As often happens in such a situation, some of the true artists suffered for remaining true to their esthetic convictions. Writers began to be judged according to a politico-economic scale of values. A left-of-center man could often get an A for effort even while he committed all the literary sins known to human society. A rightist or a middle-of-the-roader, deeply committed to serious authorship, would find his best work rewarded with an E for Escapism, or possibly an F, for failure to include some account of the latest streetcar strike in Waban, Massachusetts. Reviewers had a new measuring-stick, although, happily, many of them clung to sounder standards.

To certain members of the new Marxist clan, Hemingway began to look unfashionable in the early 1930's. *Death in the Afternoon* came out in the dead vast and bottom of the Depression. And how could he have the temerity to publish a manual of the bullfight while Americans were selling apples on street-corners, fighting over restaurant garbage cans for food, or being laid off in wholesale lots? *Winner Take Nothing,* the short-story collection of 1933, did nothing to alleviate the situation. Where, in these stories, could one read about the Gastonia strike of the spring of 1929, about General Douglas MacArthur and the bonus army rout at Anacostia Flats? What about the Russian Five-Year Plan, the inside life of union organizers, the May Day celebrations in Union Square?

"It is difficult," wrote Wyndham Lewis in 1934, "to imagine a writer whose mind is more entirely closed to politics than is Hemingway's." [10] The critic went on to say that Hemingway appeared to be interested "in the sports of death, in the sad things that happen to those engaged in the sports of love . . . in war, but *not* in the things that cause war, or the people who profit by it, or in the ultimate human destinies involved in it." Where, in *A Farewell to Arms,* could one find anything about Wilson's Fourteen Points? Why didn't the Montparnassians of *The Sun Also Rises,* in some of their aimless talk, ever analyze the causes of the war? What about the arms manufacturers who had worked behind the scenes to protract the fighting and enlarge their profits? The destinies of Catherine Barkley, Frederick Henry, Dr. Rinaldi, Jake Barnes, and Brett Ashley were not ultimate enough for Mr. Lewis's requirements.

The publication of the *Green Hills of Africa* in 1935 seemed to confirm Lewis's case. Why did Hemingway waste time and talent in Tanganyika which might better have been employed in writing of the American scene, labor strife, money barons, municipal slums like those that produced Stephen Crane's *Maggie,* or the lengthening bread-lines—not to mention beautiful, full bosomed girl-agitators who looked like Sylvia Sidney?

The year in which Mr. Lewis's book appeared saw the publication of a long short story by Hemingway. It was called "One Trip Across" and would subsequently form a unit in the novel *To Have and Have Not.* Written in Madrid in September 1933, the story was included in *Cosmopolitan* for April 1934. It introduced the person of Harry Morgan, ex-policeman from Miami, charter-boat fisherman out of Key West, a proud and independent man who took to smuggling as a means of supporting his wife and daughters in lieu of letting them go on relief. The second Harry Morgan story, in which he lost his right arm by gunfire and his boat by confiscation, and in which his cargo was contraband liquor from Cuba, was written at Key West in November 1935. When it appeared in *Esquire Magazine* for February 1936, it carried the

[10] *Men Without Art,* London, 1934, pp. 17–18.

ironic title of "The Tradesman's Return." [11] This was the second unit of the budding novel.

By the middle of July 1936, Hemingway had decided (unluckily, as it turned out) to make a novel of the Morgan story. The book as he then envisioned it would draw a sharp environmental contrast between Key West and Havana. It would contain what Hemingway had learned about the mechanics of revolution, a topic in which he had taken an artist's interest since 1931, and would attempt to show how revolutionary thought and action affects those involved. Its theme would be the decline of the individual.[12] Another Morgan story, probably longer than the first two, would combine with some additional Key West material to round out Morgan's career in a short, intense, and angry novel.

Off paper, the plan seemed excellent. One difficulty about getting the rest of the novel on paper was the outbreak of the Spanish Civil War, which occurred just about the time the decision to complete the book was made. Hemingway's heart lay in Madrid, and as an artist he was still deeply interested in war. Although he was anxious to cross to the scene of the conflict, he was equally determined to finish his work before setting sail. A writer ought always to write, he had told Perkins some years before, as if he were going to die at the end of a book. There was always an off chance that he might not come back from Spain, and he did not wish to leave a partially completed work. Under these kinds of moral pressure, he bowed out of his arrangement with *Esquire*, went out to Wyoming for peace and quiet, and worked steadily through August and September on the third Morgan story. The typescript had grown to 354 pages by early November. Back in Key West at the beginning of the New Year he completed the first draft on January 2, 1937.

Despite multiple pressures, the Morgan story had come out well. What troubled Hemingway was the companion story on the moral misfortunes of a writer called Richard Gordon. He had invented the story as a means of throwing Harry Morgan's mas-

---

[11] EH to MP, 12/7/35. Hemingway also wrote "The Capital of The World" at about the same time. This was first published in *Esquire* with the title, "The Horns of the Bull."

[12] EH to MP, 7/11/36.

culine virtues into bolder relief. There was not time enough, evidently, to make the two contrasting stories combine satisfactorily.
He continued to tinker the Gordon-Bradley story until he left
New York for Spain on February 27, 1937. But it still did not
please him. He planned to revise it further upon his return.[13]

The cause of Republican Spain made thorough revision impossible. His work on a documentary film, *The Spanish Earth,* and
his speech to the Writer's Congress in June left him only a period
of three or four weeks to put the manuscript in publishable shape.
He told Perkins that he did not consider it "a real novel," though
possibly the Morgan story alone would make a good novelette.
There was evidently some thought of using the three Morgan
items at the head of an omnibus collection of short stories and
articles. After this idea had been abandoned as unwise, Hemingway turned to a hasty reading of the proofsheets, completing the
job between July 18 and August 7. By the time *To Have and Have
Not* was published (October 15, 1937), he was back in Spain.[14]

Like his play, *The Fifth Column,* which was written in Madrid
that fall under conditions far from ideal, *To Have and Have Not*
shows marked deficiencies as a work of art. Unlike *The Fifth
Column,* however, the novel contains some of Hemingway's best
writing along with much that simply does not cohere. The intrinsic
values of the Morgan trilogy are esthetically undermined by the
story of Richard Gordon and company, as if, say, the Gordon
business were a fifth column at work within the Morgan business.
What had looked in theory like a feasible scheme of moral contrast became in practice a novel divided against itself. Once such
a distinction has been made, the reader is in a position to appreciate the worth of the good parts of the novel, and to understand
why, considered as an artistic unit, *To Have and Have Not* is Hemingway's least satisfactory book. One may notice in passing that
William Faulkner's double-focussed novel, *The Wild Palms,* published in 1939, represents a similar experiment in contrasting
characters. In Faulkner, however, the story of the doctor and his

---

[13] EH to MP, 8/26/36, 11/8/36, 12/15/36.
[14] EH to MP, 6/10/37, 8/9/37. Two weeks after publication *THAHN*
stood fourth on the national best-seller lists. By March 10, 1938, five
months after publication, the book had sold 36,000 copies.

mistress does not so much undermine as serve to enhance the story of the convict. The convict is the rough moral equivalent of Harry Morgan in Hemingway.

The novel as published contains Hemingway's notes towards the definition of a decaying culture, and his disgust with the smell of death to come. Throughout the early nineteen-thirties he had been experimenting with one technical problem after another in the attempt to develop his art. He was not only seeking to advance his dexterity with a prose instrument earlier forged and tempered, but he was also beginning to attack the problem of cultural synecdoche, the means by which the novelist, presenting and evaluating the things he has known, summarizes dramatically the moral predicament of his times. One saw this tendency at work in both *Death in the Afternoon* and the *Green Hills of Africa*. The assumption in *To Have and Have Not* was that Depressed America at large could be anatomized by using a microscope on Key West in little. America at its worst was fully visible in Key West during the period 1932–1936. If, as one gathered, the whole organism was diseased, he could examine the smear on the slide to see what malignant forces were at work.

A major difference between this novel and much depression-inspired proletarian fiction was that it really embodied the diagnostic notes on decay; it did not preach them. This was a treatise in economics and revolutionary politics which chose to present its findings, not in propagandistic set speeches or in interminable discussions between a young organizer and his experienced mentor, but in straightforward, illustrative dramatic terms. For this reason, and in spite of its serious faults, *To Have and Have Not* may be said to stand as a somewhat more persuasive social documentary than a great deal of the soap-bubble proletarian literature which appeared, shone brightly, and vanished down-wind—through inherent structural weaknesses, an internal content that was mostly air, and the pressure of changing circumstances—during the period when so many blew the Marxist pipe.

Hemingway was not out to please the "recently politically enlightened critics." What he had written about "the boys" in 1934 he could still apply in 1937. "If the book is good, is about something that you know, and is truly written, and reading it over you see that this is so, you can let the boys yip." Then the noise "will have that pleasant sound coyotes make on a very cold night when they are out in the snow, and you are in your own cabin that you have built and paid for with your work." [15]

II. SOMETHING KNOWN

To Have and Have Not was "about something" Hemingway knew. By the time of the book's publication he had been living in Key West for nearly ten years, and by 1935 his stucco house on Whitehead Street was listed in the town's guide-book as one of the points of interest for visiting tourists. He knew all about charter-boat fishing, which he regularly followed as a means of relaxing from the hard trade of writing, and he had spent some time during the spring and summer of 1933 aboard the 34-foot launch *Anita,* owned and captained by Joe Russell of Key West. When Captain Russell retired ashore to take care of his profitable bar in Key West, Hemingway continued his maritime activities with his own boat, the *Pilar,* which was built for him after his return from Africa.[16]

He also had occasion to mingle with the unemployed war veterans, several hundred of whom were at this time stationed in work camps on the Upper and Lower Matecumbe Keys. They were part of a depression-inspired FERA project building roads and bridges between Miami and Key West. On pay-days they used to come down to Joe Russell's Key West bar to refresh themselves and enjoy a general rough-house. Entering the bar one day, Hemingway was hailed by one of the drunken veterans. He had a broken leg and a pair of crutches and was enthroned on a billiard table in the rear of the room. His fun for the day was to call unsuspecting visitors over for a talk and then to attempt to knock them out with a crutch. Since that morning his ruse had worked perfectly three times. Hemingway, warned by the proprietor, kept out of range. But his memory of this and other scenes of the same general character helped him to invent one of the

[15] "Old Newsman Writes," *loc.cit.* Note 2 *supra.*
[16] *Esquire* 2 (August 1934), pp. 19, 156, 158. Cf. *Esquire* 5 (April 1936), pp. 31, 184–185.

most effective episodes in *To Have and Have Not*. The semi-comedy of the pay-dazed veterans had a tragic dénouement in the fall of 1935. On September third, a hurricane cut a wide swath east of Key West, destroying the Matecumbe work-camps and drowning more than 200 of the men. While the scandal swept across the nation and an investigation was begun in an attempt to fix the blame, Hemingway joined the volunteer workers who helped collect the dead from the watery débris all along the stricken Keys.[17]

Besides the charter-boat marlin-fishing and the depressed peoples who were cast up on the Keys like economic driftwood, a third element which was to go into *To Have and Have Not* was now borne in upon Hemingway. As the Morgan story took shape in his imagination, another began to rise up beside it. Morgan was the individualist man of action, first crippled and then killed as an indirect result of social corruption. What about that other individualist, the artist, doing his work and earning his bread in the midst of the same corruption? Between this Jamesian topic and the problems which beset Harry Morgan of Key West there appeared to be some relationship. "The Snows of Kilimanjaro," completed in April 1936, shortly before Hemingway began to push the work on *To Have and Have Not,* took as its protagonist an artist who had succumbed to the temptations of wealth and privilege. Was it merely a coincidence that his name was Harry, too?

Harry the artist had traded on his talent instead of using it. He had supposed that he could write stories about the "very rich," as if he were a kind of "spy in their country" while still remaining ethically separate from them. Instead, he had merely surrendered to creature-comfort and mental laziness. Harry's friend Julian (who was called Scott Fitzgerald in the first printed version of "The Snows of Kilimanjaro") had been wrecked by the leisure class in a way that was essentially different but hardly less devastating.[18] He thought the rich "a special glamorous race and when

---

[17] *Esquire* 4 (August 1935), pp. 19, 182. Cf. *Esquire* 2 (October 1934), pp. 21–22. For Hemingway's report on the disaster, see *New Masses* 16 (September 17, 1935), p. 9.

[18] *Esquire* 6 (August 1936), pp. 27, 194–201.

he found out they weren't it wrecked him just as much as any other thing that wrecked him."

Julian is obviously not to be confused with the artist Harry in the African story. He is a being of another order. Yet the whole problem of the cracked-up artist was dramatized for Hemingway in this period of the middle thirties by Scott Fitzgerald's losing fight against the furies that beset him. It came home to him in a special way. Between late 1933 and 1936, Hemingway had contributed twenty-five articles, chiefly in the form of "letters" on fishing and hunting, to the new men's magazine, *Esquire*.[19] Until the Spanish Civil War interrupted the arrangement, which gave Hemingway a completely free hand, these epistles, averaging about 1700 words each, held the lead position in almost every number. They earned Hemingway a following among fellow-sportsmen while enraging a lesser number of the avant-garde and leftist critics, who felt that in being fairly well paid for this form of journalism, Hemingway was lowering his literary standards. What gave Hemingway pause, during his tenure as chief letter-writer for the magazine, was that Scott Fitzgerald's graphic account of his own crack-up also ran in a series through the pages of *Esquire*.[20]

He did not, of course, take Fitzgerald as his subject. The "crack-up" articles, which are among the classic statements on the theme, left nothing more to be said during Fitzgerald's rapidly diminishing lifetime. Yet all through the early thirties the subject of the artist's jeopardy had been in Hemingway's mind, and it is at least a reasonable speculation that the Fitzgerald articles served as a kind of catalyst, being, as it were, too big to miss. The social aspect was important. "Writers should work alone," Hemingway had written in 1934. "They should see each other only after their work is done, and not too often then. Otherwise they become like writers in New York. All angleworms in a bottle, trying to derive knowledge and nourishment from their own contact and from the bottle. Sometimes the bottle is shaped art, sometimes economics, sometimes economics-religion. But once they are in the bottle they

---

[19] For a complete listing, including short stories, see Bibliography.

[20] *Esquire* 5 (February 1936), pp. 41, 169; (March 1936), pp. 35, 182; (April 1936), pp. 39, 202.

stay there. They are lonesome outside of the bottle. They do not want to be lonesome. They are afraid to be alone in their beliefs." Other writers tried to save their souls with what they wrote, or were ruined by "the first money, the first praise, the first attack." Sometimes they became frightened enough to join organizations that did their thinking for them.[21] Much could happen and most of it was bad. Now, because Hemingway was dramatizing a double indictment of American society for its predatory attitude towards both writers and individualistic men-of-action, he placed Harry Morgan and the partly invented figure of the writer Richard Gordon side by side in his depression-novel of Key West. It is of interest to discover what the contiguity produced.

III. MORGAN AND GORDON

Harry Morgan was a supreme individualist, but he was also an American type. To put it another way, he was an American type because of his individualism, his cold courage, his resourcefulness, and his self-reliance. If American readers in the 1930's could not recognize in Harry Morgan a lineal descendant of the American frontiersman, the man who made his own laws and trusted in his own judgments, they were perhaps far gone in group thinking. Both in the Far West and in Key West Hemingway had met men of the frontier temperament, so that he did not lack for contemporary models. If one wanted a historical ancestor for Harry Morgan, however, he had only to look at some of the accounts of Wyatt Earp in the 1880's. Harry had been a police officer in Miami before he came to Key West. Earp had been a Kansas sheriff before he went west to Tombstone. Fraud such as the economic royalist Johnson practiced on Harry Morgan was close to the rule of life in Tombstone. The smuggling of alien Chinese from Cuba to the United States was not far different either in principle or in practice from the rustling of cattle across the Mexican border. Harry Morgan, badly wounded by Cuban customs officials as he runs out a boat-load of illicit liquor, is in effect repeating the experience of the marauding gringos who ran afoul of armed Mexicans during raids well within living memory. Plying between

[21] GHOA, pp. 21–22 and 24.

Cuba and Key West—a Latin country and a rough American town—Morgan is a typical nineteenth-century frontiersman in a twentieth-century frontier situation.

But the Morgan story, like *A Farewell to Arms,* is a study in doom. If one wishes to see it as an instance of "cultural synecdoche," there is no difficulty in taking Morgan as the type of the old self-reliant individualist confronted by an ever-encroaching social restraint—the civil disobedient who, like Thoreau, is opposed in principle to a corrupt federalism, but is unwilling, having never heard of Thoreau's program, to content himself with passive resistance. But Morgan has two factors to contend with which did not bother the Wyatt Earps of the old frontier. One is officious bureaucracy as dramatized in the power-proud figure of Frederick Harrison, the man who loses Harry his boat. "For your information," says Harrison, "I'm one of the three most important men in the United States today." It may not be fanciful, in view of Hemingway's long familiarity with the type, to see Harrison as a notable instance of the fascist mentality.

The second force is memorably represented by the Cuban revolutionaries, in descending order from the young idealist Emilio (who very much regrets the necessity for the terrorist phase of the revolution) down to the moon-faced Roberto who has killed so much in the time of Machado that he has come to enjoy political murder for its own sake. Emilio calls Roberto a good revolutionary but a bad man. Through this pair Hemingway summarizes the revolutionary party mentality of the Comintern, Latin style.

Morgan, who bears the name of a famous pirate, entertains equal scorn for both fascism and communism, though he is wise enough to recognize their power as adversaries long before the two groups, working in quite different ways, lose him first his boat and then his life. From the time he is defrauded of honest earnings by the unscrupulous capitalist Johnson, Harry Morgan is doomed, and the steps in his destruction are clearly marked out. A plague, he might well say, on all three such houses. His dying words on the hopeless situation of "one man alone" ring the knell of nineteenth-century frontier individualism. As long as the tactics and problems remain those of the frontier, Harry can survive. But fascism and communism, like the greed of irresponsible capitalism, are more formidable enemies, too powerful for one man alone to withstand.

Hemingway made over the Morgan trilogy into a novel by two important additions. Remembering that the book, like much of his writing at this time, was experimental in nature, it might be observed that both additions have the effect of enlarging Harry Morgan's stature. The first addition is the provision of a home-life for the hero. Harry's wife Marie is a kind of faithful Molly Bloom whose closing soliloquy is Harry's personal epitaph. The second addition, quantitatively much more extensive than the story of Marie Morgan, deals with the crack-up of Richard Gordon, proletarian novelist, playboy, and sojourner in the Key West artist's colony. This was Hemingway's strategic error.

One would scarcely need Hemingway's melancholy diatribe on sold-out American writers in the *Green Hills of Africa* in order to recognize Gordon as a representative figure. His character and activities likewise serve as a foil for those of Harry Morgan. Harry's marriage is a success, Gordon's a miserable failure. Harry is tough, bitter, honest with himself; Gordon is a self-deceiver, a self-apologist, a self-pitier. One is an expert strategist in all that concerns his means of livelihood and his life as a man, while the other is a false practitioner who manages to conceal his limitations even from himself. Morgan can handle his own affairs; Gordon is a kept man in a morally unkempt society.

The climactic phase of the novel centers on the doom of both men. When Gordon enters, the time is already at hand when he will be compelled to face the facts of his life, just as Morgan, though in a quite different manner, must face up to the inexorable facts by which group-man seizes dominance over the self-starting individualist. Gordon's doom is in its way as inevitable as Morgan's. In quick succession his self-respect receives two damaging blows. One comes when his wife leaves him with a fine Irish tongue-lashing for his failure as a husband, the second sinks home when a companion at the bar who happens to be familiar with the actualities of unemployment, tells him exactly what his "proletarian" fiction is worth. The bloody figure of Richard Gordon on his way home to an empty house in the dark is neither comic nor tragic. It is an image of the writer irrevocably spoiled by the

smart-set lionizers, the ruthless bohemians, and the literary fad-
dists whose ways he has been following. Now he has met his moral
"comeuppance," a situation not unlike the confrontation of self
by self which occurs with another writer in "The Snows of Kilimanjaro." There are no degrees of chastity, but Gordon is considerably lower on the scale of the unchaste than the Harry who
dies of gangrene in Tanganyika.

Morgan is clearly impervious to the kind of corruption which
dooms Gordon. He pointedly rejects, for example, the yahoo-like
advances of a Key West literary slummer. "Shut up, you whore,"
says Harry Morgan, and the lady eventually obeys. Yet Gordon
allows himself to be taken up, and (what is worse) taken in, by
the wealthy Helene Bradley, a slummer on the grand scale and
the exact moral equivalent of African gangrene. Though both
Morgan and Gordon are victimized, it would be a mistake to
suppose that their adversaries are the same. Where the man-of-
action loses livelihood and life to something like fascism and something like communism, the parlor-pink novelist is a casualty to
capitalism's leisure class.

Strong esthetic grounds exist for the belief that the novel would
have been better without the figure of Gordon. For the story of
the writer suffers, perhaps unduly, when it is placed beside the
story of Morgan's downfall. Where the piratical smuggler credi-
bly epitomizes the self-reliant man, Gordon seems by contrast a
kind of caricature, somewhat as Francis Macomber suffers by his
proximity to the white hunter Wilson: on straight esthetic grounds.
If Gordon's pipsqueak misadventures help to bring out the stark,
tough actualities of Morgan's life and thus enlarge the boatman's
moral stature, the contrast backfires when it is looked at from the
other end. The nearness of Morgan dehumanizes Gordon to a
shadowy emblem. Although Hemingway, as in the Macomber
story, appears to feel some compassion, his scorn for the obvious
hollowness of the society life Gordon leads is finally uppermost,
and the writer's stature shrinks to that of a dwarf at the court of
the Duchess of Key West. On the other hand, in a queer way, the
author's scorn for Frederick Harrison (a caricature also) and
the Cuban terrorists only serves to increase his—and our—respect
for Morgan.

Two "exemplums" in *To Have and Have Not* operate, still somewhat oddly, in precisely the same way. One helps the novel forward; the other, esthetically speaking, is a backfire. The stories of Morgan and Gordon might be interpreted as instances in which the middle parts of fortune are invaded by the corrupting extremes. In order to emphasize for the reader the broad applicability of his social accusations, Hemingway provides two remarkable passages on the extremes of the economic have-and-have-not scale. Both are tours de force, but one succeeds as a version of the actual where the other fails because it seems obviously rigged.

The episode which backfires is the roll-call of the occupants of five yachts tied up at the Key West finger piers the night Harry Morgan is brought in from the Gulf. Two homosexuals, keeper and kept; one narcissistic adulteress; and one old economic royalist worrying over income-tax evasion are at least numerically balanced by one healthy, respectable upperclass family and two of the 324 intrepid Esthonians who are sailing around in different parts of the world and sending back articles to the Esthonian newspapers. The real imbalance is in the satire itself; this is an extreme overstatement on one of the social extremes. Instead of enhancing the effect, this piece of satire oddly cheapens the whole atmosphere when Morgan's bullet-riddled boat and body are towed past the silent yachts. The reader finds himself resenting the episode as gratuitous over-emphasis.

Much more effective is the remarkable sketch of the displaced veterans in their nocturnal drink-and-slugfest in Freddy's Bar. These men stand at the other extreme. They are the "desperate ones . . . the ones with nothing to lose . . . the completely brutalized ones." Hoover ran them out of Anacostia Flats; Roosevelt shipped them south "to get rid of them." [22] Coldly intelligent and well-educated communists are infiltrating their camps. They are as much the prey to these borers from within as the wealthy yachtsmen are prey to fascist-minded bureaucrats of the stamp of Frederick Harrison. The veterans' irrational and aimless brutality serves a better purpose in the novel than the roll-call of the

[22] *THAHN*, p. 206. According to a *New Masses* editorial for September 16, 1935, the Roosevelt administration was supposed in some quarters to have "drowned" the veterans.

yachts; for if Morgan was brutal and desperate, he was brutal to some end and desperate for good reason. These depressed peoples have been kicked around for so long that they now take a masochistic delight in their ability to absorb more punishment.

"Let us in," the bloody-faced one said. "Let in me and my old buddy." He whispered into Richard Gordon's ear, "I don't have to hand it out. I can take it."

"Listen," the other Vet said as they finally reached the beer-wet bar, "you ought to have seen him at noon at the Commissary at Camp Five. I had him down and I was hitting him on the head with a bottle. Just like playing on a drum. I bet I hit him fifty times."

"More," said the bloody-faced one.[23]

Malcolm Cowley once referred to this section of the book as a Walpurgisnacht, and the image is perfectly exact.[24] Hemingway does not spoil the direct impact of this wild scene with any contiguities. It is a terrible indictment made with a wry smile but also with an unmistakable sickness at the stomach, as if Key West had somehow got detached from its moorings and were pitching and wallowing in an ugly sea of social neglect. The same society has driven Harry Morgan to piracy and Richard Gordon to a kind of literary racketeering which passes in some circles of hell for art.

But the exemplums of the corrupt yachtsmen and the brutalized veterans, as well as the story of Richard Gordon's crack-up, have yet another function in the book. They suggest the possibility that *To Have and Have Not* is a title with a reciprocal action. Its economic meaning is clear and obvious. As one of the *Have-Nots*, Harry Morgan must take desperate measures for survival, and his adversaries are those who *Have* money, power, prestige, and unearned privilege. Yet this is a novel, not a treatise in economics. John Ruskin, whose approach to economic problems always emphasized morality over money, once defined *having* as a power whose importance lay "not only in the quantity or nature of the thing possessed" but also, and more significantly, "in its suitableness to the person possessing it and in his vital power to use it." [25]

[23] *THAHN*, p. 202.
[24] *New Republic* 92 (October 20, 1937), pp. 305–306.
[25] Ruskin, *Unto This Last,* Essay IV.

On these ultimately moral grounds, a reversed interpretation of the title suggests itself. Harry Morgan *has* a combination of social courage and personal integrity precisely suited to his character. The same qualities are notably absent among the leisure-class wastrels and other ne'er-do-wells by whom he is surrounded and with whom he is contrasted. He shows a "vital power" in putting his possessions to use. *To Have* what Harry has in the way of self-reliance, self-command, and self-knowledge is qualitatively superior, one would judge, to the strictly economic forms of having. Interpreted in this way, the Have-Nots of the title would embrace representatives of every class and occupation: wealthy yacht-owners, middle-class artists like Gordon, simple alcoholics like Harry's super-cargo Eddy, or the brutalized veterans who give and take their punishment in the Walpurgisnacht atmosphere of Freddy's Key West bar.

IV. THE MATTER OF TECHNIQUE

Few of Hemingway's critics, either in 1937 or since, seemed able to appreciate the difficulty of the technical experiments in *To Have and Have Not* or the skill with which some of them were overcome. For those who wished to pay attention, however, the Key West novel repaid the effort. One experiment which failed was the attempt to dove-tail and arc-weld two essentially disparate plots; another was the use of caricature, which seemed out of place in connection with the power and the fury of the Morgan story. But three other experiments—with the maintenance and release of emotional intensity, with the establishment of multiple perspectives, and with the building up of an ordinary Key West charter-boat fisherman to a figure of heroic proportions—were distinctly worth noticing.

For some readers one trouble with the Morgan story was that it was almost too intense—like the thumbing-out of Gloucester's eyes in *King Lear* or the axe-murder in *Crime and Punishment*. The incidents of the smuggled Chinese and the boat-battle with the Cuban revolutionaries seemed to be designed to give the reader a feeling something like that of walking in front of a battery of machine-guns manned by epileptics. Both developed a degree of tension just short of the unendurable. Fitzgerald wrote Hemingway a few months before he died that there were paragraphs and whole pages of *To Have and Have Not* which were "right up with Dostoievski in their undeflected intensity." [26]

It is not part of Hemingway's aim to deflect his intensities, but one can watch with interest his attempts to relieve them. Book I quickly establishes the atmosphere in which Harry moves by an account of a Havana gun-battle between two groups of Cuban revolutionists. This is followed with a full account of a day's deep-sea fishing, exciting in itself as a study in pursuit yet carried on at a pitch considerably lower than the man-hunt by land with which the book began. After Johnson runs out on Morgan without paying the bill, the episode of the smuggled Chinese begins to take shape, gather momentum, and develop a new and undeflected intensity. A brief account of the homeward cruise again provides relief and brings this phase of the story to a satisfactory and rounded conclusion.

The rum-running story, conducted throughout at a considerably lower emotional temperature, rises in mid-career to the time when Morgan and his Negro companion Wesley are nearly arrested by the officious Washington bureaucrat Harrison. Here the relief is provided by the humor of character, and the deflation of false pride, in a manner which anticipates the incident of El Sordo and the boastful fascist captain in *For Whom the Bell Tolls*. Captain Willie, a handsomely realized character-study, shouts his warning to the two wounded men in the booze boat:

"Listen. Get on into town and take it easy. Never mind the boat. They'll take the boat. Dump your load and get into town. I got a guy here on board some kind of a stool from Washington. More important than the President, he says. He wants to pinch you. He thinks you're a bootlegger. He's got the numbers of the boat. I ain't never seen you so I don't know who you are. I couldn't identify you—"

The boats had drifted apart. Captain Willie went on shouting, "I don't know where this place is where I seen you. I wouldn't know how to get back here."

[26] FSF to EH, 11/8/40. See *The Crack-Up*, ed. Edmund Wilson, New York, 1945, p. 284.

"O. K.," came a shout from the booze boat.

"I'm taking this big alphabet man fishing until dark," Captain Willie shouted.

"O. K."

"He loves to fish," Captain Willie yelled, his voice almost breaking. "But the son of a bitch claims you can't eat 'em."

"Thanks, brother," came the voice of Harry.

"That chap your brother?" asked Frederick Harrison, his face very red but his love of information still unappeased.

"No, sir," said Captain Willie. "Most everybody goes in boats calls each other brother."

"We'll go into Key West," Frederick Harrison said; but he said it without great conviction.[27]

The third story early achieves and steadily maintains an always mounting intensity up to the point of the gunfight with the Cuban revolutionists, then slowly decelerates through the account of Harry's dying and on to the moment of his death in the hospital. After this, in a manner somewhat like the Molly Bloom sequence at the close of Joyce's *Ulysses,* comes the soliloquy by Marie Morgan—a final chorus of lament for the slain. If one examines the Morgan trilogy as an experiment in the development and relief of emotional tension, he may find it easy to share Fitzgerald's enthusiasm, whether or not he is reminded of Dostoievski.

Besides the experimentation with emotional tensions, *To Have and Have Not* is distinguished by experiments with varying points of view. Since it must introduce the character and clarify the motives of Harry Morgan, the opening story is his own first-person narrative throughout. Part Two, on the rum-running episode, offers another perspective on Morgan, treating him almost as if he were a stranger, and gaining a special detachment by the use of the third-person narrative. We are made to share "the tradesman's return" as if somehow aboard the boat as a silent partner. This method is relieved by one shift in point of view midway in the story. When Captain Willie Adams and his two passengers are close enough to the booze boat so that Harrison becomes suspicious about what may be happening, we are taken aboard Captain Willie's boat for the comic interlude of his defiance. This

[27] *THAHN,* pp. 82–83.

double view of Morgan's predicament gives the story a length of perspective which it would lack if, like the first one, it were told entirely in the first person or entirely from the silent-partner position aboard Harry's boat.

Part Three carries the experiment further. It opens with a first-person narrative by Albert Tracy, Morgan's indigent colleague in the affair of the Cuban terrorists. This opening has a triple purpose. We get a picture of Morgan in action through the mind of someone other than Harry or the author. We learn also enough about Albert so that we are able to sympathize with him and therefore feel his loss the more when he is callously murdered by the Cubans. Finally, we are prepared, through this special knowledge of Albert, to accept the comic and almost farcical wailings and posturings of the shrewish Mrs. Tracy when she learns of her husband's death. Having treated him badly while he lived, she is prepared to put on a stirring show as the very recent widow who has lost her helpmate. Her obviously half-devised mourning is effective in the total structure of the book in that it provides a contrast with Marie Morgan's realistic and dignified acceptance of her own husband's death.

After Tracy's narrative, Hemingway introduces a short internal monologue by Morgan, the intent here being to establish with us a sense of his feeling of reluctant desperation. "I don't want to fool with it," Harry muses, "but what choice have I got? They don't give you any choice now. I can let it go; but what will the next thing be? I didn't ask for any of this and if you've got to do it you've got to do it." [28] In this mood he agrees to carry the Cubans across the straits to Cuba. From this point onwards, the third-person narrative begins again—chiefly objective, though occasionally dipping into Harry's thought-stream to show his reactions to each of the changing situations as they arise. Along with these semi-soliloquies, the author twice provides access to Marie Morgan's thoughts. This is done partly, as with Tracy, to confirm her in the reader's sympathies, and partly to provide yet another perspective on Harry Morgan.

Up through the fatal wounding aboard the *Queen Conch*, the story is therefore a straightforward third-person narrative, with

[28] *THAHN*, p. 105.

limited use of thought-reporting where it is required. After the
shooting, however, there is one very striking camera-eye snapshot
of the launch as she drifts in the Gulf Stream.

"She drifted broadside to the gentle north wind about ten miles
outside of the north-bound tanker lanes, gay looking in her fresh
white and green, against the dark, blue Gulf Stream water. . . .
There was no sign of life on her although the body of a man
showed, rather inflated looking, above the gunwale, lying on a
bench over the port gasoline tank and, from the long seat alongside the starboard gunwale, a man seemed to be leaning over to
dip his hand into the sea. His head and arms were in the sun and
at the point where his fingers almost touched the water, there was
a school of small fish . . . that had deserted the gulf weed to
take shelter in the shade the bottom of the drifting launch made
in the water, and each time anything dripped down into the sea,
these fish rushed at the drop and pushed and milled until it was
gone. . . . They had long since pulled away the ropy, carmine
clots and threads that trailed in the water from the lowest splintered holes. . . . They were reluctant now to leave a place where
they had fed so well and unexpectedly." [29]

The oppressive silence here, the *Queen Conch* with her quiet
cargo of dead men, the one still-living occupant, and the tropical
fish silently feeding in the shadow of the silently drifting launch,
provides an effective contrast to the fury of the gun-battle which
has taken place the night before. It likewise serves to remind the
reader of Hemingway that nature's quietude, nature's continuum,
nature's great age, when these are compared with the fury and the
mire of human veins, and the brevity of man's time on earth, are
something like an echo of the passage from Ecclesiastes which
was used as one of the headnotes to *The Sun Also Rises*. The sun
also ariseth in 1935, as it did in 1925 over the Pyrenees at
Burguete; the Gulf Stream, like the Irati river, still runs without
interruption; the fish still feed and swim while the generations of
mankind pass away.

We see no more of Morgan until the Coast Guard cutter tows
the launch back to Key West while the ship's officers question him,

[29] *THAHN*, pp. 178–180. The passage is too long to quote in full, and
should be read in context for the total effect.

without success, on the origin of the tragedy. His career closes, as
the book closes, with Marie's requiem-soliloquy. Basing his conclusion on the Morgan trilogy, the reader may well decide that the
virtuosity of the narrative technique alone is enough to set the
book off in a kind of lonely triumph from most of the writing of
the middle thirties.

By many carefully planned devices, Harry Morgan's stature is
raised to dimensions just short of heroic. Two of these—Marie's
silent soliloquies and the contrast which Richard Gordon un-
wittingly provides—have already been mentioned. Some of the
others may be quickly noticed. Harry's working associates serve,
for example, to emphasize his self-command (contrast Eddy the
alcoholic), his unwillingness to compromise with the truth (Bee-
lips the lawyer is the contrasting figure here), and his tough resourcefulness (as contrasted, say, with the character of Albert
Tracy, a poor hungry player who struts and frets a brief hour only
to be murdered and dumped overboard by the callous Roberto).
The rum-running story underscores Morgan's capacity for stoic
endurance—always a trait of Hemingway's heroes. Both Harry
and his assistant have been shot—he severely in the arm, Wesley
in the leg. All the way across the straits, Wesley has moaned and
complained. By morning Harry has tired of the noise.

"Who the hell's shot worse?" he asks. "You or me?"

"You're shot worse," Wesley admits. "But I ain't never been
shot. I didn't figure to get shot. I ain't paid to be shot. I don't want
to be shot."

"Take it easy, Wesley," says Harry. "It don't do any good to
talk like that."

And while his companion blubbers with his face in a corner,
Harry continues to lift the heavy sacks of liquor and to drop them
over the side with his one good arm.[30]

When the figure of Harry Morgan is looked at phlegmatically,
outside the frame of the story, he seems very much like any other
tough Key West fisherman. It would be easy to write him off as
a low-class murderer, a one-armed bandit, an inveterate opportunist whose complete callousness towards bloodshed is the measure of his moral standing. When Mrs. Laughton, drinking cuba

[30] *THAHN*, pp. 70 and 75.

libres at Freddy's Bar, casts sheep's-eyes at Morgan and admires his "beautiful face," Freddy believes that Mrs. Laughton has had one too many drinks. "Take it easy, lady," says Freddy. "He's got a face like a ham with a broken nose on it." [31] Freddy's physiognomic perceptions are clear and sharp.

It is, nevertheless, the task of any good story to enthrall the reader into certain illusions in terms of which his evaluation of character can take place. Within the illusion provided by *To Have and Have Not*, Harry Morgan emerges as a heroic and morally indefatigable figure, standing out like a stoic statue above the heads of his associates, gifted with qualities and abilities and determinations to which none of his companions can lay equal claim.

If one is compelled, in final judgment, to say that *To Have and Have Not* fails as a novel—and it does fail for the reasons already outlined—it is all the more important that the virtues of the Morgan trilogy should receive due recognition. In two respects, at least, the Morgan story looks forward to *For Whom the Bell Tolls*. One of these is the demonstrated skill in the development of emotional intensity—a skill visible also in "The Short Happy Life of Francis Macomber," which belongs to the same chronological period as the third Morgan story. The second is to be found in Hemingway's capacity for the enlargement of character to heroic proportions. What Hemingway learned from his experiments with Harry Morgan was put to excellent use in the portraits of Robert Jordan and the gypsy Pilar during the composition of *For Whom the Bell Tolls*.

[31] *THAHN*, p. 137.

X · The Spanish Tragedy

"Hemingway . . . is obviously the person who can write the great book about the Spanish War."—Cyril Connolly, 1937 [1]

I. A MATTER OF CHOICE

When Hemingway spoke to the Second American Writers' Congress in Carnegie Hall, New York City, the evening of June 4, 1937, he was newly back from two months' reporting on the Spanish Civil War. It was his first public speech. Since, in the course of it, he denounced the native and foreign fascists then operating in Spain, some of his large audience supposed that they were witnessing the wonderful transformation of a non-political writer to one who was socially conscious.[2]

Two days later, in one of the closing speeches of the Congress, Joseph Freeman thought he saw an important lesson in Hemingway's "conversion." He drew his text from an anecdote about Napoleon and Goethe. When Goethe said that he was writing a play about the destiny of man, Napoleon answered that politics is destiny. In an epoch like our own, said Freeman, politics, in its broadest sense, *is* destiny. "Even if you begin as Hemingway began, with a simple emotional desire to transmit experience, to find and convey the truth, if you follow the truth to its logical conclusion, you will end where Hemingway has ended now, in the People's Front." [3]

All this about "logical conclusions" (with the implication that the logic of history eventually forces a writer to support a political party-line) was Marxist language and typical Marxist thinking. The explosion of political circumstances in Spain had presumably blasted Hemingway out of his non-political lethargy and deposited

[1] Cyril Connolly, *New Statesman and Nation* 14 (October 16, 1937), p. 606.

[2] *Writer's Congress proceedings:* published in book form with a selection of the speeches, *The Writer in a Changing World,* ed. Henry Hart, New York, Equinox Cooperative Press, 1937.

[3] *Goethe and Napoleon: ibid.,* pp. 234–235.

him safely in the camp of the Spanish Loyalists. Gone was his "simple emotional desire to transmit experience," and perhaps his wish "to find and convey the truth." At any rate, these desires were now channelized in a political direction. According to Freeman, Hemingway was espousing a Cause. The political left, though very supercilious about his former childishness, was ready to welcome this talented if prodigal son back into the state of political awareness.

The only trouble with Freeman's conclusion was that Hemingway was still of Goethe's persuasion. "A writer's problem does not change," he told his audience. "It is always how to write truly and having found out what is true to project it in such a way that it becomes a part of the experience of the person who reads it." As to forms of government, he frankly continued, really good writers seem to have been rewarded under almost any system of government which they could tolerate. "There is only one form of government," said he, "that cannot produce good writers, and that system is fascism. For fascism is a lie told by bullies. A writer who will not lie cannot live and work under fascism." [4] Although, as a friend of Spanish democracy, Hemingway believed in the Republican side, his statement did not mean that, *as an artist,* he was pro-Republican or pro-Communist. What it emphatically meant was that as artist and man, he was anti-fascist, and had been for years.

Hemingway had followed political developments in Spain from the beginning of his career. The almost medieval country he had known in the nineteen-twenties during Alfonso's eight-year dictatorship-by-royal-decree had begun to change rapidly in 1931 with the overthrow of the monarchy and the establishment of the Democratic Republic of Workers. [5] As a student of revolutions

---

[4] *Hemingway's speech: ibid.,* pp. 69–73.

[5] The period covered was September 16, 1923, through the election of April 12, 1931. This was roughly the period of Hemingway's closest association with Spain and the Spanish, until the Civil War. The Democratic Republic was established April 14, 1931, with a new flag of red, yellow, and purple—irreverently described by Pilar and others as "blood, pus, and permanganate" (*FWBT*, p. 66).

who had watched, with an artist's eye, the development and decline of the troubles in Cuba during the early nineteen-thirties,
he had regretted not being on hand for the events which took place
in Spain during April and May of 1931, though he was in Spain
that summer and learned from his friends what had happened. As
an American and as a Catholic convert of some years' standing,
he had in general approved the separation of the Church and the
State achieved by the Democratic Republic, though he had naturally deplored the anti-clerical riotings which preceded it.[6] He had
welcomed in principal, if not in all details, the extensive program
of long-overdue reforms, covering nearly every aspect of Spanish
civil life, which was instituted by the same government.

He was in Africa when the conservative reaction—largely the
work of the landed aristocracy, the Army, and the Church—
countermanded many of the reforms accomplished in the Cortes
between the spring of 1931 and the spring of 1933.[7] In Spain
before the African trip he had gone shooting in Estremadura with
Luis Quintanilla, an ardent Republican who was later jailed by
the conservatives for his political activities.[8] At the same time
Hemingway had been embarrassed by a newspaper article which
called him "the friend of Spain" in bold capitals. The country, he
pointed out, was split wide open, and was "inhabited by too many
politicians for any man to be a friend to all of it with impunity."
Under the Republic, he saw, the country was more prosperous;
more money was coming in from taxes. But the peasants, like
some he had recently seen in Estremadura, were still the forgotten
men. Despite the newfound evidences of prosperity it was clear to
Hemingway that much of the money was going where it had always gone—into the pockets of those in power. The aims of the
Republic were just and sound, but the "great new bureaucracy"

[6] *Anticlerical riots:* In Madrid on May 12, 1931, mobs burned churches
and convents. At this time also anticlerical activity was widespread in
other Spanish cities. Martial law was proclaimed. This is the period referred to by the guerrillas in the novel as "the start of the movement."

[7] *Conservative reaction:* General election of November 19, 1933.

[8] Quintanilla, the Republican artist (born 1905) who painted Hemingway's portrait. Dos Passos and Hemingway jointly sponsored an exhibition
of Quintanilla's excellent work in New York City, November 20 to December 4, 1934. See Hemingway's article, *Esquire* 3 (February 1935), pp.
26–27.

was not, strictly speaking, selflessly devoted to the welfare of Spain. "Politics," said Hemingway, "is still a lucrative profession." To the ironist, the rise of Spain's new bureaucracy made the spectacle of Spanish government "more comic than tragic." To the friend of Democratic Spain, however, the comedy did not seem like something that would last. "The tragedy," said Hemingway, "is very close." [9]

The first act of the Spanish tragedy was in fact only a month off when Hemingway made his prediction. The failure of Spain in 1933 to extend the revolution of 1931 came about, he afterwards observed, because "the mass of the people were not ready for it and they did not want it." As late as 1937, the leftist Joseph Freeman could corroborate Hemingway's earlier view. One must face the issue frankly, Freeman told the Writer's Congress: "The majority of the Spanish people" did not even then "want socialism." They were fighting for "a democratic republic." [10] What made the events of the autumn of 1933 tragic in their results was the degree to which socialism had infiltrated the republican bureaucracy, and fascist thinking the minds of the reactionary army officers. The tragedy was launched in Spain.

Between 1933 and 1936, while Hemingway watched with care, the second act of the tragedy built up. Conservative elements formed a strong anti-Marxist alliance. The restive reform groups, including both moderates and extremists, banded together in a Popular Front organization, precipitating the bloody and desperate general strike of October 1934, which further widened the gap between the workers and the conservative groups. But when the 1936 elections produced a decisive Republican majority, the long-frustrated reformers moved rapidly to enforce the terms of their program. Further civil disorders followed. In March, the Army threatened to seize the government if order were not restored. In April the government countered with a thorough shake-up of the Army command, including the exile of some of the more dangerous general officers who showed Hitlerite ambi-

[9] "Friend of Spain": See Hemingway's letter of that title, *Esquire* 1 (January 1934), pp. 26, 136. Cf. Hemingway's remark that "Spain is an open wound in the right arm that cannot heal because the dust gets in it." *Gattorno*, foreword, Havana, 1935, p. 12.

[10] Joseph Freeman in *The Writer in a Changing World*, p. 237.

tions. But the efforts of the Popular Front, which was torn by internal dissensions, were neither strong nor extensive enough. On July 17, 1936, insurrections of army garrisons began all over Spain. Despite reprisal action and the immediate mobilization of a Loyalist militia, Mola and Franco moved quickly and according to a carefully prepared plan. The third act of the Spanish tragedy burst out in civil war.

To Hemingway, who had watched and commented on Acts One and Two, Act Three was no surprise. He had heard talk of the next European war in the Montparnasse cafés in the fall of 1933, and had been distressed, as any old soldier must be, by the widespread assumption that it was inevitable. In the summer of 1935 he had stated forthrightly that a war was "being prepared and brought closer each day with all the premeditation of a long-planned murder." This veteran correspondent knew that Europe had always fought; the intervals of peace were only armistices. Hitler's desire for war in Europe was obvious. Although Mussolini, Hemingway's old enemy through the 1920's, was not especially anxious for a war in Europe, he was very busy making Ethiopia "fit for Fiats." The general war, said Hemingway, would not come in 1935 or 1936, but in 1937 or 1938, "they [would] fight." He did not foresee, publicly at least, that Spain would become a sort of international testing-ground for Germany, Italy, and Russia before the Spanish Civil War was a year old. Otherwise, in selecting 1937 as a possible date for the outbreak of a war involving several European nations (which of course happened in Spain) he had made a fairly sound prediction.[11]

He began the year 1936 with a condemnation of the Ethiopian campaign, calling Mussolini "the cleverest opportunist in modern history," and noting that while the sons of the dictator were aviators in action against a non-existent Ethiopian air-force, the poor men's sons of Italy were dying as foot-soldiers. When would the poor men's sons learn who their real enemy was, and why? Hemingway had always regarded Mussolini, said Dean Gauss, as "a fakir and a grandstand player." The march on Rome in 1922 had

[11] See Hemingway, "A Paris Letter," *Esquire* 1 (February 1934), pp. 72, 156; "Notes on the Next War," *Esquire* 4 (September 1935), pp. 19, 156; and "The Malady of Power," *Esquire* 4 (November 1935), pp. 31, 198.

been possible owing to the "wave of disgust," Hemingway said, which "followed the farcical failure of the Italian radicals to co-operate." [12] But for a good many years now the Italian situation had been anything but a farce, and the grandstand player, though still a fakir, was also a dangerous force. Hemingway could not foresee that within a year of his public condemnation of Mussolini's activities in Ethiopia, the opportunist Mussolini would be moving his legions into Spain. Still less could he foretell the feelings with which former Tenente Ernesto Hemingway, ambulance driver, would walk through the scrub oak woods of Brihuega in the spring of 1937, inspecting the bodies of the poor men's sons who had died in the name of their real enemy, Il Duce.[13]

Hemingway's temperamental and long-term distrust of all behind-the-scenes "deals" and "arrangements" in Europe found ample evidence to support it among the Italian dead at Brihuega. The world was not run as the statesmen said it was run; one had to be able to distinguish between the poor players and the true owners. The "starry-eyed" of all countries, not to mention the conscripted sons of the Italian poor who would never see any more stars or anything else, were more than likely to be "sucked in." Both these phrases came frequently to Hemingway's mind whenever he wrote about European politics.

Why, then, did he bother with a country which was torn with "deals" and "arrangements"? Hemingway's view was forthright. "There were at least five parties in the Spanish Civil War on the Republic side. I tried to understand and evaluate all five (very difficult) and belonged to none. . . . I had no party but a deep interest in and love for the Republic. . . . In Spain I had, and have, many friends on the other side. I tried to write truly about them, too. Politically, I was always on the side of the Republic from the day it was declared and for a long time before." [14] When the Civil War broke out, it was necessary for him to make a choice of proper action.

[12] *Ethiopian Campaign:* See Hemingway, "Wings Always Over Africa," *Esquire* 5 (January 1936), pp. 31, 174–175. CG to CB, 12/26/50.
[13] See the reprinting of EH's NANA despatch in *New Republic* 90 (May 5, 1937), pp. 376–379. The crushing defeat of Mussolini's troops occurred in the period of March 11–23, 1937.
[14] EH to CB, 4/1/51.

II. THE BIG STAGE

He soon made up his mind, though not without some of the qualms which usually attend the realist in reaching such decisions. By the end of 1936 he had helped raise substantial funds for equipping the Loyalists with ambulances and medical supplies. In January 1937 he became chairman of the Ambulance Committee, Medical Bureau, American Friends of Spanish Democracy. The name of the organization fairly described Hemingway's position and the reasons behind it.

Once you are fighting a war, as he said in 1942, you have no choice but to try to win it.[15] On this principle, he worked hard for the Loyalists, among whom were many native Spaniards who shared his interest in and love for the Republic, whatever their buried feelings about the foreign communists who were moving into Madrid to join the war against the fascist aggressors, native and foreign. From the money-raising activities of 1936 through the end of the war in 1939, he was either in Spain, or working for the Republic outside Spain, or writing about the course of the conflict. His labors took him into the heart of the war on four separate occasions.[16]

His first trip began on February 27, 1937, when he sailed on the *Paris* to report the war for the North American Newspaper Alliance. From Toulouse in mid-March he flew south to Barcelona. From there a plane carried him down the east coast, over the yellow sprawl of Valencia far below, and into the airfield at Alicante, where he found the Loyalists in a holiday mood over the recent defeat of the Italians at Brihuega.

When Hemingway reached the battlefield, getting up at dawn of a late March morning and driving up from Madrid, the Italian dead still lay where they had fallen. As an objective reporter, he was compelled to conclude that, whatever his own low opinion of Mussolini, and whatever Loyalist propaganda might say to the

---

[15] *Men At War*, introd., p. xi.

[16] *Four trips to Spain:* Besides the newspaper reports of Hemingway's arrivals and departures as listed in *New York Times Index* for these years, see the further reprintings of NANA despatches in the *New Republic:* Vols. 93 (January 12, 1938), pp. 273–276; 94 (April 27, 1938), pp. 350–351; and 95 (June 8, 1938), pp. 124–126.

contrary, the Italian poor men's sons had died bravely, the victims of superior fire-power, strong air attacks, and inadequate protection from the rocky terrain. These dead did not look to an objective observer like fascist devils cowering in death before the Marxist angels of destruction. They were men who had been killed. They were another example of *Los Desastres de la Guerra*. One more of Europe's intermittent periods of armistice had ended and these were among the victims.

As a friend to the Spanish Republic, Hemingway was ready to help with the development of a documentary film, *The Spanish Earth*.[17] During April and early May he joined the young Dutch director, Joris Ivens, and his cameraman, John Ferno, working in and near besieged Madrid. Wearing a Basque beret, windbreaker, and heavy field boots, the American guide made a picturesque figure. The film-makers had set up an observation post only ten minutes' walk away, and they watched Miaja's Loyalist strikes in the depression below the city, or photographed the mangled bodies of the Madrileños in the streets and squares where Rebel artillery had permanently interrupted their civilian lives. Like every other Loyalist sympathizer who saw the results, Hemingway resented the totalitarian tactics of murdering non-participant citizenry with high explosives. The Rebels, as he told the Writers' Congress in

[17] *The Spanish Earth:* 1000 copies of the sound-film text (it was exhibited in silent form, with spoken commentary by Ivens, at the Writers' Congress) were published in Cleveland, Ohio (J. B. Savage Company, June 1938). The 60-page book contains an emotional and somewhat inaccurate introduction by Jasper Wood and decorations by Frederick K. Russell. Besides the introduction, the text consists entirely of a transcript of Hemingway's sound-track commentary, and "The Heat and the Cold," a short reminiscence of experiences in Spain during the filming, written by Hemingway and reprinted from *Verve* (Spring 1938). The film was undertaken in aid of the people of Spain by an organization called *Contemporary Historians,* including John Dos Passos, Lillian Hellman, Archibald MacLeish, and Ernest Hemingway. All of these had early recognized the threat of fascism to the free world. The film itself was designed to show the efforts of the Spanish peasantry to reclaim for agricultural purposes land which had been misused and neglected for many generations. Because of the war, their efforts were defeated and they were betrayed. The film's six-reel message could be summed up in the directive: get rid of war. The film seeks dramatic focus by recounting in part the experiences of a young Spaniard named Julian who comes from the village of Fuenteduena.

June, had been beaten in every major engagement up to that date; what they could not win in the military way, they sought to win by the mass-murder of civilian populations.

Often, at considerable personal risk, Ivens, Ferno, and Hemingway moved out into the hills of Morata de Tajuña to get pictures of tanks and infantry in action. Ivens and Ferno sometimes distressed their companion by unrealistically exposing themselves to enemy fire. Hemingway cabled MacLeish that there was some doubt about Ivens' survival because he was taking the daily risks of a regular infantry officer. In his turn, Hemingway distressed his companions by carrying strong Spanish onions in the pockets of his field-jacket as a means of assuaging hunger. For battle-thirst, the trio carried a large flat silver flask of whiskey. It was always empty by four in the afternoon until they discovered the wisdom of bringing along an auxiliary bottle.

In 1940, looking back on this spring of 1937, Hemingway said that "the period of fighting when we thought that the Republic could win was the happiest period of our lives." For the duration of that war, except for writing his play, he contented himself with NANA despatches, a few short stories, and the brief script of *The Spanish Earth*.[18] He might have agreed, if confronted with it, to the sentiments of Philip Freneau's couplet:

> An age employed in edging steel
> Can no poetic raptures feel.[19]

Poetic raptures in Freneau's sense of the phrase had never much engaged Hemingway. But during the long armistice between his discharge from the Italian base-hospital and the outbreak of new hostilities in Europe, he had felt justified in learning to write and in continuing to mind it as his proper business. Having served

[18] See "The Heat and the Cold" reference in note 17, and also the remarks by A. MacLeish, *The Writer in a Changing World*, p. 206. Ivens had left the U.S. December 26, 1936, and was in and near Madrid from January 1, 1937, until early May. See also Hemingway's preface to Gustav Regler, *The Great Crusade*, New York, 1940, p. viii.

A brief glimpse of Hemingway in Spain is provided by Constancia de la Mora, *In Place of Splendor*, New York, 1939, p. 290. See also the vignette in Stephen Spender, *World Within World*, New York, 1951, pp. 229–231.

[19] Philip Freneau, "To an Author" (1788), lines 35–36.

time "for society, democracy, and the other things quite young," he had felt no compulsion to enlist in the French Foreign Legion or to aid the Chinese in throwing back the Japanese invaders. His clear responsibility, as he saw it, was to the art of writing well, and he willingly exchanged the "pleasant, comforting stench of comrades" for the job of the individualist artist who must work alone if he is to get his work done.[20]

Now, however, he reversed the procedure, declining further writing until the war could be won and the fascist menace—with its enmity towards all honest writers—could be reduced in scale. It was a reasonably happy period for him because it was something like the old times in Italy along the lower Piave where he had served nearly twenty years earlier. The stench of brave comrades was as pleasant and comforting in the spring of 1937 as it had been in the spring of 1918. The cause was at least as good and possibly better. There was also the reasonable expectation that if one survived, with all that he had learned about the art of writing during the long armistice, he had a chance of writing a book about this war which would be better than any of the earlier books.

Though politics had brought the war on, it had little to do with the comradeship among the Loyalist soldiers in whose company Hemingway now moved. They were of all political persuasions from militant Comintern communism to the point around the center where—as artist, American, semi-detached observer, student of war, and unpartied supporter of the Spanish Republic—Hemingway stood. The Eleventh and Twelfth Brigades (really the First and Second) were his chief centers of operation. The Eleventh was German. Though they were ardent anti-Nazis and had a remarkable commander named Hans, "most of them were communists" and "they were a little serious to spend much time with." Hemingway's Republican heart was with the Twelfth Brigade, a very mixed group politically, a memorably gay assemblage as comrades. One staunch friend was Werner Heilbrun, the medical officer of the outfit. He could always provide transport, good cheer, or a hot meal at night for the dusty and famished wayfarers. Heilbrun was killed in a strafing attack at Huesca soon after the Carnegie Hall speech, and Hemingway donated to his widow the

[20] *GHOA,* p. 148.

proceeds from the printed version of *The Spanish Earth*. Another friend was Gustav Regler, calm, cheerful, tough, and one of the ablest fighting officers in the brigade. His novel, *The Great Crusade*, was published in the United States in 1940, translated by Whittaker Chambers and Barrows Mussey, and with a preface by Hemingway. The commander of the Twelfth, General Lucasz, was one of Hemingway's good friends, and a good gay man at their party of May 1, playing a tune on a pencil held against his teeth. A month later, Lucasz, too, was dead.[21]

By May 19, Hemingway was back in the United States. Between this date and his departure again on August 14 he was extremely busy. He had accepted an invitation to speak before the general assembly of the forthcoming Writers' Congress. With this out of the way he prepared the sound-track for *The Spanish Earth*, working with Ivens throughout. By July 8, the film was ready and that evening, on invitation from the White House, Ivens and Hemingway showed the film to President and Mrs. Roosevelt. Later showings brought thousands of dollars in voluntary contributions to Loyalist Spain, and the public release came in New York in August. The brawl with Max Eastman on August 11 in the office of Maxwell Perkins was a comic interlude.[22] Three days later Hemingway sailed back to the tragedy.

On this second visit (August 14, 1937–January 28, 1938) he found that the third act of the tragedy had moved well along. "Où sont les amis d'antan?" he might now have asked himself, except that he already knew. Lucasz and Heilbrun were dead and buried; Regler, wounded by a pound and a half of steel which un-

[21] Hemingway's preface to Regler, *Great Crusade*, pp. vii–x.

[22] For a dispassionate account of what happened in the office of Maxwell Perkins on the fifth floor at 597 Fifth Avenue on August 11, 1937, see the *New York Times* for August 14 (p. 15), August 15 (p. 31), and August 16 (p. 21). Of comic interest is an item in the catalogue of the House of Books, Ltd., *First Editions of Modern Authors with a Notable Hemingway Collection*, New York, n.d., p. 40. A copy of Max Eastman's *Art and the Life of Action*, New York, 1934, is there offered for $75. According to the note, this damaged copy (lacking pp. 7–84) shows on p. 95 a spot caused by contact "with Mr. Eastman's nose when Mr. Hemingway struck him with it in a gesture of disapproval of the critical essay 'Bull in the Afternoon.' " In the lower right hand corner is a presentation inscription in Hemingway's hand, "For Arnold [Gingrich] from Papa [Hemingway]," witnessed by the signature of Maxwell Perkins, August 12, 1937.

covered his kidneys and exposed the spinal cord, lived to be put in a French concentration camp after the Spanish war was over. Madrid itself, "the capital of the world," was a tangle of bitter and cynical intrigue. If the winter and spring of 1937 had been the golden age of the International Brigades, now was the winter of their discontent.

This second trip produced *The Fifth Column*. Despite its historical interest, it is a bad play. Written in the Hotel Florida in a dollar-a-day room (low price: high danger) exposed to the German batteries on Garabitas Hill, the play was completed and sent out of the country late in December 1937, just before the taking of Teruel. It sought to present Hemingway's tough-minded apprehension of the state of things in Madrid that fall. Civilians were dying in the daily bombardments, food was becoming scarcer, hopes of lifting the siege were growing dim, and the malignant growth of treason operated deep in the city. By comparison and in retrospect, the spring of 1937 had been gay.

Whatever its dramatic shortcomings, *The Fifth Column* was an attempt to draw the actual Madrid of the fall of 1937 as it might have appeared in the uncensored despatches of a very objective war correspondent. Like the film, the play showed that war is hell. Unlike the film, the play showed that at some level and out of necessity, war is waged by demons. Though still nominally sympathetic to the Republic, *The Fifth Column* could hardly be described as a vehicle for Loyalist propaganda. When he published it in 1938 (before the end of the war), Hemingway answered those "fanatical defenders of the Spanish Republic" who protested that his play did not sufficiently emphasize "the nobility and dignity of the Spanish people." This was a play about the regrettable necessity of fanaticism. It was not intended to show nobility and dignity. To present any adequate idea of the complex Spanish temperament or the even more complex Spanish predicament would require many plays and many novels. *The Fifth Column*, meanwhile, was in the nature of an on-the-spot report, and a prediction of things to come. Hemingway did not pretend that it was much more than that.[23]

[23] See Hemingway's preface to *First 49*, New York, 1938, for a short account of the composition of the play and of the author's views on his

The background action of *The Fifth Column* is, in the play,
what it was in the cellars of Madrid in 1937, a cloak-and-pistol,
spy-and-counter-spy struggle of the most ruthless and melodra-
matic kind. In the foreground of the play, however, are two of
Hemingway's familiar oppositions: home against war, and the
lover against the lonely and essentially womanless worker. The
hero is an Anglo-American soldier of fortune named Philip Rawlings. Ostensibly a blasé war-correspondent more given to playboy-
ing than to workhorsing, he is secretly a Republican agent in the
fight against fascist infiltration. Though his job sometimes nause-
ates him, he believes that he understands its importance. He performs creditably and coldly. His human sensibilities are stirred,
however, by an American named Dorothy Bridges. While she
plays at being a war-correspondent, she too has secret plans: to
marry Philip. One might construe her name as a pun. She bridges
the gap back to the past, the years before fascism turned imperialistic, and when man's inhumanity to man was at least somewhat
less spectacular than at present. "Her name," says Hemingway,
"might also have been Nostalgia."

Philip's choice is between home and war—leaving Madrid with
the girl or continuing to fight fascism. "If the play has a moral,"
writes Hemingway, "it is that people who work for certain organizations have very little time for home life." Without concurring
in the politics or G.P.U. methods of the organization he serves
(and he resembles Robert Jordan in that respect), Philip chooses
to stay on in Madrid. In the closing scene he sums up the kind of
life he might conceivably live with Dorothy Bridges:

"A thousand breakfasts . . . on trays in the thousand fine
mornings of the next three years. . . . Auteuil steeplechasing
. . . and nip back into the bar for a champagne cocktail and ride
back in to dinner at La Rue's and weekends go to shoot pheasants
in the Sologne. . . . And fly out to Nairobi and the old Ma-

---

material. "While I was writing the play," he says (p. v), "the Hotel Florida . . . was struck by more than thirty high explosive shells. So if it is
not a good play perhaps that is what is the matter with it." His view of the
play in November 1951 was that it is probably the most unsatisfactory thing
he ever wrote. After much bad luck and several false starts, the play was
adapted by Benjamin Glaser and produced by the Theatre Guild in New
York in the winter of 1940.

thaiga Club . . . [or] . . . to Lamu where the long white beach is, with the dhows beached on their sides, and the wind in the palms at night. . . . Or . . . Malindi where you can surfboard on the beach . . . [or] the Sans Souci in Havana . . . to dance in the Patio. . . ."

Sans-Souci is the word for it. Dorothy wants to know why they can't visit these places together. But they are all behind Philip like a distant past. "Where I go now I go alone, or with others who go there for the same reason I go." This is the region of man at work, man without woman. Rawlings, soldier of fortune, has given up the pursuit of happiness for the pursuit of enemies of liberty. "We're in for fifty years of undeclared wars," he tells Comrade Max, "and I've signed up for the duration."

Hemingway is not, of course, to be confused with Rawlings. As an artist whose books had been banned in Fascist Italy, and as the friend of many honest Spaniards who had suffered heavily in trying to inaugurate and consolidate the Republic, he had personal reasons for hating fascism. Russian-style communism was scarcely better, though friends of the Spanish Republic, once the war broke out, had no choice but to work with this wing of the popular front coalition. But the writer's problem was different from that of Philip Rawlings. Whatever happened to soldiers of fortune during a half-century of undeclared wars, Hemingway's obligation was still to tell the truth as he saw it.

To learn the truth he made two more extended visits to Spain. The third trip began on March 18, 1938. When he returned for the summer on May 30, he told American reporters that the Loyalists would win, though they were now clearly on the defensive. Privately, however, he must have known that they were doomed. Too much of Spain had fallen to Franco and company. Too many foreign powers were pouring in men and material on the wrong side. Fifth columns were at work in major cities. The Madrileños were starving. By far the gloomiest trip of all was the fourth, beginning August 31. That winter saw the collapse. Barcelona fell late in January, and Madrid followed at the end of March.

One had no feeling of tragic catharsis when the curtain came down on Act III of Spain's tragedy. You could already hear them shifting the scenery in preparation for the gigantic epilogue.

III. PARTISAN

The publication of *For Whom the Bell Tolls* on October 21, 1940, raised again (as Freeman had raised it in 1937) the question of Hemingway's political colors. Once more, as in the 1930's, certain critics failed to take his position as artist sufficiently into account. Mr. Edmund Wilson, for example, referred (quite erroneously) to Hemingway's "Stalinism." Hemingway flatly denied the allegation: "I had no Stalinist period." To Mr. Edwin Burgum, on the other hand, *For Whom the Bell Tolls* seemed to offer evidence that Hemingway was a fascist in spite of himself. Such claims stood at the extremes.[24]

One of the editors of *Time* magazine hailed the story of Robert Jordan as the work of a great and sensitive artist who had now safely recovered from the Red rash.[25] In spite of the compliment at the beginning of the sentence, it ended with a statement which still misrepresented Hemingway's position. He had never caught the Marxist measles. His devotion to truth in art was too effective a means of self-immunization. He knew that to propagandize is to lie, and that the complications which accompany lying may turn a simple rash to a fatal disease. He was immunized, so to speak, by esthetic principle, even if he had not been immunized by lengthy study of the European scene.

He had long since declared against the writer's making a career of politics. But to describe the effect of political forces on the individual life was quite another matter. Where the finger or the fist of power brings pressure on the human being, the artist may

[24] For Mr. Wilson's reference to Hemingway's "Stalinism" see McCaffery, *Ernest Hemingway: The Man and His Work*, p. 256. Hemingway has, it is alleged, "largely sloughed off his Stalinism" and reverted "to seeing events in terms of individuals pitted against specific odds." Hemingway denied the implication, EH to CB, 4/1/51. Burgum's essay is in McCaffery, pp. 308–328, and is generally inaccurate. Among the pejorative judgments on *FWBT* is Alfred Kazin's. He calls this novel "among the least of Hemingway's works." McCaffery, p. 202. Maxwell Geismar said of *FWBT* that it "remains inchoate in its comprehension of the central social issues of our time." McCaffery, p. 186. Malcolm Cowley, on the other hand, agreed with the judgment of the present writer that *FWBT* is Hemingway's best novel.

[25] *Time* 36 (October 21, 1940), p. 95.

legitimately move to his work. This was the situation with the old man at a bridge across the Ebro on Easter Sunday 1938. In his lone retreat from San Carlos, this old Spaniard had been obliged to abandon a cat, two goats, and eight pigeons. He was concerned for their welfare.

"What politics have you?" asked Hemingway.

"I am without politics," said the Spaniard. "I am seventy-six years old. I have come twelve kilometres now and I think I can go no further."

Because of the weather, the fascist air force was neither bombing nor strafing that day. This fact, together with the probability that the abandoned cat, at least, could look out for itself, was the grand total of the old man's Easter luck.[26]

One displaced person in the spring of 1938 helped to dramatize for Hemingway the artist the predicament of the Spanish people. About the first of March 1939 he began to write his great novel on the predicament of the Spanish people during their Civil War. He chose as his focal point a group of Republican partisans, drawn from many parts of Spain, and living under very primitive conditions in a cave on the high forested slopes of the Sierra de Guadarramas sixty miles northwest of besieged Madrid and behind the fascist lines. The time he chose was the sixty-eight-hour period between Saturday afternoon and Tuesday noon of the last week of May 1937. He worked on the book steadily for a period of eighteen months, rewriting it every day and doing the final revisions on galley proof. When his labors were over he had written the great book about the Spanish Civil War. One could not call it a book "without politics." Yet it was important to point out that the politics had been dramatically embodied in a work of fiction whose moral values transcended political affiliations.[27]

[26] *First 49*, p. 177. Mr. Kazin suggests, quite rightly, that "it was in something of this spirit" (*i.e.* of "Old Man at the Bridge") that Hemingway wrote *FWBT*.

[27] Hemingway's progress with his novel may be summarized for the record. By March 25, 1939, he had done about 15,000 words. On May 10, he was still going well, averaging 700–1000 words daily. At this time he reiterated to Perkins that the thing to do with a novel was to finish it, as the thing to do with a war was to win it. By July 10, his MS stood at 56,000 words (14 chapters); and by July 26, 64,000. He spent the summer in the west, working steadily, and by October 27 had 90,000 words. He

The driving emotion behind *For Whom the Bell Tolls* is Hemingway's sense of the betrayal of the Spanish people. Not only were they "killed in vast numbers, starved out, deprived of weapon's" but they were also "betrayed." [28] Worst of all was the betrayal. In a decade of notable betrayals the events in Spain between 1936 and 1939 dwarfed the betrayals of the Abyssinians and the Czechs. The nature of the betrayal of the Spanish people was complex in the extreme. What had chiefly caused it—internal cancer or rape by international hoodlums? The intervention of foreign powers was clearly an important factor in the prolongation of the war and the ultimate fascist victory. The wanton destruction of Guernica—an excellent example of betrayal—was evidently undertaken as a test of German bombing equipment. Hemingway's *Spanish Earth* commentary was quite possibly correct in maintaining that the Army insurrection which opened the war could have been put down in six weeks if German and Italian aid had not been made available to Franco's professionals.

Hemingway's own perspective on the fascist-communist struggle, which had been going on sporadically throughout Europe since the close of World War I, might have indicated a kind of

---

now told Perkins that the book was designed to contain what people with party affiliations could never write, or even perhaps know, or (if they knew) allow themselves to think. He was then on the point of writing a "part about Madrid" (possibly the present Chapter 18, where Madrid material is inserted as a flashback).

Chapter 23 was finished on January 18, 1940, in Havana. About this time he told Perkins that while under arms he was faithful and loyal to his side, but that, once a war was over, he was a writer—not a Catholic writer or a Party writer or anything but a writer. February 18 found him in the midst of the El Sordo story (Chapter 27). By April 6 he was well into Chapter 33, and thought briefly of *The Undiscovered Country* as a title. By April 22, however, he had settled on *For Whom the Bell Tolls* (Donne's devotion, located in *The Oxford Book of English Prose*, p. 171).

Late in May the end was in sight. He finished Chapter 40 on May 21 and ten days later was in the midst of Chapter 42. Between early June and July 12 he finished Chapter 43 (the last) and worked through his manuscript. For the next two weeks, as copy began to go to the printer, he continued reworking, chapter by chapter. The book was in galley proof by August 13. On September 10, he air-mailed the final 18 galleys from Sun Valley, Idaho, to New York. The total time for writing and revision was thus almost exactly eighteen months.

[28] Hemingway's preface to Regler, *Great Crusade*, p. vii.

tragic inevitability to foreign intervention in Spain's internal troubles. Yet these troubles had been serious before the foreign powers moved in, as Hemingway had duly noted in 1933. The outbreak of the war did not suddenly make an efficient machine from a somewhat inefficient and internally divided republican bureaucracy. Nor was it likely that the native Spanish conservatives would reject the advances of their foreign allies. Any genuinely true picture of the Spanish struggle would need somehow to embody all of these considerations, and to bring them to dramatic focus in the lives of a group of people whose backgrounds and present mode of behavior would fairly represent the total betrayal of Spain.

As he worked through the complexities of his task, Hemingway was sustained by a belief he had long held to: the job of the artist is not to judge but to understand. No matter how hard it may be to believe it in our political age, there is such a thing as the artistic "neutrality" of one who puts humanity above politics and art above propaganda. What Melville said of Captain Vere, the hero of *Billy Budd,* is applicable to the artist Hemingway. "There had got to be established in him some positive convictions which . . . would abide in him essentially unmodified so long as his intelligent part remained unimpaired. . . . His settled convictions were as a dyke against those invading waters of novel opinion, social, political, or otherwise, which carried away as in a torrent no few minds in those days." [29] Hemingway's "dyke" is a belief in the artist's obligation to truth and to art, and to humanity in its extra-political dimension.

For Whom the Bell Tolls offers many examples of the author's determination to maintain that balance without which art may degenerate into propaganda. One of the most conspicuous is Pilar's account of the massacre of the leading citizens of a town near Avila by Pablo and his mob. Pilar has the artist's observational and almost clinical interest in how each of the fascists will die. Deeper than this interest runs her sense of the humanity of the killed and the strange furious mixture of bestiality and humanity among the killers. She watches the spectacle with a cold fascination. But her humanity is revealed in the sick disgust which

[29] Melville, *Billy Budd, Foretopman,* Chapter 6.

assails her from time to time, as it troubles some of the individuals in the mob itself. One finds explicit recognition of how far out of the line of right human action this mob-murder is. But there is also a strong implicit suggestion of the criminal neglect, the inhuman apathy which has allowed the social situation in the villages of Spain to deteriorate so far that such mob action is now the sole recourse of the underdogs. After the massacre, says Pilar, "I went back inside the room and I sat there and I did not wish to think, for that was the worst day of my life until one other day." The "other day" was the day of reckoning. It came seventy-two hours later when the Fascists took the town.[30]

Pilar has led a hard life and is as tough as an old eagle. Yet the heart still beats for humankind even when the head coldly admits the need for violent activity against the enemy. Pilar's sentiments find many echoes among the more sympathetic characters of the novel. When they are put together, they show clearly that, unlike Picasso's "Guernica," *For Whom the Bell Tolls* is not a study in black and white. It is a study of the betrayal of the Spanish people—both by what lay within them and what had been thrust upon them—and it is presented with that special combination of sympathetic involvement and hard-headed detachment which is the mark of the genuine artist. One could not rightly call the novel bipartisan. Yet it is partisan in a larger way than the modern use of the term ordinarily suggests. Its partisanship is in the cause of humanity.

The artist behind his dyke of conviction must likewise be able to understand the nature of these minds which the torrent of opinion carries along in its sweep. Hemingway's grasp of the motivations which strengthened and united, but also split, the extreme leftists is well illustrated in Jordan's contrast between the two communisms of Madrid.[31] One was symbolized in Velázquez 63, the palace which served as headquarters for the International Brigades. Here was the almost puritanical, religious-crusader's side of party feeling. It gave its adherents something like "the feeling you expected to have and did not have when you made your

---

[30] Pilar's account of the massacre occurs on pp. 99–129.

[31] *FWBT*, pp. 234–235. Cf. Jordan's view (p. 230): "He liked to know how it really was, not how it was supposed to be."

first communion. . . . It gave you a part in something that you could believe in wholly and completely and in which you felt an absolute brotherhood with the others who were engaged in it." The religious reference emphasizes how far this secular substitute for religion—a substitute with its own propaganda-built hagiology and its own liturgy—had been able to go in capturing the devotions of foreign idealists.

Six months of the fighting effectively dissipated such devotions for any who kept their eyes and ears open. The idealist involved was shortly aware of the other symbol—the hotel called Gaylord's where the Russian directors of the Republican movement had congregated. Gaylord's symbolized the cold, practical, hardheaded, cynical ruthlessness of the Comintern mind, completely unsentimental and in no way deceived by the propaganda which it daily originated and disseminated. A part of the struggle in Spain lay in the attempt of the idealist to keep his devoutness whole in the face of the actualistic education he got at Gaylord's.

Another of the tensions at work under the surface of Spain's tragedy is dramatized through the boy Joaquín, one of the republican partisans on El Sordo's chancre-like hilltop. This is the conflict between the Catholic faith and the secular pseudo-religion of the communists. At eighteen, Joaquín is just old enough in 1937 to have been raised under the wing of the Church, and just young enough to have suffered irreparably when the fascists shot his parents in Valladolid. Joaquín is imbued now with party doctrine. He especially reverences La Pasionaria, the secularist Joan of Arc in Marxist Spain.

While El Sordo's men prepare their hilltop position, Joaquín admiringly quotes La Pasionaria's slogan: *Resistir y fortificar es vencer*—to hold out and to fortify is to win. The boy is obliged to endure some good-natured raillery from those of his companions to whom such propagandist watchwords are a dirty joke. Yet through the early stages of the fight on the hilltop La Pasionaria sustains him well. Then the planes come. Joaquín has not considered the vulnerability of even Pasionaria-built fortifications to attack from the air. While the drone of the fascist bombers grows in intensity, Joaquín, heavy with dread, begins to invoke

La Pasionaria once again. This time her words stick in his dry throat.

Then he shifted suddenly into "Hail Mary, full of grace, the Lord is with thee; Blessed art thou among women and Blessed is the fruit of thy womb, Jesus. Holy Mary, Mother of God, pray for us sinners now and at the hour of our death. Amen, Holy Mary, Mother of God," he started, then he remembered quick as the roar came now unbearably and started an act of contrition racing in it, "Oh my God, I am heartily sorry for having offended thee who art worthy of all my love. . . ."

When the explosions of the fascist bombs roll under the boy at the very moment of his losing consciousness, he is still repeating the petitional phrase, "Now and at the hour of our death." La Pasionaria is for other times.[32]

La Pasionaria is for bringing passionately inspired news of Marxist victories. She is the occasion for a fine travesty on senti-mental propagandists like the *Izvestia* correspondent at Gaylord's hotel.

"She was here with the news and was in such a state of radiant exultation as I have never seen. The truth of the news shone from her face. That great face . . ." says the correspondent happily. . . . "It was one of the greatest moments of the war to me when I heard the report in that great voice where pity, compassion and truth are blended. Goodness and truth shine from her as from a true saint of the people. Not for nothing is she called La Pasion-aria."

"Not for nothing," says the other correspondent in a dull voice. "You better write it for *Izvestia* now, before you forget that last beautiful lead." [33]

In the welter of opposed hatreds and in the company of senti-mental mystics, the artist must keep his human and moral values unimpaired. Of the native Spaniards in the book, none better exemplifies the right human norm than Anselmo, Jordan's sixty-eight-year-old guide and friend. Other members of Pablo's band show the range of political and moral attitudes across the popular

[32] *FWBT*, p. 134.
[33] *FWBT*, pp. 357–358.

front. At one extreme is the blood-thirst of Pablo, not unlike that of the moonfaced Cuban revolutionist in *To Have and Have Not*. Near him, though at a higher level, stands the brave, relentless, fanatical hater, Agustín, who fiercely says that he would like to swim ten leagues in a broth made from the *cojones* of all the fascists.[34] At the opposite extreme stands, or rather lolls, the irresponsible paganism of the gypsy Rafael. But Anselmo willingly endures discomfort out of loyalty to Jordan's trust, as Rafael would obviously never do. And unlike Pablo or Agustín, Anselmo, with the wisdom of his years, still hates killing even while he admits that it is necessary.

Anselmo's important function is to serve as a yardstick of human values, as Kent does in *King Lear*. "That we should win the war and shoot nobody," he fiercely cries. "That we should govern justly and that all should participate in the benefits according as they have striven for them. And that those who have fought against us should be educated to see their error." The Republic must win and Anselmo will fight for the Republic. Yet much that he must do cuts cruelly across the absolute Christian grain of this admirable old man. With Anselmo as a norm, the tragedy of Spain shows all the darker.[35]

Like Anselmo, Robert Jordan is capable of working for a cause without allowing its heretical errors to eat their way like acid into his deeper convictions. Knowing the inside of both Velázquez 63 and the hotel called Gaylord's, Jordan can qualify as the educated man who is in no way "sucked in." Working efficiently as a dynamiter with the Republican guerrillas, loving Spain, hating fascism, sympathizing with the people who have been and are being betrayed, Jordan still manages to be temperate without being at all tepid. His brain is neither dominated nor deceived by the propagandistic. He remains the free man, the man not taken in, the man doing the necessary job but also making the necessary mental reservations.

Jordan's soliloquy—as he listens from below to the hilltop bat-

[34] *FWBT*, p. 286.
[35] *FWBT*, p. 285. Cf. Jordan's comment (p. 287) that Anselmo is "a Christian. Something very rare in Catholic countries." And see the excellent Chapter 15 (pp. 191–201), containing Anselmo's soliloquy on the sin of killing.

tle in which El Sordo's partisans die—is a key passage in this connection. He reflects that he is in love with Maria, even though "there isn't supposed to be any such thing as love in a purely materialistic conception of society." Then he catches himself. Since when did he really entertain any such conception?

"Never. And you never could have. You're not a real Marxist and you know it. You believe in Liberty, Equality, and Fraternity. You believe in Life, Liberty, and the Pursuit of Happiness. Don't ever kid yourself with too much dialectics. They are for some but they are not for you. You have to know them in order not to be a sucker. You have put many things in abeyance to win a war. If this war is lost all of those things are lost. But afterwards you can discard what you do not believe in. There is plenty you do not believe in and plenty that you do believe in." [36]

Robert Jordan is with, but not of, the communists. For the duration of the war he is under communist discipline because they offer "the best discipline and the soundest and sanest for the prosecution of the [Spanish] war." [37] This is simple common sense, just as (though Robert Jordan did not live to see it) it was probably common sense for the Allies to fight side by side with the Russians in the second World War—in order to win it. But where the communist dialectic runs contrary to the older dialectics of the French and the American Revolutions, Jordan will remain as an essential nonconformist, a free man not taken in, though doing his part in the perennial attempts which free men must make if the concept of freedom is to last.

IV. THE EPIC GENRE

The structural form of *For Whom the Bell Tolls* has been conceived with care and executed with the utmost brilliance. The form is that of a series of concentric circles with the all-important bridge in the middle. The great concentration which Hemingway achieves is partly dependent on his skill in keeping attention

---

[36] *FWBT*, p. 305. With this compare Willard Thorp's remark: "Where does the democratic faith live and speak if not in the pages of *For Whom the Bell Tolls?*" See Margaret Denny and William H. Gilman, eds., *The American Writer and the European Tradition*, Minneapolis, 1950, p. 100.

[37] *FWBT*, p. 163.

focussed on the bridge while projecting the reader imaginatively far beyond that center of operations. Chapter One immediately establishes the vital strategic importance of the bridge in the coming action. Frequent allusions to the bridge keep it in view through the second chapter, and in Chapter Three Jordan goes with Anselmo to make a preliminary inspection. From that time onwards until its climactic destruction, the bridge continues to stand unforgettably as the focal point in the middle of an ever widening series of circles.

The brilliance of execution becomes apparent when the reader stands in imagination on the flooring of the bridge and looks in any direction. He will see his horizons lifting by degrees towards a circumference far beyond the Guadarrama mountains. For the guerrillas' central task, the blowing of the bridge, is only one phase of a larger operation which Hemingway once called "the greatest holding action in history." Since the battle strategy which requires the bridge to be destroyed is early made available to the reader, he has no difficulty in seeing its relation to the next circle outside, where a republican division under General Golz prepares for an attack. The general's attack, in turn, is enough to suggest the outlines of the whole civil war, while the Heinkel bombers and Fiat pursuit planes which cut across the circle —foreign shadows over the Spanish earth—extend our grasp one more circle outwards to the trans-European aspect of the struggle. The outermost ring of the circle is nothing less than the great globe itself. Once the Spanish holding operation is over, the wheel of fire will encompass the earth. The bridge, therefore —such is the structural achievement of this novel—becomes the hub on which the "future of the human race can turn." [38] Wherever the reader moves along the circumferences of the various circles, all radial roads lead to and from this bridge.

If the reader of *For Whom the Bell Tolls* is hardly cramped for space, he is also free to range in time. Jordan's action, particularized though it is, has also a significance *sub specie aeterni-*

[38] *FWBT*, p. 43. Cf. Sinclair Lewis's view that *FWBT* crystallizes "the world revolution that began long ago . . . and that will not cease till the human world has either been civilized or destroyed." Lewis, introd., Limited Editions Club reprint of *FWBT*, Princeton University Press, 1942, p. ix.

tatis. The timelessness of the central event invites the reader to compare it with all those other small and local holding actions which are stuck like gems in the web of history and tend to assume an importance out of all proportion to their size. One civil war easily suggests another, as in Jordan's memories of his grand-father who bore arms in America's war of the rebellion. Behind that, in the long perspective, is the bridge where the republican (and anti-monarchist) "peasants" of Concord fired the shot heard round the world. On a bridge across the Tiber young Horatius de-layed briefly the advance of a superior force. Still farther back is the action of Leonidas against the Persian host at the hot gates of Thermopylae. The terrain and the odds were not, after all, far different from those of Robert Jordan. There is even the prediction, comparable to Pilar's, that Leonidas will die, and there is a lone Persian cavalryman who comes, like the fascist horseman in Hemingway, to reconnoitre the mountain pass. Jor-dan could never complain with Eliot's Gerontion that he had not fought at "the hot gates." His bridge is at the center of the his-tory of holding actions; and although his problem is small in scale, it is so conceived and projected as to suggest a struggle of epical dimensions.

In making such a claim for Hemingway's novel, one must reckon with his own assertion that "all bad writers are in love with the epic." Even a few gifted writers have fallen into the error of attempting too much or going about it in the wrong way. The conscious striving for an epic magnitude, as in some of Whitman's poetry and much of Wolfe's prose, may reduce the writing to rhetoric and enlarge the people to set-piece characters whose resemblance to human beings is merely coincidental. There is also the danger that the struggle for the cosmic may backslide into the comic. The grand manner too easily inflates to the grandiose; good sense may be sacrificed to size; quantity may be mistaken for quality; and what was meant to be great will become simply gross.

As a prose epic of the Spanish people, *For Whom the Bell Tolls* commits none of these errors. Indeed the novel is a living ex-ample of how, in modern times, the epic quality must probably be projected. The failure of certain modern practitioners of the epic manner rests perhaps primarily upon ignorance of the uses of synecdoche, the device by which a part can be made to function for the whole, and the fact to gain an emblematic power without the loss of its native particularity. Hemingway's war novel, rich as it is in symbolic extensions, is somewhere near a synecdochist's triumph.

What elements of the epic manner may be successfully adapted to modern needs? Despite the obvious gap between Spain and Ilium, the student of the epic may find part of his answer in considering the Homeric parallel. A primitive setting, simple food and wine, the care and use of weapons, the sense of imminent danger, the emphasis on masculine prowess, the presence of varying degrees of courage and cowardice, the rude barbarisms on both sides, the operation of certain religious and magical superstitions, the warrior codes—these, surely, are common ties between the two sets of protagonists. Jordan is not to be scorned as the type of Achilles, and one can recognize in Pablo the rude outlines of a debased and sulking Ajax. Pilar the gypsy, though she reads the lifeline in Jordan's palm instead of consulting the shape and color of animal entrails, makes the consciousness of the supernatural an operative factor.

Nor should the technical comparisons be overlooked. One of the most interesting of these is the intentionally heightened language. Mr. Edward Fenimore has published a valuable essay on the subject. He remarks, for instance, on "the Elizabethan tone" of a number of phrases and sentences.

"That such a tone should haunt Hemingway's pages is [he goes on] inevitable. His tale has much of the epic in its breadth, in the plain fact that his characters mean more than themselves alone, the action they are engaged upon [being] unmistakably a culminating point pushed up by profound national or . . . universal forces. In the Elizabethan, the English possesses an epic language, and it is into the forms of this language that Hemingway, through the very nature of the world he is creating . . . constantly passes." [39]

[39] "English and Spanish in *For Whom the Bell Tolls*," McCaffery, pp. 205–220. See especially pp. 212 and 217. In spite of his criticism of Melville (*GHOA*, p. 20) for the over-use of rhetoric as a substitute for ob-

Yet, as Fenimore observes, this language is carefully tempered. A purely colloquial modern English and an English which belongs in its essence to the King James version of the Bible are brought together to mutual advantage. One example is a brief interchange between the rough-spoken Agustín and the supremely dignified Fernando—who is, incidentally, one of Hemingway's best-drawn minor characters.

"Where the hell are you going?" Agustín asked the grave little man as he came up.

"To my duty," Fernando said with dignity.

"Thy duty," said Agustín mockingly. "I besmirch the milk of thy duty. . . ." [40]

Several of Hemingway's short stories had made a similar collocation of the old and dignified with the new and crass. In "The Gambler, The Nun, and The Radio," for example, the contrast is used to underscore the humor of character. Now, however, with his temperamental sensitivity to the tone of language, and an intuitive feel for what would constitute the proper blend of ancient and modern idiom in the conduct of key scenes, whether they were comic or not, Hemingway developed a language suitable to his epic purposes. The masculine vigor in the march of the narrative comes about, not alone from the author's skill in the unfolding of events but also through his responsiveness to language values.

Outside the technical aspects of language one finds an over-all seriousness of conception which, though high enough to meet even Arnold's stringent requirements, does not preclude rough humor and soldierly badinage. As a means of giving depth to his characterizations, Homer knew and used (if indeed he did not invent) the device of the flashback. As for synecdoche, Homer

---

servation, Hemingway had now reached the point where an admixture of Marlovian and Shakespearean language served him in the elevation of language tone towards the epic level. Yet *FWBT* never falls into rhetoric in the expository passages, as happens frequently in *Moby-Dick*. The Elizabethan-Jacobean tone in *FWBT* is communicated exclusively through dialogue, and even there is carefully "corrected" towards modernity by the intermixture of the contemporary *lingua communis* with the slang removed. Hemingway had been speaking Spanish for 15 years, and his ear was awake to its tempos and its delicate or indelicate formalities.

[40] *FWBT*, p. 92.

was very far from limiting his range of significance by carefully centering his attention on the action before Troy. All bad writers may love the epic. A few good ones, working somewhat after the fashion of Hemingway, can succeed in keeping the epic genre in a state of good health by adapting transferable elements to the needs and expectations of the modern reader.

The principle of characterization-in-depth is strong in *For Whom the Bell Tolls*—more so than in any of Hemingway's previous work. If touch-and-go is the mark of the apprentice and the journeyman, stay-and-see may well be one of the attributes of the master. Even though the qualities which distinguished the younger writer still serve Hemingway at forty, he is now ready to move beyond them. Without, for example, sacrificing the value of *suggestion* (where the reader is required to supply his own imaginative clothing for an idea nakedly projected), Hemingway has come round to an appreciation of the value of *ingestion*. This signifies a bearing within, a willingness to put in, and to allow to operate within the substance of a piece of writing, much that formerly would have been excluded in favor of suggestion.

The result of this willingness is a notable gain in richness and depth without sacrifice of the values inherent in the principle of suggestiveness. What Hemingway allows us to know of Pilar's past, for example, enriches, activates, and deepens our sense of her vital performance in the present. The willingness, even the eagerness, to invent that past, to stay and see how it informs the present, is a mark of the transition achieved by the fully mature artist in Hemingway. The will to report has given place to the willingness to invent, though the values of the will to report have not been sacrificed in the process. There were formerly only limited vistas back through time. Now the full panoply of time past is at work in time present. This mode of operation is likewise habitual to the epic genre.

V. THE PATTERN OF TRAGEDY

If *For Whom the Bell Tolls* is a kind of epic, it is above all a tragic epic. Like the *Iliad,* it may be seen as a study in doom. Madrid, like Troy, was fated to fall. Seventeen months of hindsight on the Spanish war helped to mature in Hemingway a feeling that the republican defeat had been virtually inevitable.

"The Spanish civil war was really lost, of course, [he wrote in 1940] when the Fascists took Irun in the late summer of 1936. But in a war you can never admit, even to yourself, that it is lost. Because when you admit it is lost you are beaten." [41]

Hemingway's choice of the early summer of 1937 as the time of Jordan's action thus takes on special importance. He wanted a period deep enough into the war so that the possibility of republican defeat could be a meaningful psychological force. But the time must also be far enough removed from the end of the war so that some of his people could still believe in a republican victory. The struggle could not seem to be hopeless. Yet, as a study in doom, the novel must early isolate and dramatize those adverse powers and power-failures which would ultimately combine to defeat the Spanish republic.

Robert Jordan's first sight of Pablo gives him an insight into the nature of one power-failure. No republican, at the beginning of the movement, was more in command of himself or the situation than Pablo. Now the guerrilla leader is so far gone in defeatist "sadness" and moral cowardice as almost to doom in advance any undertaking in which he is to play a part.

"I don't like that sadness [Robert Jordan thought]. That sadness is bad. That's the sadness they get before they quit or before they betray. That is the sadness that comes before the sellout." [42]

Pablo is a specific Judas, as his stealing of the detonator will later show. But he is also a recognizable symbol for the general canker of defeatism, gnawing the tissues of republican morale from within, and leading to the larger betrayal.

A second internal danger is the inefficiency of the Republican bureaucracy. A third is an aspect of the Spanish temperament. One gets the impression that a radical inefficiency stretches all the way from the higher echelons in Madrid down to the gypsy Rafael, who is so irresponsible that he runs off to shoot rabbits when he should be standing guard near Pablo's cave. The Rus-

[41] Hemingway's preface to Regler, *Great Crusade*, p. vii.
[42] *FWBT*, p. 12.

sian General Golz, only half-believing that his attack will not be doomed to failure before it even starts, points up the larger difficulties.

"They are never my attacks [says Golz]. I make them. But they are not mine. The artillery is not mine. I must put in for it. I have never been given what I ask for even when they have it to give. That is the least of it. There are other things. You know how those people are. It is not necessary to go into all of it. Always there is something. Always some one will interfere." [43]

Tangled in red tape like Laocoon in serpents, Golz is not free enough to prosecute a war successfully. The Rafaels of the republican side are too free, and too irresponsible. Bureaucracy and temperament, two more internal foes of the republic, help to fix the doom.

But the most awesome symbol of doom is the air-power of the foreign enemy. All the Spaniards hate it, as they hate the foreigners for interfering in their civil war. When the fascist planes roar over the mountain hide-out, it is always in threes, like the weird sisters, or in those multiples of three with which practitioners of black magic used to conjure.

"The three passed and then came nine more, flying much higher in the minute, pointed formations of threes and threes and threes . . . He could still hear the receding drone. . . . By now they're well beyond the pass with Castile all yellow and tawny beneath them now in the morning . . . and the shadows of the Heinkels moving over the land as the shadows of sharks pass over a sandy floor of the ocean." [44]

When the planes return, Jordan revises his simile into something even more sinister. They have the shape but not the motion of sharks. "They move like no thing that has ever been. They move like mechanized doom." [45] It is by three such planes that

[43] FWBT, p. 5. Compare Golz's almost elegiac acceptance of reality, as he speaks over the telephone to Duval at the other end of the novel, when it is known that the plan of the bridge will not work: "Nous sommes foutus. Oui. Comme toujours. Oui. C'est dommage. Oui. . . . No. Rien à faire. Rien. Faut pas penser. Faut accepter. . . . Bon. Nous ferons notre petit possible." FWBT, pp. 428–430.

[44] FWBT, pp. 74–76.

[45] FWBT, p. 87.

El Sordo's band will be wiped out at three o'clock of the following Monday afternoon.

Hemingway's linking of the modern bombers with the ancient magic-symbol of number three greatly enhances the emotional effectiveness of the plane-passage. The old epics and the great dramatic tragedies could employ supernatural agents in the full expectation that they would intensify the emotions of pity and terror in the spectator. The rise of naturalism, and the partial decay of superstition, denied the tragic artist direct access to one of his most evocative instruments. Yet within the shadowy subconscious, the perennial human capacity for fear and awe remained to be touched by any artist who could empower new symbols with old terrors.

The book touches the edge of the supernatural also by a considered use of premonition. The primary human agent is the gypsy Pilar, who is both a woman and a kind of witch, though a witch very naturalistically portrayed and very womanly in her witchhood. Her function in part is to sharpen the reader's foreboding and thus to deepen his sense of impending tragedy. Having watched Pablo's degeneration through fear, she is both too wise and too fond of Jordan to reveal that she has seen his coming death in the lines of his hand. (Like the Circean "witch" of *The Sun Also Rises,* she is a good judge of quality.) But the reader's knowledge of Jordan's coming death gives special point to the passage in which Pilar describes, with naturalistic precision, the three blended odors of the smell of death to come.

The woman-witch dialectic is marked often in the book. In this instance, the woman withholds what the witch has gloomily discovered. Her certainty that Jordan will die has motivated her in bringing the lovers together. This is done both for the therapeutic effect of a healthy love affair on Maria, and in order to give Jordan, through Maria, as much of life as three days will hold. This, one might guess, is the tender side of Pilar. But in the passage on the smell of death to come, she adopts the very tone which will arouse Jordan's doubts as to the truth of what she is saying. He doubts and he argues, and the doubting arguments divert his thoughts at least from the probability, if not from the possibility, of death. The rough railing humor of her presentation is meant to save him from a fear which might undo his resolution, or, at any rate, spoil the closing hours of his short, happy life.[46]

This entire aspect of the novel may well remind some readers of the problem which Henry James set himself in *The Wings of the Dove*—though, as always, there is little or no overt resemblance between the two books. "The idea, reduced to its essence," said James of his own major effort, "is that of a young person conscious of a great capacity for life, but early stricken and doomed, condemned to die under short respite, while also enamoured of the world."[47] A marked "capacity for life," a full acceptance and love of the world, is always a driving motive with the Hemingway hero. It grows even stronger as one moves with Hemingway's work through the nineteen-thirties. Yet Nick Adams has it, Jake Barnes has it, Frederick Henry has it. It is strong in Harry Morgan, though he is not very articulate in expressing what he feels. The love of life—the good life—gives special point to the dying reminiscences of that other Harry, the writer on safari in Africa. Yet the two men called Harry are stricken and doomed, condemned to die under short respite, as is Colonel Richard Cantwell, a lover of life, in *Across the River and Into the Trees*.

There are other premonitions in *For Whom the Bell Tolls* than those we owe to Pilar's supersensory gifts. Jordan, as a partisan soldier, must often consider that he may die at the affair of the bridge. He is compelled to recognize the possibility of death. His life among the Guadarramas may well total three-score hours and ten—seventy hours as a substitute for seventy years.[48] In the meteorological bad luck which brings an unseasonal snowfall, in Pablo's defection, and in the bombing of El Sordo, there is a discernible "pattern of tragedy" which he is too sensible to ignore. But he has also a special soldier's talent "not to ignore but to despise whatever bad endings there could be."[49] From the point of view of the reader, therefore, Jordan's predicament is some-

[46] *FWBT*, pp. 250–257.
[47] *Works*, New York edition, vol. 19, preface, p. v.
[48] See Jordan's soliloquy, *FWBT*, p. 166.
[49] *FWBT*, p. 393.

thing like that of the torero who knows that he may be killed but despises death and enters the ring in spite of the possibility. The knowledge, derived through Pilar, that Jordan not only *may* but *will* die gives every incident in Jordan's seventy-hour span of life the special poignancy that would be felt by a spectator who knew in advance that he was watching the last fight of a torero. Through this double perspective, Hemingway gets into his novel the very "feeling of life and death" which he was seeking when he first went to watch the Spanish bullfights.

But the idea that a sane consciousness of death will give added depth and meaning to the events of life is only one of the familiar Hemingway themes in *For Whom the Bell Tolls*. Sparing but effective use is also made of the men-without-women, the father-and-son, and the home-versus-war themes. Jordan, for example, shows a kind of spiritual relationship to Pilar in that he can be, by turns, both tender and tough-minded. In one of his aspects, he can love human beings and allow himself to become involved with them, as in his good companionship with Anselmo or his love for Maria. At the other extreme, he must be the cold-minded and detached commander, reserving part of himself in all human relationships so that the necessary job can be done. It is in this detachment that he coldly judges his companions, estimating their relative dependability and expendability, and perfecting his battle-plan in accordance with these estimates. He cannot often expand warmly; as soldier he must contract coldly within himself. "I cannot have a woman, doing what I do," he tells Maria. "But thou art my woman now." After one of their encounters, Maria observes that he is now thinking of something else than love. "Yes," Jordan says, shortly. "My work." On another occasion, talking with Pilar, the men-without-women idea emerges very clearly. "You are a very cold boy," says Pilar. Jordan disagrees. "No," says Pilar. "In the head you are very cold." Jordan replies that he is preoccupied with his work. "But you do not like the things of life?" asks Pilar. "Yes. Very much. But not to interfere with my work." It is not now a liking for hardy masculine comradeship in hunting or fishing or skiing which motivates the Hemingway hero, but a preoccupation with the work a man must do, where women have no place and may even be in the way. The morning

Jordan kills the fascist cavalryman, Maria is still beside him in the sleeping-bag. As he quickly and coldly issues orders to Anselmo and Primitivo, he is aware of Maria behind him, dressing herself under the robe. "She had no place in his life now." At the end of the book, both elements are still visible. He is the republican soldier coolly drawing a bead on the fascist Lieutenant Berrendo, and the husband covering his wife's escape.[50]

The closing scene also rounds off the father-and-son theme which has been introduced in Jordan's soliloquies at various earlier times. Jordan's grandfather fought bravely and successfully in the American Civil War. His father, like the father of Nick Adams, died by his own hand. Jordan has long since forgiven his father for the act, but he is still as ashamed of it as he is proud of his grandfather's soldierly bravery. Now, at the end of the line, as Jordan lies nearly fainting under the ballooning pain from his fractured leg, the father-grandfather opposition once more commands his mind. Suicide would be permissible under the circumstances. But the memory of his grandfather, his true spiritual ancestor, helps him to hold onto his courage and to die in combat.[51]

The significance of Maria, when she is seen in the light of such other heroines as Catherine Barkley, Marie Morgan, and even Dorothy Bridges, is finally symbolic. In the lonely alien region of the Guadarramas, she comes to stand as the image of "home." Most of Hemingway's women tend to take on this special symbolic meaning. Dorothy Bridges (a fairly unsympathetic portrait) is explicitly equated with nostalgia, a somewhat untrustworthy reminder of the comforts and the joys which are so rarely possible in a world besieged by the ideology of terror. Catherine Barkley and Marie Morgan, though in different ways, represent normal domesticity vanquished by war and by the economic struggle for survival. Similarly, Maria stands for the normal in the midst of a terrible abnormality. She has been subjected to all sorts of outrages by her fascist captors. The rape is an act of supreme brutality; only the true tenderness of Jordan, as Pilar well knows, can erase the psychological scars the fascists have left. The cut-

[50] *FWBT*, pp. 73, 161, 91, 267.
[51] *FWBT*, especially Chapter 30, pp. 334–340.

ting of Maria's hair is a symbol of her loss of normal womanhood
or girlhood, just as its growing-out indicates her gradual return
to balance and health.

One might argue, of course, that the normal male-female situation in Hemingway is something like what took place in the Garden of Eden just after the eating of the fruit of the tree, but before
the malediction. All these Eves are as pleasurably ductile as the
Adams are hirsute and sexually vigorous. Like all travesties, such
a characterization would have its element of truth. But it would
tend to ignore the real tenderness with which the "good women"
in Hemingway are treated. The fate of the heroines is that they
are almost never at home; their virtue is that the best of them carry
the home-image with them wherever they go.

A fourth well-tried theme handsomely adapted to the uses of
the Spanish tragedy is that of *nada*, or nothingness militant. By
placing his action among the high slopes of the Sierra de Guadarramas, a clean, well-lighted place where the weather is cold and
the air clear, Hemingway has achieved a kind of idyll in the midst
of war, an island (like that of Nick Adams in his afternoon grove
on the way to the Big Two-Hearted River) surrounded by the
sinister. It is there that Maria, raped and probably infected by
fascist soldiery, is restored to health and sanity. This is a mountain fastness like Burguete in *The Sun Also Rises,* or like the
priest's homeland of Abruzzi in *A Farewell to Arms,* or like the
Alpine sanctuary to which Frederick and Catherine retire for
their short happy life together. One sees again the lowland-versus-
highland image; on the plain before Madrid the fascists are deployed, but here are high slopes, concealment, and something like
the good life, a veritable island in the midst of *nada*. Still, in the
words of Donne's devotion, "no man is an island." In this savage
war, no mountain can serve as a permanent sanctuary. El Sordo,
on his high hilltop position, finds no good life. Fascist cavalry
surround it, and three fascist planes destroy it from above. Similarly, when the bridge is blown, Pablo's mountain cave becomes
untenable as a refuge. The partisans plan to retreat across the
war-swept lowlands to another mountain fastness in the Sierra de
Gredos. But the planes of the enemy, in sinister "threes and threes
and threes," can presumably come there, too. "I am tired of the

mountains," says Pilar in a moment of despondency. "In mountains there are only two directions. Down and up, and down leads only to the road and the towns of the Fascists." And up, one might add, leads to the foreign bombers, assaulting even the highest and loneliest peaks.[52]

Hemingway's sense of fascism's betrayal of the Spanish people has in fact much of the nightmare quality of Picasso's allegorical painting. The mountain-sanctuary, an essentially private symbol in Hemingway's earlier books, is now shown to be open to invasion and destruction by fascist bombers, which the artist carefully establishes as symbols of the power of evil. If one follows Picasso's pictorial allegories through the order of composition from the "Minotauromachy" through the "Sueño y Mentira de Franco" up to the "Guernica," he will see how an essentially private set of symbols is made to take on political significance. In the "Minotauromachy" of 1935, Picasso employs motifs from the bullfight to express symbolically a struggle no doubt personal to himself as artist and Spaniard. The "Guernica" of 1937, occasioned by the bombing of an open Spanish city by foreign planes, regrouped the symbols of the bull and the horse and broke the calm human figures of the *Minotauromachy* into fragments of anguish and fear. In one postwar interview, Picasso refused to identify the bull-figure of the "Guernica" with fascism, though he did give it the generic meaning of "brutality and darkness"—something like Goya's "Nada." The horse, transfixed by a spear which has fallen from above, is however for Picasso a specific symbol for the Spanish people. In somewhat the same way, the destruction of El Sordo's band on the hilltop, like the roar of Heinkel bombers above Jordan's high sanctuary, suggests the horror of brutality and darkness unleashed against a betrayed people.[53]

Among those whom fascism will betray are the artists. Robert Jordan is not only a teacher of Spanish and a lover of Spain; he is also a writer. As an artist he is fully aware of the threat of fascist domination. If fascism were the kind of force which fed upon itself, remaining relatively limited in its dimensions, Jor-

[52] *FWBT*, p. 97.
[53] See Alfred H. Barr, Jr., *Picasso: Fifty Years of His Art*, New York, 1946, p. 202.

dan's manifest duty would belong to the development of his art—
a task so huge that it takes a lifetime to accomplish. During the
years of peace, Jordan wrote one book on Spain and the Spanish people.[54] Presumably he would not be averse to doing another.
But this is not the time.

In the deeper meaning of *For Whom the Bell Tolls,* the invasion
of the high sanctuary *from above* marks a transition in the affairs
of the artist. Unless the force is stopped, it can mean the death of
art as it can mean the death of everything else the artist values
and needs. Fascism has become militant, imperialistic, and international. The artist, devoted though he must be to the development of his art, can no more ignore it than he could ignore a storm
blowing in at his study window and scattering the pages of his
work in progress. His move must be to shut the window against
the storm. Still it will not leave him alone. The lightning strikes
his house, and it is his obvious duty to save his manuscript and
put out the fire. The *blitz* is not what he asked for or what he
wanted. Since it has come, he must take arms against it, and end
it as soon as possible by opposing it. Then he can go back to his
work, if he survives.

VI. THE GREAT WHEEL

In his account of how he went about writing *The Awkward
Age,* James says that he "drew on a sheet of paper . . . the
neat figure of a circle consisting of a number of small rounds disposed at equal distances about a central object." [55] This central
object was his "situation." The small rounds disposed about it
were like a series of small searchlights centering on the situation,
and seeking to illuminate it from all sides. As often in James, the
problem of the artist was to draw, by a geometry of his own,
the limited circle in which his demonstration would transpire. If
he drew his circle well and directed his searchlights with a sufficient intensity, the human relations on which he concentrated
would "stop nowhere." [56]

[54] *FWBT,* p. 248.
[55] Henry James, *Works,* New York edition, vol. 9, preface, p. xvi.
[56] *ibid.,* vol. 1, p. vii.

The central organizing image of *For Whom the Bell Tolls* is also geometrical. We have, of course, in the chief characters, a series of smaller rounds disposed at equal distances about the central object or situation. But beyond these, and spreading out to the edge of the world, we have a whole series of concentric circles. The human relations of the war in Spain "stop nowhere,"—any more than the tragic implications of the art of the bullfight stay confined within the two hours' traffic of a particular afternoon. In fact Hemingway's novel follows an architectural plan comparable to that of a Spanish bullring, which is constructed in a series of concentric circles, so arranged that from any point one can watch the action taking place at the center.

Remembering that Picasso and Hemingway have as artists a common interest in the bullfight, and noting that their separate reactions to the Spanish Civil War produced so remarkable a set of symbolic parallels, one might expect to find Hemingway making use of symbolism derived from the bullfight. That is, one might find both the geometrical *and* the pictorial use of images. To a limited extent this happens, and as usual the pictorial images are fully justified by the psychological situation. All the native Spaniards in the book are of course well acquainted with the terminology of their national sport, as a similar group of Americans might be with that of baseball or football. A few even know the sport from the inside. Before the war began, Pablo worked around bullrings. The boy Joaquín planned a career as torero. And by her own boast, Pilar lived for "nine years with three of the worst-paid matadors" in the business.

One of the most striking and memorable parts of the novel is organized in terms of a pictorial metaphor of the bullfight.[57] This is Pilar's account of the murder of the fascists in the village square at the hands of Pablo's lynch-mob. The natural resemblance between the square and an arena has been furthered by piling carts before the several street-entrances to the square. This is the usual custom in preparation for a *capea*, or amateur bull-baiting show, at the time of a fiesta. The resemblance to a feast-day celebration is emphasized by the fact that some of the peasants, just in from the country, are dressed in their Sunday clothes. The

[57] *FWBT*, pp. 109–129. See also p. 55.

caretaker of the plaza hoses down the dust as would be done for a *capea,* and when the dust has settled a peasant shouts, "When do we get the first fascist? When does the first one come out of the box?"

The eyes of the whole company are fixed on the doorway of the *Ayuntiamento,* where the fascists have been herded, as if by sweating workers at a bullring. The concentration is comparable to that with which a *capea* crowd would watch the cage-door through which a bull was to be released. Once the crowd has tasted blood through the murder of the first fascist, Mayor Don Benito Garcia, it is as though they waited tensely and impatiently for the second bull. Howling in a great voice, a drunkard summarizes the sentiments of a considerable part of the crowd. *"Qué salga el toro! Let the bull out!"*

But this is one of those almost unendurable "bullfights." It will produce no sense of tragic catharsis, no genuine purgation of the emotions. Pilar says that after it was over she felt sick, hollow, ashamed, and oppressed. There was no experience, as happens in a good bullfight, of anything "profound as any religious ecstasy." The total effect was as nasty as that of a jungle grove through which a tribe of baboons have just passed.

Even though, as such affairs often will, this *capea* produced some isolated instances of courage, *pundonor,* and the allied virtues—instances which Pilar describes along with the rest—these are not enough to redeem the total performance. Pilar's feeling is itself a fitting symbol for the reaction of many a reluctant observer to the tragedy of the Spanish war, the international bullfight with a poorly armed matador arrayed against the "brutality and darkness" of Pan-European fascism. If one at this instant remembers "Guernica," he sees that the artists Picasso and Hemingway, drawn as by a magnetic attraction to the pictorial imagery of the bullfight, move along lines precisely parallel. The major difference is that Hemingway, working with a different and more extendable medium, can take care to paint both sides of the picture. He has, to return to the Jamesian metaphor, an opportunity to draw more circles, more wheels of fire.

Within the scope of man's world, turning like a great wheel through empty space, there are in fact many small and large wheels turning for ever. In the quiet of his last Sunday evening inside the cave of Pablo, while Jordan draws his circles and makes his mathematical computations for the dynamiting of the bridge, the simile of a wheel comes into his mind.

"It is like a merry-go-round, Robert Jordan thought. Not a merry-go-round that travels fast, and with a calliope for music, and the children ride on cows with gilded horns, and there are rings to catch with sticks, and there is the blue gas-flare-lit early dark of the Avenue du Maine, with fried fish sold from the next stall, and a wheel of fortune turning with the leather flaps slapping against the posts of the numbered compartments, and the packages of lump sugar piled in pyramids for prizes. No, it is not that kind of a merry-go-round; although the people are waiting, like the men in caps and the women in knitted sweaters, their heads bare in the gaslight and their hair shining, who stand in front of the wheel of fortune as it spins. Yes, those are the people."

Those are the people, French or Spanish or any other, watching the two revolving circles—the temporal merry-go-round and the wheel of fortune. But Jordan has in his mind yet another wheel.

"This [he reflects] is like a wheel that goes up and around. It has been around twice now. It is a vast wheel, set at an angle, and each time it goes around and then is back to where it starts.

"One side is higher than the other and the sweep it makes lifts you back and down to where you started. There are no prizes either, he thought, and no one would choose to ride this wheel. You ride it each time and make the turn with no intention ever to have mounted.

"There is only one turn; one large, elliptical rising and falling turn and you are back where you have started. We are back again now, he thought, and nothing is settled." [58]

Call it the wheel of human conflict. For Jordan, as for all men, the turn of the wheel shows tragic implications. When it has completed its revolution, the rider is back where he started, as on the little wheel of Jordan's relations with Pablo. He has been twice now on *that* wheel, "and twice it has gone around and come back to where it started." Jordan wants no more rides with Pablo, though he will have them before his day is done. In the giant

[58] *FWBT*, pp. 225–226.

clockwork of human relations, the turning wheels may be as small as the arguments with Pablo, or as vast as the elliptical rise and fall in the action of a year of war.

In either of these instances, in three days or three years, you come back to where you began—"and nothing is settled." This is the wheel-like turn of Spain's tragedy, indeed, that after all the agony and all the blood, nothing should be settled, and that Spain should be back where it began, in a medieval situation.

XI · The River and the Trees

> "To be poised against fatality, to meet adverse conditions gracefully, is more than simple endurance; it is an act of aggression, a positive triumph."—Thomas Mann, *Death in Venice*

I. THROUGH THE IRON GATES

Ten years after the publication of his tragic epic on the Spanish civil war came Hemingway's *Across the River and Into the Trees*. It was his fifth novel, and some readers were prepared to rank it fifth in the order of his prose-fiction work of the period 1925–1950. It was clearly less effective in the conversion of readers to a special point of view than *A Farewell to Arms* and *For Whom the Bell Tolls*. It lacked some of the vernal freshness of *The Sun Also Rises*. Its almost elegiac mood prevented it from achieving the dramatic intensity of some of the Morgan stories in *To Have and Have Not,* though the novel of Venice, as a work of art and artifice, was generally superior to the novel of Key West. For those, however, who were prepared to take it seriously, and to read it often enough to grasp its full intention, the book was a genuine contribution to the Hemingway canon. Its intrinsic form was that of a prose poem, with a remarkably complex emotional structure, on the theme of the three ages of man.

It was important to notice that much of the book was composed in Europe. Hemingway began composition early in 1949 among the mountains in the valley of Cortina d'Ampezzo, one of his more ancient haunts, and therefore a kind of proper seat for reminiscence. In 1918 he had gotten to know the Italian lakes during week-ends from Milan, and he once told Ernest Walsh that he had always liked Stresa (which appears in *A Farewell to Arms*), as well as Sermione and Pallanza. But Cortina had for years been a favored spot, psychologically right for the kind of work on which he was then engaged.

Composition continued in Cortina and afterwards in Cuba, where Hemingway had been living for ten years at Finca Vigia, the large breeze-swept farmhouse at San Francisco de Paula in the hills outside Havana. As in the writing of *The Sun Also Rises* nearly a quarter century earlier, the long first draft was finished in Paris towards the end of the year. On location in Venice during the winter of 1949–1950, he completed the revision, chiefly by means of extensive cutting. After serialization in *Cosmopolitan,* beginning in February and ending in June, the novel was published in book form on September 7, 1950.[1]

In order to complete *Across the River and Into the Trees,* he had interrupted work on a novel of considerably greater size and scope. Its subject, as he told curious inquirers, was the Land, the Sea, and the Air, and he characteristically hoped that the inquirers would not think his subject too ambitious for his talents. Although the book would by no means confine itself to the second world war, his experiences in that war must inevitably affect, in various ways, the development of this major work. As always, it would deal with what Hemingway knew. He knew something about the Land War, having accompanied elements of the First Army through France and into Germany during the summer, fall, and winter of 1944–1945 after the St. Lô break-through. He had also been extremely active in the Sea war from the summer of 1942 to the spring of 1944, having offered his own services, as well as those of his launch, the *Pilar,* to help maintain the anti-submarine cordon in American and Cuban coastal waters under the direction of Naval Intelligence. In the Air war, he had flown at least one mission over Festung Europa in a Mitchell bomber of the Royal Air Force fairly soon after the invasion of Normandy late in June of 1944. It was evident that he knew a representative portion of the war as a novelist must know it—from the inside.[2]

---

[1] EH to Ernest Walsh (fall 1925), and EH to CB, 4/1/51. The reader may note Malcolm Cowley's footnote, McCaffery, p. 35, which briefly refers to Hemingway's serious illness at this time. It was a bad infection in one eye (Hemingway had consistently bad luck with his eyes from boyhood) resulting from a piece of gunshot wadding.

[2] For an account of Hemingway's experiences during the war, from

It was the third war in which he had been actively engaged within the span of thirty-three years. An experience of such magnitude and of such bitter intensity was not immediately adaptable to the purposes of fiction. Even as late as 1949, when he turned aside from his major task to work on his novel of Venice, the traumatic effects of his life in the second world war still rankled in his mind. The story of Colonel Cantwell emerged as a way of exorcising what for Hemingway still had the aspect, and the terrorizing atmosphere, of a recent nightmare. *Across the River and Into the Trees* was a necessary first step in the process of objectifying not only World War II, but also the other wars and the periods of armed truce between the wars which Hemingway had personally known.

The life-story of Colonel Cantwell contains a rubric of the course of time. First is the youth who thinks that life will be better than it is. Then comes the man of experience who finds that it is sometimes—or often—worse than he had anticipated. Finally there is the man who reaches the age and status when death may come at any time through causes that are generally called natural. As he looks back along the closing circle of his days (for the structure of *Across the River*, like that of *For Whom the Bell Tolls,* is that of the closed circle), he is ready to concede that since it might have been worse, it was on the whole good enough, and he is glad (though with certain reservations) to have had it.

Mourir, à Venise, c'est être bien mort was an adage with Henry James [3] who, like Thomas Mann, had given some thought to the subject. Hemingway's version of "death in Venice" could not have been more completely the opposite of Mann's in tone and manner if he had set himself at every turn to contradict the older story. Mann's story is set in the languid dog-days when the foreign vacation-trade is in full and decaying bloom, the bathhouses along the Lido are busy, and the growing threat of the plague must be concealed in order to drive no one away. Hemingway chooses Venice in winter. The cold, gray, sharp air (which

his arrival in England in May, 1944, to his flight home on March 6, 1945, see Baker, *Ernest Hemingway: A Life Story*, New York, 1969, pp. 387-445.

[3] James, *Works,* New York edition, vol. 1, preface, p. vi.

for him has often been associated with physical and moral courage) drives steadily across the northern mountains and down the Grand Canal. Mann's hero is a famous writer, Hemingway's a professional soldier. Mann's writer sits and dreams. Hemingway's Colonel acts and remembers.[4]

But the themes of the two stories have much in common. Both ring with the overtones, though they do not accept the didactic limitations, of parables. They have in common the subject of youth contemplated by age, the emotional sense of innocence looking to and longing for experience (this is more marked in Hemingway than in Mann), and the object of exploring the nature and power of imaginative illusion. In Mann, the protagonist interests himself in studying, always from a little distance, a young child of almost angelic beauty. Cantwell spends roughly half the waking hours of his last week-end in the company of a young Italian countess. She is named, of all names, Renata. In her character, as in that of the child in Mann, may be found bloom and beauty and innocence, but also a strong suggestion of old-worldly wisdom. Renata is both as credible and as incredible as the child, and for the same reasons. Though both achieve a degree of actuality within the respective parables, Renata and the boy are both symbolic figures.

The mirror in both stories is held up chiefly to the face of experience. Mann's aged and tiring writer carries the weight of a successful career on his shoulders. Twenty years of fighting in the professional army of the United States have marked the Colonel with the almost innumerable scars he bears. Each of the men is of the indomitable type of Saint Sebastian (well known to the iconology of Venice). Mann calls this saint "the most beautiful figure, if not of art as a whole, at least of the art of literature." He is thinking of Sebastian also when he says that "to be poised against fatality, to meet adverse conditions gracefully, is more than simple endurance; it is an act of aggression, a positive triumph." Cantwell's aggressiveness is not enough to overcome in any but a moral way the eventual triumph of death. But when he comes to rest in the shade of the willows beside the road, he has crossed all his

---

[4] The Mann comparison is suggested in Northrop Frye's judicious review of the novel in *Hudson Review* 3 (Winter 1951), pp. 611–612.

rivers and met all adverse conditions with as much poise and grace as Mann could wish.

The reader of the *Meditations* of Marcus Aurelius should be able to recognize under Cantwell's profanely rugged exterior the type of the Roman stoic. The Colonel has the further distinction of a sense of humor. He is full enough of wounds, indeed, to have earned the right to jest at scars, though he respects them. They mark, in a way, the stations of his progress, and are the signs of the present state of his maturity. One could call them the stigmata of all that he has met of adversity, and all that he has so far overcome of fatality. One of them will not heal. The right hand, the hand of the non-dreamer, the hand of hard experience, is deformed and split. It has been twice shot through, like the hand and arm of Stonewall Jackson, from whose dying words the title of the novel is taken. Like General Jackson, ex-General Cantwell dies of an inward disease, a smothering paroxysm which he can not confront with his wild-boar truculence, or he might have a chance of facing it down.

He finds himself at fifty with high blood-pressure, occluding coronary arteries, a pocketful of nitroglycerine pills, and the extreme probability that his death may be waiting round any corner of Venice he happens to turn. His problem is not unlike Robert Jordan's—to roll his soldier's universe into a ball and squeeze it as rapidly as possible through the iron gates of life. Renata helps him to immerse himself as strenuously and wholeheartedly in the present as his coronary arteries will allow.

II. THE RAZOR'S EDGE

At the center of the Colonel's character, as possibly also at the center of this time, is a tense Manichean opposition between the tough and the tender, between the brutal and the delicate, between the rude and the remorseful. When W. B. Yeats undertook a somewhat similar character analysis, he used the terms Hic and Ille.[5] They are of use in understanding Colonel Cantwell.

[5] "Ego Dominus Tuus" in *The Collected Poems of W. B. Yeats,* New York, 1940, pp. 183–185. See *FWBT,* p. 304.

Ille is that whole aspect of the Colonel's nature which partakes of the nature of love. This side is shown not only in his relations with Renata, but also in his friendships with bartenders and waiters, motor-boatmen and gondolieri, or with various members of the Venetian nobility. Nobility in the Colonel's Venice is a nonrestricted term. It includes both the modest bearers of inherited titles, like the Barone Alvarito, and those who belong, like the Gran Maestro at the Gritti, to the natural *aristoi*. The Colonel's heart beats for all of these.

Ille has also a capacity for pity. It is the side of Cantwell which makes him love best those who have fought or been mutilated. "Other people were fine," he reflects, "and you liked them and were good friends; but you only felt true tenderness and love for those who had been there and received the castigation that every one receives who goes there long enough." The Colonel's summarizing expression is as tough as the emotion is tender. "I'm a sucker for crips," says he. "And any son of a bitch who has been hit solidly, as every man will be if he stays, then I love him." One of the arrows of outrageous fortune has lost the hotel-waiter Arnaldo his left eye, and he belongs accordingly in the category of the "cripples." [6] Nothing could be more thoughtful than the treatment of Arnaldo by the Colonel, or of Cantwell by Arnaldo. For the Colonel has known the castigation, and though he can draw Inferno-circles and populate them with his enemies as unjustly as Dante did, there is still room for love.

The side that Yeats called Hic is uppermost in the battle with the drunken sailors. Though these are certainly "hit solidly" by the Colonel—so solidly that his wounded hand nearly splits open again—they are anything but loved. They have whistled at Renata, and the chivalric impulses of Ille rise at once to meet the implied insult. But Hic loves to fight, and uses his fists with effectiveness and enjoyment, playing only to win as the true fighter sometimes must. In the end, he walks away without any contrition, or even a backward glance at the fallen sailors. "Let's walk," he tells Renata, "so we make even the backs of our legs look dangerous." [7]

[6] *ARIT*, p. 67.
[7] *ARIT*, pp. 283–285.

The wild-boar attitude is visible, too, in his treatment of the occasional Venetian fascists. There is one in particular, a backstairs servant at the Gritti Palace Hotel, whom the Colonel once caught in the act of going through his luggage. When this citizen slides the morning paper under the door, Cantwell likes to startle him by taking it before the servant has let go of the other end. It is the Colonel's pleasure and custom not to be caught napping by the always-present opposition.[8]

The soldierly vigilance which never lets him sit down without having both flanks covered is apparent also when he encounters the two ex-fascists during his morning walk to the market. As they come up behind him, the Colonel hears them talking about him on the supposition that he does not understand their language.

"They are making it pretty personal now. It isn't just Americans, it is also me, myself, my gray hair, the slightly crooked way I walk, the combat boots (those, of that stripe, disliked the practicability of combat boots. They liked boots that rang on the flag stones and took a high black polish)."

After turning the next corner and waiting for the former fascists to come up in order to face them down, the Colonel reflects that it was hardly intelligent of them "to think old Infantrymen would not fight this early in the morning against the simple odds of two to one."

"I'd hate to fight in this town where I love the people. I would avoid it. But couldn't those badly educated youths realize what sort of animal they were dealing with? Don't they know how you get to walk that way? Nor any of the other signs that combat people show as surely as a fisherman's hands tell you if he is a fisherman from the creases from the cord cuts."[9]

It was a pity that they were not ten to one instead of only two, the Colonel says to himself. They might have fought then, like the murderers of Matteotti back in the most high and palmy state of Rome, long before their leader was strung up in a filling station.

The love of fighting is part of what the Colonel sums up as the *sale métier* of his profession. Yet this side of him does continuous

[8] *ARIT*, p. 115.
[9] *ARIT*, pp. 186–188.

Manichean battle with what, thinking of Hamlet, one might call the fighting of love. "Sir, in my heart there was a kind of fighting that would not let me sleep." [10] But the Colonel is himself, not a latter-day Hamlet. Though his fifty-year-old modern world is out of joint, he never imagines that he was born to set it right. He has only contrived to do his best along the way. The best, as the rule runs, was none too good, and he knows all about the bitterness of remorse. "It is the mistakes," he says, "that are no good to sleep with. . . . They can certainly crawl into a sack sometimes. They can crawl in and stay in there with you." [11] Even when the horrors come, however, the Colonel is very far from wishing that his beat-up and sullied flesh would melt. He is glad to occupy it as long as luck allows. He accepts without protest the Almighty's edict against self-slaughter. He is content to prepare stoically for "the best way to be over-run," but he is in no hurry.[12] There is always the fighting of love.

One of his deepest affections is for his old comrade-at-arms, the Gran Maestro, who resembles the Colonel in carrying his afflictions gracefully, and in contriving to be happy despite his ulcers and the "small cardiac condition." The two men are "brothers in their membership in the human race, the only club that either one paid dues to, and brothers, too, in their love of an old country, much fought over, and always triumphant in defeat, which they had both defended in their youth." As a badge of the brotherhood, they have invented a fictitious order with the resounding Spanish title, *El Ordine Militar, Nobile y Espirituoso de los Caballeros de Brusadelli*. The knights of Brusadelli pay ironic homage to their "leader" and patron, a notorious Milanese profiteer who once accused his young wife, through due process of law and in public, "of having deprived him of his judgment through her extraordinary sexual demands." [13]

The Order of the Caballeros is, however, much more than a joke on its patron. Its regular members are admitted only on unimpeachable evidence that they have received (and gracefully

---

[10] Act V, scene ii.
[11] *ARIT*, p. 188.
[12] *ARIT*, p. 104.
[13] *ARIT*, pp. 55–57. This organization parodies that of the Carbonari.

survived thus far) the castigation that flesh is heir to. They are the
uncomplaining fardel-bearers, who understand the whips and
scorns as part of time's earthly business. They are the occupants
of the inner circle which always stands at the center of masculine
relationships in Hemingway; they have been "hit solidly, as every
man will be if he stays." And the Knights of Brusadelli are among
those who have stayed.

The admission of Renata is a revealing act of the Order. One
way of describing the extended conversations between the countess
and the Colonel is to say that they represent the indoctrination of
youth by grizzled experience.

"What would you like to know, Daughter?" asks the Colonel
at one point in the story.

"Everything," says Renata.

"All right," says the Colonel. "Here goes." [14]

What he has to tell her, as the type of the non-initiate, are some
of the more recent events in his "sad trade" of war-making. She
hears of the Normandy break-through, the bombing of American
troops by their own air support, the serio-comic *opera* of the taking of Paris, and the destruction of an infantry regiment in the
forest at Hürtgen. After she has been properly indoctrinated into
the intricate ironies by means of the Colonel's recital, it is significant that Renata should be admitted to the Order. "You are
a member now," says the Gran Maestro. *"Por merito di guerra."*
But it is only an honorary membership. The countess is too young.
She still wears the bloom. She cannot show, like Cantwell and the
Gran Maestro, "the ever happy face of the old soldier who is still
alive and appreciates it." The experience is not really available,
in short, except to those who have been there, and had it, and
managed to survive without being ruined by it. [15]

Henry James interested himself in the "whimsical theory of two
distinct and alternate presences . . . in two quite distinct and
'water-tight' compartments." [16] In Hemingway's portrait of the
Colonel we move slightly beyond the area of whimsy, and the
compartments of the character are neither wholly distinct nor

water-tight. In fact one keeps breaking in on the other. Among the questions implicit in this complex character is, "How much of all that is good here can survive the onslaughts of evil without being spoiled?" The answer, supplied by the Colonel, is that very much can survive—courage, love, a chivalric code, generosity, the sense of beauty and the sense of the ridiculous, and the capacity for soundly based belief. The distinct and alternate presences of the Colonel's character agree, though not without obstinate questionings, on the necessity for such qualities as these. They constitute the unwritten by-laws of the *Ordine Militar, Nobile y Espirituoso de los Caballeros de Brusadelli.*

Of utmost importance is the capacity for soundly based belief, for what might well be called the desirability of informed illusion. "Every day is a disillusion," says the very young Countess. "No," says the Colonel, flatly. "Every day is a new and fine illusion. But you can cut out everything phony about the illusion as though you would cut it out with a straight-edge razor." [17]

The illusion must be informed, evaluated, tested for the truth it bears. "My Colonel," says the night porter at the Gritti, "I have so little political development that I believe all honorable men are honorable." "Oh you'll get over that," the Colonel assures him. "Don't worry, boy." [18] Cantwell is employing, of course, his usual rough brand of jocularity, but he is making, at the same time, an important point about informed illusion. He well knows that the necessary thing to retain, after the loss of any illusion, is the capacity for belief which made the original illusion possible. It may be that all honorable men are not honorable. It is even very likely. This does not, however, add up to anything like permanent disillusionment with mankind. One gets out the straight-edge razor and performs a delicate operation. Afterwards, if the operation has been well done, the patient will recover.

The Colonel's remark to Renata probably brings the reader somewhere near the center of his complex character as it is presented in the novel. He has the marked ability to combine a mature intellectual toughness and resilience with a deeply felt love for the world extant. He faces with courage and equanimity the

[17] *ARIT*, p. 232.
[18] *ARIT*, p. 182.

evils that surround him and are even inside him. During the heart attack in the lobby of the Gritti, he will not even sit down, though he is gray-faced and sweating. Afterwards he rests "lightly and without illusion," as a hawk might rest, against a corner of the concierge's desk. When he feels well enough to move, he walks carefully and at the proper speed through the streets of Venice to join his girl—the complex image for nearly all that he really loves in the past of his life.[19]

To embody these and other facets of the Colonel's character in a book which carries the exposition almost entirely through dialogue and monologues would have been a sufficient task for an ordinary artist. In a year of hard work, Hemingway not only did this job; he likewise developed, with a craft subtler than one at first suspected, the symbolic pattern in which the Colonel moves.

III. PAST AND PRESENT

As the reader of the novel immerses himself beneath its surface ebb and flow, he soon finds that much more is required of him than a quick and cursory tourist-gondola ride among the urban canals of Venice. He needs to be prepared for the probability that any scene actually carries at least twice the significance he had at first supposed. Having accepted that probability, and having placed himself on the watch for it, he will discover that in Colonel Cantwell's mind nearly all the every-day aspects of Venice operate quite as fully at the level of symbolic meaning as they do in their outward-seeming and easily recognizable selves. In its deeper reaches, *Across the River and Into the Trees* is meant as a symbolic study of a complex state of mind, embodied in a carefully ordered prose poem. It represents the recollection of things past in a state of imaginative hypertension almost the equivalent of a spell.

Hegel once wrote that the necessary precondition for the best lyric poetry was the "poet's ability to absorb the real content absolutely, converting it thereby into his own possession," and grasping certain "relations in the light of his poetic individual-

[19] *ARIT*, p. 196.

ity." [20] This is precisely what has happened with the author, and therefore with the protagonist, of this lyric-poetical novel. In Colonel Cantwell's hypersensitive state of mind, there is special connotative meaning to all the tides and rivers and canals, all the boats and gondolas and gondolieri, all the bridges and mooring-stakes in this lovely "town." The north wind and the far snow-capped mountains, the Countess Renata and her portrait and her heirloom emeralds, the bars and the hotels and the old associates of Venice all mean more to the Colonel than Hemingway will say. But for those who can take a hint, the novel shows an almost absolute absorption of the "real" content into the poet's, and hence the sympathetic reader's, own possession.

Even the most cursory reader of the book knows that every event in Colonel Cantwell's last week-end in Venice has for him a special savor. He is in an intense state of awareness, like the hero of Mann's story. One agent of intensification is the near, consciously accepted, morally scorned, but never ignorable approach of death. Before his departure from Trieste the Colonel has dosed himself heavily with one of the common medications for high blood-pressure, technically known as hypertension. The technical term is almost a metaphor for the Colonel's state of mind. As with Robert Jordan in *For Whom the Bell Tolls* and the dying writer of "The Snows of Kilimanjaro," the emotional hypertension of the recognized approach of death gives every observed detail of remaining life a special sharpened value.

The other factor which illuminates his Friday, his Saturday, and his Sunday is not the end but the beginning: his constant, joyous awareness of the way it was for him in the country round Venice in the days of his youth. This is not a mere sentimental heightening of the good parts of the past. For Cantwell, like his inventor, refuses to cry over departed youth. (Everybody loses all the bloom, Hemingway once told Fitzgerald.[21] A gun or a saddle or a person are all better when they are worn and the bloom is off them. You may lose everything that is fresh and everything that is easy. But you have more *métier* and you know more and when you get flashes of the old juice you get more results with them.)

[20] Hegel, *Philosophy of Fine Art*, London, 1920, vol. 4, p. 201.
[21] EH to FSF, 9/13/29.

But this is not to say that the past is to be rejected. Its value consists in its holding a light behind the present. To be conscious of it in and through the present is to sharpen the meaning of every present incident, and to define in profile the nature of illusion.

For some time before he wrote the Venice novel, Hemingway had shown a marked interest in the effects which may be gained by the collocation of two widely separated periods of time. Such an effect enters very movingly into the short story, "Fathers and Sons." The dying writer of "The Snows of Kilimanjaro" places his two lives side by side—the old free one and the more recent life that has been bought and sold so thoroughly and completely that, shopworn, it can never serve as anything but a sorry contrast to the fine, fresh life of the old days. Harry the writer, dying of gangrene with his work undone, has cause for regret. And there are certain regrets, including a half-buried remorse, which Cantwell feels in bringing together, as in a kind of spell, the time of his youth and the time of his death, in and around the ancient city of the Adriatic.

But Venice for the Colonel is a city of happy spells. His weekly visits, on leave from his command post at Trieste, have always a force like a magical incantation. Driving in from the north-east through the city's ugly suburbs near Mestre he feels again, this Friday, the old exultation. "We are coming into my town," he says silently. "Christ, what a lovely town." His love for the city is nothing new. As a young lieutenant, fighting in the Italian army through a whole wet winter to head off a series of Austrian assaults against the high-road to Venice, he went back to Noghera one clear cold day to have a "gift-wound" dressed. Although he did not enter it at that time, he then first saw the city in the sea, far off like a vision. "It is my city," he now reflects, "because I fought for it when I was a boy, and now that I am half-a-hundred years old, they know I fought for it and am a part owner and they treat me well."

Part of the spell lies in his hospitable acceptance as a Venetian by the Venetians. Though cynics might suppose so, it has nothing to do with his being "a chicken colonel on the winning side." "We all love Venice," says the Barone Alvarito after the duck-shooting expedition. "Perhaps you do the best of all." It is this love which deeply informs the Colonel's Venetian relationships. The anarchist bartender near the *imbarcadero* is an example. He might hate the Colonel as a foreign intruder (like the "over-liberated" boatman in the Veneto). But his real hatred, which the Colonel shares, is for the still recognizable *fascisti*, or for fat, sleek *pescecani* like the postwar rich from Milan who are down for a week-end of gambling on the Lido. The bartender's salute (and it has many echoes) is "My Colonel," a phrase in which the practiced ear might catch the slightest loving stress on the possessive pronoun. There is, indeed, a pride of possession on both sides. The Venetians recognize him as "part owner," even though all of them do not know that he took out a mortgage on a piece of Venice in 1918, depositing his blood and his right knee-cap like permanent collateral at the bank of the Basso Piave near Fossalta.[22]

As a loving man of property, the Colonel reflects that Venice would be a good place to retire to; he might even be buried somewhere near the great villas of the Brenta. In retirement he could do with a simple room in a house where he could look out and watch the boats going by on the canals. "I could read in the mornings and walk around the town before lunch and go every day to see the Tintorettos at the Accademia and to the Scuola San Rocco and eat in good cheap joints behind the market." Venice offers more than a banquet of the senses for a soldier as well educated as Cantwell.

Later, when his spare body fails him finally, he can be "part of the ground where the children play in the evenings, and in the mornings, maybe, they would still be training jumping horses and their hoofs would make a thudding on the turf, and trout would rise in the pool when there was a hatch of fly." As he thinks of it in connection with his departed youth and his approaching death, Venice and the country round it mean very much to him, "more than he could or would ever tell anyone." They mean, in fact, something like the circular entwinement of alpha and omega, the rounding out of a life. For the life of Cantwell has properly begun

[22] *Cantwell's love of Venice*: Cf. *ARIT*, pp. 26, 34, 45, 301.

where it will fittingly end, beside the rivers which drain into the Adriatic and mingle with the tides which ebb and flow among the stones of Venice.[23]

For one in so intense a state of awareness, Venice is full of symbolic reminders. A noteworthy instance is the two mooring-stakes on the canal which leads into the Rio Nuovo.

"They went under the white bridge and under the unfinished wood bridge. Then they left the red bridge on the right and passed under the first high-flying white bridge. Then there was the black iron fretwork bridge on the canal leading into the Rio Nuovo and they passed the two stakes chained together but not touching: like us the Colonel thought. He watched the tide pull at them and he saw how the chains had worn the wood since he first had seen them. That's us, he thought. That's our monument. And how many monuments are there to us in the canals of this town?" [24]

The "us" of this emblem-packed passage would be Lieutenant Cantwell of 1918 and Colonel Cantwell of 1950, chained together by the fact that they are the same person, but separated by the thirty-odd years that have come between. The Colonel is careful to notice that the emblematic stakes are "not touching." In another sense they are very touching indeed. For in the symbolic language of the passage, if one is awake to it and sympathetic with it, is the sum of a lifetime. The tide (take it doubly) pulls at the stakes. The chains (take them doubly) have worn the wood. The stakes (take them doubly, too) are as good a monument as a man could ask.

There are also the bridges, structures of wood and metal arching over Venetian canals and wrenching the Colonel's laboring heart whenever he climbs them to cross. But they are more than obstacles. Because the Colonel is in the state of recollection, they serve him as symbolic reminders of certain milestones in his youthful experience. He never identifies them precisely, merely noting them as they pass, but one might guess that the first white bridge is childhood, the unfinished wooden bridge interrupted adolescence, the red bridge the first far-off war, and the high-flying white bridge an aspect of youthful ambition. At the end of

[23] *Retirement and burial in Venice:* Cf. *ARIT*, pp. 33, 35, 45.
[24] *ARIT*, p. 46.

all these comes the black iron bridge. It is no symbolic accident that this crosses the canal which leads into the Rio Nuovo—the New River. Across the river is where the Colonel will be going before the week-end is out. And here, by this black iron bridge, like a wordless summary of the whole, are the two stakes chained together but not touching.

IV. THE CRAFT AND THE ARMOR

The Colonel's disorder is mechanical, a heart that may go at any time but is kept in action until that time by the kind of tinkering that nitro-glycerine pills can provide. He ought, says his doctor, to drag a chain like a high-octane gasoline truck. The mechanical parallel is not inept. In postwar Venice the Colonel finds any number of similar mechanical disorders. As one who has schooled himself to appreciate all nice ironies, whether comic or tragic, he is prepared to accept each disorder tacitly, bitter-humorously, as an emblem of his own. One, for example, is the elevator in the Gritti-Palace Hotel. It halts, after one ascent, with a "slight hydraulic inaccuracy at the top floor." "Can't you run an elevator properly?" asks the Colonel. "No, my Colonel," the boy said. "The current is not stable." Neither is the Colonel's, as every bridge he crosses in Venice stabbingly shows him.[25]

The most memorable parallel is the old motor in the launch which carries the Colonel to his hotel when he arrives in Venice. Although it resembles a speed boat, being "radiantly varnished and lovingly kept," it derives its power from a tiny, reconditioned Fiat engine, bought from an automobile graveyard and sounding like a stricken tank except that its noises are minute in comparison. As they move through the familiar canals, the Colonel watches the valiant prow of the "delicately brass-striped" craft. He has formerly been striped with brass himself as a general officer, and is both as neatly kept and as "beat-up" as the boat in which he is riding. Therefore he listens to the "metallic agony" of the laboring engine with a specially conditioned sympathy. Even though the Colonel makes no obvious comparisons between the boat and himself, Hemingway's ironic intention is clear:

[25] *ARIT*, p. 66.

"The motor boat came gallantly up beside the piling of the dock. Every move she makes, the Colonel thought, is a triumph of the gallantry of the aging machine. We do not have war horses now like old Traveller, or Marbot's Lysette who fought, personally, at Eylau. We have the gallantry of worn-through rods that refuse to break; the cylinder head that does not blow though it has every right to, and the rest of it." [26]

There is quite a lot to the rest of it. For we have the gallantry also of Old Traveller Cantwell, who has fought, personally, in many places, and can feel, accordingly, a kind of fraternal sympathy with the agony of the vital engine and the still-proud forward motion of the beat-up boat. Again silently, but like a delayed-action corroboration, we have Renata's reaction when she bids the Colonel goodbye two hundred pages later. As they stand on the *imbarcadero,* the Colonel suggests that she return in a faster launch than this "old displaced-engine boat" which has brought them across the river. "I'd rather," says the countess, "take the displaced engine boat if you don't mind." The Colonel does not mind. He knows her choice for what it is—a tacit compliment, a loving gesture, to the gallantry of that cylinder head in his own chest which does not blow, though it has every right to do so. "It's just a muscle," the Colonel has remarked the day before. "Only it is the main muscle. It works as perfectly as a Rolex Oyster Perpetual. The trouble is you cannot send it to the Rolex representative when it goes wrong. When it stops, you just do not know the time. You're dead."

Death is symbolized also in a far more ancient image than a blown cylinder head or a chronometer. *"Fa brutto tempo,"* says the night porter as Cantwell leaves for his early morning game of *solitaire ambulante. "Bruttissimo,"* answers the Colonel, stepping into the wind. And *bruttissimo* is precisely the word for it, since the wind of winter, which plays like a dark undersong throughout the surface gaiety of this last week-end, is also the wind of death. "It's from the high mountains," says Renata as the north wind lashes at the gondola and helps to raise the tide. "Yes," says Ricardo. "And beyond there it's from somewhere else." It is, in-

[26] *ARIT,* pp. 45–52. Cf. the Countess's remark, p. 277, and the Colonel on the Rolex Oyster Perpetual, p. 138.

deed, whether we interpret the remark as simple meteorology or as a form of religious symbolism.[27]

The wind is blowing hard from the mountains on the Friday afternoon of the Colonel's drive by way of Latisana to Venice. It sharpens all the outlines of the buildings on Torcello, Burano, and Murano so that they look "geometrically clear," as the consciousness of approaching death might clarify the vision of a dying man. When the Colonel asks the waiter to open all the windows of his hotel room, the waiter protests that the wind is too strong. But the Colonel will have them open and the wind enters the room as if it were implacably defying the soldier's implacable defiance.

Sometimes, for those who are paying attention, the wind almost identifies itself. When the Colonel and Renata ascend the first bridge of their walk together, the wind lashes at them. Immediately the answering twinge is felt in the Colonel's laboring heart. All through his days in Venice, the wind does its work of buffeting the soldier. He goes about his business and his pleasure, not as if the wind did not exist as an adversary, but as if he scorned it.

His attitude is much the same with respect to the high tides. Like the wind, these have a double meaning for the Colonel. Twice during the gondola ride with Renata, where he comports himself in a manner better becoming his manhood than the state of his health and blood-pressure, he checks the height of the underside of the bridges through which they pass. The first time, while the wind rips wildly under the edges of the blanket, the strain on the Colonel's heart has been such that the gondola is only "inches free" of snagging its bowsprit against the bridge-girders. A little later, when they have turned and are going "with the wind" and have been quiet for a considerable time, he checks "on the bridge that [is] coming up" and notes with relief that there is "clearance." As happens subtly all the time in this novel, the reader may safely assume a symbolic intention behind both passages.[28]

The wind and the tide, the motor-boats and the gondolas, the canals and the bridges and the mooring-stakes, the far mountains and the spreading plain, the hotel-room home, the elevator, the unstable electric current, and perhaps especially the sea-city itself,

[27] *ARIT*, pp. 25, 28 (and cf. 48), 68, 105, 152, 183.
[28] *ARIT*, pp. 155 and 159.

are all of them for the Colonel in his state of heightened awareness, signs and symbols of more than themselves. Each of them in its smaller way (like the city in its total way) is one of his monuments.

As always in Hemingway, death has its opposite numbers—the images of home and the presence of love. Cantwell walks the streets of Venice with his "same old stride" and even breathes deeply as he faces the wind. But he is glad of the welcoming door of Harry's bar. "He had made it again and was at home." Equally welcome is the main entrance at the hotel, where one comes "out of the wind and the cold . . . into the light and warmth of the lobby." Even in the dark of the gondola the home-feeling is re-created. Outside, unremittingly, the wind lashes at the waves. Under the blanket there is no wind. "We are in our home and I love you," says the Countess Renata.[29]

The love is important. Once, in a natural emblem, it is called the island in the great river with the high steep banks. At another time it is presented in the more complex mechanical image of an armored tank. "Don't you feel better to be loved?" asks the girl. "Yes," says the Colonel. In a soldierly metaphor he compares the feeling to that of being within range of enemy fire on a hill "where it was too rocky to dig, and the rocks all solid, but with nothing jutting, and no bulges, and all of a sudden instead of being there naked, I was armoured. Armoured, and the eighty-eights not there. . . ."[30]

This bare and rocky hill, with never a foxhole or a possibility of digging one, and with the enemy all round the base, is a special nightmare of the Colonel's, as it was one of El Sordo's in *For Whom the Bell Tolls*. But he knows the armor that will clothe his nakedness, just as he knows the clean, well-lighted bars and hotels of Venice where a man can be at home even while the north wind blows. In his familiar room at the Gritti—"really home, if a hotel room may be so described"—Richard Cantwell might well echo the feelings of Nick Adams, bedded down in his shelter-half on the bank of the Big Two-Hearted River. "It had been a hard trip. He was very tired. . . . He had made his camp. He was settled.

[29] *ARIT*, pp. 78–79, 106, 151–152.
[30] *ARIT*, pp. 129 and 153.

Nothing could touch him. . . . He was there, in the good place. He was in his home where he had made it." The Colonel, thirty years nearer death than the young Nick Adams, is otherwise in no different a state of happiness. With a decanter of Valpolicella, a portrait of his girl, and a sports column by Red Smith, he is merely a little more comfortable, as is fitting.[31]

V. OPERATION COMPLETED

"You are making the discovery," says the Countess Renata once, politely, to her lover. "I am only the unknown country." [32] The lady might be addressing the reader over the Colonel's shoulder. The discovery to be made about Renata is that, like so many other people and things in the book, she is a symbolic figure. Her portrait and her square-cut emeralds, both of which she lends to the Colonel, are extensions of her symbolic meaning.

Renata exists, of course, merely as a young woman of Venice in love with an aging soldier. Lewis Gannett was thinking of this phase of her existence when he called her "the dream-girl who is a dream of all fair women and never more than a dream." [33] But the real point about Renata is that she is more than a dream.

The Countess is more than Nostalgia, though the sense of the past is one of the gifts she brings to the Colonel. To his imagination, she is like a presiding genius of Venice. One clue to her identity is the translation of her name. She is the figurative image of the Colonel's past youth, still living in the vision-city he once saw from a distance when he fought for Italy on the plains of the Veneto long ago.

A second important clue to her symbolic identity is Renata's age. She is "nearly nineteen," which is precisely the age of the young Cantwell when he got his big wound—the wound that still makes him walk crookedly—at Fossalta in 1918. Her youth, her freshness, and her bravery, like the seemingly inborn wisdom she sometimes displays, are qualities which evidently belonged to young Lieutenant Cantwell in that winter of his rapid growing-up.

[31] *ARIT*, p. 164. Cf. *First 49*, p. 313.
[32] *ARIT*, p. 155.
[33] *New York Herald Tribune*, September 7, 1950.

Renata carries the bloom which he, likewise, owned before the *sale métier* of war-making substituted the scarred, leathery, and battle-smoked patina he now shows.

In Renata's presence (the psychological situation is common), Cantwell is able to return imaginatively to the freshness of his youth. This is the meaning of what at first seems to be a mere passing incident in the Colonel's room at the Gritti-Palace Hotel. The couple have come to wash up before dinner. The Colonel examines his woeful countenance, very critically and in passing, before the bathroom mirror. It looks, he tells himself, like something "cut out of wood by an indifferent craftsman." All of it is covered with ridges, welts, and the thin lines of plastic operations after head-wounds. The Colonel is a *gueule cassée* in spite of all the doctors could do. If the *gueule* is that of experience, and therefore respectable, it does not fit the Colonel's mood of that special moment. "The hell with you," he says to the mirrored image. "You beat-up, miserable. Should we rejoin the ladies?" When he reenters the room where Renata waits, he is "as young as at his first attack,"—*fraîche et rose comme au jour de la bataille*.[34]

The man-woman relationship between the Colonel and his girl is clear, and as simple as these things can ever be. The symbolic relationship is not so clear, though it is revealed by a sufficient number of hints and allusions to make the guessing game a fair one. "I want to be like me, only much, much better and I want to have you love me," says the Colonel's youthful image to the Colonel's aged image during dinner. "Also," she says ("suddenly and unmaskingly"), "I want to be like you. Can I be like you a little while tonight?" The request could be read as a way of phrasing the longing youth feels for experience. The "unmasking" should be noticed because it reveals the process by which the symbolic relationship is to be grasped by the reader.

---

[34] The incident is in *ARIT*, pp. 111–112. The phrase, "as young as at his first attack," is a rough translation of Edgar Quinet's "fraîche et rose comme au jour de la bataille." When Hemingway was in Paris on the way to Africa in the fall of 1933, James and Nora Joyce came to dinner the last night before the hunters entrained for Marseille. They ate a roast pheasant and a quarter of the chevreuil which Hemingway had shot in the Sologne. The Quinet line was running in Joyce's head that night. See *GHOA*, pp. 71 and 195. Cf. *ARIT*, p. 272.

In Venice, the city of spells for the Colonel's intensified imagination, it is possible for youth and age to come together, though always only briefly because the realities of this day keep breaking in. The evanescent feeling of union with the past is underscored again in the gondola. "Please hold me very tightly so we can be part of each other for a little while" is the double-edged request of the Countess. The Colonel's answer is likewise doubled-edged, and one of the edges is tipped with irony. "We can try," says Cantwell. In the special, magical atmosphere and mood of Venice, a degree of success is possible.[35]

When the Colonel and his image walk home afterwards across the cold and windswept square in the winter night, they hold together "close and hard in their sorrow and their happiness." If the happiness is in the nature of an illusion, the sorrow is the straight-edge razor that will cut out the false parts. The sorrow originates in the Colonel's awareness of the errors he has made in the course of his hard-bitten life—the women and the soldiers and the countries he has lost, through cruelty and faulty judgment and bad luck, since the days when the bloom was on him and he was starting out. He readily agrees to Renata's suggestion on the following morning: "Please hold me very close and let's not talk, or think, about how things might have been different." The suggestion is sound. The Colonel has already told himself the same thing in the gay and bitter version of Villon: "Où sont les neiges d'antan? Où sont les neiges d'autrefois? Dans le pissoir toute la chose comme ça." Yet the sorrow and the remorse cannot be disposed of so easily. Cantwell must purge himself by confession.[36]

Even when one fully accepts the idea of the Venetian spell, it would be possible to accuse the Colonel of a sentimental romanticization of the days of his youth. This matter is handled by means of Renata's symbolic portrait.[37] "While it is not truly me," says the Countess, "it is the way you like to think of me." The Colonel also assists in the identification of the meaning of the portrait. "Portrait," he says once—"Boy or daughter or my one true love

[35] *Renata's symbolic identity: ARIT*, pp. 82, 91, 96, 142, 156, 160, 210.
[36] *ARIT*, pp. 94, 242, 294, and 112. I owe the confession-idea to Malcolm Cowley.
[37] *ARIT*, pp. 97, 114, 147, 170, 173, 178, 180, 196, 209.

or whatever it is." The picture is interwoven, for him, with the happiness he feels if he looks far enough backward—skipping the *sale métier* of the intervening years. "I'll be damned if I'll turn that in," says he. "I keep that." But at the close of the book, since he cannot take it with him, the Colonel gives back the portrait.

Even while he has it, however, he is quite clear in his mind that it is no substitute for the real thing. There is even a kind of commentary on the relation between life and art in what the Colonel says of the portrait. "The portrait is lovely to have," says he in one of his boar-like moments. But in comparison with the real thing, the living Renata, "it is like skinning a dead horse." He recognizes in the painting a "static" quality which makes it an inadequate substitute for the moving thing. He reflects, evidently, that one can lose himself so far and so long in the past that he gets out of touch with the salutary present. Looking at his own scarred face in the mirror, the Colonel draws the contrast: "Portrait was a thing of the past. Mirror was actuality and of this day."

In a very womanly fashion, knowing the answer in advance, the Countess puts the crucial question about her portrait. "Do you love her more than me?" This is another way of asking the Colonel if he prefers the art to the actual. "I'm not abnormal yet," says the Colonel. "But she's lovely." Later he adds (and the remark is still double-edged): "There's no comparison of course. I don't mean likeness. The likeness is excellent." All art, the argument would run, can be valued because it provides fresh insights into the conglomerate of good and bad which the actual offers to us. Yet all art needs the corrective which can be supplied only by a direct and often-renewed attention to the actual. The Colonel prefers the actual, but he cherishes the art.

Renata's square emeralds have likewise a double function.[38] These are the stones of Venice, cut long ago by master craftsmen. They embody in a lasting art form something, at least, of the deep past of the city. As heirlooms, handed down from mother to daughter through the generations, they represent a history familiar to the Colonel. Being part owner of the city, it is proper that he should be part owner of the emeralds, and the Countess insists on lending the stones to her lover. They are to be kept in his pocket

[38] *ARIT*, pp. 103, 105, 108, 117, 166, 181, 195–197.

like a lucky piece. They are something durable given him by his youth and something tangible for one in the imminent presence of death. "Put your hand in your right-hand pocket and feel very rich," says Renata. "I am rich," says the lover of Venice. The Gran Maestro, sensing that this is a private joke between them (as it is also between the author and the reader), silently departs.

Yet it is a serious kind of joke. Later on, and the action is symbolic, the Colonel transfers the emeralds, "whatever they are," from his right-hand pocket to the inside left pocket of his tunic, beside the old chronometer of his heart. But in the end, having no further use for them where he is going, he gives them back. Like the surrender of his youth and age, as death over-runs his position, the turning-back of the stones is a gesture. It signifies, perhaps, the complete independence of the Colonel's inner self (a Stoic doctrine), and the final aloneness of his being. Like the portrait, the stones have only been lent—as Venice has been lent, as the life itself has been lent. Cantwell is very careful to pay his debts in full and in kind. He knows that after the squaring-up will come the rounding-off. The circle of his days will be closed and completed, and he can die, as he dies, under perfect control and without impediment, in what Mann called a "positive triumph."

Across the River and Into the Trees is not one of Hemingway's major novels. It was not meant to be, any more than Eclogue X was meant to match the *Aeneid*, or *Paradise Regained* to duplicate *Paradise Lost*. One might construct a rough table of correspondences in order to place the book in its relations to the best of his earlier work in long fiction. If *A Farewell to Arms* was his *Romeo and Juliet*, and *For Whom the Bell Tolls* his *King Lear*, this mid-century novel could perhaps be called a lesser kind of *Winter's Tale* or *Tempest*. Its tone is elegiac. It moves like a love-lyric. The round within which its forces are deployed is the rough shape of a life.

The country a novelist knows, said Hemingway, is the country in his heart. Another Venetian, Robert Browning, remarked that if you opened his heart you would "see graved inside of it—Italy." Though the lion-like Colonel with his wild-boar's irascibility would make a surly joke about letting anyone tinker with his own un-tinkerable chronometer, he shares the love that Browning felt.

De gustibus. For the opening of one's heart, as for its closing, Italy is as good a place as any. To the north, where the cold wind comes from, are the mountains. All around Venice stretches the plain where the young lieutenant lost his feeling of immortality at the age of eighteen, and where the Colonel at fifty completes the operation with a death.

XII · The Ancient Mariner

"Old men ought to be explorers
Here and there does not matter
We must be still and still moving
Into another intensity
For a further union, a deeper communion
Through the dark cold and the empty des-
olation,
The wave cry, the wind cry, the vast wa-
ters
Of the petrel and the porpoise. In my end
is my beginning."

—T. S. Eliot [1]

I. TRUTH AND POETRY

Goethe called his autobiography *Dichtung und Wahrheit,*
Poetry and Truth. The reverse of Goethe's title, as a strategy of
emphasis, admirably fits the collected works of Hemingway.
From the beginning he was dedicated as a writer to the rendering
of Wahrheit, the precise and at least partly naturalistic presentation of things as they are and were. Yet under all his brilliant
surfaces lies the controlling Dichtung, the symbolic underpaint-
ing which gives so remarkable a sense of depth and vitality to
what otherwise might seem flat and two-dimensional.

The literary histories commonly credit Hemingway with being
the "archpriest of naturalists." This is something less than a half-
truth because it tends, as a designation, to ignore what is always
taking place down under. That Hemingway the technician
achieves effects simply impossible to his naturalistic forebears or
current imitators has sometimes been noticed. The cause behind
the majority of these effects, the deep inner Dichtung which runs
through all of his work from *The Sun Also Rises* to *The Old Man
and The Sea,* has not until very recently been fully recognized or
systematically explored.

[1] "East Coker," in *Four Quartets,* New York, 1943, p. 17.

Hemingway's conception of the meaning of Wahrheit steadily changed in breadth and depth over a thirty-year period, attaining a kind of apogee in *The Old Man and the Sea*. His earliest conviction, to which he always held with one facet of his artistic consciousness, is well summed up in a remark of Albert Schweitzer's on the *Naturphilosophie* of Goethe: "Only that knowledge is true which adds nothing to nature, either by thought or imagination; and which recognizes as valid only what comes from a research that is free from prejudices and preconceptions, from a firm and pure determination to find the truth, from a meditation which goes deeply into the heart of nature." [2]

As a partial summary of Hemingway's esthetic and moral position, Schweitzer's statement would have to be qualified only by adding human nature to the rest of nature. Hemingway was very rarely interested in the passing show of the non-human universe unless it could serve him in some way to gain further understanding of one of nature's more complex phenomena, the human mind. A meditation which goes deeply enough into the heart of nature, whether along the banks of the Big Two-Hearted River, on the high slopes of the Guadarramas, or among the vast waters of the Gulf Stream, will often end, as it does in Hemingway, with a meditation which goes deeply into the heart of man.

Its grasp of reality, its content of Wahrheit, is one guaranty of the survival power of Hemingway's art. A second guaranty, not less important, is the use and control of Dichtung. The Dichtung in Hemingway might be provisionally defined as the artist's grasp of the relationship between the temporal and the eternal. That grasp is expressed, in his fiction, through the considered use of imaginative symbols. Most of these come, by the way of the artist's imagination, from the visible material universe— the mountains and the plains, the rivers and the trees, the weather and the seasons, the land and the sea. To such natural images Hemingway attached the strong emotional power of his artistic apprehension of them. With Wordsworth, he knew that natural "objects derive their influence, not from properties inherent in them, not from what they are actually in themselves,

[2] Schweitzer, *Goethe: Four Studies*, transl. by Charles Joy, Boston, 1949, pp. 70–71.

but from such as are bestowed upon them by the minds of those who are conversant with or affected by those objects. Thus the poetry . . . proceeds, whence it ought to do, from the soul of man, communicating its creative energies to the images of the external world." [3] At the same time, Hemingway continuously managed to render with fidelity each of the natural objects or scenes precisely for what, in itself, it really is. As a result of their union with imagination and emotion, the various phenomena rise up as operative symbols in all his art. They become thereby not less real but more real than they are in themselves because of the double or triple significations with which they have been imbued.

Hemingway hinted strongly at this point when he said in 1942 that the writer's "standard of fidelity to the truth should be so high that his invention, out of his experience, should produce a truer account than anything factual can be." [4] The *invention* here could be defined as that form of symbolic logic which is the artist's rough equivalent to the rational logic of the philosophers. Hemingway understood, with Niebuhr, that "the relation of time and eternity" cannot be expressed in simple rational terms, but "only in symbolic terms." [5] In some writers, the symbols are made over from antecedent literatures. In Hemingway they are usually, though not invariably, derived from the nexus of nature by means of the imaginative apprehension of human experience in natural environs.

The conjunction of a "naturalistic" Wahrheit with the non-literary symbols of the Dichtung gives Hemingway's best work its special strength and staying power, as well as its special distinction of being the most truly "original" writing in the field of twentieth-century fiction. Alfred Kazin once remarked that "it is hard to think of Hemingway and Faulkner as naturalists, their sensibility is too wide." [6] Hemingway's poetic "sensibility" in fact carries his work far beyond the area of the simple naturalist. Yet

[3] Wordsworth to Wrangham, January 1816.
[4] Introduction to *Men at War*, New York, 1942, p. xv.
[5] Reinhold Niebuhr, *Beyond Tragedy*, New York, 1938, p. 4.
[6] Alfred Kazin in *The American Writer and the European Tradition*, ed. Margaret Denny and William H. Gilman, Minneapolis, Minnesota, 1950, p. 121.

the clear seeing and the level-headedness of the undeceivable naturalist is not finally sacrificed to the requirements of the poetic sensibility. The two powers cooperate.

One is what nature gives to the artist who has the clairvoyance to recognize it and the patience to select it out from the mass of available impressions. The other is what the artist gives to nature when his sensibility is broad and deep enough to endow natural phenomena with an emotional significance which they do not in themselves possess. Either one, taken by itself, would involve a falsification of experience, a unilateral objectivity or a unilateral subjectivity in the apprehension of what we know. Goethe's title is, however, particularly apposite in that it implies both a distinction and a collaboration. It is through the reciprocal interaction of a natural Wahrheit and a natural Dichtung that Hemingway so often seemed to get, as Emilio Cecchi said, "the illusion of having finally hit upon a literature which has nothing to do with literature, which is not spoiled or weakened by literature." [7] His two-handed grasp on the actual, with the right hand of the head and the left hand of the heart, is the chief of many reasons why his work is likely to last when that of most of his contemporaries in fiction and poetry has been forgotten.

II. SANTIAGO AT SEA

The Old Man and The Sea earned its author the Pulitzer Prize in fiction for 1952, and was instrumental in winning him the Nobel Prize two years later.[8] This short novel, in the words of

[7] Emilio Cecchi in *Americana: Raccolta di Narratori,* ed. E. Vittorini, Milan, 1943, introd., p. xvi.

[8] Award of the Pulitzer Prize was announced May 4, 1953. News that Hemingway had been awarded the Nobel Prize for Literature was first published October 28, 1954. Between these two awards came another when, in recognition of his long residence in Cuba and his authorship of a novel about a brave Cuban fisherman, he was given the Order of Carlos Manuel de Cespedes, the highest honor that the Cuban government could bestow on a foreigner. The day chosen for the award, which took place at the International Yacht Club in Havana, was July 21, 1954, Hemingway's fifty-fifth birthday. This triple recognition of the author's prowess, coming as it did nearly thirty years after the first American publication of *In Our Time,* could be thought of under the rubric of "better late than never." See below, Chapter XIII.

Eliot, explores yet "another intensity" beyond those which can be located in Hemingway's previous fictions. Among the vast waters of the petrel and the porpoise, he seemed to many of his readers to have found the means of establishing "a further union" and "a deeper communion" between Wahrheit and Dichtung than he had achieved before.

The old man of the title is a fisherman by trade. He bears the fitting name of Santiago.[9] Early one morning after months of bad fishing luck, he rows out alone into the mile-deep Gulf Stream where it swings in above the long island of Cuba. Towards noon of the first day out, he hooks a gigantic marlin. For two days and two nights it pulls him in his boat far to the northward and the eastward, while he hangs for dear life onto the heavy line, a human towing bitt, fighting a battle of endurance against the power of the fish. On the third day out, again nearly at noon, he succeeds in bringing the marlin to the surface and killing it with his harpoon. Since it is too large to put aboard, he lashes it alongside his skiff and sets his small, patched sail for the long voyage home. Then, one by one, two by two, and later in rapacious ripping packs, the sharks move in on his trophy. By the time he has reached his native harbor, there is nothing left of it except the skeleton, the bony head, and the proud, sail-like tail.

The old man loses the battle he has won. The winner takes

---

[9] Literally *Saint James*. Professor Robert M. Brown first noted the point. Melvin Backman in *Modern Fiction Studies* 1 (August 1955), p. 10, observes the connection between Santiago and the "fisherman, apostle, and martyr from the Sea of Galilee." See *Matthew* 4: 18–22. "When we reach *The Old Man and the Sea*," says Professor Backman, "we seem to have come a long way from the early works, but there is a pattern into which all of them fall. It is true that the old man is the only hero who is not left alone, at the end of the story, with death or despair. He is old and womanless and humble. Yet in him we have a blending of the two dominant motifs—the matador and the crucified." Santiago's suffering is, however, more remarkable than his matador-like act of killing. "Etched on the reader's mind," says Backman, "is the image of the old man as he settled against the wood of the bow . . . and took his suffering as it came, telling himself, *Rest gently now.* . . . Suffering and gentle and wood blend magically into an image of Christ on the cross."

nothing but the sense of having fought the fight to the limits of his strength, of having shown what a man can do when it is necessary. Like many of the rest of us, he is undefeated only because he has gone on trying. There is no need for the corrupting forces of moth and rust: thieves have broken through Santiago's lines of defence and made off with all there is. As for the mariner himself, he has reached a condition of absolute physical exhaustion as well as, on the moral plane, an absolute but not an abject humility. Both have cost him very little less than everything, which is of course the price one must always finally pay. Santiago's victory is the moral victory of having lasted without permanent impairment of his belief in the worth of what he has been doing.

In its main outlines, the story is simple in the extreme. Stripped, like the marlin, down to its bare bones, it looks not unlike the 200-word version which Hemingway first recorded in an article on the Gulf Stream during the spring of 1936. "An old man fishing alone in a skiff out of Cabanas hooked a great marlin that, on the heavy sashcord handline, pulled the skiff far out to sea. Two days later the old man was picked up by fishermen 60 miles to the eastward, the head and the forward part of the marlin lashed alongside. What was left of the fish, less than half, weighed 800 pounds. The old man had stayed with him a day, a night, a day and another night while the fish swam deep and pulled the boat. When he had come up the old man had pulled the boat up on him and harpooned him. Lashed alongside the sharks had hit him and the old man had fought them out alone in the Gulf Stream in a skiff, clubbing them, stabbing at them, lunging at them with an oar until he was exhausted and the sharks had eaten all they could hold. He was crying in the boat when the fishermen picked him up, half crazy from his loss, and the sharks were still circling the boat." [10]

[10] "On the Blue Water," *Esquire* 5 (April 1936), pp. 31, 184–185. The story as finally told evolved slowly in Hemingway's mind. On February 7, 1939, he told Maxwell Perkins of his wish to write the story of the old fisherman. In developing the character of Santiago, he seems to have appropriated some of the personal qualities of an acquaintance, since dead, who lived in Casablanca on the eastward side of Havana harbor where (until the area was razed by fire) many commercial fishermen made their

The difference between this anecdote and the finished work of art is of course immense. What makes the difference is the manner of the narration. Concentrating on the shape of the anecdote alone, the unsympathetic reader might argue that, except for its presumptive basis in historical fact, the story is nearly incredible. Or he might find too neat a balance in the narrative of a determined old man doing battle, first against an almost equally determined marlin, and then against a band of predators determined to make off with the catch. Such a reader might ask what the whole matter comes to. After the sharks' assault, the tangible loss precisely cancels out the tangible profit, leaving the reader neither in the red nor in the black, neither plus nor minus, but exactly at zero.

Yet the novel does not leave us that cold. The manner of its telling controls, one might say, the thermogenetic factor. The warmth of our sympathy can be traced in part to the way in which the portrait of Santiago himself has been drawn. "He was an old man," the story begins, "who fished alone in a skiff in the Gulf Stream and he had gone eighty-four days now without taking a fish. In the first forty days a boy had been with him. But after forty days without a fish the boy's parents had told him that the old man was definitely and finally *salao,* which is the worst form of unlucky, and the boy had gone at their orders in another boat which caught three good fish the first week. It made the boy sad to see the old man come in each day with his skiff empty and he always went down to help him carry either the coiled lines or the gaff and harpoon and the sail that was furled around the mast. The sail was patched with flour sacks and, furled, it looked like a flag of permanent defeat.

"The old man was thin and gaunt with deep wrinkles in the

---

headquarters. "The book is fiction," said Hemingway, "based on many actual occurrences." See *Life* 33 (September 22, 1952), p. 12, also for the picture of a marlin caught by Hemingway himself and partially destroyed by sharks. After more than fifteen years, Hemingway felt prepared to tell the story. It was in first-draft typescript by April 1, 1951. The MS was received by Scribner's on March 10, 1952, published in full in *Life,* Sept. 1, 1952, and in book form by Scribner's on Sept. 8 in a first printing of 50,000 copies. Originally it stood as the concluding section of the book first called *The Island and the Stream,* posthumously published in October 1970 as *Islands in the Stream.* See below, Chapter XV.

back of his neck. The brown splotches of the benevolent skin cancer the sun brings from its reflection on the tropic sea were on his cheeks. The blotches ran well down the sides of his face and his hands had the deep-creased scars from handling heavy fish on the cords. But none of these scars were fresh. They were as old as erosions in a fishless desert.

"Everything about him was old except his eyes and they were the same color as the sea and were cheerful and undefeated."

In a strictly objective view, the man Santiago is only a simple fisherman, like his namesake the son of Zebedee, mending his nets by the shore of Galilee. As Laurence Housman remarked of Wordsworth's leech-gatherer, another old man going about his lonely professional work on the undulating stretches of a British moorland, he is probably not in himself an exceptionally noble character.[11] What has happened is that in both instances an individual has been singled out against such ancient backdrops of sea or moorland, and then staged so memorably, and in terms of a contest of endurance that seems itself a paradigm of human life, that he enters immediately, and perhaps not even tentatively, into the gallery of literary immortals.

Sean O'Faolain once commented on Hemingway's love for the spirit of gallantry, which has made him rove the world "in search of the flame of the spirit in men and beasts."[12] Within the structure of the story, it may be said at once, the gallantry of Santiago is defined in part by the gallantry of his adversary. Aside from the essential valiance of the marlin's towing operation, which Santiago knows all too well because he is on one end of it, the adversary's courage and power are underscored in three stages. When he first sees one of his bobbing green sticks dip sharply, and feels the slight, nibbling, tentative yank on his line, Santiago knows that an event of some importance is in the offing. For this is the line set for a hundred fathoms, and six

[11] Laurence Housman, ed., *A Wordsworth Anthology*, New York, 1946, introd., pp. 15–16. "Wordsworth has here staged a type so wonderfully that he stands out and becomes a great figure in literature—just as, in sculpture or painting, rough types of labor by Meunier or Jean François Millet become things of significant and permanent beauty."

[12] Christian Gauss Seminar, Princeton University, 1954.

hundred feet down in the darkness a marlin is eating the sardines impaled on the point and shank of the hook.[13]

After the gentle tugging comes the hard pull and heavy weight when the huge fish swims off with the bait in its mouth. As Santiago braces himself against the thwart and leans against the pull, weight against weight, the skiff moves slowly off towards the northwest. Four hours later the fish is still swimming steadily and the old man is still solidly braced with the line across his back. Like other Hemingway characters in not dissimilar positions, he is by now trying "not to think but only to endure." At sunset it is still the same. "I wish I could see him only once," thinks Santiago, "to know what I have against me." And again, near midnight: "We are joined together and have been since noon. And no one to help either of us." Gallantry against gallantry: but neither of them has seen his adversary.[14]

The second stage comes with Santiago's first sight of the fish, in royal purple as befits a king, near noon of the second day. "The line rose slowly and steadily and then the surface of the ocean bulged ahead of the boat and the fish came out. He came out unendingly and water poured from his sides. He was bright in the sun and his head and back were dark purple and in the sun the stripes on his sides showed wide and a light lavender. His sword was as long as a baseball bat and tapered like a rapier and he rose his full length from the water and then re-entered it, smoothly, like a diver and the old man saw the great scythe-blade of his tail go under and the line commenced to race out." With awe, Santiago observes that the marlin is two feet longer than the skiff.[15]

But Santiago knows, has known all along, that there are other standards of measurement than feet or inches on steel tape. That morning, at first light, while the boat still moved steadily, inexorable as the tick of time, he had spoken to the fish of his love and respect: "But I will kill you dead before this day ends." It is the huntsman's code—as in the pursuit of the kudu among the

[13] *The Old Man and The Sea*, p. 45.
[14] *Ibid.*, pp. 47–55.
[15] *Ibid.*, p. 69.

green hills of Africa—to admire the courage and the strength of that which one is out to kill. Breakfasting on raw bonito, the old man had reflected that he would like to pass some down to the fish his brother. Yet he knew he must kill the fish and keep strong to do it, and that by the same token the fish's strength must be worn down.[16]

From his new knowledge of "what I have against me" Santiago becomes newly aware of what he has inside him that will enable him to win. It is this sense of proving worth against a worthy adversary which, as much as any other means at his disposal, sustains the old man in his time of stress. The first breaching, like the various slight changes in the slant of the line, suggest that by almost imperceptible degrees Santiago is gaining the advantage. The sight of the fish itself is a further spur, for here at last, expansed before his eyes, is the enormous quarry, the goal towards which he moves. But the chief way in which the power outside enlarges the power inside is through Santiago's resolute comparisons. "Let him think I am more man than I am, and I will be so." Or again: "I will show him what a man can do and what a man endures." [17] If the old man wins, he has proved his own worth to himself once more, which is the proof men need in order to continue with the other and perpetual endurance contest into which birth precipitates them all.

Stage the third, the zenith of Santiago's struggle, which is also close to the nadir of his strength, comes on the morning of the third day. Now the marlin rises and slowly circles the boat while the old man sweats and strains to get him close enough for harpooning. "You are killing me, fish, the old man thought. But you have a right to. Never have I seen a greater, or more beautiful, or a calmer or more noble thing than you, brother. Come on and kill me. I do not care who kills who." But he does care. Though his hands are pulped and he is nearly blind with fatigue, he tries one final time on the ninth circle. "He took all his pain and what was left of his strength and his long gone pride and he put it against the fish's agony and the fish came over onto his side and swam gently on his side, his bill almost touching the plank-

[16] *Ibid.*, pp. 60–65.
[17] *Ibid.*, pp. 71 and 73.

ing of the skiff." Now Santiago drives home the harpoon, the fish leaps and falls in death, and the first forty-eight hours are over.[18]

In this movement of the story, as in the phase of the sharks that is yet to come, Santiago bears a significant relationship to other characters in the Hemingway canon. For many years prior to the composition of *The Old Man and The Sea,* Hemingway had interested himself in the proposition that there must be a resemblance, in the nature of things, between Jesus Christ in his human aspect as the Son of Man and those countless and often nameless thousands in the history of Christendom who belong to the category of "good men," and may therefore be seen as disciples of Our Lord, whatever the professed degree of their Christian commitment. The young priest, friend to Lieutenant Henry in *A Farewell to Arms,* is an early example; the old Spaniard Anselmo, friend to Robert Jordan in *For Whom the Bell Tolls,* is a more recent instance.

Santiago shows, in his own right, certain qualities of mind and heart which are clearly associated with the character and personality of Jesus Christ in the Gospel stories. There is the essential gallantry, a kind of militance. There is the staying-power which helps him in his determination to last to the end of whatever is to come. There is the ability to ignore physical pain while concentrating on the larger object which is to be achieved. "Etched on the reader's mind," writes a recent commentator, "is the image of the old man as he settled against the wood of the bow . . . and took his suffering as it came, telling himself, 'Rest gently now against the wood and think of nothing.' " The suffering, the gentleness, and the wood it is noted, "blend magically into an image of Christ on the cross." [19] So it may be. As the old man moves into and through the next phase of his operation, the force of the crucifixion idea is gradually intensified.

Besides the qualities already enumerated, three others deserve particular notice in this connection: Santiago's humility, his

[18] *Ibid.,* pp. 102–103.
[19] Melvin Backman, "Hemingway: The Matador and the Crucified," *Modern Fiction Studies* 1 (August 1955), pp. 2–11. See esp. p. 10.

natural piety, and his compassion. His humility is of that well-tested kind which can co-exist with pride. "He was too simple to wonder when he had attained humility. But he knew he had attained it and he knew it was not disgraceful and it carried no loss of true pride." When his own disciple, the boy Manolo, calls him, as Jesus has many times been called, "the best fisherman," Santiago answers in character:

"No. I know others better."

"Qué va," the boy said. "There are many good fishermen and some great ones. But there is only you."

"Thank you. You make me happy. I hope no fish will come along so great that he will prove us wrong."

The great fish that Santiago is soon to be engaged with will not, of course, prove Manolo to be in error. Quite the contrary. But when the old man finally outfights his marlin, we are told that his pride has been gone for a long time—forced out through the openings in the sieve of his suffering. The humility remains as the natural companion of his immense fatigue.[20]

However jocular he may be about his religion, however much, in his humility, he may deny himself the guerdon, Santiago is evidently a pious old man. The piety appears unobtrusively in his constant, accepted, and unquestioning awareness of supernal power, at once outside and potentially inside his personal struggle. His allusions to Christ, to God, and to the Virgin are never oaths, as one might expect to find them in the mouth of a professional fisherman out of Havana. They are rather simple petitions to a presumably available source of strength of which he feels the need. "Christ knows he can't have gone," he exclaims in the parlous interval before the fish is actually hooked. "God let him jump," he prays, soon after dawn on the second day, for if God will permit or urge the great fish to leap high and twist, "he'll fill the sacs along his backbone with air and then he cannot go deep to die." "God help me to have the cramp go," says Santiago once again, when his left hand has become temporarily useless. But he does not depend solely on God's intercession: he massages the hand, he exposes it to the sun, he eats raw tuna in the expectation of benefit. If he has to compel the hand to open, he

[20] The Old Man and The Sea, pp. 14, 25, 103.

will, "cost whatever it costs." He prefers to "let it open by itself and come back of its own accord." But like sun, diet, and massage, prayer may help.

One finds also the more formal prayers. "I am not religious," says the old man untruly. "But I will say ten Our Fathers and ten Hail Marys that I should catch this fish, and I promise to make a pilgrimage to the Virgen de Cobre if I catch him. That is a promise." As he begins to say his prayers, he discovers that he is so fatigued that he cannot always remember the word-sequences. Concluding that "Hail Marys are easier to say than Our Fathers," he tries one of the former and completes it, appending a further petition to the Blessed Virgin: "Pray for the death of this fish. Wonderful though he is." Then, "with his prayers said, and feeling much better, but suffering exactly as much and perhaps a little more," he leans once more against the wood of the bow of his boat, mechanically working the fingers of his recently uncramped left hand. Much later, at the battle's climax, prayer enters his mind again. This time he raises the ante of promised prayers tenfold. "Now that I have him coming so beautifully, God help me to endure. I'll say a hundred Our Fathers and a hundred Hail Marys. But I cannot say them now." [21]

According to the ancient mariner of Coleridge, "he prayeth best who loveth best all things both great and small." Along with humility, pride, and piety, Hemingway's ancient mariner is richly endowed with the quality of compassion. Of course he is not so foolish as to love all creatures equally. He dislikes, for example, the Portuguese men-of-war, whose beautiful "purple, formalized, iridescent, gelatinous" bubbles serve to buoy up the "long deadly purple filaments" which trail a yard behind them in the water and contain a poison which will paralyze unwary passersby. *"Agua mala,"* says the old man to one of them. "You whore." Outwardly handsome, inwardly lethal, these beings strike him as the falsest things in the sea. It is his landside sport "to walk on them on the beach after a storm and hear them pop when he stepped on them with the horny soles of his feet." He has another set of enemies in the waters of the tropic sea. For he genuinely hates, and gladly destroys, the voracious sharks

[21] *Ibid.,* pp. 47, 59, 66–67, 71–72, 96.

which attack and disfigure the marlin he has fought so long to win.[22]

But his hatred is more than overbalanced by his simple love and compassion for all those creatures which swim or blindly soar. His principal friends on the ocean are the flying fish. He loves the green turtles and the hawksbills "with their elegance and speed," and though the loggerheads are huge and stupid, happily gobbling the Portuguese men-of-war with shut eyes and an air of heavy contentment, the contempt he feels for them is friendly. Porpoises delight him. "They are good," he says. "They play and make jokes and love one another. They are our brothers like the flying fish." Several times in the course of his struggle he feels pity for the great marlin he has hooked—so "wonderful and strange" in his power to pull the skiff for so many hours, without sustenance, without respite, and with the pain of the hook in his flesh.[23]

For the lesser birds his compassion is greatest, "especially the small delicate dark terns that are always flying and looking and almost never finding." The birds, he reflects, "have a harder life than we do except for the robber birds, and the heavy strong ones. Why did they make birds so delicate and fine as those sea swallows when the ocean can be so cruel? She is kind and very beautiful. But she can be so cruel and it comes so suddenly and such birds that fly, dipping and hunting, with their small sad voices are made too delicately for the sea." [24]

His grateful sense of brotherhood with the creatures of the water and the air is, though full of love, essentially realistic and unsentimental. His implied or overt comparisons between sub-human and human brothers often open out, therefore, in as many directions as our imaginations wish to follow. A memorable example of this tendency appears in the incident of the land-bird, a warbler, which comes to rest on Santiago's skiff far out at sea. "A small bird came toward the skiff from the north. He was a warbler and flying very low over the water. The old man could see that he was very tired. The bird made the stern of the boat

---

[22] Ibid., pp. 39–40.
[23] Ibid., pp. 32, 40, 53, 83.
[24] Ibid., p. 32. The poetry of this passage is worth special notice.

and rested there. Then he flew around the old man's head and rested on the line where he was more comfortable."

"How old are you?" the old man asked the bird. "Is this your first trip?"

The bird looked at him when he spoke. He was too tired even to examine the line and he teetered on it as his delicate feet gripped it fast.

"It's steady," the old man told him. "It's too steady. You shouldn't be that tired after a windless night. What are birds coming to?"

The hawks, he thought, that come out to sea to meet them. But he said nothing of this to the bird who could not understand him anyway and who would learn about the hawks soon enough.

"Take a good rest, small bird," he said. "Then go in and take your chance like any man or bird or fish."

This gently humorous monologue with its serious undertone of implied commentary on the human condition encourages the old man at this stage of his struggle. "Stay at my house if you like, bird," he said. "I am sorry I cannot hoist the sail and take you in with the small breeze that is rising. But I am with a friend." It is just at this point that the marlin gives a sudden lurch, the tautened line jerks, and the warbler flies away—towards whatever it is that awaits him on the long voyage home. Hawks or sharks, the predators wait, whether for tired young birds or tired old men.[25]

Coleridge's ancient mariner comes, one might say, to share with Hemingway's this quality of compassion. A major difference between the novel and the poem is that Santiago already owns compassion as by a natural gift; Coleridge's wanderer must achieve it through an ordeal. The act of shooting the albatross is in no way comparable to Santiago's killing of the marlin. One is meaningless and wanton; the other is professional and necessary. In Coleridge's poem, the broken circuit, the failure of spiritual electricity, leads immediately and sequentially to the ordeal, which is by hunger and thirst, cold and heat (like Santiago's), but is chiefly an ordeal by loneliness. Precisely balancing the horror of aloneness is the sense of brotherhood and at-

[25] *Ibid.*, p. 60.

one-ment which floods in upon the mariner when by a simple act of contrition he subconsciously blesses the watersnakes as they coil and swim in the phosphorescent ocean of Coleridge's imagination. The central theme of the poem resides exactly here: in that projected sense of a breakable but reparable solidarity between us and the other life that is around us on the earth, or in the waters beneath the earth.

To their hazard or their sorrow, Hemingway's heroes sometimes lose touch with nature. Jake Barnes in the Parisian café-circle and Fred Henry in the toils of war on the plains of Italy are two memorable examples. Their health ordinarily returns when they re-ally themselves with the natural laws and forces which wait unchanged for the errants' return. But Santiago is never out of touch. The line which ties him to the fish guarantees that the alliance will remain unbroken. Saint Francis with his animals and birds is not more closely allied to God's creation than this Santiago with his birds and his fish. These are his brothers, in all the sizes. "I am with a friend," he cheerfully tells the warbler. When the bird has departed, he is momentarily smitten by a sense of his aloneness on the vast waters. Then he looks ahead of his skiff to see "a flight of wild ducks etching themselves against the sky over the water, then blurring, then etching again." Once more he is convinced of what he has only momentarily forgotten: no man is ever alone on the sea. This sense of solidarity with the visible universe and the natural creation is another of the factors which help to sustain him through his own long ordeal.[26]

III. THE BOY AND THE LIONS

The relationship between Santiago and the boy Manolo is of a special and memorable kind. In the light of the experiment in symbolic doubling which Hemingway tried in *Across The River and Into The Trees*, the meaning of this other relationship becomes clear. In one of her aspects, Renata stands for Colonel Cantwell's lost youth. Manolo fulfills a similar purpose, and with greater success in that we do not have to overcome the

[26] *Ibid.*, p. 67.

doubt raised by the difference of sexes between the Colonel and his lady. To claim such a purpose for Manolo is not, of course, to discount his dramatic function, which is to heighten our sympathy with the old fisherman. At the beginning and end of the story, we watch Santiago through the boy's admiring and pitying eyes. From the charitable (and again fittingly named) Martin, owner of The Terrace, Manolo brings Santiago a last supper of black beans and rice, fried bananas, stew, and two bottles of beer. On the morning of the expedition, Manolo arranges for the simple breakfast of coffee in condensed milk cans. He also procures the albacores and sardines which Santiago will use for bait. After helping to launch the skiff, the boy sees Santiago off in the dark with a wish for his luck on this eighty-fifth day. At the close of the story, after the ordeal, Manolo brings coffee and food for the old man's waking, and ointment for his injured hands, commiserating on the loss, and planning for a future when they will work side by side again. The love of Manolo for Santiago is that of a disciple for a master in the arts of fishing.[27] It is also the love of a son for an adopted father.

But from Santiago's point of view the relationship runs deeper. He has known the boy for years, from the period of childhood up to this later time when Manolo stands, strong and lucky and confident, on the edge of young manhood. Like many other aging men, Santiago finds something reassuring about the overlay of the past upon the present. Through the agency of Manolo he is able to recapture in his imagination, and therefore to a certain degree in fact, the same strength and confidence which distinguished his own young manhood as a fisherman, earning him the title of *El Campéon*.[28]

[27] The disciple-master relationship is established early with a playing upon the words *doubt* and *faith*. See the colloquy between man and boy, pp. 10–11.

[28] Santiago uses two other images to give himself confidence during the ordeal. One is the great DiMaggio of the New York Yankees, himself the son of a fisherman, and just then suffering from a bonespur in his heel. The old man gains strength from the idea of DiMaggio's performing with a champion's grace despite the pressure of his affliction. See esp. pp. 75 and 114. Santiago's second image is of himself in his prime, handwrestling with the great negro dockworker from Cienfuegos. See pp. 76–77. But it is to the image of the boy that the old man returns most often.

During the old man's ordeal, the two phrases, "I wish the boy was here," and "I wish I had the boy," play across Santiago's mind often enough to merit special attention. In each instance he means exactly what he says: the presence of the boy would be a help in a time of crisis. But he is also invoking by means of these phrases the strength and courage of his youth. Soon after he has hooked his marlin and knows that he must hang onto the line for some time, Santiago says, "I wish I had the boy." Immediately his resolution tightens. During the first night he says it again. He is just reflecting that "no one should be alone in their old age," though in this case it is unavoidable. Again, and as if the mere mention of the boy were a kind of talisman, he then resolves to eat the tuna he has caught, though the thought of the raw fish sickens him, "in order to keep strong." Later the same night, he says aloud, "I wish the boy was here"—and promptly settles himself against the planks of the bow for another period of endurance. Near dawn he says again, "I wish I had the boy." Then he upbraids himself for wishful thinking. "But you haven't got the boy, he thought. You have only yourself and you had better work back to the last line now . . . and cut it away and hook up the two reserve coils." So he does exactly that.

As he summons the courage to eat the raw tuna for his breakfast on the second day, he links the boy and salt in what amounts to a metaphor: "I wish the boy were here and that I had some salt." Then he proves to himself that he has enough of both in their metaphorical meaning to eat the tuna and renew his waning strength. While he wills to unknot the cramp, he thinks that "if the boy was here" a little massaging would loosen the muscles of the forearm and maybe help the still useless gnarled claw of the hand. Yet when, soon afterwards, his great marlin breaches, Santiago summons the strength he needs to play his fish.

On the next breaching it is the same. While the marlin leaps again and again, unseen in the darkness of the second night, and while the old man and his line are both strained and stretched almost to the breaking-point, he triples the refrain: "If the boy was here he would wet the coils of line . . . Yes. If the boy were here. If the boy were here." Once more the effect of the invocation is nearly magical as if, by means of it, some of the strength of youth flowed in to sustain the limited powers of age. Always, just after he has said the words, Santiago manages to reach down into the well of his courage for one more dipperful. Then he goes on.

From this point onwards, having served its purpose, the refrain vanishes. It is not until the return voyage, while the old man reflects Job-like on the problem of the connection between sin and suffering and while the sharks collect their squadrons unseen in the dark waters, that the boy's image returns again. "Everything kills everything else in some way," he tells himself. "Fishing kills me exactly as it keeps me alive." Then he corrects the misapprehensions that can come from false philosophizing. "The boy keeps me alive . . . I must not deceive myself too much." It is good, at this point, that the old man has the thought of the boy to keep him alive. For the sharks wait, and a very bad time is just ahead.[29]

In the night in which he is preparing for betrayal by the sharks, though he does not yet absolutely know that they will come, Santiago has recourse to yet another sustaining image—a pride of lions he once saw at play on an African beach when he was a young man like Manolo. Hemingway early establishes a clear symbolic connection between the boy and the lions. "When I was your age," Santiago says, "I was before the mast on a square rigged ship that ran to Africa and I have seen lions on the beaches in the evening." Manolo's answer—"I know. You told me."—indicates not only that the reminiscence has arisen before in their conversations, but also that the incident of the lions is a pleasant obsession in Santiago's mind. "There is for every man," writes the poet Yeats, "some one scene, some one adventure, some one picture that is the image of his secret life, and this one image, if he would but brood over it his life long, would lead his soul." Santiago finds such an image in the lions of his youthful experience.

The night before his ordeal, after the boy has left him to sleep, the old man dreams of the lions. "He was asleep in a short time and he dreamed of Africa when he was a boy and the long golden beaches and the white beaches, so white they hurt your eyes, and

[29] For allusions to the boy, see esp. pp. 49, 52, 55, 57, 62, 68, 117.

the high capes and the great brown mountains. He lived along that coast now every night and in his dreams he heard the surf roar and saw the native boats come riding through it. He smelled the tar and oakum of the deck as he slept and he smelled the smell of Africa that the land breeze brought at morning. Usually when he smelled the land breeze he woke up and dressed to go to wake the boy. But tonight the smell of the land breeze came very early and he knew it was too early in his dream and went on dreaming to see the white peaks of the Islands rising from the sea and then he dreamed of the different harbours and roadsteads of the Canary Islands."

Santiago "no longer dreamed of storms, nor of women, nor of great occurrences, nor of great fish, nor fights, nor contests of strength, nor of his wife. He only dreamed of places now and of the lions on the beach. They played like young cats in the dusk and he loved them as he loved the boy."

Early in the afternoon of his second day out, having strengthened his resolution by the saying of the prayers, Santiago thinks again about his lions. The marlin is pulling steadily. "I wish he'd sleep and I could sleep and dream about the lions," thinks Santiago. "Why are the lions the main thing that is left?" Much later the same day, "cramping himself against the line with all his body," and "putting all his weight onto his right hand," the old man manages to sleep. Soon then he begins to dream of the long yellow beach, and in the dream, we are told, "he saw the first of the lions come down onto it in the early dark and then the other lions came and he rested his chin on the wood of the bows where the ship lay anchored with the evening off-shore breeze and he waited to see if there would be more lions and he was happy." In his old age and the time of his suffering, Santiago is supported by the memory of his youth and the strength of his youth. Living so, in the past, he is happy. But there is the further realization that "the child is father to the man." Luckily for this old man, he has also the thought of the strength of the boy Manolo, a young lion of just the age Santiago was when he first sailed to Africa. These together help him to endure.[30]

They help in a very notable way. For the boy and the lions

[30] For allusions to the lions, see pp. 24, 27, 73, 90, 140.

are related to one of the fundamental psychological laws of Santiago's—and indeed of human—nature. This is the constant wave-like operation of bracing and relaxation. The boy braces, the lions relax, as in the systolic-diastolic movement of the human heart. The phenomenon is related to the alternation of sleep and waking through the whole range of physical nature. But it is also a law which fulfills itself on the level of mentality. Its effects can be traced in our reaction to works of literature like this story of the acquisition and loss of the great marlin. The basic rhythms of the novel, in its maritime sections, are essentially those of the groundswell of the sea. Again and again as the action unfolds, the reader may find that he is gradually brought up to a degree of quiet tension which he is barely able to accept, as in the ascent by a small craft of a slow enormous wave. When he has reached the theoretical peak of his resistance, the crest passes and he suddenly relaxes into a trough of rest. The rhythm of the story appears to be built on such a stress-yield, brace-relax alternation. The impression is furthered by the constant tension which Santiago and his fish maintain on the line which joins them. Again and again one finds the old man telling himself that he has stretched the cord to a degree just short of the breaking-point. Then the stress relaxes, and the involved reader relaxes with it. This prolonged tug-of-war involves not only the fisherman and his fish but also the reader and his own emotions.

The planned contiguity of the old man with the double image of the boy and the lions converts the story of Santiago, in one of its meanings, into a parable of youth and age. It may be suggested that Hemingway, who read the whole of Conrad during the days of his writing apprenticeship in Paris and Toronto, has recollected the central strategy of Conrad's long short story, "Youth." For that story is built upon a brilliant contrast between young and old manhood. The ill-fated voyage of the barque *Judea*, out of London bound for Bangkok, shows young Marlow, with all the illusions and prowess of his youth, working side by side with old Captain Beard, the ship's master and a brave man. "He was sixty, if a day," says Marlow of the captain. "And he had blue eyes in that old face of his, which were amazingly like a boy's, with that candid expression some quite common men preserve to the end of their days by a rare internal gift of simplicity of heart and rectitude of soul." Again Marlow says, as the fated ship beats her way through a sea of trouble, that Beard was "immense in the singleness of his idea."

It may of course be a coincidence that these are qualities which Santiago shares. If so, it is a happy one. Two "quite common men" rise to the level of the heroic through simplicity of heart, rectitude of soul, and that immensity which is gained for them through the singleness of their concentration on a particular object. "Do or die" is the motto which adorns in flaking gilt the stern-timbers of the old *Judea.* The same words might with equal justice be carved into the weather-beaten wood of Santiago's skiff.

Conrad's story depends for its effect not only upon the contrast between young Marlow and old Beard but also, since the story is told some twenty years after the event, upon the contrast between the aging Marlow and his remembrance of his own youthful self. Santiago happily recalls the lions on the shore of Africa. Marlow recollects the brown men on the jetty of a Javanese port. This was where the small boats from the wrecked *Judea,* filled with exhausted men, at last reached the land. "I remember my youth," says Marlow, "and the feeling that will never come back any more—the feeling that I could last for ever, outlast the sea, the earth, and all men; the deceitful feeling that lures us on to joys, to perils, to love, to vain effort—to death; the triumphant conviction of strength, the heat of life in the handful of dust, the glow in the heart that with every year grows dim, grows cold, grows small, and expires." This feeling, which William Hazlitt has well described as the feeling of immortality in youth, is closely associated in Marlow's mind with the East—"the mysterious shores, the still water, the lands of the brown nations." As he tells his auditors: "For me, all the East is contained in that vision of my youth. It is all in that moment when I opened my young eyes on it. I came upon it from a tussle with the sea— and I was young—and I saw it looking at me. And this is all that is left of it! Only a moment; a moment of strength, of romance, of glamour—of youth!"

For Santiago it is not the coast of Java but that of Africa, not the faces of the brown men crowding the jetty but the playing lions, which carry the associations of youth, strength, and even immortality. "This is all that is left of it," cries Marlow of his youthful vision. "Why are the lions the main thing that is left?" cries Hemingway's old man in the midst of his ordeal. For both of them, in Marlow's words, it is "the time to remember." Santiago manages to put his vision to work in the great trial of his old age. "I told the boy I was a strange old man," he says. "Now is when I must prove it." And the author adds: "The thousand times that he had proved it meant nothing. Now he was proving it again. Each time was a new time and he never thought about the past when he was doing it." If he does not, at such times, think about the past to brood over it, he periodically calls back what it means to him through the double vision of the boy and the lions. If he can prove his mettle for the thousand-and-first time, there is no reason short of death why he cannot continue to prove it, as long as his vision lasts.

Of how many events in the course of human life may this not be said? It is Marlow once more who reminds us of the way in which one account of one man on one journey can extend outwards in our imaginations until it easily becomes a paradigm of the course of all men's lives. "You fellows know," says Marlow, beginning his account of the *Judea,* "there are those voyages that seem ordered for the illustration of life, that might stand for a symbol of existence. You fight, work, sweat, nearly kill yourself, sometimes do kill yourself, trying to accomplish something—and you can't. Not from any fault of yours." If it is so with the *Judea,* bound for Bangkok, do or die, it is so with Santiago of Havana, bound for home, with the sharks just beginning to smell the blood of his great fish. Do or die. In such works as these we all put to sea. Santiago makes his voyage on what used to be known as the Spanish Main. But it is also, by the process of synecdoche, that more extensive main, or mainstream, where we all drift or sail, with or against the wind, in fair weather or foul, with our prize catches and our predatory sharks, and each of us, perhaps, like the ancient mariner of Coleridge, with some kind of albatross hanging round his neck.

IV. THE CAUTERY OF CIRCUMSTANCE

It is provided in the essence of things, writes the stoical philosopher, that from any fruition of success, no matter what, shall come forth something to make a greater struggle necessary. With such a sentiment Santiago would no doubt agree. For the second major movement of the novel confronts him with a struggle which, though shorter in duration, is at least as intense as the fight with the marlin just brought to a successful conclusion. This comes, too, at a time when he has used all his strength, and as much more as he could summon, to attain his object; when his hands are stiffening round the edges of his wounds, when the muscles of his back and shoulders are knotted with pain, and when his fatigue runs bone-deep.

Having secured his catch alongside, stepped his mast, rigged his boom, and moved off with the beneficent tradewind towards the southwest and home, Santiago enjoys (though not to the full because of his tiredness) that brief respite which follows work well done. Side by side like brothers the old man and the marlin move through the sea. Up to now, they have been, as Santiago believes, friendly and mutually respectful adversaries. Now they join together in league against the common enemy. "If sharks come," the old man has long ago reflected, "God pity him and me." It is a full hour before the first shark arrives.[31]

With its arrival begins a tragedy of deprivation as piteous as that which King Lear undergoes at the hands of his shark-hearted daughters. Lear's hundred knights, the only remaining sign of his power and the badge of his kingly dignity, are taken from him in batches of twenty-five. A series of forty-pound rippings and tearings are now gradually to reduce Santiago's eighteen-foot, fifteen-hundred-pound marlin to the skeleton he brings finally to shore.

The first of the sharks is a Mako. "Everything about him was beautiful except his jaws. . . . Inside the closed double lip . . . all of his eight rows of teeth were slanted inwards. They were not the ordinary pyramid-shaped teeth of most sharks. They were

[31] *The Old Man and The Sea,* pp. 75, 109.

shaped like a man's fingers when they are crisped like claws. They were nearly as long as the fingers of the old man and they had razor sharp cutting edges on both sides." Santiago, standing poised with his harpoon, hears the clicking chop of these great jaws and the rending and tearing of the marlin's flesh just before he drives the point of his weapon "with resolution and complete malignancy" into the Mako's brain. Death is immediate but the loss is heavy. When the shark sinks, he takes with him forty pounds of the marlin, the harpoon, and all the rope. The marlin's blood will attract other sharks. But worse than this is the mutilation of the long-fought-for prize. Santiago "did not like to look at the fish anymore since he had been mutilated. When the fish had been hit it was as though he himself were hit." The process of crucifixion is now intensified.[32]

At first sight of the second shark, Santiago utters the single word *Ay*. "There is no translation for this word," writes Hemingway, "and perhaps it is just a noise such as a man might make, involuntarily, feeling the nail go through his hands and into the wood." For some hours now, of course, Santiago's hands have shown the fisherman's equivalent of the stigmata of a saint. Both have been cut in the "working part," which is the palm, by the unpredictable lurchings of his quarry. The right hand is cut first, at a time when the old man's attention is momentarily diverted by the warbler's visit. Another of the marlin's sudden accelerations awakens him from the only sleep he permits himself. The line is burning out through his already wounded right hand. When he brings up his left for use as a brake, it takes all the strain and cuts deep.[33]

The old man's involuntary epithet, and Hemingway's explanation of it, is fully in line with what had gone before. Throughout the ordeal, Santiago has been as conscious of his hands as any crucified man might be. He speaks to them as to fellow-sufferers, wills them to do the work they must do, and makes due allowances for them as if they were, what he once calls them, "my brothers." He also carefully distinguishes between them in a manner which should not be lost on any student of paintings

[32] *Ibid.*, pp. 111–113.
[33] *Ibid.*, pp. 61, 63, 118.

of the Crucifixion. The right hand is the good one, dextrous and
trustworthy. The left hand, the hand sinister, has "always been a
traitor." [34]

Our Lord might well have entertained a similar reflection about
the man who was crucified on his own left. The allusions to Santiago's hands are so carefully stylized that such a statement becomes possible. On the naturalistic plane, of course, the meaning
of the distinction between the two hands is apparent to all normally right-handed persons; the left is never as good as the right.
But on the plane of what we have called Dichtung, and in the
light of the tradition of Christian art as it pertains to the Crucifixion, it is clear that a moral judgment is to be inferred. Of the
two who were crucified with Jesus Christ, the one on the left
failed Him, insulting and upbraiding Him. But the man crucified
on Jesus's right hand rebuked his companion, and put his fortunes
into the hands of the Savior. In paintings of the Crucifixion, as
Hemingway is well aware, the distinction between the two malefactors is always carefully maintained. It even carries over into
pictures of the Last Judgment, where those who are to be saved
are ranged on the right hand of the Savior, while the damned
stand dejectedly on the left. [35]

Santiago vanquishes the second and third sharks, hateful, bad
smelling, "scavengers as well as killers" with his knife lashed to
an oar. But when the *galanos* sink into the sea, they take with
them fully a quarter of the marlin's best meat. "I wish it were
a dream and that I had never hooked him," says the old man.
"I'm sorry about it, fish. It makes everything wrong." The fourth
shark, a single shovel-nose, adds yet another degree to our sense
of wronged rightness. "He came like a pig to the trough if a pig
had a mouth so wide that you could put your head in it." This

[34] *Ibid.*, pp. 70, 78.
[35] See Luke 23: 39ff.: "And one of the malefactors which were hanged
railed on him saying, Art thou not the Christ? save thyself and us. But the
other answered and rebuking him said, Dost thou not even fear God, seeing
thou art in the same condemnation? And we indeed justly; for we receive
the due reward of our deeds: but this man hath done nothing amiss. And
he said, Jesus remember me when thou comest into thy kingdom. And
he said unto him, Verily I say unto thee, Today shalt thou be with me in
Paradise."

one breaks Santiago's knife, bearing the blade in its brain-pan as it follows the *galanos* to death.

By the time the old man has clubbed the fifth and sixth sharks into submission just at sunset, a full half of the marlin has been gouged away. "What will you do now if they come in the night?" asks the voice inside Santiago. "Fight them," says the old man aloud. "I'll fight them until I die." But when he tries to stand off a whole ravaging pack at midnight, striking at whatever heads he can see, he knows the fight is almost useless. Something seizes his club and it disappears; he hits out with the unshipped tiller until it breaks, and then lunges at another of the sharks with the splintered butt. When this one lets go of the marlin and rolls away, the massacre is ended. A few more come to hit the carcass in the night, "as someone might pick up crumbs from the table." But the old man ignores them and sails on. There is nothing left of the great fish except the skeleton, the bony head, and the vertical tail.

This story of great gain and great loss is esthetically satisfying partly because of its symmetry. Hemingway has little trouble, either, in persuading his readers of the inevitability of the process. For with so fine a prize in a tropical sea where hungry sharks constantly swim, Santiago's return with a whole fish would be nothing short of miraculous. In assessing the old man's total experience, one is reminded of the experiences of younger men in some of Hemingway's earlier novels: Lieutenant Henry's gain and loss of a new wife, for example, in *A Farewell to Arms,* or Robert Jordan's gain and loss of a new life in *For Whom the Bell Tolls.* Yet in this latter-day return to the theme of winner-take-nothing, on which Hemingway has so often and so successfully played his variations, he seems to have added a new dimension. This is the dimension of transfiguration, anticipated (it is true) in the story of Robert Jordan, but never made quite so explicit as in the instance of Santiago.

Santiago's experience is a form of martyrdom. We do not object to it: it is his by right of eminent domain. The old man's only fault, if it is a fault, consists in doing to the best of his ability what he was born to do. When the man on the right rebuked his companion for crass raillery at the expense of Jesus Christ, he raised the essential moral problem. "We receive," said he, "the due reward of our deeds: but this man [Jesus Christ] hath done nothing amiss." Neither has Santiago, but this does not prevent his martyrdom. Tried out through an ordeal by endurance comparable to a crucifixion, he earns, by virtue of his valiance, a form of apotheosis.

His humility and simplicity will not allow entry to any taint of conscious martyrdom. "Man is not made for defeat," he says at one point. "A man can be destroyed but not defeated." His resolution is always stiffened by some such thought as this, and he acts in accordance with it. Being native to his character, these qualities of resolution and action sustain him up to that point when he knows that his only remaining recourse is to take what comes when it comes. Arrival at this point does not unbalance him. He is not a rebel, like the mariner Ahab, against the ruling powers of the universe. Nor does he imagine, as he drives his harpoon into the marlin's heart, that he is destroying anything except a prize fish with whom he has fought long and fairly. The arrival of the sharks on the scene does not surprise him. He does not expect for a moment that they will let him run their saber-toothed gauntlet unscathed. Santiago is a moral realist.

Yet he is too human not to be troubled, like Job before him, by certain moral and metaphysical questions. One is the problem of whether any connection exists between sin and suffering. "It is silly not to hope," he thinks to himself after the killing of the Mako shark. "Besides I believe it is a sin." In this way he launches himself into a consideration of the problem. At first his realistic capacity for self-criticism cautions him that this is dangerous ground. "There are enough problems now without sin. Also I have no understanding of it and I am not sure that I believe in it . . . Do not think about sin. It is much too late for that and there are people who are paid to do it. Let them think about it."

The problem will not be put down so easily. "Perhaps," he speculates, "it was a sin to kill the fish. I suppose it was even though I did it to keep me alive and feed many people." After all, "San Pedro was a fisherman," and who would accuse him of sin? But once more the cautionary voice chimes in. "You did not kill the fish only to keep alive and to sell for food, he thought. You killed him for pride and because you are a fisherman. You loved him when he was alive and you loved him after. If you love him, it is not a sin to kill him. Or is it more?" [36]

On this double allusion to pride and to love, greatest of sins and greatest of virtues, hangs the philosophic crux of the problem. Was his real motivation the blameless one of doing his professional duty and feeding people? Probably not basically. He did it for pride: to show that he was still El Campéon. "I'll kill him," he boasted during the battle. "In all his greatness and his glory . . . I will show him what a man can do and what a man endures." Yet all through the struggle he was never without love and compassion for his marlin, or for most of the lesser creatures in God's marine creation.

As in other tragic literatures, the whole process consists ultimately in the readjustment of moral proportions. What begins as a balanced mixture of pride and love slowly alters through the catalysis of circumstance. When Santiago brings his marlin to the gaff, his pride has been gone for a long time. Statements like "I'll fight them until I die," made during the encounter with the sharks, are not so much the evidence of pride as of the resolute determination to preserve something loved and earned from the distortion that comes with mutilation. The direction of the process then comes clear. Where pride and love exist together, the pride must be burned out, as by the cautery of fire. Love will remain as the natural concomitant of true humility.[37]

Though Santiago admits to pride and lays claim to love, his moral sense is not fully satisfied by this way of resolving the problem. He looks for some other explanation of the profit-and-loss pattern. What he seems finally to settle on is the notion that he had gone, as he often puts it, "too far out." This concept of "too-far-outness" is not simply what Colonel Cantwell might describe as over-extension: lines of communication stretched past the breakingpoint, possible support abandoned, danger courted for its own sake, excess of bravery spilling over into foolhardiness.

[36] *The Old Man and The Sea*, pp. 115–116.
[37] Compare the conversation between Lt. Henry and the Italian priest in *A Farewell to Arms*, Chapter 26.

It is rather what Melville described as "the intrepid effort of the soul to keep the open independence of her sea"—a willingness to take the greater risk where the greater prize is involved.[38]

Very early in the book the contrast is established between the lee shore and the Gulf Stream. There are the inshore men, those who work within sight of land because it is easier, safer, and less frightening, and those like Santiago who have the intrepidity to reach beyond the known towards the possible. "Where are you going?" Manolo asks him, on the eve of the eighty-fifth day. "Far out," replies Santiago, "to come in when the wind shifts." The boy hopes to persuade his father to work far out that day in order to provide help for Santiago if it should be necessary. But this will not happen. Manolo's father is plainly an inshore man, one who does not like to work far out, one who prefers not to take chances, no matter how great the potential gain might be.

Santiago does not hesitate. On the morning of the eighty-fifth day, we are told, he "knew he was going far out." This is why he passes over, even before dawn, the inshore fishing-ground which fishermen call "the great well"—an easy place teeming with provender, where thousands of fish congregate to feed and to be caught. By seven he is already so far out that only three fishing boats are remotely visible inshore; by noon only the tops of the blue Cuban hills show on the horizon. No other boats are now in sight. Here, somewhere, lurk the great fish of this September season. When Santiago is passed by a school of dolphin, he guesses that marlin may be nearby. "My big fish," he tells himself, "must be somewhere."

Even as he speaks the marlin is approaching, the lordly denizen of this far-out domain. In coming there, in the process of invasion, the old man has made his choice—not to stay inshore where the going might be easier but to throw out a challenge to what might be waiting, far out and down deep at the hundred-fathom level. As for the marlin, "his choice has been to stay in the deep dark water far out beyond all snares and traps and treacheries." Yet he accepts, in effect rises to, the old man's challenge. From then on Santiago is tied by a strong line to his doom. "My choice,"

[38] *Moby-Dick,* Chapter 23.

he reflects, "was to go there to find him beyond all people. Beyond all people in the world. Now we are joined together." The long battle is also joined. Since it came about through Santiago's free choice, he has no alternative but to accept the consequences.

These follow inevitably. For to have gone far out is to have invited the depredations of the sharks on the equally long homeward voyage. When the first three have done their work, Santiago apologizes. "I shouldn't have gone so far out, fish. Neither for you nor for me. I'm sorry, fish." When the mutilation has developed to the point where he cannot bear to look at it, he apologizes again. "You violated your luck," says his speaking self, "when you went too far outside." Inshore again, with the marlin destroyed and the old man's weapons gone, there is another dialogue of the soul with itself. "And what beat you?" "Nothing," answers the second voice. "I went out too far." Urged on by pride, by the love of his trade, by his refusal to take continuing bad luck as his portion, and by a resurgent belief that he might win, Santiago made trial of the impossible. In the tragic process he achieved the moral triumph.

It is not necessarily a Christian victory. Yet it is clear that Hemingway has artfully enhanced the native power of his tragic parable by enlisting the further power of Christian symbolism. Standing alone on the rocky shore in the darkness before the dawn of the fourth day, Santiago shows the wounded hands. Dried blood is on his face as from a crown of thorns. He has known the ugly coppery taste in his mouth as from a sponge filled with vinegar. And in the agony of his fatigue he is very much alone. "There was no one to help him so he pulled the boat up as far as he could. Then he stepped out and made her fast to a rock. He unstepped the mast and furled the sail and tied it. Then he shouldered the mast and started to climb."

Once he paused to look back at the remains of his fish. At the top of the hill "he fell and lay for some time with the mast across his shoulder. He tried to get up. But it was too difficult and he sat there with the mast on his shoulder and looked at the road. A cat passed on the far side going about its business and the old man watched it. Then he just watched the road." The loneliness of the ascent of any Calvary is brilliantly emphasized by the presence of the cat. The Old Masters, as Auden wrote long ago, were never wrong about suffering. "How well they understood its human position; how it takes place while someone else is eating or opening a window or just walking dully along. . . . They never forgot that even the dreadful martyrdom must run its course anyhow in some corner, some untidy spot where the dogs go on with their doggy life"—and where the innocence of ignorance never so much as bats an eye.[39] The cat on the far side of the road from Santiago is also proceeding about its private business. It could not help the old man even if it would. Santiago knows and accepts this as he has accepted the rest. There is nothing else to be done—except to reach home, which he manages at last to do, though he has to sit down five times to rest between the hilltop and the door of his shack.

On the newspapers that cover the springs of the bed, and below the colored chromos of the Sacred Heart of Jesus and the Virgin of Cobre, the old man now falls heavily asleep. He sleeps face down with his arms out straight and his body straight up and down: cruciform, as if to sum up by the symbolic position, naturally assumed, all the suffering through which he has passed. *In hoc signo vinces.* Santiago has made it to his house. When Manolo looks in next morning, he is still asleep. There is a short conversation as he drinks the coffee the boy brings, and they lay plans for the future even as they allude laconically to the immediate past. "How much did you suffer?" Manolo asks. "Plenty," the old man answers. Outside, a three-day blow has begun. Inside the shack, the book concludes, the old man falls again into the deep sleep of renewal, of diurnal resurrection. "He was still sleeping on his face and the boy was sitting by him watching him. The old man was dreaming about the lions." In my end is my beginning.

V. OPEN AND CLOSED LITERATURE

During over a quarter-century of experiment and speculation, Hemingway discovered ways of opening out the literature he

[39] "Musée des Beaux Arts," in *The Collected Poetry of W. H. Auden,* New York, 1945, p. 3.

wrote, of universalizing the significance of the stories he had
to tell. We have heard much in our time about open and closed
universes, and open and closed societies. Such a book as *The
Old Man and The Sea* clearly demonstrates by example the difference between open and closed literatures. It is characteristic
of a closed literature to be fact-bound. Its factual texture may
be so tightly woven, so impenetrable to light, so opaque to the
contemplation, that we are unable to see through it to any larger
implications. The distinction is naturally a matter of degree: no
literature is entirely closed. But one knows by experience the
kind of book which too seldom offers the imagination a constructive opening, the book by which one feels bound or uncomfortably
limited. In the midst of such a work the reader may find himself
squirming with esthetic claustrophobia.

Open literature is the literature of agoraphilia. It recognizes
the necessity of fenestration. Out through its windows we continu-
ally catch glimpses of a larger world than that immediately encompassed by the story we are reading. We look out towards
the sea that is all around us, the vast waters crowded with life
and joined forever, as Melville tells us, to contemplation. Hemingway early discovered and then steadily experimented with the
means by which closed literature could be converted into open
literature. The particular kind of fenestration he provides began
to develop at that point where the sensibility of the artist revolted
against the limits which factualistic naturalism necessarily im-
poses. In *Death in the Afternoon,* he asserted that the writer of
prose ought to aim at "architecture, not interior decoration." [40]
Hemingway's study, as one of the architects of modern prose,
was not completely devoted to this matter of fenestration. But
in the process of the development of his powers, it was plainly
promoted to the rank of a key element.

One characteristic of open literature is its tendency to take
on certain stylistic overtones of the parable. Readers of *The Old
Man and The Sea* appear to have been impressed by its parable-
like aspects, an impression traceable in part to echoic resemblances between the language of the novel and that of the
Bible. The language is not in fact truly Biblical, as anyone can

[40] *DIA*, p. 191.

discover by reading the story of Jonah immediately before or after an encounter with Santiago. Yet the language does share two qualities with that of the Old and New Testaments: first, a slightly stylized vocabulary and movement long familiar to readers of the King James or the Douai translations, and secondly, what D. H. Lawrence once called the essence of poetry—"a stark, bare, rocky directness of statement." It is this latter quality which brings the story of Santiago closest in tone to such parables in the synoptic gospels as those of the sower, the lost sheep, the laborers in the vineyard, or the Pharisee and the publican.

Novels do not commune or communicate only by style or tone any more than men live only or commune mainly by the utterances of the logical intellect. What *The Old Man and The Sea* carries for the close reader is the conviction, sporadically renewed, that this story means more than it directly says. Those off-the-cuff allegorists who suggested that there was, for example, a one-for-one correspondence between Santiago, his marlin, and the sharks and Hemingway, his fiction, and the critics seem to have been content to rest triumphantly on this perception. A far more careful statement of the matter may be found in the words of Mark Schorer. "For those who, like this reviewer, believe that Hemingway's art, when it is art, is absolutely incomparable, and that he is unquestionably the greatest craftsman in the American novel in this century," *The Old Man and The Sea* may well appear to be "not only a moral fable, but a parable, and all the controlled passion, all the taut excitement in the prose come, I believe, from the parable. It is an old man catching a fish, yes; but it is also a great artist in the act of mastering his subject, and, more than that, of actually writing about the struggle. Nothing is more important than his craft, and it is beloved; but because it must be struggled with and mastered, it is also a foe, enemy to all self-indulgence, to all looseness of feeling, all laxness of style, all soft pomposities." [41]

Such a view of Santiago's adventure can be made to stand up fairly well under hard-bitten scrutiny. Yet even so forthright a statement falls into the possible error of too greatly constricting the available meanings of the story. Another view is ably sum-

[41] *New Republic* 127 (October 6, 1952), p. 20.

marized by Harvey Breit. What Hemingway has sought to do "is to fuse under a sustained pressure the opposite elements of experience and vision, of prosaic event and dramatic or poetic insight. Say it how you will, in his continuous, exacting, and independent operations in prose Hemingway has attempted to annihilate the shadow which, according to T. S. Eliot, falls between the idea and the reality, between the essence and the descent." The realities in *The Old Man and The Sea* have to do with the craft of fishing. But in all Hemingway's best work, "these special areas, these particular professions and occupations, are transposed inexorably into universal meanings. In *The Old Man,* the mystique of fishing, with its limited triumphs and tragedies, is transposed into a universal condition of life, with its success and shame, its morality and pride and potential loss of pride." [42]

The voyage Santiago undertakes seems, in fact, naturally ordered for the illustration of a larger experience of life than was even intended in some of the New Testament parables. Its theme has been well pointed up by the Christian stoic Samuel Johnson, both in the title and the substance of his poem on the vanity, which is to say the vain-ness, of human wishes. The story of Santiago shows not only a natural tragic pattern, as the individual human life may do when seen as a whole; it also can stand as a natural parable. In this story, as in the life of man, the battle commences, grows, and subsides between one sleep and another. In human experience there are many forms of both marlin and shark. Much is to be endured, and perhaps relatively little is to be enjoyed between our human setting-forth and our return to port. A provisional means of describing the effect of Hemingway's novel may be found in Yeats's opinion that "the more a poet . . . purifies his mind with elaborate art, the more does the little ritual of his verse resemble the great ritual of nature, and become mysterious

[42] *Nation* 175 (September 6, 1952), p. 194. See Hemingway's remark to a reporter: "No good book has ever been written that has in it symbols arrived at beforehand and stuck in. That kind of symbol sticks out like raisins in raisin bread. Raisin bread is all right, but plain bread is better." In *The Old Man and The Sea,* "I tried to make a real old man, a real boy, a real sea and a real fish and real sharks. But if I made them good and true enough they would mean many things." *Time* 64 (December 13, 1954), p. 72.

and inscrutable. He becomes, as all the great mystics have believed, a vessel of the creative power of God." [43]

Although Hemingway might have questioned the temerity of Yeats's last sentence, he could not, after *The Old Man and the Sea*, deny the first. For his best work, like that of any great creative artist, is in a happy conspiracy with permanence. The language, the subjects, the underlying symbolic structures all belong to that area of human thought and belief which survives virtually without change from age to age. This area, this continuum, this current flowing unchanged below the surface disturbances, is the true artist's gulf stream. After his return from the green hills of Africa in 1934, he found an image for his point of view among the blue depths of Atlantica.

"When, on the sea, [he wrote] you are alone with it and know that this Gulf Stream you are living with, knowing, learning about, and loving, has moved, as it moves, since before man . . . [then] the things you find out about it, and those that have always lived in it, are permanent and of value because that stream will flow as it has flowed, after the Indians, after the Spaniards, after the British, after the Americans and after all the Cubans and all the systems of governments, the richness, the poverty, the martyrdom, the sacrifice and the venality and the cruelty are all gone as the high-piled scow of garbage . . . spills off its load into the blue water. . . . The stream, with no visible flow, takes five loads of this a day when things are going well in La Habana and in ten miles along the coast it is as clear and blue and unimpressed as it was ever before the tug hauled out the scow; and the palm fronds of our victories, the worn light bulbs of our great discoveries and the empty condoms of our great loves float with no significance against one single, lasting thing—the stream." [44]

In all things as permanent as this blue river in the sea, the writer who means his work to last must sink his nets, cast his lines, and bring his giants to the gaff. Let the garbage go. It will disappear as all such things have always gone. But the stream

[43] W. B. Yeats, *Essays*, New York, 1924, pp. 248–249.
[44] *GHOA*, pp. 149–150.

will last. This is the area where Hemingway, the compleat angler, has chosen to fish.

Much of Hemingway's language, like much of his imagery, belongs to the area of the permanent. One of the poets of Genesis said for the land what this modern artist said for the Gulf Stream: "While the earth remaineth, seedtime and harvest, and cold and heat, and summer and winter, and day and night shall not cease.[45] The point of the passage is not alone the images—what the Lord God Jehovah promised not to change—but it is also the language, the permanent *lingua communis* which resists change because it is the expression of those things that do not change. "Some of [Hemingway's] writing has gone bad," said Malcolm Cowley, "but surprisingly little of it." [46] At all times a living language carries a vast burden of the temporary, not only the slang of the current moment, but also faddism, technical jargon, trickery, and the cheap fashionable ornamentation that soon turns green. Under this burden, which vanishes periodically like Havana's garbage in the Gulf Stream, the elder and timeless language moves majestically along, changing very slowly where it changes at all. It is the language of seedtime and harvest, bread and wine, heat and cold, the rising-up and going-down of the sun, and the slow turn of the seasons. Hemingway has it, or at any rate enough of it to carry the content of the impermanent, the temporariness of the contemporary, which even the world's greatest artists, being also men, have been unable to avoid.

Hemingway's services to the permanent also required him to unite what Cyril Connolly once referred to as his "courageous, heart-whole emotional drive"·and his "adult and lively intellectual toughness." [47] Both the heart-wholeness and the toughness must be operative, as Hemingway had realized from the beginning. The first and final thing you have to do in this world, he once told Maxwell Perkins, is to last in it and not be smashed by it, and it is the same way with your work.[48] This is at once a rule

[45] Genesis 8: 22.
[46] *The Portable Hemingway*, New York, 1944, introd., p. xxiv.
[47] Introduction, *Horizon*, vols. 93–94, October 1947.
[48] EH to MP, 4/4/32.

for the conduct of life and a rule for the conduct of art: to last, and to do work that will last. In line with this conviction, Hemingway almost literally wrote his heart out in every major book he brought into being. He seized as his ruling idea the determination never to write a false line. Naturally he committed a few; the determined seeker can find lapses of taste, failures in clear communication, instances where the emotional drive overshot esthetic distance and brought the artist too close to his material for the reader's comfort. Pity has sometimes overflowed and irony has sometimes been overplayed. Yet such instances are neither numerous nor, in the end, very consequential. Hemingway was very possibly our best meteorologist of emotional climates because he retained the tough determination to correct his reports for subjective error. As practical esthetician, he managed so firmly to combine in his work the Wahrheit and the Dichtung of the world as he knew it that his art as a whole, if not in all its constituent parts, is likely to stand relatively impervious to the shifting weather of the future.

A conspicuous irony in the present age is the recurrent notion that Hemingway's name belongs on the list of irresponsibles. During the course of his career this accusation twice erupted, once in the early thirties, and again in 1950. What it meant, it seems, was that Hemingway was "socially irresponsible" because he had failed to carry the banner of a particular social group, and to write his novels in terms of a particular social program. To be responsible in this sense he would have had to commit his writing to some form of didacticism, and to hope that history would bear out his interpretation of history. When an artist *as an artist* is not disposed to assume this kind of responsibility and even goes so far as to imply that those who do are not being faithful to their duty as writers, a degree of unpopularity is probably inevitable for him. This will be true even if, as a man living in society, he does all else that is in his power (by expending money, time, and energy) to ameliorate the evil conditions which other writers may be attempting to overcome through various forms of propaganda-art, closed literature in its tightest form.

If, on the other hand, one defines the artist's social responsibility as the presentation of the reality of man's experience, no artist of our time has been more responsible than Hemingway, both to his art itself, and to the strong foundation of esthetic and moral conviction on which the art is built. What Mr. Allen Tate has written of the poet's responsibility in our own and other time applies equally to the prose artist of Hemingway's persuasion.

"*To whom* [Mr. Tate asks] is the poet responsible? He is responsible to his *conscience*, in the French sense of the word: the joint action of knowledge and judgment. . . . No crisis, however dire, should be allowed to convince us that the relation of the poet to his permanent reality can ever change. And thus the poet is not responsible to society for a version of what it thinks it is or what it wants. *For what* is the poet responsible? He is responsible for the virtue proper to him as poet, for his special *arête:* for the mastery of a disciplined language which will not shun the full report of the reality conveyed to him by his awareness: he must hold, in Yeats' great phrase, 'reality and justice in a single thought.' " [49]

Between the truth of things and the poetry of things no necessary antagonism exists. The total accumulation of Hemingway's work amply proves and documents this point. His proper virtue as an artist consists in the willing assumption of a responsibility to hold the reality of what is knowably real in steady conjunction with the justice of what is esthetically just. What one might call his art-enlightened empiricism is, however, further strengthened and informed by the consistent operation of a kind of stoic morality. One finds implicit in all his work the half-humorous, half-bitter acceptance of what the act of living brings, though with him merely to endure is never enough. With the endurance and acceptance comes a recognition of the necessity of right action for the soul's sake, the counsel of freedom from perturbation and fear, and the constantly renewed assertion of the complete independence of the inner self.

There is also a visible though unobtrusive natural piety. If it seems non-Christian despite the grave allusions to our Lord, this is chiefly because Hemingway carefully refrained from taking doctrinaire sides in all his dramatizations of religious motifs. As one held back by esthetic principle from talking of what he did

[49] *Hudson Review* 4 (Autumn 1951), p. 333.

not know, he offered few speculations on the unknown country
at the other side of the grave. But he was neither a moral nor
metaphysical nihilist. The consciousness of God is in his books.
The tragic view of life comes out in his perennial contrast of
the permanence of nature and the evanescence of man.

XIII · The Death of the Lion

"Tir n'a N'Og is not far from any of us."
—W. B. Yeats
"It is when the damned wheel comes
down that it gets you."—Robert Jordan

I. LOOKING BACKWARD

In providing an account of Hemingway's career for the period 1951–1961, the emphasis must fall far more upon what he did than upon what he wrote. Between the completion of the type-script of *The Old Man and the Sea* and his sudden death slightly more than ten years later, he did not see fit to bring to publication any major work of fiction. Although he worked as the spirit moved him, and spoke happily to his friends of the fund of finished manuscript which he had deposited in the vaults of the Trust Company of Cuba in Galiano Street, Havana, so little of what he wrote in these years was allowed to emerge into print that even those who knew him best might have been forgiven for wondering, as they did, whether his powers were not beginning to decline.

Relatively speaking, the surmise was justified. Hemingway in his later fifties, no matter how he might choose to drive himself, had not that fund of strength and resilience on which he had been able to draw in his twenties, thirties, and forties. Several of those who had known him longest privately guessed that his version of the meaning of life required youth and health, that the retention of these was fundamental to his literary power, and that as time and its accidents ravaged brain and body he sought, with gradually increasing desperation, to repeat and even to relive the years when nothing could stop or defeat him.

What he retained, as he was fond of saying, was the benefit of all those preceding years of experience, like an old and crafty lion in the African veldt. He knew his limits, as well as how, with luck, it might be possible to transcend them. If he was privately troubled or morose—and he frequently was—he considered it a matter of moral duty to give no outward sign of cracking up. For his many correspondents he continued to provide the most recent figures on his increasingly troublesome hypertension, always matching them with the number of words he had managed to do in successive mornings of labor at the stand-up desk where he regularly wrote at Finca Vigía.

In short, he kept busy. Around the time when he composed *The Old Man and the Sea*, he had more or less completed three other parts of a long sea-novel, relating phases in the life story of Thomas Hudson, a painter, on Bimini in 1936, and during the war in Havana, and at sea hunting submarines. The various foreign-language translations of *The Old Man and the Sea* sporadically occupied his attention. When the Ringling Brothers Circus came to Havana in the winter of 1952–1953, Hemingway wrote an essay on the joys of circus-going for boys of all ages, and permitted himself to be photographed in companionable poses with several of the larger and fiercer of the circus's trained bears.

But he now began to complain to friends that he had lived too long at sea-level. He was beginning to wish for high ground once more: the Alps, perhaps; certainly the high Spanish plateau of Navarre which he had not seen since the end of the Spanish Civil War; and finally the hill-country of Africa, where he had known what he called "pursuit as happiness" during a climactic kudu-hunt twenty years before. By the late spring of 1953, his plans were close to realization. In a decade of turning and looking backward, this one would be triple: back to Spain, the European country he had always loved best; back to Paris, the scene of his earliest triumphs; back to Africa, where the stirrings of new nationalism, and the rise of the Mau-mau terror, might soon put an end to the kind of hunting he still recalled with sharp nostalgia.

The purpose of the trip, he said sententiously, was travel and study. His Spanish was already in shape from daily use; he began a jocular recall of Swahili, which he termed the "most comic" of languages, and found that his oral knowledge came back quickly. The Mau-mau insurrection did not strike him as a par-

ticular deterrent. The natives, he suggested, would have no reason to kill his wife Mary or himself; if he should happen to be
wrong, he would not have to write any more books. Though the
possibility of extra danger intrigued him, he had other reasons
for wishing to return to Africa. His second son, Patrick, had
recently bought a farm at a place called John's Corner in central
Tanganyika, and he looked forward happily to a father-and-son
reunion in the African highlands six thousand feet above sea-
level.

But first there was Spain. The Hemingways left Cuba in mid-
June, sailed from New York for Le Havre, and by early July
were in Pamplona for the "usual rough seven days" of the fiesta
of San Fermin. The author of *The Sun Also Rises* was treated
there, as he said, "like local boy makes good." Though the
weather was foul, with much rain and cold, he managed to convince himself that it was otherwise just like old times. The bright-
est event of the visit was a first meeting with the brilliant young
matador, Antonio Ordoñez, son to that Niño de la Palma, otherwise Cayetano, whom he had pictured under the name of Pedro
Romero in the later pages of *The Sun Also Rises*. Like father,
like son. Fathers and sons ran much in his mind that summer.

Madrid, afterwards, seemed filled with the ghosts of former
times. They revisited the Prado, watched further bullfights, and
walked over some of the battle-sites of 1937. He showed his wife
the mountainous locale which had served as the setting of *For
Whom the Bell Tolls:* the pass, the cave, El Sordo's vulnerable
hilltop, and the now mended bridge which the fictional Robert
Jordan had successfully dynamited before he died in defense of
Spanish democracy.

Africa still waited, vast in the southern sun. After a quick run
to Paris for yellow-fever shots and hasty repacking, they sailed
from Marseilles for Mombasa at the end of the first week in
August. Before the month was out they had been outfitted for
a long safari and were on location with Hemingway's old friend
Philip Percival, the white hunter whose calm bravery had been
celebrated in *The Green Hills of Africa,* and who had come out
of retirement to accompany the expedition. Once more Hemingway felt that he was retracing former steps. Although M'Cola,

his gun-bearer and blood-brother from 1933–1934 was dead, Hemingway managed, after a few quick questionings, to convince himself that N'Gui, his new gun-bearer, was one of the sons of M'Cola. Following two days of master-and-servant relationship, they settled into the ancient and even atavistic blood-brother pattern, and "we had more fun," as Hemingway wrote later, "than I ever had in my life."

The four-month hunting expedition began on the banks of the dry river at Salengai. Here in September, Earl Theisen, the official photographer, shot many good pictures of a herd of some dozens of elephants as they trampled and trumpeted at a water-hole in the streambed where a modicum of moisture still seeped up. The three weeks in this area was broken briefly by a side trip to the Kimana Swamp region to which Hemingway would return when the hunting was over. Then the party moved south to the edge of the Rift Valley. Here, relaxed and happy at an idyllic site which they called Fig Tree camp, Hemingway drafted a letter to his soldier-friend, General C. T. Lanham, in which he noted that the Oleibortoto River was clear as an American trout-stream, that all members of the party were healthy and sleeping well, that reveille was usually at 0500, and that he had not once been bored since starting from Cuba.

In mid-October they paid a visit to Philip Percival's home at Kitanga. Here Hemingway left his wife to complete a piece of writing and set out to meet his son Patrick in the high rolling land of central Tanganyika. Early in November the enlarged party established a base camp still further south on the Moarali River, hunting there until the arrival of the rainy season drove them north once more to John's Corner. From there, their relaxed itinerary carried them in easy stages to Dodoma, Babati (another haunt from 1934), Arusha, and Kajiado until by Thanksgiving time they were once more back at Selengai. For the next six weeks, while Christmas passed and the new year arrived, Hemingway took considerable satisfaction in serving as volunteer Ranger at the Masai game preserve at the foot of Mount Kilimanjaro, stationed near the village of Laitokitok on the edge of the mile-high Kimana Swamp, assisting, as he proudly said, "in the Emergency."

But the expedition, which had begun so well and continued so happily with all the reunions and without the amoebic dysentery which had assaulted Hemingway in 1933–1934, was now about to conclude in near disaster. Having left the Kimana region in mid-January, Hemingway and his wife slowly made their way back to Nairobi. Hunting was over, sightseeing in the great national parks was now their object, and they were planning a flight to the Belgian Congo as a belated Christmas gift for Mary Hemingway. To this end they engaged a Cessna 180, piloted by Roy Marsh, and left Nairobi's West Airport on Friday, January 22nd.

The first day's trip carried them over the wild and Edenlike Ngorongoro Crater, the vast and swarming Serengeti Plain where Hemingway had formerly hunted in the company of his second wife Pauline, and across the southernmost tip of Lake Victoria to Costermansville. On the twenty-third, they flew over the Ruwenzori Range, spent the night in the Lake Victoria Hotel at Entebbe, and took off belatedly next morning for the Congo, detouring slightly from their westward course in order to admire and photograph the spectacular gorge of Murchison Falls on the Victoria Nile in north-west Uganda.

Here, without warning, disaster struck. As Marsh banked the plane sharply to accommodate the picture-takers, the tail-assembly bounced sickeningly against an abandoned and nearly invisible telegraph line three miles from the Falls. Only the pilot's skill kept them from flipping and burning as he crash-landed the plane in heavy brush. Even as it was, the damage to both plane and people was severe. Mary Hemingway sustained two broken ribs and multiple contusions, spending the greater part of Saturday night in a state of shock. Hemingway's injuries, which might have killed a lesser man, included yet another full-scale concussion, complete, as he said, "with solid-gold handles," as well as a ruptured liver, a ruptured kidney, complete stoppage of peristalsis in the intestines, damage to the lower vertebrae and the sphincter muscle, and severe sprains in the right arm and shoulder and the left leg. According to his wife Mary, both his scalp and his skull were laid open, and cerebral fluid oozed from the wound. Indeed, as Hemingway later put it, blood and water flowed from all the bodily orifices; for some time he was afflicted with double vision, and the concussion caused the temporary loss of hearing in one of his ears.

That night they huddled beside the plane while a herd of elephants roved nearby and voracious crocodiles could be heard moving on the adjacent river-bank. They were fortunate enough on the Sunday to hail a chartered launch, the *S.S. Murchison*, which carried them to Butiaba on Lake Albert. Here, while the world waited for news and all the journalistic morgues were raided for obituary materials, it might have been supposed that they had earned the right to a quiet period of recuperation.

But Hemingway's injuries, despite his outward sick bravado, required better treatment than could be found in Butiaba, and the decision was reached to go to Entebbe. Once more bad luck pursued them. Taking off just after sunset aboard a lightly loaded twin-engined De Havilland Rapide piloted by Captain Reginald Cartwright and capable of seating twelve passengers, they crashed for the second time. This time the plane caught fire. To his previous injuries Hemingway now added substantial areas of burned skin and badly singed hair, making the need of immediate hospitalization even more nearly absolute. Twice vanquished in the air, they were driven by car to Masindi and afterwards to Entebbe from which, after several days of extreme discomfort, Hemingway was flown out on the 29th to Nairobi.

Harking back again to the safari of 1933–1934, which had concluded with a fishing-expedition once the hunting-season was over, the party had laid plans and selected a coastal locale as base of operations prior to the air-accidents. While Hemingway remained in Nairobi trying to regain his strength and his normal vision, his wife took the motor vehicles and the safari servants to the tiny port of Shimoni and summoned the already chartered fishing-boat down from Mombasa. Once the new camp was in running order, Roy Marsh flew Hemingway down to the beach and the whole party, including Patrick and his wife, made a valiant pretence of enjoying a season on the water after the adventures on land and in the air. But Hemingway could not participate. He was able to move only with the greatest difficulty owing to the as yet incompletely diagnosed internal injuries, and his pain was both constant and severe. When a forest fire suddenly burst out on the outskirts of Shimoni, he was foolish enough to try to help the other fire-fighters. But his condition was so poor that he stumbled and fell into the flames. When they pulled him out, his clothes smouldering, it was found that he had once again sustained severe burns on top of those from the second plane-crash which had so recently been healed. The bout of amoebic dysentery from which he had suffered and slowly recovered twenty years before, his ears ringing with the effects of emetine, was as nothing to the physical state in which Hemingway now found himself—smashed, blistered, and (as he said) "punch-drunk"—halfway through the fifty-fifth year of his life.

That astonishing resilience on which he had always hitherto depended managed to reassert itself, to some degree at least, even on the gloomy and uncomfortable voyage in mid-March from Mombasa to the port of Genoa. Ensconced once more in his favorite Venetian hotel, the Gritti Palace, where he had been severely ill with erysipelas in 1949–1950 and where he had put the fictional Colonel Cantwell through the final adventures of a doomed life, Hemingway received callers and read with ironic relish the obituary clippings which the papers of the world had solemnly printed at the time of the airplane crashes two months before. Yet all through the spring season in Italy and afterwards in Spain, under the constant scrutiny of friendly doctors, he was visibly far below his normal physical par—a condition still evident when he returned in June to the comparative quiet and order of life in Cuba after an absence of thirteen months divided almost equally between the extremes of pleasure and pain.

II. THAT SWEDISH THING

Upon his return to the Cuban finca, Hemingway's immediate task was to set down his recollections of the African tour while the events and the savor of the country were still fresh in his mind. Remembering his enthusiastic labors in preparing *Green Hills of Africa* twenty years earlier, he now began a story based on the second tour of Kenya and Tanganyika. Except for the loosely written journalistic articles for *Look* magazine, one of which he had dictated from his sickbed in Nairobi following the airplane accidents, this was his first extended attempt at composition since well before his departure from Cuba in 1953. Yet he was now prepared, as he said, to settle philosophically for the prospect of one good working year out of every three or four. His still considerable physical discomfort in the lumbar region of the back, which he sardonically rated between Force 5 and Force 7 on the Beaufort wind velocity scale, caused him to regard whatever progress he made in writing as a piece of good fortune. The twenty-five-day voyage home from Europe had been, he now said, both restful and healthy but also "boring as hell," and he threw himself with such zest into the new project that by mid-July he had completed some 10,000 words of a first draft.

Thinking and writing about East Africa only served to sharpen his nostalgia. During much of that summer he seriously considered making another two-month visit as soon as his physical condition would allow. The project was the preparation of a documentary film about the country and its animals, and some reasonable haste seemed desirable before the rise of African nationalism and the spread of civilization or war or greed overran those happy hunting-grounds where twice in his lifetime he had disported himself. But the hope came to nothing. In the end, angered by what he thought of as an ill-considered and premature news release by some of his associates, he rejected the proposal.

It was perhaps just as well. However great his love of Africa, however often he might dream of reassuming his self-imposed duties as acting game warden over the teeming preserves in the shadow of Kilimanjaro, or of buying a Cessna 180 in which he could make patrol flights over the Kimana Swamp, counting wild-life heads or scaring away native poachers, he was not yet in proper physical shape for anything of the kind.

Although his closest friends continued to believe that his life was protected by some special talisman, the near-débâcle of the January crack-ups had alerted the rest of the world to the fact that he had no absolute lien on physical immortality, whatever the survival powers of his books. Whether or not such considerations entered the minds of those in charge, the summer and fall of 1954 were signalized by two major awards, one in Cuba and the second in Stockholm.

For the first he had to go no further than the International Yacht Club in Havana. The date was his fifty-fifth birthday at the end of the third week of July. With his head completely shorn and shaved for the occasion, and wearing a jacket, a necktie, and even a handkerchief in his breast pocket, he bowed and smiled as the Cuban Subsecretary of State, Señor Gonzalo Guell, presented him with the medal of the Order of Carlos Manuel de Cespedes, the highest honor for a foreigner that Cuba could then bestow. The citation made clear the nation's pride in this famous American who for the better part of twenty years had chosen to make his home in Cuba. According to those who knew him best, Hemingway's pride in this decoration was genuine and heartfelt. No presentation since that of the Bronze Star for his work in France during the second World War pleased him so deeply.

The second award was of far greater magnitude. For years Hemingway had speculated, privately and sourly, about the methods employed by the Swedish Academy in selecting recipients of the Nobel Prize for Literature to which he sometimes alluded, with studied carelessness, as "that Swedish thing." His opinions of previous American winners were not high. The cruelly satirical fictional portrait of Sinclair Lewis, who had won the prize nearly a quarter-century before, had been duly recorded in *Across the River and Into the Trees.* As early as 1924 he had made known his views on T. S. Eliot, another Nobel Prizeman from the United States, while as recently as August of 1954 he had expressed his personal scorn over Faulkner's account, in *A Fable,* of Christ reincarnate in the guise of an army corporal. Was this, he hinted, the kind of thing they liked in Sweden? Past winners of the award had followed a consistent pattern: nothing any of them wrote afterwards was worth an obscenity. In certain moods he was not above suggesting darkly that some degree of political log-rolling might have governed previous selections.

But he either forgot or repressed his previous suspicions on the morning of October 28 when the news reached Cuba that he was in fact the fifth American (the sixth if one counted T. S. Eliot) to have won the Nobel Prize for Literature. The morning was cool and windy, gilded with bright sunlight, his favorite weather. Reporters who came in droves to see him at San Francisco de Paula found him relaxed and exuberant, glad to join them in drinks after a long dry season, though still favoring his painful back and limping as he walked through the rooms of the finca, showing his visitors where he worked. He listened with pride to the Academy's official citation, which spoke of his "forceful and . . . style-making mastery [of the art of narration], as recently evinced in *The Old Man and the Sea*." He modestly mentioned others who in his opinion deserved the prize: Lincoln's biographer Carl Sandburg, the Swedish baroness and novelist Isak Dinesen, the art collector and critic Bernard Berenson. He said frankly that he would use $8,000 of the $35,000 prize-money to pay off personal debts and that he would find good use for the rest. But he made it clear at once that his physical condition would prevent his going to Stockholm for the ceremonial presentation in December.

Non-attendance in person did not relieve him of the obligation of writing a speech of acceptance. Two weeks after the announcement he was still telling his friends that the task looked "impossible" and that he had no idea what ought to be said. In the end, however, he managed to set down and to polish a wryly serious and wholly typical seven paragraphs, totalling 335 words, and setting forth opinions with which his name had long been associated. In the minds of some critics, his opening reference to rhetoric and oratory looked like a slur upon the acceptance speech of William Faulkner. In the minds of others, his allusion to the deterioration of a writer's work as he grows in public stature might have been meant as a criticism of himself. Whatever his intentions, he duly recorded the speech at home in Cuba, and it was forwarded to John Cabot, the United States Ambassador to Sweden, to be read in the Town Hall at Stockholm on the evening of December 10.

"Members of the Swedish Academy, Ladies and Gentlemen:

Having no facility for speech-making and no command of oratory nor any domination of rhetoric, I wish to thank the administrators of the generosity of Alfred Nobel for this prize.

No writer who knows the great writers who did not receive the prize can accept it other than with humility. There is no need to list these writers. Everyone here may make his own list according to his knowledge and his conscience.

It would be impossible for me to ask the Ambassador of my country to read a speech in which a writer said all of the things which are in his heart. Things may not be immediately discernible in what a man writes, and in this sometimes he is fortunate; but eventually they are quite clear and by these and the degree of alchemy that he possesses he will endure or be forgotten.

Writing, at its best, is a lonely life. Organizations for writers palliate the writer's loneliness but I doubt if they improve his writing. He grows in public stature as he sheds his loneliness and often his work deteriorates. For he does his work alone and if he is a good enough writer he must face eternity, or the lack of it, each day.

For a true writer each book should be a new beginning where he tries again for something that is beyond attainment. He should always try for something that has never been done or that others have tried and failed. Then sometimes, with great luck, he will succeed.

How simple the writing of literature would be if it were only necessary to write in another way what has been well written. It is because we have had such great writers in the past that a writer is driven far out past where he can go, out to where no one can help him.

I have spoken too long for a writer. A writer should write what he has to say and not speak it. Again I thank you."

For well over a year after the Nobel Prize award, Hemingway's writing program was severely inhibited by two factors—persistent pain and insistent fame. Although he crept slowly forward with the African story, his injuries were still so troublesome that he found concentration difficult. In February, 1955, he wrote his old friend Dorman-O'Gowan that the discomfort in his back was still bad, and after the second long recuperative year had ended he complained privately to another correspondent that a cold had settled in the kidney he had ruptured in Africa and knocked him out from Thanksgiving of 1955 until well into January 1956. His fame was another major deterrent to progress. For the well-publicized award had reawakened such curious probing interest in his private life that even the well-insulated Cuban retreat had begun to seem increasingly untenable. Drunks on holiday in Cuba or Florida habitually telephoned him at all hours of the day and night. A newspaper man took public offence over some remarks Hemingway had made and challenged him to a duel which he was wise enough to reject. Many a stranger came to Cuba with the avowed purpose of interviewing him, asking a favor, or merely catching a glimpse of the latest Nobel laureate at work or at play. Their motives, said Hemingway, were much the same as those of Sunday afternoon zoo-visitors wishing to examine the elephant at close quarters.

Although it was a further interruption of his true work, he welcomed the opportunity of serving as adviser in preparing the film version of *The Old Man and the Sea*. From March through the middle of June, 1956, he threw his still considerable energies into the long business of helping the Warner Brothers organization to prepare the first movie made from one of his books in which he was able to take a strong personal interest. Authenticity was his chief concern. He looked closely at the shooting script by Peter Viertel, sought to instruct Spencer Tracy in creating the role of Santiago, and worried a good deal over the problem of finding a suitable living model for the great marlin of the book.

The game-fish in the Caribbean that spring refused to co-operate with the film-makers. After consultation, it was decided to try the livelier fishing-grounds off Parina Point below Talara in northern Peru. Wearing capacious white shorts, well-scuffed brown loafers, a generously pocketed hunting-jacket, and a long-billed fisherman's cap, Hemingway led the expedition into

Pacific waters, hooked and played four or five giant marlin while the cameras recorded their leaps and contortions, and assisted in the exposure of thousands of feet of color-film from which a composite portrait of Santiago's huge adversary could be put together. Upon his return to Cuba in May, he declared that the trip had done him good, that his injured back had stood up well under the stress of big-game fishing, and that he was glad to be finished at last with what he was now calling "the bloody picture."

Experience was clearly confirming his earlier prediction that one good working year out of every three or four was all he had reason to count on. His wife's health as well as his own now seemed to warrant a return to Spain for a change of climate and altitude. In the winter of 1956–1957 they took up residence in the "lovely hotel" at El Escorial outside Madrid. Hemingway found the food excellent, the out-of-season rates welcome, and the suite of rooms "super-comfortable." Yet there were spectres, as in the previous visits to Spain in 1953 and 1954. Their good friend Juan Madinaveitia of Madrid, the doctor who was treating Mrs. Hemingway, insisted also upon examining Hemingway himself, discovering, to his dismay, that the blood pressure and cholesterol count were both at dangerous levels while the aorta seemed to have assumed a different contour from that of 1954. Under strict dietary regulations, these disorders came under control. But it was not until the spring of 1957 that Hemingway resumed serious writing.

Once again, he seemed to himself to be entering what he was accustomed to call a "belle époque." Although in writing to his friends he habitually exaggerated his actual productivity, he did manage to make substantial progress with two new enterprises. In both, one discovers a repetition of the same pattern of backward turning which had governed his imagination for the better part of ten years. For the first was a novel with a setting on the southern coast of France in the middle 1920s, while the second was a non-fiction book about the early days in Paris and the Austrian Vorarlberg. It contained, he said, what many people had previously tried to relate, even though no one but himself could know how it had actually been. By

mid-September, the non-fiction book was well along. At the
end of the month he took it with him to Ketchum, where the
Hemingways stayed until March 1959, and continued work on
it in Cuba until the departure for Spain in April.

So began the long nostalgic summer in which fell his sixtieth
birthday. He and his wife disembarked at Gibraltar on the first
of May and were driven to Malaga to stay with friends at a
capacious villa in the outskirts of the city until the opening of
the San Isidro bullfights in Madrid. As the season matured,
there were other *corridas* to attend in Seville, Aranjuez, and
Algeciras, as well as the memorable first encounter between
Antonio Ordoñez and Luis Dominguin under the heavy June
sunlight at Zaragoza. In July came Pamplona, about which Hemingway managed to be as romantically nostalgic as ever. With
evident delight he revisited the ancient forest road along which
he had hiked in 1925. "Finding the country unspoiled and being
able to have it again," he wrote, "I was as happy as I had ever
been." All through the summer, which included an elaborate
double birthday party for Hemingway and the handsome wife
of Antonio Ordoñez, the happiness seems to have continued.
As he entered the sixty-first year of his life, he managed to
convince himself that he was "having it" all again, much as he
had known it far away and long ago in the kingdom of his
youth.

III. TIR N'A N'OG: THE LAND OF GOD KNOWS WHERE

Although members of his immediate family were well aware
that the state of his health was something less than good, the
year preceding his death seems otherwise to have begun normally enough. In the fall of 1959 and the winter and spring of
1960 he completed the typescript of *The Dangerous Summer*,
which had grown far beyond its originally expected dimensions,
shipped it off to the editors at *Life* magazine to be serialized in
the fall, and completed plans for yet one more visit to Spain.
When he and his wife Mary left San Francisco de Paula late in
July for Key West and New York, international relations be-

tween the United States and Cuba had not reached anything like the emergency status which they would assume in the fall and winter of 1960–1961. The Hemingways instructed the servants at Finca Vigia to guard the household and their pets, saw their voluminous baggage through customs, and departed for the mainland in full expectation of returning soon after Christmas, as had been their custom in former years.

Hemingway left his wife to organize and settle the New York apartment which they had leased some months before, and in August set off alone for Madrid, where he was met by his friend Nathan Davis and where unhappily he showed severe symptoms of advanced paranoia. As in 1959, he was soon as involved as ever in the febrile night-time journeyings from city to city, the late Spanish dining and wine-bibbing, and those vicarious but not less painful agonies to which he subjected his sensibilities while assuming once more the fiercely avuncular role of trainer-manager-counselor-and-wound-dresser to his brave young friend Ordoñez.

The season was waning and he was in Malaga on September 5 when the first installment of *The Dangerous Summer* was published in *Life* magazine. Next day he cabled his magazine editors in New York an admiring account of Antonio's refusal to follow the doctor's orders after his right forearm had been rendered nearly useless by a hard blow from a bull's horn during a rough *corrida* at San Sebastian. Twenty-four hours later, said Hemingway, the matador had insisted on fulfilling his contract at Bilbao, achieving there what seemed to his mentor to have been "one of the finest and most truly valiant faenas I have ever seen— using only his left hand because the right was crippled." In spite of a "brutally severe concussion," suffered when he was caught and tossed in the arena at Bilbao, Ordoñez was back at work five days later, fighting in France yet another *mano a mano* in the company of his brother-in-law and arch-rival, Luis Miguel Dominguin. Hemingway's latest hero had not let him down.

But by the beginning of October, his own much-tortured physique had deteriorated badly and his mind had slipped alarmingly. Even his friend Ordoñez took private notice of the unusual "sadness" that had come upon him. After his return to

New York in mid-October, he stayed only a week before leaving by train for the house on Wood River in Ketchum, Idaho, which he and his wife had purchased in the spring of the preceding year. The ostensible reason for haste was that the pheasant-shooting season was already on. Behind this public reason lay the increasingly troublesome hypertension and an ever more severe tendency towards mental depression. Although the Hemingways climbed at once into their western clothes and got as quickly as possible into the open air, it was clear that Hemingway was in abnormal physical and psychic difficulties.

At first gradually, but at last with pitiful rapidity, he had begun to look and sometimes to act like an old man. From the full-fleshed vigor of early 1959, he had now turned gaunt. His muscular arms were beginning to look wasted. His boyish voice had lost much of its former timbre, and though he had always spoken with deliberation, his speech was now marked by increasing hesitancy and lapses between words. The hair, now almost white, was combed carefully forward from the back of his head to cover a baldness he had once scorned to conceal. People who had known him for years were shocked at his pallor, the sagging flesh beneath his eyes, the spreading network of wrinkles. Even the broad shoulders had begun to stoop, the erect carriage to move forward and downward as if to protect the internal organs where the seat of his disorder lay.

Nor was he certain about the quality of what he had lately been writing. Despite the labor he had expended at the beginning of the year over the bull-fighting book, he seemed to be well acquainted with its limitations. He would later refer to it as a piece of journalism undertaken for *Life* in order to meet his income tax obligation, and in retrospect it now struck him as a "bad mistake." Many of those who read between the lines of the lengthy excerpts which *Life* printed that fall had sensed the fatigue behind the brave front. The editors had played the game, made the selections, printed the pictures, paid the substantial contracted price. But the full-length version, locked away at Charles Scribner's Sons, was only more of the same, much of it not as good as what was selected for magazine publication.

At the start, in its seminal stages, it had been planned as

another *Death in the Afternoon*—another backward turn, in a whole decade of turnings and returnings, to the glories he had known in his far-off youth of thirty years ago. But somewhere between the two books, the old emotion had gradually waned, the shadows had deepened, the light had turned crepuscular. This Hemingway knew. He was not anxious to rush the volume into print, as his publishers would have been prepared to do if he had insisted upon it. He did not wish to damage with an admittedly inferior product the latter-day reputation he had earned with *The Old Man and the Sea*. The new book was written, it was behind him, it had been a strategic error. Now he seemed almost bored by it.

If this was true, it was a boredom induced in great part by the development of his disease. As November waned and his physical torpor took increasing command, it was apparent that something drastic must be done. The limited resources of the small hospital at Sun Valley caused Dr. Saviers to recommend the Mayo Brothers Clinic in Rochester, Minnesota. Arrangements were completed quickly and in secrecy. On the last day of the month, slightly more than three weeks before Christmas, a large bearded man who gave his name as George Saviers was admitted to a private room in St. Mary's Hospital, subjected to a battery of tests, and placed under the care of two doctors. Besides the persistent hypertension, Hemingway was found to have a lingering case of jaundice. He was also suffering from partial loss of memory and periods of profound depression.

Under electric shock treatments and medication, he presently began to rally. Less than a month after admission to the Clinic he was well enough to accept an invitation to take Christmas dinner at the home of one of his doctors. By the beginning of 1961, his weight and blood-pressure had both been substantially reduced, his astonishing life-long resiliency had begun to reassert itself, and he turned with some semblance of good cheer to attack the always heavy pile of correspondence.

But the situation was anything but cheerful. Steady deterioration in Cuban-American affairs had resulted on January 3rd in the severance of diplomatic relations. Castro had long since proclaimed his adherence to Marxist doctrine, and it was unlikely that the incoming American administration would be able to solve the Cuban problem through any prompt and simple methods. The chances, as Hemingway now saw and said, were that he and his wife would lose their estate at San Francisco de Paula, as well as all its contents. Nor was he in any condition to accept the invitation to the inaugural ceremonies for John F. Kennedy. As the sixth and seventh weeks of his hospitalization came and went, he spoke often of his desire to get back to Idaho and the house on Wood River which had now perforce become his American home. Bad weather and a bad cold in the third week in January held up his departure, but by the twentieth of the month he was looking forward happily to a flight back to the west as soon as the storms and the virus had subsided. They would go, he said, straight across by way of Rapid City and Casper, south of the Wind River Range, then past the Tetons and across the ancient lava beds until they reached Hailey, just south of Ketchum. On January 22nd, seven years to the day after he left Nairobi's West Airport on the ill-fated flight to the Congo, the plane set him down in Idaho without accident or incident, and he spent the next two and a half months at home in the care of Dr. Saviers.

Once again now, as steadily as his afflictions would allow, he resumed work on the non-fiction sketchbook about some of the people he had known in Paris, or along the Côte d'Azur, or among the snow-covered slopes of the Vorarlberg region of Austria thirty-five or forty years earlier. Already finished, though not to his complete satisfaction, were enough of the sketches to make a short book. With the addition of another piece about the six-day bicycle races which he had watched from the sidelines as a youngster of twenty-three, the volume would print up to something like two hundred pages of prose, about equally divided between sardonic reflections and romantic recollections of days which were now receding ever more swiftly into the distance.

To his dismay, he discovered a lessening ability to recall in detail the events of the past. His memory, once so sharp and so readily at his service, was now beginning to be invaded by shadows. The man who had once been able to call hundreds by name could no longer remember the shape of circumstances or the names of former acquaintances. Most men past sixty have been so troubled. But Hemingway had always hitherto taken pride in his memorial powers; and if his remembrances were often inexact, as befitted one who had spent his life writing fiction, he nevertheless believed, and had often boasted, that that part of his equipment was both more intense and more trustworthy than is common. Once in March, in something close to desperation, he telephoned long distance to his first wife, with whom he had shared some of the experiences he was now seeking to relate, in order to ask her help in remembering certain names and episodes. To her ears his voice seemed pitifully distant, ringed with doubts, tinged with sadness. Once more, in fact, the hypertension was assuming potentially dangerous levels and the moods of depression were becoming more protracted.

Two suicide threats early in April required his return to Minnesota and two further months of hospitalization. This time the greater part of his correspondence piled up unanswered. He read newspaper accounts of the abortive Bahia de Cochinos invasion attempt on April 17–19, as well as Castro's May Day Speech, calling Cuba a socialist state and ordering the immediate expulsion of all foreign-born Catholic priests. Hemingway's earlier prediction on the likelihood of his own losses as a result of the twists and turns of Castro's foreign policy now seemed closer to fulfillment. Even more depressing was the news that Gary Cooper, Hemingway's friend for more than twenty years and the actor who had portrayed Robert Jordan in the film version of *For Whom the Bell Tolls,* was dying of cancer in California.

Once more, because he had little choice, Hemingway submitted to treatment and tried to follow the advice of his doctors. Once again, outwardly at least, he seemed to be making such progress in the last month of his stay that his release seemed sensible. Mrs. Hemingway asked her husband's old friend George Brown to assist in driving the patient back to Ketchum. On Sunday, June 25th, they left Rochester by car for Idaho, reaching home five and a half days later after a leisurely and uneventful trip.

But Hemingway, without the certain knowledge of either his wife or his friends, had entered Tir n'a N'Og. They had scarcely unpacked their gear when the report of the shotgun in the morning quiet of the house on Wood River went echoing across the airways to every corner of the world. Once more, as had happened after the airplane crashes in Africa, obituary notices spelled the news out darkly on all the front pages in most of the languages around the globe. Hemingway had read the first ones at the New Stanley Hotel in Nairobi, ironically amused over his survival though bitterly certain that there were many who had long wished for the opposite. Now he was past amusement or any further bitterness. To the astonishment and dismay of many thousands of his admirers, the embattled old lion was dead. It was Sunday morning, July 2, 1961.

XIV · Looking Backward

> "If you are lucky enough to have lived in
> Paris as a young man, then wherever you
> go for the rest of your life, it stays with
> you, for Paris is a moveable feast."
> —Hemingway to Aaron Hotchner, 1950[1]

I. THE TRUE GEN

The first semi-serious intimation that Hemingway might one
day undertake the writing of his memoirs was stimulated by the
appearance of Gertrude Stein's *Autobiography of Alice B. Toklas*
in 1933. He told Maxwell Perkins that his own memoirs would
be damned good because he was jealous of no one, owned a real
"rat-trap" memory, and possessed the relevant documents.[2] Almost exactly sixteen years later he returned to the subject in a
letter to Charles Scribner. He wanted, he said, to give his own
version of what happened, even though he knew that no one
could set down the truth about himself because of his natural
personal bias. As to subjects, he would like to try Ezra Pound,
James Joyce, Ford Madox Ford, Gertrude Stein, André Gide,
Valery Larbaud, André Malraux, Pablo Picasso, Georges Braque,
Joan Miró, Juan Gris, Clemenceau, Lincoln Steffens, various
Russians, and a scattering of admirals and generals. He would
also say something about Fitzgerald, Thomas Wolfe, Sherwood
Anderson, Faulkner, Dos Passos, Charles Ritz of the Paris Ritz,
and all the dead bartenders and whores he had known. Along
with these portraits of people, he would include the "inside gen,"
known only to himself, on the Spanish Civil War; offer a sketch
of "my life in the church"—about his nominal conversion to
Catholicism; and provide an account of the low-level bombing
operations of the Royal Air Force in 1943-1944, when their
targets were often Gestapo headquarters in the French country-

---

[1] This quotation from a letter of Hemingway's to A. E. Hotchner,
written in 1950, was used as epigraph for *A Moveable Feast*.

[2] EH to Maxwell Perkins, 7/26/33.

side, or launching platforms for the buzz-bomb attacks on England. This was already a large order, but he wanted to add some "information pieces" on his personal discoveries about cats; the way in which gambling houses are run; the "true story" of the taking of Paris in August, 1944; and, perhaps best of all, "the real gen on the old days in Paris."[3]

Very little of this, except the last, ever got into publishable form, although his letters, both before and after this one to Scribner, were replete with anecdotes about many of the people and some of the events in his long list of possible subjects. A few reminiscences of Paris in the early days of 1921-1926 had found their way into *Green Hills of Africa*, "The Snows of Kilimanjaro," and some of the pieces he had done for *Esquire*. But he had never set down what he variously called the "true," the "inside," or the "real gen" on those far-off times. "Gen" was a term he had discovered in young manhood and adopted thereafter as his own. It means something like intelligence in the military sense, and is probably a shortened form of "genuine." The genuine truth about the past was, in any case, what he proposed eventually to deliver. Meantime he had squirreled it away against a time when he felt like digging it up and telling it out as only he could do.

The event that finally activated him in the direction of a memoir took place seven years after his letter to Scribner and was almost literally a digging-up of something long hidden away. With his wife Mary he had spent the fall of 1956 in Spain. Late in November they reached Paris and stayed at the Ritz. The hotel porters lost no time in reminding him that two small trunks marked with his name had been moldering in the Ritz basement for many years. It was high time he reclaimed them: they were beginning to fall apart. On inspection they turned out to be a pair of steamer trunks, covered with rotting fabric. Inside, along with a few books and pictures and articles of clothing, he found sheaves of typewritten pages and a varicolored batch of notebooks partly filled with his handwriting. He had stored them there more than a quarter-century before, perhaps as early as the spring of 1928 when he had left Paris for Key West, Florida, with his second wife Pauline. Reading them through was like a chance

[3] EH to Charles Scribner, 7/28/49.

meeting with a former self. There lay the half-forgotten literary relics of his young manhood in Paris.[4]

At home in Cuba he received a letter from Edward A. Weeks, editor-in-chief of *The Atlantic Monthly*, reminding him of his promise to contribute to the hundredth-anniversary number of the magazine. Weeks had first approached him on the subject in the summer of 1955. After a considerable lapse of time, Hemingway had sent word that he would be pleased to cooperate. Weeks had all along had in mind a new short story. But Hemingway's imagination was now aglow with memories of the old days in Paris. Sometime in the spring he wrote an account of his first meeting with Fitzgerald at the Dingo Bar in 1925, and went on to tell the very funny story of their trip to Lyon to pick up Fitzgerald's Renault. He soon discovered that it was easy to remember but hard to write about, and spent a month finishing and polishing it to his satisfaction. Then, reading it over, he began to have second thoughts. As he explained in June, he was afraid that people would think he was doing the same kind of thing to a dead friend that John Malcolm Brinnin had done after Dylan Thomas's death in bringing out an "intimate journal" about Thomas's exploits in America. This fear was enough to dissuade him from his first plan, and he set the Fitzgerald piece aside in favor of two mediocre short stories. These came to Weeks's desk in the middle of August, and were printed in the centenary number of the *Atlantic* that November.[5]

[4] Mary Hemingway, "The Making of the Book: A Chronicle and a Memoir," *New York Times Book Review*, May 10, 1964, p. 26. No listing of the exact contents of the trunks was made, although a number of such notebooks, both blue and tan, have been preserved in Mary Hemingway's collection of her husband's papers. A preliminary census of this manuscript and typescript material was prepared and edited by Philip Young and Charles W. Mann, *The Hemingway Manuscripts: An Inventory*, University Park, Pennsylvania, 1969.

[5] Hemingway's dealings with *The Atlantic Monthly* at this time may be summarized as follows. Edward Weeks to EH, 8/30/55, first invited him to contribute to the centenary number. Weeks to EH, 4/16/56, acknowledged receipt of an oral message from Frank Hatch of Boston that Hemingway would be glad to cooperate. Weeks to EH, 2/4/57, reminded him of his promise. Weeks to EH, 8/16/57, thanked him for having sent the stories. EH to Weeks, 8/20/57, asked for a double fee, since there were two stories instead of one. Weeks agreed in writing a

The account of Fitzgerald had, however, served the important purpose of getting Hemingway launched on his Paris sketchbook. During the fall of 1957, he completed three more "chapters" and in December handed them to his wife Mary for typing. One told how it was to be living with his first wife Hadley in the flat at 74, rue du Cardinal Lemoine, near the Place de la Contrescarpe; how it was to be writing "The Three-Day Blow" at a table in a café on the Place St.-Michel; and with what pleasure Hadley had reacted to his proposal that they take a winter's holiday at the Gangwisch pension in Chamby-sur-Montreux, Switzerland. The second piece discussed his meetings with Gertrude Stein early in 1922 after the Swiss holiday. The third one skipped ahead in time to the early spring of 1924, when they had returned from Canada and were living above the sawmill at 113, rue Notre Dame des Champs. Hemingway was then using the Closerie des Lilas as a place to write in, and the sketch told amusingly of one of his meetings there with Ford Madox Ford, at which they learnedly discussed, *inter alia*, the differences between cads and gentlemen.

Mary was somewhat disappointed to discover that the sketches contained so little that was straightforwardly autobiographical. Hemingway explained that he was using a special technique, like a cushion shot in billiards or a double-wall bounce in jai alai. The analogy was fairly exact, since what one learned about the young Hemingway, from the four sketches so far completed, was revealed in part by watching him rebounding from the personalities of Miss Stein, Ford, Fitzgerald, and the wine-sozzled habitués of the Café des Amateurs in the rue Mouffetard.[6]

---

week later, and EH to Weeks, 8/31/57, thanked him for the payment. I am indebted for copies of these letters, along with a valuable running commentary, to Robert Manning, Weeks's successor as editor-in-chief: Manning to CB, 6/30/70. Hemingway's account of the writing of the piece on Fitzgerald and his reasons for withholding it are in EH to Harvey Breit, 6/16/57. John Malcolm Brinnin's *Dylan Thomas in America: An Intimate Journal* was published in 1955. The short stories that replaced the Fitzgerald memoir were "A Man of the World" and "Get a Seeing-Eyed Dog," *Atlantic*, 100 (November, 1957), pp. 64-68.

[6] Mary Hemingway, "The Making of the Book," *New York Times Book Review*, May 10, 1964, p. 27.

Through the winter he made few allusions to the book, although he reported at the end of July, 1958, that Mary had typed out his longhand version, and that he must now accomplish the final corrections and revisions. He spoke also of the possibility of resurrecting two further chapters, which he had begun and then put aside when he grew stale from overwork. During a future visit to Paris he still wanted to "check some things"—evidently exact locales and place-names, which had been an obsession with him since the days of *The Sun Also Rises*. Still unsettled in his mind was "the best way to handle" the book, whether by serialization in a magazine or first publication in book form.[7] At some time, either now or later, he wrote an amusing word-portrait of his son Bumby as he had been in the fall of 1925 at the age of two. It mentioned the Rohrbachs, Marie and Ton-Ton, who had often taken care of the child while his parents were traveling, spoke with admiration of "Silver" Beach, Bumby's name for the lady who ran the Shakespeare and Company bookshop, and ended with some further comments on Scott Fitzgerald's drinking habits. Hemingway labelled it "After Chapter 17"—which meant that he intended it to appear late in the book directly following the long essay on Fitzgerald—and put it aside for further consideration.[8] Both he and Mary told correspondents on September 18 and 19 that the whole book was done and copied. It was both his boast and his belief that it contained "the true gen" on what everyone else had written about, but that no one but he really knew.[9]

He was curiously reluctant to submit the book to his publisher.

[7] EH to L. H. Brague, 7/31/58. At this time he reported having once shown some of the sketches to George Plimpton, who liked them. This was probably about mid-December, 1957, when Plimpton was in Cuba. EH to Plimpton, 12/13/57. According to Valerie Danby-Smith (*Saturday Review*, 47, May 9, 1964, pp. 30-31 and 57), Hemingway "rechecked places and scenes" during walks around Paris in September, 1959.

[8] The unpublished MS bears no title but begins, "My first son, Bumby." It is complete and runs to eight pages in Hemingway's longhand. The notation, "After Chapter 17," is also in Hemingway's holograph.

[9] EH to General C. T. Lanham, 9/18/58, and Mary Hemingway to Gianfranco Ivancich, 9/19/58. For a different version of the chronology of composition, see Mary Hemingway's "Note" in the front matter of *A Moveable Feast*, 1964.

He accounted for his procrastination by saying that he did not want to follow the example of John Steinbeck, getting out a book each year made up of his toenail parings, or writing little fantasies about King Poo Poo, the last in scornful allusion to Steinbeck's *King Pepin the Third*.[10] He also seems to have been fearful that the contents of the book might precipitate some lawsuits.[11] In any case, he took the completed typescript with him to Ketchum in the fall of 1958, and kept it within arm's reach for a full year, tinkering with it occasionally, possibly shifting the order of the sketches a little here and there, but otherwise making few substantive changes. At last, touching base in New York in early November, 1959, en route from Spain to Cuba to Ketchum, he gave it over to be read by Charles Scribner, Jr., with instructions that it be sent afterwards to Ketchum for his final revisions.[12] Although he evidently continued to look it over from time to time, he never reached the point of sending it back to Scribner through all the period of his last illness and death.

After his suicide, Mary found the typescript in a blue box in the walnut-paneled back bedroom he had been using as a study whenever he was in Ketchum. He had prepared a prefatory statement, dated from his house at San Francisco de Paula, Cuba, 1960, in which he spoke chiefly of how much had been left out of the book, "for reasons sufficient to the writer," a phrase not without those overtones of tragedy that are always present among the effects of a writer who has died. "There is no mention," he had written, "of the Stade Anastasie where the boxers served as waiters at the tables set out under the trees and the ring was in the garden. Nor of training with Larry Gains [a colored prizefighter whose welfare Hemingway had sought to defend against allegedly crooked entrepreneurs], nor the great twenty-round fights at the Cirque d'Hiver. Nor of such good friends as Charlie Sweeney, Bill Bird and Mike Strater, nor of André Masson and Miró. There is no mention of our voyages to the Black Forest or of our one-day explorations of the forests that we loved around

[10] EH to L. H. Brague, 2/22/59.
[11] Mary Hemingway to CB, 8/3/64.
[12] Hemingway's note to Charles Scribner accompanying the MS is dated 11/3/59.

Paris. It would be fine if all these were in this book but we will have to do without them for now."[13]

He was saying in effect that it was impossible, however desirable it might have been, to provide anything like an exhaustive autobiography of those supremely significant years when he was really getting started, and that time and circumstance had obliged him to settle for a good deal less. Except for the long chapter on his early meetings with Fitzgerald and the concluding section on his two winters in the Austrian Vorarlberg, which ran to twenty-eight and fourteen pages respectively, the average length of the sketches was only six pages—roughly the size of a long anecdote—and two of them were only three pages long.

Hemingway could tell himself, of course, that he had already dealt with many people and events, whether by name or in thin fictional disguise, in the course of his other writings. Harold Loeb, Kitty Cannell, Donald Ogden Stewart, Duff Twysden, Ford, Cayetano Ordoñez, and Juanito Quintana had all appeared in *The Sun Also Rises*, and Maera and Villalta, as well as Ordoñez, in *Death in the Afternoon*. Pound had been the subject of a laudatory sketch in *This Quarter* as long ago as 1925. Bill Smith had appeared by name in some of the early short stories. Gertrude Stein had been scorned, and Joyce and Captain Dorman-Smith had been praised, in *Green Hills of Africa*. McAlmon and Bird had been saturninely commemorated in a poem in *Der Querschnitt*, and Henry (Mike) Strater, the painter, had been the subject of an article in *Esquire*. Fitzgerald had nodded briefly in the first published version of "The Snows of Kilimanjaro." And

---

[13] I have not seen the original of this prefatory note. If, as the date indicates, it was written in 1960 in Cuba, it must have been done between the middle of January, when he returned there from Idaho, and late July, when he left Cuba finally and went to New York en route to Spain, where his paranoia became severe. During much of this period, he was intensely occupied with completing *The Dangerous Summer*, his book about Ordoñez and Dominguin in 1959, of which *Life* magazine published excerpts in 1960. The preface is careless enough in small details, such as the misspelling of Charlie Sweeny's name (which appears as Sweeney) and the reference to "our voyages to the Black Forest" (there was only one, and it was not a "voyage"), so that one might be justified in concluding that he was not in good shape when he wrote it, or that he did not regard it as final.

so on. But many stories that Hemingway remembered sharply were' still untold, and the Paris sketchbook might have offered a fresh opportunity to set them down.

The twenty sketches that Mary Hemingway found in the blue box ranged in time from around Christmas of 1921, when Hemingway and Hadley first reached Paris, until about Easter of 1926, when they returned to Paris after their second winter in the Vorarlberg. This period of slightly more than four years had been crucial for Hemingway's career. It was the time of his marriage to Hadley, before the break-up over Pauline Pfeiffer, who was to become his second wife. It was a time when, besides much journalism and some minor poetry, he had written the eighteen miniatures that William Bird brought out in the Paris edition of *in our time*. It was in this same period that he had completed a dozen superlative and in a real sense epoch-making short stories, ranging from "Indian Camp" to "Big Two-Hearted River." To the same years belonged the Anderson parody, *The Torrents of Spring*, and the first major novel, *The Sun Also Rises*. It was the time when he explored not only provincial France and Germany but also Switzerland, Spain, and Austria, besides making a pilgrimage to the 1918 battle-sites of northern Italy and taking a month-long trip to Asia Minor. It was a time when he had first welcomed and then rejected newspaper work as a means of support, when he met and interviewed many of the leading statesmen of Europe, the Middle East, and the U.S.S.R. It was the time when he first discovered the joys and some of the responsibilities of fatherhood, and when he had helped with the editing of such little magazines as the *transatlantic review* and *This Quarter*.

It was a time when he was first befriended by people as various as Pound and Joyce, Gertrude Stein and Alice Toklas, Ford and his then wife, Stella Bowen; of the development of close friendships with Lewis Galantière, who accompanied the Hemingways to the Black Forest, Mike Strater, with whom Hemingway often boxed, Charlie Sweeny, the soldier of fortune, whom he first met in Constantinople, and T. H. (Mike) Ward, who worked for a bank and loved six-day bicycle racing. It was a time of renewal of older friendships with Bill Smith and Krebs Friend, John Dos Passos and Captain Dorman-Smith. In these years he knew boxers like Larry Gains, bullfighters like Villalta, Maera, and Ordoñez, and *aficionados* like Juanito Quintana. He consorted occasionally with painters like Joan Miró, Jules Pascin, and Bertram Hartman. Among the editors and publishers he knew were Maxwell Perkins, Robert McAlmon, Horace Liveright, Ernest Walsh and Ethel Moorhead, Edward J. O'Brien, Jane Heap, and Margaret Anderson. Then there were the kindly booksellers, Sylvia Beach and Adrienne Monnier, and newspapermen like William Bird, Guy Hickok, Sisley Huddleston, Max Eastman, and Lincoln Steffens. And the writers, of all sorts and conditions: Harold Acton, Nathan Asch, Natalie Barney, Robert Benchley and Dorothy Parker, Donald Ogden Stewart, Janet Flanner and Solita Solano, Sinclair Lewis and Wyndham Lewis, as well as the poets Evan Shipman and Ralph Cheever Dunning. Large in his memory stood his long friendship with Scott Fitzgerald, fifteen years in duration, his profound distrust of Zelda, his adoption and ultimate repudiation of Gerald and Sara Murphy, and perhaps most of all his love for Hadley, who was going to emerge as the heroine of his sketchbook.

So, as he said, there was much, very much, that did not get into his memoirs, not even that memorable day when he scratched around to assemble enough francs to buy Miró's "The Farm" as a birthday present for Hadley. Not the story of his first interview with Mussolini during an otherwise nostalgic trip back from Paris to Milan. Not the truth about his adventures in Asia Minor, which he had handled fictionally in some of the miniatures and most memorably in "The Snows of Kilimanjaro." Not the history of his dealings with Krebs Friend in Chicago and in Paris. Not the reasons for his victimization of Harold Loeb and Chard Powers Smith.[14]

[14] A short account of buying Miró's "The Farm" appears in John Dos Passos, *The Best Times*, New York, 1966, p. 144. Hemingway's first interview with Mussolini was printed in the Toronto *Daily Star*, June 24, 1922, p. 16. His opinion of Il Duce changed markedly at the end of this year when he saw him again in Lausanne and called him "Europe's Prize Bluffer." Toronto *Daily Star*, January 27, 1923, p. 11. For some of the facts about Hemingway's trip to Asia Minor, see Baker, *Ernest Hemingway: A Life Story*, New York, 1969, pp. 97-99. Same source (pp. 77, 79, 131, and 136) for the story of Krebs Friend. Same source (pp. 124, 133, 142, 145, 148-151, and 154) for the story of Hemingway's relation-

But the typescript in the blue box was as close to final form as it would ever be. It included, as was his custom, a list of possible titles, among them *A Moveable Feast*, spelled as written. This and several others bore his checkmarks in the margins, as if to indicate that he had not yet finally made up his mind as to what the book should be called. When Mary Hemingway showed the contents to Malcolm Cowley in 1963, he urged her to publish it as the first of the posthumous volumes. She went over the book with care, correcting spelling and punctuation, and "sometimes but rarely" deleting repetitious words and phrases. Afterwards, with the assistance of L. H. Brague of Scribner's, she made a few further cuts and changed the order of two chapters for the sake of continuity. One important omission, evidently inadvertent, was the sketch of Bumby, meant to appear as chapter 18 just after the account of the Hemingway-Fitzgerald trip to Lyon. It had not been typed and remained in Hemingway's longhand on a bound pad of writing paper. Finally, as Hemingway himself had done in the fall of 1959, Mary flew to Paris for one last thorough check of place-names and terrain. The book was published on May 5, 1964, thirty-eight months after his death.[15]

II. ENEMIES AND OTHERS

By the time he set to work on the Paris sketchbook, Hemingway's tendency to remember himself as an intrepid, humorous, poverty-stricken, and lone-going fighter against the stupidities of many of his former associates had congealed into a stereotype. He was no longer jealous of most of the people he had known thirty years earlier because he believed, not without reason, that on the record he had succeeded better than they. The emotion

---

ship with Harold Loeb. Same source (pp. 133 and 181) for Hemingway's attack on and quarrel with Chard Powers Smith. See also the present volume, Ch. II, note 4, above.

[15] Mary Hemingway, "The Making of the Book," *New York Times Book Review*, May 10, 1964, p. 27, mentioned the list of titles. Charles Scribner, Jr., to CB, 7/6/70 accounted for the omission of the Bumby sketch. Valerie Danby-Smith accompanied Hemingway on a walking-and-checking tour of the Left Bank in September, 1959. *Saturday Review* 47 (May 9, 1964), pp. 30-31.

that erupted in him when he thought about many of them was not jealousy but scorn—scorn of their pretentiousness, their snobbery, their childish tantrums. This emotion was funneled into approximately half the sketches, enough to give the whole collection an acidulous tone, despite the humor and despite the fact that the other half took on an aureate coloration from his habit of romanticizing the far-away and long-ago. The percentages of attraction and repulsion were about average for Hemingway. He was a good hater who had always shown a tendency to divide the people he knew into categories of good and bad, honest and false, and to nurture grudges against those who had crossed him in fact or in his imagination.

Among those whom he remembered as enemies from the vantage-point of the late nineteen-fifties were Harold Acton, Nathalie Clifford Barney, Ralph Cheever Dunning, Zelda Fitzgerald, Ford Madox Ford, Percy Wyndham Lewis, Gertrude Stein, Ernest Walsh, and, in a more complicated fashion, John Dos Passos and Gerald and Sara Murphy. Sometimes, as in the case of Dunning, the sketch was simply an excuse to relay a good anecdote, one that Hemingway had evidently treasured for years and perhaps had often repeated to his friends. At other times, as with Acton and Wyndham Lewis and Gertrude Stein, a motif of vengeance appears to be central, since all three had insulted him in print. The attack on Zelda Fitzgerald was evidently occasioned by Hemingway's belief, which was formed early and changed little from first to last, that Zelda was jealous of her husband's literary talents, and that she tried to counteract the time and energy he gave to writing by encouraging him in his drinking and his irresponsible social conduct, and by assuring him (as an irritant) that he was sexually incompetent and inadequate. Although Dos Passos and the Murphys are not alluded to by name, it is clear enough that Dos Passos is blamed (quite unfairly) for having introduced Hemingway to the Murphys at a time when he was still innocent and impressionable. It is also clear that the Murphys, scornfully characterized as "the rich," are held culpable for having encouraged Hemingway to break with Hadley and to take up with Pauline Pfeiffer—an accusation equally unfair.

Hemingway had little reason to malign Ford Madox Ford, who had always gone out of his way to praise him in print. In the twenties Ford had done nothing worse than to make a public apology for Hemingway's slur on T. S. Eliot and to allow the *transatlantic review* to die young when Hemingway had counted on it as an outlet for more of his short stories. Yet in Hemingway's memory Ford stood as a physical slob and an egocentric snob who somehow managed to embody many of the worst traits of the English intellectual.

In form, the sketch on Ford turned out to be fairly typical. It opened with two pages of introduction on the pleasures of sitting alone at the Closerie des Lilas, a café that Hemingway had come to think of as his eminent domain. Then Ford appeared. "On this evening," wrote Hemingway, "I was sitting at a table outside the Lilas watching the light change on the trees and the buildings and the passage of the great slow horses of the outer boulevards. The door of the café opened behind me and to my right, and a man came out and walked to my table. 'Oh here you are,' he said." The happy and peaceful light-and-horse-watching séance was suddenly and permanently destroyed.

Hemingway's capacities for scorn and derision then came strongly to the fore. He began by selecting unpleasant physical terms with which to damn the interloper. Ford's mustache was *stained*; his eyes were a *washed out blue* under eyelashes and eyebrows that were unnaturally colorless. He was built like a *hogshead*. His breath was so sour that one must sit to windward of him, even out-of-doors. "I took a good look at him, repented, and looked across the boulevard," wrote Hemingway. It even occurred to him that Ford's coming might have fouled his drink, though an exploratory sip reassured him.

Ford's obtuseness and egocentricism came out in conversation. Noticing that Hemingway looked glum, he attributed the glumness to overconcentration on work rather than to its real cause, his own thoughtless interruption of his young friend's evening observations. With every appearance of kindness, he next invited him to relax at an amusing Bal Musette he had recently discovered. It was located, he said, at the top of the rue du Cardinal Lemoine near the Place de la Contrescarpe. Hemingway assured him that he knew the place well, since he and Hadley had often danced there when they lived in the flat just above it. But Ford was not listening. He offered to draw a sketch-map so that Hemingway could find the place. Something of the same sort occurred when Ford ordered a drink, first asking for a vermouth-cassis, then changing the order to brandy and water, and finally upbraiding the waiter for not having brought vermouth. Hemingway, who knew and sympathized with the waiter, offered to drink the brandy and water and quietly suggested that Ford would like a vermouth instead. Encased in his ego like an egg in its shell, Ford not only ignored the inconvenience he had caused but also assured Hemingway that it was fatal for a young writer to drink brandy.

The sketch closed with an anecdote by which Hemingway summed up Ford's social gaucherie. He told it well because he had already written it out at least once before in the uncut version of *The Sun Also Rises* in the part that was lopped off before publication. This version gave an account of a conversation between Jake Barnes and his snobbish friend Braddocks. They were in the midst of it when a man in a cape walked past. Braddocks said that the man was Hilaire Belloc, and then began crowing over the skill with which he had just "cut" Belloc by not greeting him. He was obviously very proud of this piece of one-upmanship. After Braddocks had gone, the man in the cloak went past again. "There's Belloc," Jake told a friend. Not at all, the friend said. It was Aleister Crowley, the renowned diabolist.[16]

The Closerie des Lilas was the scene of another intrusion by an unwanted visitor, this time in the morning rather than the evening. Again the sketch commenced in sweetness and then turned sour. "The blue-backed notebooks," wrote Hemingway, "the two pencils and the pencil sharpener (a pocket knife was too wasteful), the marble-topped tables, the smell of early morning, and luck were all you needed." All that, and not being interrupted in your labors. "Then you would hear someone say, 'Hi, Hem. What are you trying to do? Write in a cafe?' Your

---

[16] *AMF*, pp. 81-88. (Unnumbered Chapter 9). The Braddocks-Barnes-Belloc incident appeared in the MS of *SAR* and was deleted before publication.

luck had run out and you shut the notebook. This was the worst thing that could happen. If you could keep your temper it would be better but I was not good at keeping mine then and said, 'You rotten son of a bitch what are you doing in here off your filthy beat?' "

The target of this vituperation was "a tall fat young man with spectacles," identified merely as Hal. The only Hal of Hemingway's known acquaintance who fitted that description was Harold Acton, novelist, poet (chiefly in couplets), translator, erstwhile Oxonian, and later professor of English Literature at Peking. He was also, later, the author of *Memoirs of an Aesthete*, published in London in 1948. In this book Acton had listed Hemingway as one of the "chief pupils" of Gertrude Stein to whom, it was said, he paid "clumsy homage"—even though he feared her because "she saw through his matador poses" to the cowardice beneath. This in itself would have been enough to place Acton forever in Hemingway's black book. But Acton also said that Hemingway had thought it "essential to look tough . . . to make a cult of the hair" on his chest. Acton was "suspicious of this vaunted virility" and chose to shun all such "bogus Broncho Bills." It is of course impossible to be sure that the Hal who intruded upon Hemingway in the morning quiet at the Closerie was meant to be Acton. If it was, Hemingway's posthumous vengeance was complete.[17]

Yet another of those whom Hemingway marched out for flaying was Wyndham Lewis. This enmity also went far back in time. He was only just back in Paris from his first African safari of 1933-1934 when he paid a visit to Sylvia Beach's bookshop and read an essay of Lewis's called "The Dumb Ox." The intent of the piece was to impugn Hemingway's anti-intellectual pose. "The sort of first-person-singular that Hemingway invariably evokes," Lewis wrote, "is a dull-witted, bovine, monosyllabic simpleton. This lethargic and stuttering dummy he conducts or pushes from behind, through all the scenes that interest him . . . like a moronesque version of his brilliant author." Further, he said, "the expression of the soul of the dumb ox would have a penetrating

[17] *AMF*, pp. 91-96. (Unnumbered Chapter 10). See Acton, *Memoirs of an Aesthete*, London, 1948, pp. 161 and 173-175.

beauty of its own if it were uttered with genius—with bovine genius (and in the case of Hemingway this is what has happened): just as much as would the folksong of the baboon." There was more of the same, and even some that was laudatory, but Lewis, like Acton, made the highly injudicious error of calling Hemingway a pupil of Gertrude Stein's. "This brilliant Jewish lady," he wrote, "had made a *clown* of him by teaching Hemingway her babytalk. . . . And it is very difficult to know where Hemingway proper begins and Stein leaves off as an artist." Reading Lewis' essay so enraged Hemingway that he struck out at a vase of tulips on Sylvia Beach's table, breaking the vase and scattering the flowers. He settled the matter with Miss Beach by paying her 1,500 francs' damages. But the matter with Lewis was not settled until the publication of *A Moveable Feast* thirty years later.

His long-simmering dislike then boiled over. According to Hemingway, he was at Ezra Pound's studio teaching him to box on the afternoon when he met Lewis for the first time. Lewis was wearing "a wide black hat, like a character in the quarter," and was dressed "like someone out of *La Bohème*." His face reminded Hemingway of a frog, "not a bullfrog but just any frog, and Paris was too big a puddle for him." It was an embarrassment merely to see him, and he looked on "superciliously" while Pound and Hemingway boxed. Hemingway watched him narrowly, with veiled eyes, as his custom was. He did not think that he had ever seen "a nastier looking man." On the way back to his flat in the rue du Cardinal Lemoine, he tried to think of metaphors for Lewis' appearance, and they all came out like the pictures of diseased organs in his father's medical books. When he sought to break down Lewis' face into its component elements, he found that what he recalled with most horror was the eyes. Under that histrionic black hat, "the eyes had been those of an unsuccessful rapist." Later, said Hemingway, he had tried to like Lewis because he was a friend of Pound's. But that first impression lingered: a supercilious frog-face with the slightly exophthalmic look of a frustrated degenerate.[18]

[18] *AMF* pp. 108-110. (Unnumbered Chapter 12). See Lewis, *Men Without Art*, London, 1934, esp. pp. 28-29. The tulip episode is given in

In the same essay Hemingway mildly satirized Nathalie Barney, "a rich American woman and a patroness of the arts" who "had a salon at her house on regular dates"—none of which Hemingway felt any inclination to keep. According to her friend Magdeleine Wauthier, Miss Barney was "une femme très blonde, d'un blond lunaire," and glacier-cold blue eyes. In 1939 she had brought out a book of *pensées,* in one of which she typically said, "L'amour est l'unique communisme auquel je crois." It was not, however, the kind of love in which Hemingway believed. Unlike her friend Harold Acton, she had never made the mistake of attacking Hemingway in print, although she did say, after his death, that she had always envied Gertrude Stein such "chevaliers servants" as Hemingway, Fitzgerald, and Thornton Wilder. If Hemingway had been alive when this remark was published, it is likely that his treatment of Miss Barney would have been a good deal less chivalric.[19]

That he still had a score to settle with Gertrude Stein was evident from the fact that three of the chapters were largely devoted to her. His account of his early meetings with her in the spring of 1922 was not unkind. "She had beautiful eyes," he wrote, "and a strong German-Jewish face . . . and she reminded me of a northern Italian peasant woman with her clothes, her mobile face, and her lovely, thick, alive immigrant hair." But this vibrant creature soon betrayed her Dutch-uncle dogmatism, adversely criticizing "Up in Michigan," urging him to buy pictures rather than clothes, and instructing him about the ins and outs of homo-

---

Sylvia Beach's holograph note dated 3/24/34 in the Beach Collection, Princeton University Library. One of Hemingway's gestures of friendship toward Lewis came after publication of *SAR* when he asked Lewis whether Brett's English speech had been faithfully reproduced. Lewis reassured him that his ear and memory were both excellent. See W. K. Rose, ed., *The Letters of Wyndham Lewis,* London, 1963, p. 454. In October, 1927, Lewis had praised *The Torrents of Spring* and Hemingway rejoined by praising Lewis's *Paleface.* See Lewis, *Rude Assignment,* London, 1950, p. 203.

[19] *AMF,* pp. 110-111. Miss Barney's remark on love appears in *Nouvelles Pensées de l'Amazone,* Paris, 1939, p. 35; her description of Hemingway as one of Gertrude Stein's "chevaliers servants" is in her *Traits et Portraits,* Paris, 1963, p. 66. Miss Wauthier's description of Miss Barney is in the introduction to this volume.

sexuality. She said that the acts committed by male homosexuals were ugly and repugnant, but with women it was just the opposite. "They do nothing that they are disgusted by and nothing that is repulsive," she insisted, "and afterwards they . . . can lead happy lives together."

The second sketch told of his habit of dropping in to talk literature at her apartment. Again her opinions were firm but biased. Aldous Huxley's books were "inflated trash," D. H. Lawrence wrote like a "sick man," and, as for Joyce, if a visitor brought up his name as much as twice, he would no longer be welcome in the rue de Fleurus. She liked and recommended *The Lodger*, Marie Belloc Lowndes's Jack the Ripper story, and always spoke warmly of Sherwood Anderson, Ronald Firbank, and Scott Fitzgerald. Hemingway not only received but retained the impression that she was both dictatorial and professionally jealous.

The sketch concluded with Miss Stein's story about "the lost generation." Once in the south of France her old Model T Ford had developed ignition trouble. The young man who worked on it proved to be so inept that she complained to the manager of the garage. The manager then scolded the young mechanic in a memorable phrase: he and all his kind belonged to a "génération perdue." These words, as Miss Stein pontifically asserted, were applicable to the members of Hemingway's generation. "Don't argue with me," she said. "It does no good at all. You're all a lost generation, exactly as the garage keeper said." Walking home to the sawmill flat, said Hemingway, he got to thinking "of what a warm and affectionate friend Miss Stein had been" in the two years since they had met. But he could not help resenting her insistence that he himself belonged to a lost generation. It fell under the rubric of "dirty, easy labels." Gertrude Stein was nice, he told Hadley that evening, but she did talk "a lot of rot" sometimes.

What Hemingway did not reveal in *A Moveable Feast* was that he had once seriously considered using Miss Stein's "dirty, easy label" as the title of his first novel. He was down in Chartres on September 27, 1925, when he wrote a boyish foreword headed, "The Lost Generation: A Novel." Here he told a different version of the anecdote about the garage-keeper. A valve was stuck in Miss Stein's Ford and a very young mechanic fixed it fast and well. She asked the man in charge how he found such good men. The very young ones were good, he said, because he trained them himself. Not so those in the age-group of twenty-two to thirty, who were all a "génération perdue." Although the novel was finally named *The Sun Also Rises* and the foreword rightly discarded, Hemingway's revelation of his thought-processes on the way home, as set down in *A Moveable Feast*, was an obvious misrepresentation.[20]

The final sketch on Miss Stein had been carefully prepared for by the conversation on homosexuality and Lesbianism set forth in the first. By the time it alluded to, a bright spring morning in 1925 or 1926, Hemingway had been given a standing invitation to stop in at any time, whether or not Miss Stein was at home. The servant had instructions to offer him *eau de vie*. He would drink his drink, admire the paintings, and then leave if the mistress of the house had not returned. On the morning in question, Miss Stein was upstairs with a companion. He could not help overhearing the companion's voice speaking to Miss Stein as he had never heard anyone anywhere speak before. Then came Miss Stein's voice, begging and pleading and saying, "Don't, pussy. . . . Please don't. I'll do anything, pussy, but please don't do it." Hemingway drank his *eau de vie* and beat a retreat. Although he continued to do the customary small favors and make the required appearances, he knew that eventually he would be dismissed along with the rest of Miss Stein's male entourage. So came the end—"a strange enough ending"—to an association that had begun so well. If this anecdote was his final reply to the attack she had made in *The Autobiography of Alice B. Tok-*

[20] The sketches largely given to Miss Stein are "Miss Stein Instructs," pp. 11-21, "Une Génération Perdue," pp. 25-31, and "A Strange Enough Ending," pp. 117-119. (Unnumbered chapters 2, 3, and 13). Hemingway's contemporaneous foreword was written in longhand in a brown *cahier* dated in his holograph, "Chartres. Sept. 27, 1925." For yet another version of the lost-generation anecdote, see Hemingway to CB, Easter Sunday, 1951, printed with his permission in the present volume, Chapter IV, pp. 80-81. It is clear, and also of course understandable, that the story underwent several transformations between the middle twenties and the late fifties.

las, as it seems to have been, it was the unkindest cut he could have made in response to her statement that he was yellow.

Hemingway's feelings of disgust carried over into the following account of Ernest Walsh, "The Man Who Was Marked for Death." Among the twenty sketches it was perhaps the least inspired, as well as the most pointless and tasteless. The two young men had met in the summer of 1922. In the early months of 1925, Walsh and his friend Ethel Moorhead, a painter, established a new "little magazine," *This Quarter.* Hemingway volunteered his editorial assistance in preparing the first number, which was dedicated to Ezra Pound and included brief tributes from Joyce, Hemingway, Walsh, and Miss Moorhead. He worked hard on the project, with no other compensation than the sale of two stories to the magazine. When he tried to persuade the editors to employ his friend Bill Smith to perform the same labors that he had been doing gratis, they refused in such a manner that he was angry and hurt. The rather foolish poem and the highly flattering review of *In Our Time* that Walsh wrote for the second number did not help, since Hemingway professed to find all such overpraise almost literally nauseating.

Some of the nausea was unhappily reflected in the sketch of Walsh, which depended on a sick pun to portray Walsh as a "con-man" in two senses. One was Walsh's consumption, of which he died in October, 1926. "He knew I knew he had the con," wrote Hemingway, "not the kind you con with but the kind you died of then. . . . I was wondering if he ate the flat oysters in the same way the whores in Kansas City always wished to swallow semen as a sovereign remedy against the con." Then there was Walsh as confidence-man. He had conceived a plan to offer a literary prize for contributors to *This Quarter,* to be awarded to the writer whose work was adjudged best at the end of the first four issues. In the course of a sumptuous oyster lunch, Walsh promised him the prize, even though, later on, Hemingway learned that he had given similar assurances to James Joyce, and possibly to Ezra Pound.[21]

---

[21] *AMF,* pp. 123-129. (Unnumbered Chapter 14.) On Hemingway's association with Walsh and Miss Moorhead, see Baker, *Ernest Hemingway: A Life Story,* pp. 101, 137, 140-143, and 148. Walsh's poem, "Ernest

Among female enemies, Zelda Fitzgerald stood out at this period, less for what she did or said to Hemingway than for her repressive attitude towards her husband's work. For Scott himself Hemingway had already conceived an avuncular affection, despite the fact that he was the younger of the two, and the theme of his oral discourse often turned upon the writers' need to join forces against their common enemies. Scott candidly mentioned the words killjoy and spoilsport, which Zelda hurled at him whenever he began working hard. On the day in 1925 when the Hemingways came to lunch in the rue Tilsitt, Zelda seemed "jealous of Scott's work," and ready to complain of her boredom in order to "get him off on another drunken party." Some years later, Fitzgerald told of another method by which Zelda had sought to undermine his confidence. She had said, he confided, "that the way I was built I could never make any woman happy. . . . I have never felt the same since she said that." Hemingway did his best to reassure Fitzgerald: Zelda had merely been using "the oldest way in the world of putting people out of business." But even a tour of the Louvre to inspect the unfigleaved statues was not antidote enough against Zelda's poisonous accusation.[22]

Fitzgerald himself was more friend than foe, although he could sometimes be a very trying friend. When they first met, Hemingway was embarrassed by the unbelievable fulsomeness of Scott's praise, his barrage of too-personal questions, and the fact that he passed out from drinking a little champagne. The second meeting went better, Fitzgerald being "cynical and funny and very jolly and charming and endearing, even if you were careful about anyone becoming endearing." The third meeting took

---

Hemingway," *This Quarter*, 1 (Autumn-Winter, 1925-1926), p. 67, begins: "Papa soldier pugilist bullfighter/Writer gourmet lionhead aesthete/ He's a big guy from near Chicago. . . ." The same number carried a picture of Hemingway and Bumby on skis in Schruns (p. 107) and Walsh's review of *In Our Time*, pp. 319-321. Walsh died of tuberculosis in Monaco, Oct. 16, 1926, and was buried there. Miss Moorhead dedicated the third number to Walsh and carried on as editor.
[22] *AMF*, pp. 179 and 190 (unnumbered sketches 18 and 19). Hemingway had relayed the measurements anecdote to Fitzgerald's biographer, Arthur Mizener, in a letter of 4/22/50.

place in Lyon, followed by the high-low comedy of driving Scott's topless Renault through ten showers of rain between Lyon and Châlon-sur-Saône—a story too long, too funny, and too good to be read in any other version than Hemingway's. This was the piece he had written for the centenary of the *Atlantic Monthly*, and it was by far the best and most sustained in *A Moveable Feast*. At the end of it, Hemingway remarked that Fitzgerald had many more friends than anyone else he knew. He himself was glad enough to enlist in these ranks with the hope of being of some use to a beleaguered fellow-writer.

But Fitzgerald often transformed the use to abuse. "When he had very bad times," wrote Hemingway, "I listened to him about them and tried to make him know that if he could hold onto himself he would write as he was made to write, and that only death was irrevocable." When he came to Paris from the Riviera in the fall of 1925, Scott was drinking more heavily than ever, and made a habit of dropping in on the Hemingways, unannounced, whenever he was drunk by day or by night. On one of these occasions he sat in the fireplace until the tail of his overcoat caught fire. He seemed, in short, to be taking "almost as much pleasure" in interfering with Hemingway's work "as Zelda did interfering with his."[23]

Fitzgerald was always a special case. The friends to whom Hemingway was kindest included Evan Shipman, poet and trotting-horse fancier, Sylvia Beach the bookseller, Pascin the painter, and Ezra Pound. Pound, as Hemingway had written much earlier, was "always a good friend . . . always doing things for people." At its best, his writing was "so perfect, and he was so sincere in his mistakes and so enamoured of his errors" that Hemingway "always thought of him as a sort of saint." Even

[23] *AMF*, first meeting, pp. 149-152; second meeting, 152-154; Lyon trip, 154-174; Hemingway's enlistment among Fitzgerald's friends, 176; Fitzgerald's drunken misbehavior, 183-184. When Hemingway wrote *The Torrents of Spring* in November, 1925, he inserted a note: "It was at this point in the story, reader, that Mr. F. Scott Fitzgerald came to our house one afternoon, and after remaining for quite a while suddenly sat down in the fireplace and would not (or was it could not, reader?) get up and let the fire burn something else so as to keep the room warm." *Torrents*, New York, 1926, p. 119.

his occasional irascibility might have been construed as a saint-like quality. Besides this, his only fault was the cacophony he produced while learning to play the bassoon. It was less a fault than a Homeric nod when he confessed that he had never read "the bloody Rooshians"—such, for example, as Turgenev, Gogol, Chekhov, Dostoievski, and Tolstoi. This seemed all the more strange to Hemingway, since Miss Beach had introduced him to the major Russian writers in the spring of 1922, making him feel as if she had opened a chest and given him "a great treasure." Toward Sylvia he remained unequivocal in his praise. He liked her "sharply sculptured face," her lively eyes and wavy hair, both brown in color like his own, her pretty legs, her kindness and good cheer, her love of jokes and gossip, and (though he only hinted at this) the fact that she was somewhat inclined to mother him. She urged him to eat properly, lent him books on credit, received and forwarded his mail, and bucked him up when he felt depressed. "No one that I ever knew was nicer to me," he wrote.[24]

For all their slightness of content, two of the most charming of the essays were those on Pascin the painter and Shipman the poet. Both opened, like so many of the others, with brief autobiographical set-pieces. In the first, having worked hard all one bright spring day, Hemingway allowed himself a small social adventure in the evening. Later he would dine with Hadley on the *plat du jour* at the Nègre de Toulouse, but now he went along to make a quick survey of the major cafés, settling for the Dôme, where most of the assemblage had spent the day as he had done, in honest and productive work. Pascin was there with the sisters who modeled for him, one fair, one dark. Hemingway had not been at his table for two minutes before Pascin was gaily inviting him to "bang" the dark sister and proffering his studio for the purpose. In declining the invitation, Hemingway was yet uncomfortably aware of the charms of the brunette, who amused herself by showing off her handsome profile and displaying her breasts under the tight black sweater for his special benefit. The blonde sister pretended to be upset by her employer's "piggish"

[24] On Pound, *AMF*, pp. 93, 107-108, 110, 134. On Sylvia Beach, *AMF*, pp. 35, 70-72, 133-134.

talk. Only Pascin was at ease. "Let's be comfortable," he said. "The serious young writer and the friendly wise old painter and the two beautiful young girls with all of life before them." Sitting there with a grin on his face and his hat on the back of his head, he looked (thought Hemingway) "more like a Broadway character of the Nineties than the lovely painter that he was." Later, when Pascin had hanged himself, Hemingway liked to remember him as he had been, gay and insouciant, that springtime evening at the Dôme.[25]

The sketch about Shipman, far better and more closely known to Hemingway than Pascin was, took place one evening in the fall of 1924 at the Closerie des Lilas. The autobiographical opening concerned Hemingway's enthusiasm for the Russian novelists, but the bulk of the sketch was a characterization of Shipman— tall, slender, and pale, with stained fingers and bad teeth, wearing a wrinkled gray suit, a shirt that had once been white, and a tie that was as carefully knotted as if he had been a *boulevardier.* Over the first whiskey they spoke of Tolstoi and Dostoievski. But the talk soon turned to the predicament of the waiters at the Lilas, which had recently acquired a new management. On pain of dismissal, the waiters had been ordered to spruce themselves up by wearing white jackets and shaving off their mustaches. This came especially hard to the one named Jean, a war veteran who had been decorated for gallantry in action with his cavalry regiment. It took him some time to reconcile himself to the sacrifice of his sweeping dragoon's mustache. Meantime, in secret protest against the new management, he insisted on serving the Americans with very large glasses of whiskey at a reduced price. It was typical of the kindly Shipman to console Jean for the loss of his mustache by helping him cultivate his vegetable garden at Montrouge in the leafier purlieus of Paris.[26]

Even though Hemingway devoted minimal space to the physical environment, he managed to surround the ancient city with a romantic aura. There were the subdued colors: the tans, greens, and flaking whites of the race-course at Enghien; the saffron and brown nightcarts in the rue du Cardinal Lemoine looking, under

[25] *AMF*; pp. 99-104 (unnumbered sketch 11).
[26] *AMF*, pp. 133-140 (unnumbered sketch 15).

the moonlight, like something Braque might have painted. He came to like the sculptured forms of the black trees in the Luxembourg Gardens when the "branches were bare against the wind and the cold, wintry light"; he admired the quiet square of St.-Sulpice, with its lion-guarded fountain and the pigeons that perched (unaware of irony) on the statues of bishops. Interiors, too, pleased him—the "smoky afternoon light" in the Vélodrome d'Hiver where the bike-riders fiercely circled the steeply banked wooden track; the somber rooms of the Musée du Luxembourg with its Manets, Monets, and incomparable Cézannes; even the sight of James Joyce dining with his family at Michaud's and "peering at the menu through his thick glasses," for Joyce was part of the scenery, too. No book on Paris could be complete without some allusion to the swift gray river that bisected the city. One of the shorter sketches, "People of the Seine," was designed to meet that need. He visited the bookstalls along the *quais*, looking for volumes to assuage his ever-present hunger for reading. He liked to walk the narrow streets of the Île St. Louis, or to gaze across at the "old, tall, beautiful houses" that stood in serried rows on the small island where Bird had established his printing-press and Ford maintained the office of the *transatlantic review*. Sometimes he took a simple lunch and a book to the head of the Île de la Cité below Pont Neuf, where fishermen were sure to congregate in fine weather. Seated there in the sunlight, shading his eyes against the glare, he reveled in the vistas of the Seine—the absorbed and serious fishers, the tugs with folding smokestacks, the great smooth-running barges, and above them all the elms and plane trees and chestnuts that stood along the high stone banks.[27]

Some of the best writing in the sketchbook was not about Paris at all. The city in winter was too damp and cold for the new baby. Not so the "sunny market town" of Schruns, in the Austrian Vorarlberg, where they lived in simple luxury at a hotel called the Taube (Dove), as if its very name promised a softer nest than

---

[27] *AMF*, Braque, p. 4; Luxembourg trees, 11; Musée, 13; Enghien, 52; Joyce, 56; Vélodrome, 64; St.-Sulpice, 69; and unnumbered sketch 5, 41-45.

could be found at the Adler down the street from the Kirchplatz. It was in any case "a healthy place for Bumby, who had a dark-haired beautiful girl [Mathilde Braun] to take him out in his sleigh and look after him" while his parents explored the Monta-fon Valley or made longer skiing trips into the high mountains.

In retrospect, the two winters in Austria struck Hemingway as a kind of paradise. He remembered the excellent breakfasts, the wines and beers, the occasional wild game for dinner, and the skiing trips into the upper country. During the first winter, all went well, but the second saw the invasion of this private Eden. It was perhaps from this feeling of being moved in upon that Hemingway was nowhere more unfairly cruel than in what he said, without naming names, about his second wife, Pauline, and the Murphys, Gerald and Sara, and John Dos Passos. Pauline had paid a visit to Schruns during the Christmas season of 1925, and in March of 1926 Dos Passos came along with the Murphys. Hemingway blamed them all, in great or less degree, for having encouraged the break-up of his marriage to Hadley. In the long view, they had become his scapegoats, and he sought to establish a curious kind of counterpoint between the penurious innocence of his life with Hadley and the evil that came upon them once they had been adopted and befriended by "the rich."

He saw Dos Passos not as one of the wealthy but rather as the man responsible for seducing Hemingway into admiration for them. He appeared as the "pilot fish" of the closing chapter in a vicious and slashing portrait of one who was "shy, comic, elusive" —always "going somewhere or coming from somewhere," enter-ing and leaving "countries and people's lives" with equal slipperi-ness. Only those who trusted him were caught and killed: he always eluded the trap. Even his talk was a come-on. "But I like them. I like them both. . . . I see what you mean but I do like them truly. . . . No, Hem, don't be silly and don't be difficult. . . . You'll like him (using his baby-talk nickname) when you know him." Gerald Murphy's baby-talk nickname was Dow-dow, but Dos Passos' mode of speech (according to Hemingway) was that worst form of baby-talk, an innocence masking evil. The dark motivations behind this false caricature, not one of them just, had grown up in the years between 1926 and 1956, but chiefly in the period of the Spanish Civil War, when Hemingway had quarreled with Dos Passos.[28]

III. AUTOBIOGRAPHY BY REFLECTION

In spite of its value as a personal record by a very well-known writer about the days when his career was just getting started, and in spite, too, of the interest which such a memoir must always have for future generations, the question of the truth of Hemingway's report hovers over the whole book. Although he had assured Perkins in 1933 that his memory was good, he had said just as flatly the year before that "memory," of course, was "never true." His reaction to John Groth's *Studio: Europe* in 1945 reiterated his skepticism. Groth gave an account in prose and pictures of Hemingway as war correspondent in the Schnee Eifel in the fall of 1944. "I do not remember it that way," wrote Hemingway in his preface to Groth's book, "but nobody ever remembers it the way it was." His remark to Scribner in 1949 that one's personal bias often colors the truth was yet another admission of the inevitability of error, especially when, as in *A Moveable Feast*, the events described had taken place more than thirty years back. All these doubts, set down in earlier times, help to explain Hemingway's statement in his brief preface that the book ought probably to be "regarded as fiction," even though there was "always the chance that such a book of fiction" might "throw some light" on what others had set down as fact.[29]

[28] *AMF*, pp. 197-211 (unnumbered sketch 20). Deleted before publication were some cruel remarks on the Murphys' having been punished for their part in the divorce from Hadley through the death of their son by tuberculosis.

[29] EH to Perkins, 7/26/33. On the falseness of personal memory, *DIA*, New York, 1932, p. 100. EH's preface to John Groth, *Studio: Europe*, New York, 1945, pp. 7-9, dated from San Francisco de Paula, Cuba, Aug. 25, 1945. EH to Scribner, 7/28/49. Apart from those of judgment, Hemingway's errors were few and of small importance. He misspelled the name of his Swiss pension-keeper Gangwisch as Gangeswisch, p. 55; he made himself speak anachronistically of having published writing in the *Frankfurter Zeitung*, though this came later, p. 71; he identified Fitzgerald's companion the first time they met as a former Princeton athlete named Dunc Chaplin, who was not present, pp. 149-150; and he stated,

He had designed it as his portrait of the artist as a young worldling. Joyce had done his own in fictional form, and Hemingway chose also to work in the gray area between fiction and fact. What he said had happened probably did, though not invariably in just the way he told it. Changes must inevitably have crept in to alter memories both in spirit and in detail. The conversations reproduced after the lapse of so long a time obviously could not be accepted as exact. But the preface advised the reader, at least by implication, to differentiate between fiction wholly invented and that other kind, familiar enough to his followers, in which people bore their actual names and where the author tried to recall their traits of character, their customary ways of speaking, and the substance, if not the letter, of what they had said.

"By reflection" was the phrase he used in 1957 to describe his autobiographical method. In practice it meant that many clues to his personal character were meant to emerge either in conversation or in response to scenes and events in which he was observer, participant, or both. When he detailed his reactions to various kinds of stimuli—a glimpse of a handsome girl with raven-black hair, the taste of a dozen fresh oysters, or the feel of the well-worn rabbit's foot carried in his pocket as a talisman—he told the reader how and what he felt. But for subtler effects he counted on their guessing at the qualities of his mind by seeing him in contrast to someone else—Ford or Walsh or Gertrude Stein. Ordinarily, in such cases, it was he who was meant to come out on top.[30]

---

in connection with the trip to Lyon with Fitzgerald, that he had "never before accepted an invitation to go on any trip that was paid for, instead of the cost split," though in fact he had done so with Robert McAlmon, who footed all bills for the Spanish tour in the spring of 1923, p. 157.

[30] According to Mary Hemingway, "The Making of the Book," *New York Times Book Review*, May 10, 1964, p. 27, her husband told her in December, 1957 that he was doing "biography by *remate*" or "by reflection." Two things seem wrong about this statement. He was doing autobiography rather than biography; and *remate* in jai alai normally means a kill-shot, sent with such speed and so low against the front wall that it does not bounce enough to be retrieved by the opponent. Hemingway's tongue may have slipped when he meant to say *rebote*, the back wall or a rebound off it. The term itself is less important than his applica-

Without being precisely an *apologia pro vita sua*, the book contained few passages of self-reproach. In the encounter with Acton, or whoever it was, he admitted to having a bad temper, and proved it in the language he hurled at the hapless interloper. Pound, he also noted, could be "kinder and more Christian about people" than he was. Two other passages reflected self-condemnation. One came when Hadley, who seldom complained over the stringent conditions in which he made her live, had gently asked if they had enough money to bet on the races. "I know," said her husband. "It's been terribly hard and I've been tight and mean about money." In the second passage, after having complained to Svlvia Beach about the rejection of his early stories, he upbraided himself in an interior monologue: "You God damn complainer. You dirty phony saint and martyr. . . . You quit journalism of your own accord." This point, which was made by implication elsewhere in the book, meant that he must never compromise his integrity as a writer by protesting against the conditions under which he had freely chosen to live.[31]

It was, in fact, just here, in the tacit assumption of his own superiority, accomplished through the persistent denigration of others, that the tone of the book sometimes turned sour. "We thought we were superior people," he wrote, "and other people that we looked down on and rightly mistrusted were rich. It had never seemed strange to me to wear sweatshirts for underwear to keep warm. It only seemed odd to the rich." This was the old disdain, on which he had leaned so often when he was a young aspirant on the way up and when so many others were like steps who to their dismay had felt the imprint of his ascending heel. Such stated or implied comparisons between superior and inferior people was "autobiography by reflection" with a vengeance. It was one measure of Hemingway's condition of mind in the nineteen-fifties that this vengeance-motif, subtly but corrosively

tion of it. The evidence that he was writing autobiography by showing himself rebounding from the personalities of others is everywhere in the book. But perhaps he meant that he was treating some of his former enemies to verbal "kill-shots." The term *rematado*, used in *IITS*, p. 338, clearly means "killed."

[31] *AMF*, tight and mean, p. 50; saint and martyr, 72; bad temper, 91-92; ᵓound's kindness, 108.

at work among so many of the sketches, should have kept them from achieving that degree of magnanimity which at least some of his readers would have liked to find in an author of his proved caliber.

Examples were many, as when Miss Stein presumed to instruct him in aberrant sexual customs. Hemingway at once made it plain, though not to her, that years of observation had taught him more about the subject than she would ever know. On another topic, he said that she invented "skilful and malicious ways" to account for her dislike of Pound, yet without indicating that this very sketch was as ingeniously malicious towards her as she had ever been about Pound. Despite his own respect for Pound, he could not help preening himself on having read the Russian novelists as Pound had not done, thus establishing a momentary superiority over his erstwhile mentor.[32]

On at least half a dozen occasions, Hemingway flaunted his youthful poverty like a badge of honor, stressing his need to wear old clothes or to skip meals in order to save money. To add poignancy to his poverty, which was of course never so abject as he made it seem, he confessed to a liking for luxury, for good food and wine, for crisp oysters and tender steaks. At the more expensive restaurants, he was more often guest than host, having usually been invited by someone who needed his advice. During the meals with Walsh and Fitzgerald, for example, it was he who did the ordering in French, assuming command of the menu and the wine list, and afterwards serving as doctor, psychiatrist, or sexual counselor in return for the favor of having been well fed. By such means the poor young man could be shown by "reflection" to be the social and moral superior of those who were staking him.

His brusque assumption of the role of European initiate—the experienced wayfarer in two hemispheres—led him sometimes to overstate the roughness of his own upbringing, which, at least through his seventeenth year, had been the epitome of midwestern bourgeois *politesse*. He constantly sought to show his fellowship with the *demos*, proving it by his friendly interest in

[32] *AMF*, Miss Stein instructs, p. 18; her dislike of Pound, 28; superior people, 51; Pound and the Russians, 133-134.

the welfare of waiters and his disparagement of the rich and snobbish. This anti-snobbism had, however, another side, in which he indulged his veteran's prejudice against those who had never heard a shot fired in anger, while proudly associating himself with others who had been more or less permanently mutilated in the recent war. He was at pains to show his uprightness as a husband. The dark-haired girl in the café off the Place St. Michel disturbed him until he made the moral choice of siphoning off his sexual excitement into the story he was writing. Far too virile to be unaware of the posturings of predatory women, he chose to dine with his *légitime*, Hadley, instead of accepting the invitation of Pascin's brunette model. In the account of Pauline late in the book he presented himself less as culprit than as victim of an ancient trick in which a young unmarried woman attached herself to a married couple and then "unknowingly, innocently, and unrelentingly" set out to catch the husband. It was to this temptation that he had succumbed finally, even though he had found no special difficulty in shrugging off lesser and earlier ones. Hemingway did not see—or, if he saw, did not seem to care—that his self-portrait here as the innocent victim ran contrary to the picture of the man of experience which he had built up so carefully in the earlier chapters of his "autobiography by reflection."[33]

[33] *AMF*, poverty, pp. 51, 100, 134, 156, 197, 211; Walsh, 127; Fitzgerald, 168, 173-174; EH's alleged rough upbringing, 18; veteran's pride, 82; girl in the café, 5-6; Pascin's model, 104; Pauline as temptress, 209.

XV · Islands in the Stream

"Continue searching carefully westward."
—A message from Guantánamo, 1943[1]

I. EVOLUTION OF A THREE-DECKER

Apart from the reprints issued under the titles of *By-Line* and *The Fifth Column and Four Stories of the Spanish Civil War*, Hemingway's next posthumous work after *A Moveable Feast* was the long three-part novel, *Islands in the Stream*. It was written at intervals in 1946-1947 and 1950-1951. In point of publication, if not of composition, it was his seventh major work of fiction.

At the time of his death in 1961 it had stood virtually untouched for about ten years. His generic working title for the manuscript had been "The Sea Book,"—by which he meant that he thought of it as one segment of a huge trilogy on the Land, the Air, and the Sea. He commonly referred to this super-novel with some show of modesty, since his enterprise would embrace at least three of the four classical elements. At intervals, however, he mentioned it with reasonable confidence, as if the grand design were etched somewhere along the walls of his imagination. But the part relating to the sea was the only one of the three that he contrived to finish. The sections on the land and the air remained unwritten and apparently unplanned.

He seems to have begun the opening section as early as 1946. It told the story of a painter named Thomas Hudson who owned a large house on the island of Bimini, another in Cuba, and a ranch in Montana. Much of the action grew out of a visit paid to Hudson by his three sons during the summer of 1936. Hemingway called it *The Island and the Stream* in allusion to Bimini's position along the curve of the Gulf Stream well to the north of Cuba. Having run the total of pages up to 977, by his own count,

---

[1] *Islands in the Stream*, New York, 1970, p. 368.

he put it aside at the time of his son Patrick's illness in April, 1947.[2]

His determination to get on with the book was not reaffirmed until the late fall of 1950, when a sudden influx of creative energy enabled him to complete a second and much shorter section, accomplished largely in the three weeks before Christmas Eve. Thomas Hudson's days on Bimini now lay far behind him, and he had taken up permanent residence at his Cuban *finca*. From this as a home-base, with the coming of the war, he had begun volunteer service as skipper of a Q-boat, with the mission of cruising Caribbean waters in search of German submarines. But the sea, as such, figured very little in the action of Part II. Hudson had come ashore after a long and fruitless voyage, and his activities centered mainly on a relaxational and reminiscential visit to his favorite restaurant in the old part of Havana.[3]

The afflatus that had struck Hemingway with such force early in December survived the Christmas season and extended into the new year. Now for the first time he judged himself capable of attempting to tell a story he had first heard in 1935 from his former mate and fishing-guide, Carlos Gutiérrez. By January 17th he was a quarter of the way into it, and by the same date in February he was nearly done. His aging hero, Santiago, had caught and killed his giant marlin and then lost it piecemeal to a

[2] The date of composition for the Bimini section is somewhat conjectural. Hemingway to Scribner, 5/16/51, said that he must rewrite this part which he had been away from since the end of the war in Europe [May, 1945]. On 7/4/51 he told Scribner that he had not looked at it for six years [since July, 1945]. But on 7/8/51 he stated that he had not looked at it since 1947. Hemingway to his son Patrick, 8/16/51, said he stopped working on Pt. I "when you were laid up that summer"—in evident reference to Patrick's severe illness of April-May, 1947. If he had completed 977 pages of MS by April 1947, it is likely that he must have begun work on it no later than 1946, and possibly as early as late 1945.

[3] Hemingway to E. E. Dorman-O'Gowan, 12/22/50, said that he had been working on a new book to keep from thinking. Hemingway to Bernard Berenson, 12/31/50, said his labors on it ended Dec. 23rd. Hemingway to Dorman-O'Gowan, 1/4/51, said that he finished the book ("one of a three-decker") on Christmas Eve, 1950, the allusion being clearly to Pt. II, the Havana episode. He may have been spurred to this new effort, as he told Adriana Ivancich (letter of 3/4/51), by her presence at the Finca through Christmas. But the poor reception of *ARIT* in the fall of 1950 doubtless spurred him also.

parade of marauding sharks on the way home. Hemingway was always afterwards astonished by the relative ease with which he had been able to tell the Santiago story, which was wholly finished in final typescript by the first of April.[4]

His writing streak continued unbroken. After a short holiday, he had set to work again by March 5th on the concluding section of his story of Thomas Hudson. This third part followed directly on the Havana episodes, and told of Hudson's pursuit of the crew of a sunken German submarine. It ended with Hudson's possibly fatal wounding during a firefight in a narrow channel among the lonely keys off the north coast of Cuba. After two and a half months of fairly steady work, he asserted on May 17th that the story was finished. At roughly 45,000 words, it was almost twice as long as the story of Santiago. But he felt that it seemed shorter than it was because of the intensity of the action. He said that the dialogue had been set down with great precision, and that the quality of the whole book was as high as that of the fishing story.[5]

Early in February, while he was still deeply engaged with Santiago and his marlin, and well before he had decided to attempt the sea-chase story, he had spoken of his sea book as a trilogy and given titles to the parts. The first, Hudson and his sons on Bimini, would be called *The Sea When Young*; the second, Hudson on holiday in Havana, would be *The Sea When Absent*; and the third, on Santiago, would be called *The Sea in Being*. But by May, being driven, harassed, and enthralled "as though I had the devil up" by the sea-chase story, he knew that he had a tetralogy on his hands and that his previous plans would have to be modified.[6]

Although in March he had hopefully assured Charles Scribner that "The Sea Book" would be in shape to publish in the fall of

[4] See also Chapter XII, pp. 294-295 and note, above.

[5] Hemingway's allusions to his writing of the sea chase section appear in Hemingway to Carlos Baker, 3/31/51; to Scribner, 5/5/51, 5/16/51, and 5/18/51 ("finished book yesterday"). He described its quality in another letter of 10/5/51.

[6] His tentative titles for the several parts were given in Hemingway to Lillian Ross, 2/3/51. His allusion to the devil inside him was in Hemingway to Scribner, 5/5/51.

1952, he presently began to doubt the wisdom of such a move. In July he told Scribner that there was no need to rush into print. For one thing, the story of Hudson and his sons on Bimini, though it contained some "wonderful parts" that he would hate to delete, was in need of much reshaping to bring it into conformity with "the tempo" of the other three novels. The ideal plan might be to set the whole project aside until he could get some perspective on it. Nothing would be lost. If anything happened to him before the task was done, the story of Santiago, which he rightly regarded as the most finished novel of the four, could be brought out as one small book.[7]

But Hemingway was too much in the grip of his sea book to relinquish it now. By the first week in August he reported to Scribner that he had reduced 484 of the original draft pages of Part I to 305. He believed that the whole book might run, after revision, to some 150,000 words, a figure that he subsequently revised upwards to roughly 177,000 and then to 183,000—as if the episodes in the Bimini section that he hated to cut out had proved to be so "wonderful" that he found himself unable to sacrifice them after all. Although he continued to worry about the comparative quality of *The Sea When Young* (Bimini) and *The Sea When Absent* (the partly humorous interlude in Havana), he assured his publisher that his accounts of Santiago and of the sea-chase were both "impregnable to criticism." Once known, they would prove how wrong were those reviewers who had been saying that his writing had entered a state of decline.[8]

A series of fortunate events soon caused a change in his original plans for "The Sea Book." During the summer and fall of 1951, he quietly showed the typescript of the Santiago story to a number of sympathetic readers, and was reassured by the universally affirmative response. In the spring of 1952, his friend Leland Hayward urged him to consider serializing it in *Life* magazine.

---

[7] His suggestion for fall publication was in Hemingway to Scribner, 3/5/51. The idea was withdrawn in Hemingway to Scribner, 7/8/51, where he mentioned publishing *OMATS* as one small book.

[8] Hemingway's word-counts on the total length were numerous and sometimes contradictory, as in Hemingway to Scribner, 5/16/51, 8/7/51, and 9/9/51; to Lillian Ross, 9/15/51; to Carlos Baker, 10/7/51; and to Harvey Breit, 10/23/51.

By May it was agreed that it would appear in September, first in
Life, printed entire in a single number, and a week later as a
book from Scribners. The tetralogy on the sea was once more
reduced to a trilogy, and the story of Thomas Hudson, separated
from that of Santiago, with which as a whole it had never really
belonged, was preserved intact for possible future use.[9]

In June of 1953 he told a correspondent, as he afterwards told
many others, that his three novels on the sea were safely locked
up in the vaults of the Trust Company of Cuba in Havana.[10]
There they languished, apparently untouched, for the rest of
his lifetime. When Mary Hemingway paid a visit to Cuba late in
July, 1961, she brought them back to New York along with such
other unpublished materials as had not already been shipped to
their house in Idaho.

From this date until 1970 the materials of the book came to
the surface only once. This was when President and Mrs. John F.
Kennedy honored the American recipients of the Nobel Prize at
a reception held in the White House on April 29, 1962. The two
Nobel Laureates who had recently died were represented by their
widows, Mrs. George C. Marshall and Mrs. Ernest Hemingway.
As part of the evening's entertainment, the actor Fredric March
read aloud some excerpts from Hemingway's story of the sea-
chase. Then the trilogy sank back once more into the obscurity
from which it had so briefly emerged.[11]

During the winter of 1969-1970, after consultation with Mary
Hemingway, Charles Scribner, Jr., undertook a preliminary reading of the whole book with a view to deciding whether it did,
indeed, form a publishable unit and a worthy addition to the
Hemingway canon. The Bimini materials, though still somewhat
inchoate, with several false starts and a number of confusing
name-changes among the leading characters, told a story that,
with more of the extensive cutting that Hemingway himself had

[9] For a more detailed account of the sale, publication, and reception
of *OMATS*, see Baker, *Ernest Hemingway: A Life Story*, New York,
1969, pp. 493, 499, and 501-506.

[10] Hemingway to Carlos Baker, 6/11/53.

[11] For an account of this reception, see *New York Times*, April 30,
1962. Hemingway read excerpts from *The Sea-Chase* on Caedmon Record,
TC 1185, which was published in 1965.

begun in 1951, could be made into a book. Although some of the conversations in the Havana section ran on too long, this part could survive the few block-deletions that were judged necessary. The sea-chase story stood up so remarkably well that little beyond the customary copy-editing was required. Working together and separately, Hemingway's publisher and his widow completed their editing and cutting operations in the spring of 1970. At Scribner's suggestion, the three parts were named simply "Bimini," "Cuba," and "At Sea." Hemingway's sometime title for Part III, "The Sea-Chase," was accordingly dropped in favor of the shorter designation. Bearing in mind that her husband had long thought of calling Part I *The Island and the Stream*, but recognizing that more islands than Bimini were involved in the trilogy, Mary Hemingway suggested that by changing the title to *Islands in the Stream*, his original intentions could be best served. The trade edition was published by Scribners in October, 1970, eighteen years after the publication of *The Old Man and the Sea*, with which it had once been so closely associated in Hemingway's mind.[12]

II. THE NARCISSUS PRINCIPLE

"One is prepared for art," wrote T. S. Eliot in 1924, "when one has ceased to be interested in one's own emotion and experience except as material."[13] This dictum can hardly be accepted as an absolute, since no one, least of all the artist, can achieve quite that degree of disinterestedness toward the circumstances of his past life or his emotional response to them. The observation does, however, raise a problem very pertinent to the course of Hemingway's development. For a time in the twenties and early thirties, he seemed to share Eliot's view, aggressively assuring Fitzgerald, for example, that the thing to do with a personal misfortune was to use it as material for fiction rather than allowing oneself to be smashed by it. In those days, his program as a writer called for and often got a hardheaded

[12] Charles Scribner, Jr., to Carlos Baker, June, 1970.
[13] T. S. Eliot, introduction to Paul Valéry, *Le Serpent*, London, 1924, p. 12.

sublimation of emotion and an objectification of personal experience. The first two novels and many of his early short stories proved how successfully he was able to follow his own counsel.

Yet as his life grew longer, his adventures accumulated, and his sense of his place in literary history grew stronger, a subtle change of attitude became gradually visible. To his original impulse to transform his personal past into material for art was added an ulterior and perhaps mainly subconscious determination to exploit it as a means of justifying himself and his actions in the eyes of the world. It was precisely the tendency he had condemned in Joyce's *Ulysses* in an unpublished fragment of 1924: "That was the weakness of Joyce. Daedalus [*sic*] in *Ulysses* was Joyce himself, so he was terrible. Joyce was so damn romantic and intellectual about him."[14] Although Hemingway could seldom be said to have intellectualized his heroes, he fell with increasing frequency into Joyce's implicit narcissism. Nostalgia of various kinds and degrees shadowed and colored his perspectives on his past, romanticizing his fictional self-portraits and even giving prominent place to some of his own personal idiosyncrasies, as if he hoped to persuade readers to accept these, along with the rest, in lieu of the genuinely objective art he had once been able to achieve. Not only was he beginning to be impressed, like the legendary Narcissus, with the splendor of his reflected image, but he was also obliged to contend with the most dangerous problem of all—the same that he had clairvoyantly recognized in Joyce—the tendency to fall in love with the images he was making out of the materials that his life had foisted upon him.

This change of perspective did not come all at once, nor did Hemingway altogether lose that tight grip on experience and emotion that had distinguished the best work of his youth. The first unassailable evidence of the shift occurred in *The Fifth Column*, written in the fall of 1937. Hemingway weighted down

---

[14] These remarks occur in an internal monologue by Nick Adams in the original conclusion to "Big Two-Hearted River," which was deleted by Hemingway before publication. This monologue is printed in part in *Ernest Hemingway: A Life Story*, New York, 1969, p. 131, by kind permission of Mrs. Ernest Hemingway.

his hero, Philip Rawlings, with so many of his own personal traits, desires, and illusions that the feeble dramatic structure of the play buckled under the load. Yet his resilience was such that he was able, in *For Whom the Bell Tolls*, written in 1939-1940, to present Robert Jordan in so strong a context and at such a level of action and emotion that both novel and hero transcended the limitations that had bent and broken *The Fifth Column*.

Between this pair of works and the next intervened the world war. After the lapse of half a dozen years in which his skills had been employed only in the writing of war despatches and a handful of poems, Hemingway set himself the task of making a novel out of his adventures on Bimini and his relations with his sons during the early summer of 1936. Here the Narcissus principle intruded once again. For he seems to have assumed that the story of his marriages and the characterization of his growing sons could become, with certain minor fictional alterations, a work of art that would engage the attention of others to the degree that it preoccupied him.[15]

Rummaging the closets of his memory, he emerged with a series of episodes to be strung on the string of Thomas Hudson's personality. He had always chosen to work close to his own experience. Yet ordinarily his sense of form, his powers of invention, and his ability to suggest without explaining had helped to transform that experience into the stuff of art. Now his trust in the interest-value of experience for itself alone had taken over, and the tricks by which he sought to project it were becoming mechanical. Any reader who knows something of the real-life sources on which the story drew feels sometimes like a spectator watching from the wings, rather than from the pit, the performance of a sleight-of-hand magician.

Like Hemingway at this period, Hudson had been married

---

[15] At about the same time that he began work on the Bimini story, Hemingway started another novel, *The Garden of Eden*, also based in part on his memories of his first two wives. The chief locales were Paris and the village of Le Grau-du-Roi in the south of France. The story was concerned with the love-relationships of two couples: David Bourne, a novelist, and his wife Catherine, and Nick Sheldon, a painter, and his wife Barbara.

twice. The prototype of his first wife, the mother of his eldest son, Tom, was Hadley Richardson, the mother of Hemingway's own son John, called Bumby. The brief account of his second wife was based on Pauline Pfeiffer, whose two children by Hemingway, Patrick and Gregory, served as models for Hudson's younger boys, David and Andrew. One temporal switch took place, in that Hudson's estrangement from his second wife anticipated rather than duplicated Hemingway's separation and divorce from Pauline, which did not occur until 1939-1940. Like Hemingway, Hudson sometimes reflected that he had "behaved stupidly and badly with women"—his excuse being that he had formerly been "undisciplined, selfish, and ruthless."[16] We are given to understand that Hudson has now overcome these faults.

Among the many parallels between Hudson and Hemingway were their youthful apprentice years in Paris. These years were diversified in both instances with skiing trips to Switzerland and afterwards to Austria where the child Tom, like his prototype Bumby, had a pretty, dark-haired nursemaid and a pet dog called Schnautz. Young Tom was made to recall his father's association with Joyce, Pound, and Ford, as well as Miró, Pascin, and Waldo Peirce. When Hemingway took up the second part of Hudson's story a few years later, he added other parallels in which Hudson shared Hemingway's memories of boyhood summers in Michigan, and recalled a winter's voyage to Europe with his wife and infant son aboard a creaky old Cunarder, a clear reminiscence of Hemingway's own transatlantic passage with Hadley and the three-month-old Bumby on the *Antonia* in January, 1924. There were supplemental allusions to the studio above the sawmill, where the child was guarded in his crib by a large pet cat called F. Puss, and to the poverty of the youthful family, who were often reduced to making meals off *poireaux*, as the young Hemingways had sometimes done. Yet in neither case was the penury very severe, for both Hudson and Hemingway were acquainted with the Berlin art-dealer, Alfred Flechtheim, from whom they bought the same canvases, partly for love and partly as an investment. We also learn that Hudson once made an expensive safari in East Africa, followed by a return voyage

[16] *Islands in the Stream*, pp. 9 and 98.

aboard a luxury liner from Mombasa to the south of France. Except for Hudson's adulterous affair with a princess during their time at sea, which Hemingway seems to have invented to spice up our sense of his hero's worldliness, this account was obviously based on Hemingway's own voyage on board the *Gripsholm* in the spring of 1934.[17]

None of this, naturally, is either surprising or reprehensible, since Hemingway had long been firm in his belief that an author must use what he knows. What was damaging, however, was his tacit assumption that the remembered details of his own career, slightly modified here and there, could supply the same degree of interest as a more freely invented fable might have done. His determination to follow the autobiographical course, come hell or high water, helps to explain his extreme response at this time to a public statement by William Faulkner. He was just completing the first draft of the Bimini section when he heard that Faulkner had rated five American novelists according to the degree to which they were willing to take chances, going beyond the level of known experience and making "splendid failures" in striving for "the impossible." This, said Faulkner, Hemingway did not do, and his name was accordingly at the bottom of the list.[18]

But Hemingway felt no yearning to achieve a splendid failure, or indeed a failure of any kind. The date he had chosen for the opening scenes of his novel was May 24, 1936, the birthday of the late Queen Victoria of England, still being celebrated on the island of Bimini. At this time, Hemingway's three sons were thirteen, eight, and five years of age. It was typical of his attitude that the only liberty he took with this fact was to make the sons of Thomas Hudson a year or two older than the Hemingway boys. Even the tragic conclusion to Part I, where Hudson

[17] Switzerland and Austria, pp. 59, 318, and 320; friendships with painters and writers in Paris, 63-67 and 71; memories of Michigan summers, 285-286; winter voyage, 379-380; life above the sawmill, 57; *poireaux* and poverty, 65; Flechtheim and pictures, 237-238; safari and return, 222-225. The remarks on Ford, Joyce, and Pascin anticipate their portraits in *A Moveable Feast*.

[18] For an account of Hemingway's over-reaction to Faulkner's remarks, see *Ernest Hemingway: A Life Story*, New York, 1969, pp. 461, 464, 503, and 647.

learned of the death of his two younger sons in a car-crash in the south of France, would seem to have been suggested by an actual automobile accident at Key West in the spring of 1947. Both the younger Hemingway boys were hurt, Gregory only slightly but Patrick with a concussion so severe that he remained in serious condition well into the summer. It was this same illness that caused Hemingway to interrupt work on the rough draft of his Bimini novel. His use of the accident motif in the death of Hudson's sons represents a curious—and some would say a callous—reversion to his former belief that a writer must use his misfortunes instead of succumbing to them.[19]

The shift of geographical locale and the substitution of death for injury was evidently as far from the norm of actual experience as he was willing to go. Nor did he try to devise a supporting symbolic structure for the novel, as he had done so skilfully seven years before in *For Whom the Bell Tolls*. Instead, formally speaking, he seemed content to let day follow day and incident succeed incident with only minimal attention to that fusion of imaginative and emotional powers that might have given unity to his diverse materials. Narrative progression was now linear rather than cubic, and depth was sacrificed to surface. Even his mastery of the art of dialogue for characterization and advancement of the action had suffered a change. Although conversations filled page after page in the longhand manuscript of the Bimini section, they were too often repetitive and banal, as if Hemingway were prepared to assuage his rather touching desire for productivity at the expense of quality.[20]

Part II, "Cuba," took place in February, 1943, nearly seven years after the action on Bimini. Although it was written at the end of 1950, much later than Part I, the Narcissus principle was

[19] The Key West accident and its consequences: *Ernest Hemingway: A Life Story*, pp. 460-463.

[20] A number of heavy cuts in the original manuscript version of Pt. I were made by Charles Scribner, Jr., working in concert with Mary Hemingway. Comparison of the manuscript with the published version indicates that the deletions were very skilfully accomplished, and that they reduced the length by about 25-30%, a process Hemingway had begun in 1951. But the published novel gives grounds for belief that the cutting was not carried far enough.

still apparent. Hudson's Cuban *finca*, for example, was an exact replica of Hemingway's Finca Vigia, even to the Samoan matting on the living-room floor, the second-best bed where he slept alone during marital quarrels, the Chinese cook in the kitchen and the ceiba tree in the patio, the rain-eroded driveway, the chained entrance gate, and the westward view of Havana. The "information piece" on his domestic cats, which he had once proposed to include in his memoirs, emerged in this section with the desperate love affair between Hudson and Boise, the black-and-white male that he had acquired as a kitten at Cojimar in 1941. Not content with immortalizing his favorite pet, Hemingway referred by name and personality to many of the other cats and dogs that roamed his house and grounds during the war years and after.[21]

In the period since Bimini, Hudson had also acquired a third wife. She remained unnamed and stayed offstage during the whole course of the action, and Hemingway's allusions to her were not nearly so acidulous as Cantwell's remembrances of his former spouse in *Across the River*. Yet it is clear that both were associated in Hemingway's mind with his own former wife, Martha Gellhorn. Since nothing in the action of Part II required either the presence or the absence of such a person, one can only conclude that the Narcissus principle was again at work. In 1943 Hemingway was unhappily married to Martha Gellhorn: therefore a figure which stood for her had somehow to be worked into the texture of his novel.[22]

As in the larger, so in smaller matters, down to the least important personal tastes and attitudes, Hudson was twin to Hemingway. Even their sizes, at a fighting weight of 192 pounds, were approximately the same. The favorite drinks of both were tall, unsweetened frozen daiquiris, served in endless succession at that most beloved of restaurant-bars, the Floridita, or else mixtures of gin, coconut milk, fresh lime juice, and Angostura bitters—to be held up to the light, praised for their combination

---

[21] Hudson's *finca* and Hemingway's: matting, p. 205; bed, 237; cook, 218; ceiba tree, driveway, and gate, 243; pets, 203-218, 221-222, 242.

[22] Allusions to the third Mrs. Hudson appear on pp. 203, 274, 297, 307, and 325.

of smoothness and strength, and then consumed in sips with fervor. Their table wine, when they were given a choice, was Tavel rosé, and in times of stress they could be counted on to call for sandwiches of meat or peanut butter fortified with thick slices of raw onion. Their interests ran the gamut from sport to art. They loved to fish and hunt or to relax with *Ring* magazine. Yet none of this damaged their esthetic sensibilities, and they shared a belief in Cézanne as the king of modern painters. During internal monologues, they were likely to address themselves as "kid," but they reveled exceedingly in the homage of their sons and in the loving title of Papa. They were much given to bouts of remorse, especially at night, and resorted to double seconal capsules as a remedy. Both were outspokenly scornful of F.B.I. agents while insisting on having their flanks well covered whenever they sat down. They loved showing off their powers of stoical endurance by steering their cabin cruisers at all hours and in all weathers, and they both enjoyed command. They commonly uttered such epigrams as, "There's only one thing you don't get over and that is death." But neither of them was above slipping into outmoded slang, witty plays on old advertising slogans, or puerile high school humor.[23]

None of this really mattered except to show how often Hemingway looked at his own mirrored reflection while drawing his portrait of Thomas Hudson. One of the most curious aspects of this on-the-record evidence was his flat assertion to his publisher, Charles Scribner, that he did not put autobiography into his novels. No writer, said he, could keep his knowledge, whether personally experienced or picked up from other sources, from the pages of his books. But to try to prove that he, Ernest Hemingway, could write only about himself was, in his opinion, "utter balls." In taking and defending such a position, he was obviously deceiving either his publisher or himself, and the strong likelihood is that it was a little of both.[24]

[23] For example: fighting-weight, p. 12; wine, 230; sandwiches, 220; *Ring* magazine, 200; Cézanne, 382; "kid," 296; remorse, 294; seconal, 216; F.B.I. agents, 215, 336; covered flanks, 258; epigram on death, 296; slang and high-school humor, 260, 271, 321.

[24] Hemingway to Charles Scribner, 10/29/51.

III. EPISODES AND ANECDOTES

The first two parts of *Islands in the Stream* consist largely of episodes and anecdotes, held together by the ligatures of Thomas Hudson's history and personality. In Part I the chief events include the Queen's Birthday celebration on board Goodner's yacht *Narwhal*, culminating in the bloody fistfight between Hudson's friend Roger Davis and the unnamed northern industrialist; the killing of the hammerhead shark that threatens young David as he fishes along the reef; and, most notably, David's long fight with the broadbill. Taken together, the two fishing episodes represent stages in the boy's progress into maturity, and his conduct in both instances goes far toward making him the true hero of the novel. Indeed, the fight with the broadbill, which requires all his courage and staying power, reads almost like a dress rehearsal for Santiago's lonely struggle with the marlin, which in 1946-1947 had not yet been written. There is, however, one important difference. David's fight is carried on in the midst of company—too much company, as it turns out, and all of them talking so reassuringly and repetitively as a cheering section that they lessen instead of heightening the reader's appreciation of the boy's bravery and skill.[25]

These episodes, along with the others that make up the first two novels, might have attained greater unity and force if Hemingway had been able to impose upon them or discover in them a strong and consistent theme. The only one that fully emerges is Hudson's loneliness. He sorrowfully anticipates the dark pall that will descend on his life when his sons have ended their vacation and left the island, but he cannot, of course, predict the absolute gloom that follows the news that the heroic David and his brother Andrew have been killed. Shortly before the opening of Part II, he also loses his eldest son, "shot down by a flak ship" while piloting an RAF Spitfire over the English Chan-

---

[25] Queen's Birthday, Chapter IV; hammerhead shark, Chapter VII; David's broadbill, Chapter IX. One reviewer called the broadbill episode *The Young Man and the Sea*. A curious anticipation of *OMATS* appears in a remark of David's after his fish escapes. "Don't make yourself some sort of special guilt about it," he tells his father. "I just went too far out," p. 96. Compare *OMATS*, New York, 1952, p. 133: "I went out too far."

nel.[26] This multiplication of bereavements, supplemented in a minor way by his separation from his third wife, leaves Hudson inwardly distraught, outwardly cynical, and above all, lonely. Having now given up his painting and devoted himself to the Q-boat command, he has exchanged the creative role of artist for that of man of action, with nothing to fill the vacancy caused by his abandonment of his true profession—nothing, that is, except the consolations to be gained from the worship of his pets, the friendly admiration of his houseboy, Mario, and the sentimental sympathies of Honest Lil, his oldest friend at the Floridita. Facing these two great gaps in his life, both allied to his capacities for creativity, he is kept from staring into an empty abyss only through his pride in the sea-command. It is by this that he is to be rehabilitated, if at all, during the chase sequence of Part III.

A lesser anticipation of this larger theme appears in Part I through the saving of Roger Davis, whose past psychological and amatory misfortunes are revealed in a series of anecdotes given to Hudson in conversation. Hemingway's intent was apparently to portray a spoiled writer not unlike Harry in "The Snows of Kilimanjaro." Roger has demeaned his talents by writing for the films, entered into an incredible series of maladroit sexual adventures, and behind everything else is tortured by the guilty remembrance of a boyhood canoeing accident in which his younger brother was drowned. None of this was beyond Hemingway's ability to make credible. But the episodes relating to Roger's past are on the whole so thinly imagined as to suggest that Hemingway's powers of invention had temporarily atrophied in the immediate postwar period.

One of Davis' functions is clearly to serve as foil to Hudson, who, while rising to eminence in his profession, has outgrown psychological problems not unlike those of his friend. World-famous and financially at ease, Hudson is still able to surround himself with a "carapace" of honest work each day while Davis remains vulnerable to the memory of his multiple misfortunes. Yet it is possible that Hemingway meant Davis to stand as an *alter ego* for himself, not as he was in 1946-1947, married to his

---

[26] Death of Tom Hudson, p. 322.

fourth wife Mary and taking up his writing where he had dropped it when the war began, but rather as he had been in the middle thirties, socially truculent, full of hatreds, including that of self, not at all certain that he had made the best use of his talents, and often masking his doubts beneath the outward manner of the roaring boy. Such a conjecture would help to explain why it is Davis, rather than Hudson, who allows himself to be drawn into the fist fight, as Hemingway himself was when he knocked out Joseph Knapp on the Bimini docks in May, 1935.[27]

This intrusion of yet another autobiographical episode, now transferred to Davis, could reasonably represent Hemingway's rejection of the way he had behaved in that distant Bimini period, a bravo and bully-boy who was then as inwardly troubled as the gentler Davis is here made to seem. But the real fault with the presentation of Davis, putting aside this psychological guesswork, is that he is not a fully fledged and credible character. If Hemingway did in fact divide his personality to evolve the twin figures of Davis and Hudson, the Davis aspect lay too far off in time to be grasped with real conviction.

Another phase of the theme of rehabilitation is carried by Eddy the cook, Hudson's servant at sea and ashore. In handling such minor characters as Eddy, Hemingway seems more assured than he does with men like Davis, whose life-style is complex in a way that Eddy's could never be. It is just possible that the personal history of Hudson's Eddy dates back to his namesake, Eddy Marshall, the "rummy" who served Harry Morgan as deckhand in *To Have and Have Not*.[28] Although Eddy the Second has found himself through association with Hudson and the three sons, he has still to reckon with his alcoholic tendencies. His finest hour comes during the shark incident, when he handles himself and his submachine gun so well that he saves young David's life. Eddy becomes boring only in his over-conscientious care for David during the fight with the broadbill. If Hemingway meant Eddy's rehabilitation to run parallel on a lower level to that of Davis, he did not emphasize the connection, and the theme

---

[27] For an account of the Hemingway-Knapp fight, see *Ernest Hemingway: A Life Story*, p. 273.

[28] *THAHN*, Part I, *passim*.

accordingly becomes so attenuated that it is never fully realized in the book.

Another lesser character, Mr. Bobby, the owner of the Ponce de León, figures memorably in the two humorous episodes of Part I. The best is the first, which begins when Bobby asks Hudson to paint him a large picture of a waterspout to hang behind his bar. When Hudson promises to begin, Bobby launches at once into an account of another huge painting on the theme of the end of the world. "Hell is just opening," cries Bobby. "The Rollers are rolling in their church up on the ridge and all speaking in unknown tongues. There's a devil forking them up with his pitchfork and loading them into a cart. . . . There's a big sort of hatch open . . . and they go out of sight. . . . Rummies are taking their last swigs and beating on the devils with bottles. . . . You and me standing in the center of the picture observing all this with calm. You make a few notes and I refresh myself from a bottle and occasionally offer you refreshment. . . . I'll offer the devil a drink as he passes, sweating and grimed . . . and he'll say, 'No thank you, Mr. Bobby. I never touch the stuff when I'm working.' " When Hudson names Bosch and Breughel as the real masters in this genre, Bobby is not impressed. "Oh hell," he says, "no old-timer will touch us."[29]

This vein of tall-tale-telling, where the narrator's ingenuity takes flight and fantasy takes over, is perhaps the most admirable aspect of Hemingway's humor. His natural instinct for incremental inventiveness was given little scope in his published work after *The Torrents of Spring*, partly because he did not write the kind of books where it properly belonged, partly owing to his prejudice against fantasy in fiction. Yet his letters are filled with examples of his easy, laughing ability to develop mere suggestions into such large and graphic scenes as Mr. Bobby's "The End of the World."

The second humorous episode is a practical joke designed to confound the members of a yachting party at the Ponce de León. Hudson calls it "the pretend-rummy scene," and apparently thinks it very funny indeed. He and Roger Davis play the confirmed adult alcoholics. Young Tom's role is to dissuade Davis

[29] Bobby's End of the World picture, pp. 17-20.

from getting drunk again, and young David's is to pretend to have gone on the wagon after a spectacular binge the night before. Andrew, the smallest of the lot, is given the pleasant task of drinking gin as if it were water, as of course it is. The idea for this episode seems to have arisen from a series of play-acting routines perfected by Patrick and Gregory Hemingway in their schoolboy days. "Did you ever see me do the [mongolian] idiot brother?" David asks his father just before the barroom hoax begins. Patrick had actually played such a part, with Gregory as straight man, while returning by train from Florida to their school in Connecticut. Their story of the exploit vastly amused Hemingway, who described it in a letter to a friend early in 1946.[30]

The dramatic function of the hoax incident is to introduce Audrey Bruce, one of the two female members of the yachting party. Unlike her companion, who weeps angrily over Andrew's supposed gin-drinking, Audrey at once suspects the truth. Her common sense, as well as her beauty, causes Hudson to invite her to join his group after the joke is revealed. In the end she has a revelation of her own. By the most astonishing of coincidences, she is the former schoolgirl who fell half in love with both Davis and Hudson in the days when they were working in Paris and vacationing on the Riviera.[31]

The purpose for which Audrey is introduced is soon evident. She is to be the agent of Roger Davis's rehabilitation. His belated courtship moves along with astonishing speed, and she falls a shade too easily into the position of *dea ex machina*, or perhaps more exactly the good girl who can rescue him from his lifelong tendency to engage in a series of alliances with bitch-like and predatory women. When the three Hudson boys reach the end of their holiday, they are flown back to the mainland in the old Sikorsky amphibian. It is only a matter of days before Roger and Audrey depart the island by the same means. Their destination is Hudson's ranch in Montana, where Davis will presumably finish his "great novel," and where, as soon as Audrey has been

---

[30] "Pretend-rummy scene," pp. 162-174. Like much else in Parts I and II, this goes on too long. One account of Patrick and Gregory play-acting is in Hemingway to General C. T. Lanham, 1/20/46.

[31] Audrey's personal history, Chapter XII.

able to divorce her wealthy but otherwise objectionable husband, the lovers will be married.[32]

Coming so late in the action of Part I, the introduction of Audrey has an air of plotted contrivance of the kind that Hemingway was careful to avoid in the books he wrote between the wars. So does the account of Davis' personal background, which nearly fills two earlier chapters. On the other hand, the portraits of the three sons are drawn with considerable skill, as if Hemingway felt far more at home in writing from his close knowledge of members of his family than in imagining a career for Roger Davis or portraying the former life of Audrey Bruce. Once again, as so often in Part I, he placed his trust in known autobiographical fact rather than risking the possible pitfalls of wholesale invention.

Yet he did take what was for him a notable risk in offering the most extended treatment of children to be found anywhere in his work. Except for half a dozen stories on the boyhood and adolescence of Nick Adams, he had done only two directly involving the young. The central figures in both were himself and Bumby, only slightly disguised.[33] Tom Hudson is this same child grown older, proudly recalling his childhood in Paris and his friendships with the great. "After you've spent your life with men like Mr. Joyce and Mr. Pascin," he says, "being with boys seems sort of juvenile."[34] Although he makes this remark apropos of preparatory schools, it applies by extension to much of the action of Part I. In spite of Hemingway's implicit belief that it was unwise for a writer like himself to give much fictional space to children or adolescents, he was ready and eager to do so in the case of his own sons. Apart from their personal charm, the Hudson boys do help to show their father and Roger Davis in a sympathetic light, and their presence also enables Hemingway from time to time to invoke that mild irony which often results in fiction when innocence is knowingly contrasted with experience.

[32] Departures, Chapter XIII. A long story about Davis's drive from Florida to Louisiana, accompanied by a girl who resembles Audrey, though she bears a different name, was wisely deleted before publication.
[33] These are "A Day's Wait" and "Fathers and Sons," collected in WTN, 1933. There is also the boy waiter in "The Capital of the World."
[34] IITS, p. 108.

The voice of experience, as well as a certain kind of boyish exuberance, is evidently intended to pervade Part II, which shows us Hudson ashore between voyages, trying to throw off the loneliness occasioned by the recent death of his only remaining son. By midmorning on the day in question, having consoled himself as well as possible with the pets at the *finca*, he summons his chauffeur for the drive to the old city of Havana and a day on the town. "Come on," he tells himself. "You're going to have fun today. Relax and enjoy it."[35] Enthroned in his familiar seat at the Floridita, he manages to relax with a succession of visitors. These include a local man of wealth named Ignacio Natera Revello, two members of his sub-hunting crew, and Honest Lil, the aging prostitute.

Although Hudson secretly regards Don Ignacio as a rummy, a snob, and a bore, they roll dice for drinks cheerfully enough until Ignacio mentions young Tom, only to be flatly told that he is dead.

"He was a splendid athlete and a fine sportsman," says Ignacio, comfortingly.

"There's only one thing really wrong with him," says Hudson.

"What's that?"

"He's dead."[36]

The irony here has nothing to do with innocence. It is Hudson's way of meeting destiny by adopting a verbal stance that parallels his sense of destiny's ruthlessness. That these words should be uttered to someone like Ignacio, whose entire character Hudson deplores, is proof that Hudson can be ruthless, too. The irony is further compounded by the fact that the portrait of Ignacio is based on a real-life resident of Havana, Alvaro González Gordon. The portrait is exact, even to the green-tinted spectacles, and it was doubtless in Hemingway's mind, when he caused Ignacio to advance polite arguments meant to console Hudson for the loss of his son, that Alvaro González Gordon had no sons—and indeed no children—of his own.

The portraits of Hudson's next three visitors are likewise drawn more or less from life. Two of them are members of his sea-going crew now happily embroiled in their land-side social

---

[35] *IITS*, p. 259.   [36] *IITS*, p. 264.

life. Henry Wood's huge build, his unfailing good cheer, and his excellent manners perfectly evoke the corresponding qualities of Winston Guest, who served as executive officer aboard the *Pilar* in 1942-1943. The account of Willie, the one-eyed former Marine, somewhat more remotely points to the figure of Don Saxon, a Marine master-sergeant who was assigned to the *Pilar* as gunner. The third visitor, Honest Lil, was well known in Havana as Leopoldina, and her name appears with some frequency in Hemingway's letters of those days. When the others go, Lil remains, happily settled at Hudson's elbow, listening to his store of anecdotes, and kindly convinced that by getting him to talk, she can help him to shed his burden of sorrow.[37]

Hudson's anecdotes are all set forth in Hemingway's inimitable conversational style, and a few of them, as was to be expected, are autobiographical. The first, apparently invented, tells of his narrow escape from drowning under logs in a boom on the Bear River near a lumbering settlement in western Wyoming. Another, plainly based on fact, is the story of his Atlantic crossing on a ship closely resembling the *Antonia*, which carried Hemingway, Hadley, and Bumby back to France in 1924. The most space is devoted to a trip to the Far East some months before Pearl Harbor, for Hudson, like Hemingway, has also been there. He alludes in passing to Morris Abraham Cohen, formerly of London, who began as bodyguard to Sun Yat-sen and was serving as "general" in the Chinese army when Hemingway met him. Under prodding from Lil, who longs for love-stories, Hudson responds with a tall tale of his frustrated affair with a beautiful Chinese girl, only to cap it with another, even taller, about his adventures with three more Chinese girls who were sent to his hotel room in Hong Kong by one of the local millionaires. A similar yarn was

[37] Mario Menocal to CB, 11/18/70, identifies Ignacio Natera Revello with his prototype, Alvaro González Gordon, and adds that Alvaro was the youngest son of the old Marqués de Torre Soto, patriarch of the González family of Jerez de la Frontera, owners of the González Byass sherry house. The same letter suggests the connections of Wood with Guest and Honest Lil with Leopoldina. It is a curious coincidence that the ship which carried Hemingway and his wife Hadley to Europe in 1921 was the *Leopoldina*. According to Señor Menocal, the real Leopoldina was born about 1900, and her "essential goodness" is perfectly suggested in Hemingway's portrait of Lil.

often related by Hemingway after his return from the Far East, and Hudson enthusiastically elaborates it into the crowning set-piece of his conversation with Honest Lil.[38]

The adventitious arrival of his first wife interrupts his afternoon at the Floridita. Like the sudden appearance of Audrey Bruce in Part I, this one seems contrived, since it has not been prepared for except by Hudson's nostalgic memoir of his ocean crossing in the lady's company years before. She is a famous actress, a composite of Hadley Richardson and Martha Gellhorn, but with the face, figure, and profession of Marlene Dietrich, who worked in wartime as a U.S.O. entertainer, the very activity which has brought the first Mrs. Hudson to Camagüey and thence to Havana.

Their reunion is not, however, very satisfactory. At Hudson's *finca*, after a passage of lovemaking which Hemingway meant to be as cursory as he makes it seem, she suddenly asks for news of their son Tom. "He's fine," lies Hudson. But she divines the truth and forces it from him. "Tell me. Is he dead?" "Sure," says Hudson, as crudely laconic as he has been with Ignacio. Even though he presently expands on the circumstances, and although they speak with tenderness of Tom as a child, riding on his father's shoulders as they skiied down through the orchard behind the inn at Schruns, the conversation echoes throughout with the essential hollowness of their predicament, and they have begun to quarrel bitterly, as of old, when the houseboy appears to call Hudson back to sea.

The summons is more welcome than Hudson would admit. In the action ahead, whatever its shape, in the renewal of contact with the sanative sea, he has some hope of shoring up the ruins of his career as lover, father, and artist. On the way back to Havana in the car, he allows himself some moments of reflection. Perhaps, he thinks, it would have been good to stay ashore. But he knows at once that this, like so much else, is an illusion. The facts stare him in the eyes. "Get it straight. Your boy you lose. Love you lose. Honor has been gone for a long time. Duty you

---

[38] Hudson's near-drowning, pp. 277-278; Atlantic crossing, 279-280; General Cohen, 289; Chinese girls, 290-295.

do."[39] A mere score of words is enough to sum up his past failures and his present obligations, and he turns with half-reluctant anticipation to a future whose dimensions he does not yet know how to measure.

IV. PURSUIT AS HAPPINESS

"Hemingway," said Wyndham Lewis in 1950, "is an obvious instance of a writer whose muse is married to action." As if to confirm the justice of Lewis's observation, the final third of Hemingway's trilogy concentrates almost wholly upon a single action. He himself described it as the pursuit and destruction of the crew of a German submarine where the objective was to make them prisoners and where everything possible was done to accomplish this mission. Like the earlier sections of his tripledecker, this one contains episodes and anecdotes. Yet these are few, and the action sweeps always onwards from east to west towards that obscure Cuban islet where the chase is to be consummated in blood and death.[40]

The climactic section of *Green Hills of Africa*, centering on the hunt for the elusive kudu, was called "Pursuit as Happiness." Hemingway's Jeffersonian pun, which was not so much a joke as a sentiment deeply engraved in his hunter's heart, could apply as well to Hudson's final mission. So could his original subtitle for the African book: "Hunters Are Brothers." In *The Old Man and the Sea*, written just before the sea-chase story, he had even experimented with the notion that hunted and hunter are brothers —a view repeatedly enunciated by Santiago and clearly hinted at by Thomas Hudson in his fraternal and gentle treatment of the one dying German sailor whom they manage to capture.[41]

Hemingway's claim for his sea-chase story was that it had

---

[39] Hudson's synoptic reflections: p. 326.

[40] Wyndham Lewis, *Rude Assignment*, London, 1950, p. 31. Hemingway's description of Part III was in a letter to Charles Scribner, 10/5/51.

[41] *Green Hills of Africa*, Part IV. The original subtitle is quoted from the MS version, in the Library of the University of Virginia. On the brotherhood between hunters and hunted, compare *OMATS*, pp. 65, 70, 83, 102, and 109 and *IITS*, pp. 362-365.

"the same quality" as *The Old Man and the Sea*, except that the action was much faster. In one way he was right, for the two novellas could have been placed side by side in the same book as a pair of pursuit stories, one in war, the other in peace. Both engaged the theme of profit and loss; both were stripped down for action, with little in the way of side issues to encumber their forward motion. The aged fisherman and the aging painter share a determination to endure to the end, to do what they have set out to do, no matter what it takes, even to try to think their way into the heads of their respective quarries so as to anticipate whatever moves they make.

On the other hand, as with the difference between David Hudson's fight with the broadbill and Santiago's with the marlin, there is the profound difference between going it alone and fighting it out in company. Santiago, solus in his small skiff, is at almost the other extreme from Hudson, accompanied by a crew of eight in a sleek, fast, seaworthy cabin cruiser. Santiago has only the tools of his civilian trade—oar, knife, gaff, and club—but Hudson is armed with light and heavy machine-guns as well as grenades and canister bombs. Santiago has no food but what he can catch, no clothes but those he set out in. Hudson, however, lives like a nautical king, or at least a captain, with dry clothes whenever he gets wet, with food and drink whenever he calls for it. Finally, and it is an important point of contrast, the novel of Hudson lacks (perhaps intentionally) that fourth or fifth dimension that strengthens and universalizes *The Old Man and the Sea*, the very point that Bernard Berenson made about it when he said that Hemingway's "short but not small masterpiece," like "every real work of art," *exhaled* "symbols and allegories."[42] With very few exceptions, the exhalations from the Hudson story are neither symbolic nor allegorical.

It is action, rather, action virtually unencumbered by thought, that sustains it. During the last week of February, 1943, Hudson and his crew have stopped at a lonely island some three hundred miles east of Havana along the north coast of Cuba. The place has been recently invaded, the inhabitants massacred, their cabins burned to the ground. Ballistic and other evidence proves that

---

[42] Bernard Berenson to Hemingway, 9/21/52. Italics in original.

the invaders were the survivors of a sunken German submarine. They have commandeered the two Bahaman turtle-boats with which the dead islanders made their living. Even now they are sailing westward in the desperate hope of getting ashore and taking ship from the Matanzas or Havana to return to the Fatherland. Hudson's task is to run them to earth before they can escape homeward by sea.

The story, fictional in essence though autobiographical in certain details, was Hemingway's second attempt to make use of his wartime adventures. He referred to the first attempt, in *Across the River and into the Trees*, as a "distillation" of his experiences on the Continent with the Fourth Infantry Division, set down in case he never found time to write more extensively about the land war.[43] This left the war in the air, about which he wrote nothing beyond a single article on the Royal Air Force, and the war on the sea, as he had known it aboard the *Pilar* during his sub-hunting days of 1942-1943. He was eager to use the sea material, even though his cabin cruiser had never managed to close with a German craft during all her months of patrolling, and had certainly never given chase, as Hudson does, to the survivors of a U-boat destroyed by a plane.[44]

In this connection it gave Hemingway pleasure to commemorate some of the men who had served under his command aboard the *Pilar* nine years earlier. Guest and Saxon, who briefly enter the Havana section under the names of Henry Wood and Willie, are not the only recognizable members of Hudson's crew. Ara, the broad-shouldered Basque, is a straightforward and admiring portrait of Francisco (Patxi) Ibarlucia, a jai alai player who accompanied Hemingway on many wartime cruises, as did Juan Dunabeitia, another Basque who later captained a ship of his own and who appears in the novel under his own name. Antonio, Hudson's first mate, was in real life Gregorio Fuentes, a Canary Islander who held a similar position on the *Pilar* before, during, and after the war.[45]

[43] Hemingway to General C. T. Lanham, 1/8/51. Hemingway also wrote some short stories on the land war.

[44] For an account of Hemingway's subhunting activity, see *Ernest Hemingway: A Life Story*, New York, 1969, pp. 373-380.

[45] Besides these, Hudson's crew includes two other Basques named

As with the people, so with the north coast of Cuba, which Hemingway knew like his own back yard from years of fishing expeditions—a wild region of open sea and narrow channels, diversified with mangrove keys, banks of marl, and occasional stretches of lonely beach, populated here and there by fishermen and lighthouse-keepers, as well as tropical birds, turtles, iguanas, huge landcrabs, and legions of voracious insects. Even though the coastal keys stretch for hundreds of miles, there is hardly a landfall, a lighthouse, or a major island between Cayo Sabinal and Cayo Francés that does not figure somewhere in Hudson's mission. Apart from the fish and the birds, which Hemingway always describes with the trained and loving eye of a confirmed naturalist, he is able to provide memorable accounts of such strange domains as Cayo Romano, due north of Camagüey, a large island where the French once attempted colonization. Hudson has no doubt as to why the colony was aborted: "It was a wonderful key when the east wind blew day and night," but "when the wind dropped, the mosquitoes came in clouds from the marshes." Once, going ashore for water, he had had a shocking experience. The native dogs and pigs were huddled together hopelessly in the mud, their bodies uniformly gray from "the solid blanket of mosquitoes that covered them."[46]

In spite of such hazards as mosquitoes and sand flies, the whole region is ideally suited to the desperate drama of running and hiding, search and pursuit that is the real center of Hemingway's story. From the afternoon of discovery on the island of the massacre to the time of the ambush behind Cayo Guillermo, the chase occupies six days. The turnings of day and night, the rising and ebbing of the tides, and the alternating periods of bracing and relaxation are comparable to the wave-like rhythms that Hemingway had so well exploited in his narrative of Santiago a month or two earlier. But the excitement of this chase-sequence

---

Gil and George, and the radioman, Peters, the only casualty besides Hudson. None of these can be positively identified with members of the *Pilar's* wartime crew. I am indebted to Mario Menocal, letter of 11/18/70, for some of the identifications.

[46] Cayo Romano mosquitoes: p. 393. Señor Menocal (see note 45) called Hemingway's account of the north coast "marvelously described."

is far more intense. Each time Hudson gets positive information on the condition and location of the enemy, he is that much closer on their heels. At the radio station on Confites, he is three days behind; at Cayo Cruz, where they find the dying German sailor, there is evidence that the quarry has been there only the day before; and the native woman in the shack on Guillermo has seen the turtle-boat enter the inner channel less than two hours earlier. As Hudson and his men close the time-gap, the suspense gradually mounts, reaching a peak on the afternoon of the fifth day when they locate and board the enemy's craft in an action that kills both Peters, the radio operator, and one already wounded German sailor. Willie's lone scouting expedition, where his friends can follow his progress by means of the birds he scares up, reaches yet another peak of suspense, while the sequence of events that leads up to the final ambush next day is taut with rising expectation.[47]

The ambush episode is marked by a curious reminder of Hemingway's early literary idol, Joseph Conrad. Just as Conrad's "Youth," Marlow's story of a valiant battle against heavy odds aboard the old *Judea*, came into Hemingway's mind when he wrote *The Old Man and the Sea*, so here, in the final chapter of the Hudson story, it was evidently a memorable passage from Conrad's "The Heart of Darkness" that helped Hemingway to shape the climactic action.[48]

No reader of "The Heart of Darkness" is likely to forget Charlie Marlow's account of the native ambush on a bend of the Congo just below Kurtz's Inner Station. As the *Roi des Belges* rounds the curve, Marlow sees an "islet, a mere grassy hummock of bright green." This proves to be "the head of a long sandbank . . . stretching down the middle of the river." He has a choice of channels, and elects to follow the one on the western side, which soon becomes both narrower and shallower than he had supposed. He is in the pilot house beside his steersman when the

---

[47] Confites, p. 350; Cruz, 379; Guillermo, 410; capture of turtle-boat and Willie's scouting foray, 423-429.

[48] On the relation between *OMATS* and "Youth," see above, Chapter XII, section iii. Both Conrad's novellas were written and published shortly before Hemingway's birth.

air is suddenly filled with what at first seem to be sticks. But the sticks are actually flights of arrows from the tangled gloom of the bush. Marlow's crew responds with a fusillade from their Winchester rifles. The helmsman is stabbed by a spear and falls dead at Marlow's feet. "A pool of dark blood" spreads out on the deck, "gleaming dark-red under the wheel."[49]

When Hudson enters the backwaters behind Guillermo, he at once picks out Cayo Contrabando, "looking small and green and cheerful," though he soon notices the long sandspit that runs north and south of it. At this point, like Marlow, he has a choice of channels, but the water is so muddy and the tide is falling so fast that he can neither see nor maneuver adequately and the boat soon runs aground. The final ambush is delayed both by this and by the capture and booby-trapping of the Germans' one remaining turtle-boat. But next morning, afloat once more, Hudson moves into a channel so narrow that his boat nearly grazes the mangroves on either bank. It is here that the attack suddenly explodes. Hudson, serving as his own steersman, is wounded in the leg, and the deck below the wheel soon turns "very slippery" from his own "dark" blood.[50]

The overt resemblances between the two actions are plain enough—an armed boat in a narrow reach beside a bright green islet with an attached sandbar, a choice of channels, the matted trees almost close enough to touch, the sudden attack, the wounding of the helmsman, the deck beneath the wheel gone slippery with his blood. Hemingway's treatment is far more elaborate than Conrad's, and there are, of course, many other differences in the conduct of the two stories. Conrad once said of "The Heart of Darkness," which was itself autobiographical to a marked degree, that it represented "experience pushed a little (and only a little) beyond the actual facts of the case."[51] Hemingway was inventing out of his experience as a boat-captain, but pushing that experience well beyond the actual facts. It is therefore not at all

[49] Conrad, *The Heart of Darkness*, ed. Robert Kimbrough, New York, 1963, p. 44.

[50] Green of Contrabando and choice of channels, pp. 412-413; final ambush, 453-458.

[51] Conrad's "Author's Note" to the volume of 1917 in which "The Heart of Darkness" was reprinted.

surprising that he should have turned for assistance, whether consciously or not, to his distant recollection of that other ambush in Conrad's masterly novella.

The heart of Hudson's darkness is his double sense of loss. For not only has he lost his sole remaining son, he has also lost his sentimental illusion that it might have been possible to recapture in maturity his love of the boy's mother as he had known it long ago in his youth. Although no action that he can ever take will "bring back anything" from his past, he is "glad to have something to do" in this command at sea, and takes pleasure in having such "good people to do it with." Duty is now his carapace against the incursions of melancholy. "I do not know," he thinks, "what I would have done without duty since young Tom died." He has, as he puts it, "traded in remorse" for this other horse that he is riding now.[52]

Once he has learned the identity of his quarry and the direction he must follow, he is ready for an action he half-suspects may be final. Pocketing the four black-nosed bullets that he has dug with knife and spoon from the corpses on the island of the massacre, he thinks that they may possibly represent "the rest of his life." Murder has been done by the German sailors in their desperate attempt to get free. Other murders, perhaps even Hudson's own, may lie ahead. Although "no good will come of any of it," the chase itself is challenge and joy enough. "I love doing it," thinks Hudson. "I just don't like the end."[53]

His devotion to action is so intense and relentless that three of his closest friends among the crew feel compelled to warn him against it. Henry Wood says simply that Hudson must take some rest: "You've been driving yourself past what a man can stand." Willie is characteristically forthright. "You," he says. "Flogging yourself to death up there [on the bridge] because your kid is dead. Don't you know everybody's kids die?" But Ara suspects another motivation. "All a man has is pride," he says. "Sometimes you have it so much it is a sin. We have all done things for pride that we knew were impossible. . . . But a man must implement his pride with intelligence and care. Now that you have ceased

[52] Something to do, p. 348; duty, 418; remorse, 383.
[53] Four bullets, p. 337; murder, 356; love of action, 379.

to be careful of yourself, I must ask you to be, please. For us and for the ship."[54]

Pride of command, pride of endurance, pride in the ascetic abnegation of creature comforts, pride in having overcome remorse and gloom (if never the innermost sorrow) not once but many times, pride in his expectation of outwitting a resourceful enemy, pride in his potential ability to accomplish the impossible—these are the major instruments in Hudson's unstated and largely unplanned program of self-rehabilitation. All of them are summed up in the only military order that comes through to Hudson, twice for emphasis, from the naval base at Guantánamo: "Continue searching carefully westward." For it is not only a military but also a moral directive. It is precisely what Hudson and all others like him must do until the end. It is also a way of describing what Hemingway himself was seeking to do in this last of the novels he was able to complete in his lifetime as a writer.[55]

[54] Advice from Henry and Willie, pp. 360 and 366; Ara on pride, 358.
[55] Guantánamo directive: pp. 368 and 384.

A Working Check-List

OF HEMINGWAY'S PROSE, POETRY, AND
JOURNALISM—WITH NOTES

The following check-list is retained for the convenience of readers who may need a quick guide to the major publications by Hemingway during his lifetime. For more detailed guidance, readers are referred to Audre Hanneman's ERNEST HEMINGWAY: A COMPREHENSIVE BIBLIOGRAPHY, Princeton University Press, 1967, which supersedes all other compilations.

I. BOOKS

1. *Three Stories and Ten Poems*. Summer [probably July] 1923. 300 copies. Published by Robert McAlmon (Contact Publishing Company), Paris and Dijon. Contains stories: Up in Michigan, Out of Season, My Old Man. Contains poems: Mitragliatrice (P), Oklahoma, Oily Weather (P), Roosevelt (P), Captives, Champs d'Honneur (P), Riparto d'Assolto (P), Montparnasse, Along with Youth, Chapter Heading (P). Note: The six poems labelled (P) had first appearance in *Poetry: A Magazine of Verse* for January 1923. See below, section III.

2. *in our time*. January 1924. 170 copies. Published by William Bird (Three Mountains Press), Paris. Contains: 1. "Everybody was drunk . . ."; 2. "The first matador got the horn . . ."; 3. "Minarets stuck up in the rain . . ."; 4. "We were in a garden at Mons . . ."; 5. "It was a frightfully hot day . . ."; 6. "They shot the six . . ."; 7. "Nick sat against the wall . . ."; 8. "While the bombardment . . ."; 9. "At two o'clock in the morning . . ."; 10. "One hot evening in Milan . . ."; 11. "In 1919 he was traveling . . ."; 12. "They whack whacked the white horse . . ."; 13. "The crowd shouted all the time . . .";

14. "If it happened right down close . . ."; 15. "I heard the drums coming . . ."; 16. "Maera lay still . . ."; 17. "They hanged Sam Cardinella . . ."; 18. "The king was working. . . ."

Note: This is the uncapitalized or Paris edition of *in our time,* a 32-page book consisting entirely of the miniatures which have since formed the inter-chapters of the American editions of *In Our Time* (1925 and 1930: see below, items 3 and 8), and appear also in the collected edition, *The Fifth Column and the First Forty-nine Stories* (1938). The chapters numbered 1–6 inclusive first appeared in *The Little Review* for April 1, 1923. See below, section III.

3. *In Our Time.* October 5, 1925. 1,335 copies. Published by Boni and Liveright, New York. Contains all the miniatures from *in our time,* though in a slightly different order, together with two of the three stories from *Three Stories and Ten Poems.* Two of the *iot* miniatures have been elevated to the status of short stories (miniature chapter 10 has been titled "A Very Short Story," and miniature chapter 11 has been titled "The Revolutionist"). The untitled miniatures alternate with the titled stories. Besides those already mentioned, there are ten new stories. All but four of these had been printed previously in several of the "little magazines" and in McAlmon's *Contact* anthology (see below, section III). In the following list of contents, the arabic numerals in parentheses represent the *iot* miniatures, and the other stories are represented by their titles.

    Contains: (1); Indian Camp; (3); The Doctor and the Doctor's Wife; (4); The End of Something; (5); The Three Day Blow; (6); The Battler; (7); A Very Short Story; (8); Soldier's Home; (9); The Revolutionist; (2); Mr. and Mrs. Elliot; (12); Cat in the Rain; (13); Out of Season; (14); Cross Country Snow; (15); My Old Man; (16); Big Two-Hearted River, Part One; (17); Big Two-Hearted River, Part Two; (18). The stories which appear in this volume for the first time are The End of Something, The Three Day Blow, The Battler, and Cat in the Rain. The order of miniatures and stories followed in this edition was continued in the two later editions.

4. *The Torrents of Spring.* May 28, 1926. 1,250 copies. Published by Charles Scribner's Sons, New York. Note: With this book Hemingway began his long association with Scribner's. Six years later the book was reprinted in Crosby Continental Editions, Paris, 1932. See Caresse Crosby's interesting prefatory epistle.

5. *The Sun Also Rises.* October 22, 1926. 5,090 copies. Published by Scribner's. Note: This was the novel which caused Scribner's to agree to publish *The Torrents of Spring,* which the firm undertook, as Perkins said, "with some misgivings." In a letter to

Perkins dated 4/24/26, Hemingway refers to *SAR* as "the pig that you bought in a poke."

6. *Men Without Women.* October 14, 1927. 7,650 copies. Published, like the rest of Hemingway's work, by Scribner's. Note: By this date Hemingway's reputation as a writer was fairly firmly established. In a letter to Perkins dated 10/1/27, he pointed out that he now had 2 British, 1 Danish, 1 Swedish, 1 French, and 1 German publisher. It is also interesting to recall that in a letter to Perkins of 2/3/30 Hemingway recorded that motion picture interests had paid him $500 for the title, *Men Without Women.* They wanted it to tack on to a picture about men in a disabled submarine, which of course had nothing to do with the contents of Hemingway's short story collection. The order of the stories in *Men Without Women* was the same as that followed in the collected edition of 1938, pp. 331–469. The hitherto unpublished stories in *MWW* were: A Simple Enquiry, Ten Indians, A Pursuit Race, Now I Lay Me. The other ten had appeared before. See below, section III.

7. *A Farewell to Arms.* September 27, 1929. 31,000 copies. Scribner's. Note: This book was Hemingway's first conspicuous success in terms of sales. By 2/14/30, roughly four months after publication, sales stood at 79,251, an average of about 20,000 copies a month.

8. *In Our Time.* October 24, 1930. 3,000 copies. Scribner's. Note: This is a Scribner re-issue of the Boni and Liveright edition of 1925, from which it differs in several particulars, chiefly a new "introduction" by Hemingway, consisting of a miniature later entitled "On the Quai at Smyrna" (see *First 49,* pp. 185–186), and a specially prepared critical essay by Edmund Wilson. For data on minutiae in this connection see Cohn's bibliography, pp. 39–40.

9. *Death in the Afternoon.* September 23, 1932. 10,300 copies. Scribner's. Note: Besides the account of bullfighting, this handbook is diversified with a few short stories, mostly not otherwise "collected." The exception is "A Natural History of the Dead," which was included as a separate story in the *First 49* (1938).

10. *Winner Take Nothing.* October 27, 1933. 20,300 copies. Scribner's. Note: This collection of short stories follows the same order as those on pp. 470–597 of the *First 49.* This was the first appearance of six of the fourteen stories: The Light of the World, A Way You'll Never Be, The Mother of a Queen, One Reader Writes, A Day's Wait, Fathers and Sons. It may also be noted that The Gambler, The Nun, and The Radio was a new title; the story when it first appeared in *Scribner's Magazine* for April, 1933, had been called by the much less apt title: Give Us a Prescription, Doctor.

11. *The Green Hills of Africa.* October 25, 1935. 10,550 copies. Scribner's. Note: Despite serialization in *Scribner's Magazine,* this book went less well than had been anticipated. Perkins wrote Hemingway 2/27/36 that the public had chosen to take *GHOA* as an "interlude." Another factor, which likewise had worked against *DIA* three years earlier, was the Depression.
12. *To Have and Have Not.* October 15, 1937. 10,130 copies. Scribner's. Note: Two of the three stories of Harry Morgan had already appeared as short stories: One Trip Across in *Cosmopolitan* for April 1934 (cf. *THAHN,* pp. 3–64); and The Tradesman's Return in *Esquire* for February 1936 (cf. *THAHN,* pp. 67–87).
13. *The Spanish Earth.* June 15, 1938. 1,000 copies. J. B. Savage Company, Cleveland, Ohio. Note: This book consists of a transcript of the spoken commentary prepared by Hemingway for the Loyalist film of the same title, together with a reprint of the autobiographical essay, "The Heat and the Cold," from the magazine *Verve.* For further information on this book see the footnote on *The Spanish Earth* in the tenth chapter of the present volume.
14. *The Fifth Column and the First Forty-nine Stories.* October 14, 1938. 5,350 copies. Scribner's. Note: This is the collected edition of the short stories, and comprises the contents of *IOT, MWW,* and *WTN.* This is the first printing of the play, and there are four hitherto uncollected stories: The Capital of the World, Old Man at the Bridge, The Short Happy Life of Francis Macomber, The Snows of Kilimanjaro. These had all, however, been printed before in magazines. The Capital of the World is a new title, replacing the title, The Horns of the Bull, which the story had when it first appeared in *Esquire* for June 1936. Old Man at the Bridge, originally a news despatch, had appeared in *Ken* in May 1938.
15. *The Fifth Column.* June 3, 1940. 1,174 copies. Scribner's. Note: This is a separate edition of the play. It was apparently brought out in connection with the production of the play on Broadway in this year.
16. *For Whom the Bell Tolls.* October 21, 1940. 75,000 copies. Scribner's. Note: This was Hemingway's most successful book. By December 28, about nine weeks after publication, sales stood at 189,000 copies. By April 4, 1941, sales had risen to 491,000 copies, and some 565,000 copies were in print.
17. *For Whom the Bell Tolls.* October 1942. 1,500 copies. Printed by Princeton University Press for the Limited Editions Club of New York. Contains a prefatory appreciation by Sinclair Lewis, and decorations by Lynd Ward.
18. *Men at War.* October 22, 1942. Crown Publishers, New York. Edited and with an introduction by Hemingway. Contains the Caporetto retreat sequence from *FTA* and the El Sordo hilltop episode from *FWBT,* as well as "The Chauffeurs of Madrid."

19. *A Farewell to Arms.* November 15, 1948. 5,300 copies. Scribner's. New illustrated edition with a short introduction by Hemingway.
20. *Across the River and Into the Trees.* September 7, 1950. 75,000 copies. Scribner's.
21. *The Old Man and the Sea.* September 8, 1952. 51,700 copies. Scribner's.
22. *A Moveable Feast.* May 5, 1964. 83,800 copies. Scribner's. The first posthumous publication.
23. *Islands in the Stream.* October 6, 1970. 75,000 copies.
24. *The Nick Adams Stories.* April 17, 1972. 25,000 copies. Stories appear in chronological order, with eight previously unpublished items.

II. PAMPHLETS

1. *Today Is Friday.* Summer [probably July] 1926. 300 copies. The As Stable Pamphlets, Englewood, New Jersey. Hemingway's first "play" appeared in *MWW* (and in the *First 49*) as a story.
2. *God Rest You Merry Gentlemen.* 1933. 300 copies. The House of Books, Limited, New York. Note: This is a special limited edition of a short story which was evidently based on Hemingway's experiences as a cub reporter for the *Kansas City Star* in 1917.

III. WORK WHICH FIRST APPEARED IN PERIODICALS OR ANTHOLOGIES

This section includes short stories (ss), poems (P), articles (A), letters (L), and despatches (D). Initials following a number of the entries indicate the book in which the stories were first collected. It should be noted that those stories which first appeared in the various collections are not included here. For a listing of these, see section I, items 2, 3, 6, 8, and 10. Abbreviations used here follow the custom of the present volume: *iot* (*in our time*, Paris, 1924); *IOT* (*In Our Time*, New York, 1925); *MWW* (*Men Without Women*); *WTN* (*Winner Take Nothing*); and *First 49* (*The Fifth Column and the First Forty-nine Stories*).

American Caravan: A Yearbook of American Literature, ed. Van Wyck Brooks, New York, September 1927. Contains (ss) "An Alpine Idyll," pp. 46–51. *MWW.*

Atlantic Monthly:
ss Fifty Grand. Vol. 140, July 1927, pp. 1–15. *MWW.*
ss Get a Seeing Eye Dog. Vol. 200, November, 1957, pp. 66–68.
ss Man of the World. Vol. 200, November, 1957, pp. 64–66.

The Boulevardier (Paris):
A The Real Spaniard. Vol. 1, October 1927, p. 6.

Collier's:
D Voyage to Victory. Vol. 114, July 22, 1944, pp. 11–13, 56–57.
D London Fights the Robots. Vol. 114, August 19, 1944, pp. 17, 80–81.
D Battle for Paris. Vol. 114, September 30, 1944, pp. 11, 83–86.
D How We Came to Paris. Vol. 114, October 7, 1944, pp. 14, 65–67.
D The G.I. and the General. Vol. 114, November 4, 1944, pp. 11, 46–47.
D War in the Siegfried Line. Vol. 114, November 18, 1944, pp. 18, 70–73.

Contact Collection of Contemporary Writers, published Paris, 1925. Contains (ss) "Soldier's Home," pp. 77–86. *IOT.*

Cosmopolitan:
SS After the Storm. Vol. 92, May 1932, pp. 38–41, 155. *WTN.*
SS One Trip Across. Vol. 96, April 1934, pp. 20–23, 108–122. (The first section of *THAHN.*)
SS The Short Happy Life of Francis Macomber. Vol. 101, September 1936, pp. 30–33, 166–172. *First 49.*
SS Nobody Ever Dies. Vol. 106, March 1939, pp. 29–31, 74–76.
SS Under the Ridge. Vol. 107, October 1939, pp. 34–35, 102–106. (This story turns on the Spanish hatred of foreign interlopers, a point very well underlined in *FWBT.*)

Double Dealer (New Orleans):
FABLE A Divine Gesture. Vol. 3, May 1922, pp. 267–268.
P Ultimately. Vol. 3, June 1922, p. 337.

Esquire (This listing prepared by Mr. Stephen Parker):
L Marlin off the Morro. Vol. 1, Autumn 1933, pp. 8, 39, 97.
L The Friend of Spain. Vol. 1, January 1934, pp. 26, 136.
L A Paris Letter. Vol. 1, February 1934, pp. 22, 156.
L a.d. in Africa. Vol. 1, April 1934, pp. 19, 146.
L Shootism vs. Sport. Vol. 2, June 1934, pp. 19, 150.
L Notes on Dangerous Game. Vol. 2, July 1934, pp. 19, 94.
L Out in the Stream. Vol. 2, August 1934, pp. 19, 156, 158.
L Defense of Dirty Words. Vol. 2, September 1934, pp. 19, 158B, 158D.
L Genio after Josie. Vol. 2, October 1934, pp. 21–22.
L Old Newsman Writes. Vol. 2, December 1934, pp. 25–26.
L Notes on Life and Letters. Vol. 3, January 1935, pp. 21, 159.
L Remembering Shooting Flying. Vol. 3, February 1935, pp. 21, 152.
L Sailfish off Mombasa. Vol. 3, March 1935, pp. 21, 156.

L The Sights of Whitehead Street. Vol. 3, April 1935, pp. 25, 156.
L a.d. Southern Style. Vol. 3, May 1935, pp. 25, 156.
L On Being Shot Again. Vol. 3, June 1935, pp. 25, 156–157.
L The President Vanquishes. Vol. 3, July 1935, pp. 23, 167.
L He Who Gets Slap Happy. Vol. 4, August 1935, pp. 19, 182.
L Notes on the Next War. Vol. 4, September 1935, pp. 19, 156.
L Monologue to the Maestro. Vol. 4, October 1935, pp. 21, 174A, 174B.
L The Malady of Power. Vol. 4, November 1935, pp. 31, 198–199.
L Million Dollar Fright. Vol. 4, December 1935, pp. 35, 190B.
L Wings Always Over Africa. Vol. 5, January 1936, pp. 31, 174–175.
ss The Tradesman's Return. Vol. 5, February 1936, pp. 27, 193–196. (The second section of *THAHN*.)
L On the Blue Water. Vol. 5, April 1936, pp. 31, 184–185.
L There She Breaches. Vol. 5, May 1936, pp. 35, 203–205. Also Gattorno-Program Note, pp. 111, 141, reprinted from *Gattorno,* Havana, 1935.
ss The Horns of the Bull. Vol. 5, June 1936, pp. 31, 190–193. (*First 49,* where it was retitled: The Capital of the World.)
ss The Snows of Kilimanjaro. Vol. 6, August 1936, pp. 27, 194–201. *First 49.*
ss The Denunciation. Vol. 10, November 1938, pp. 39, 111–114.
ss The Butterfly and the Tank. Vol. 10, December 1938, pp. 51, 186, 188, 190.
ss Night Before Battle. Vol. 11, February 1939, pp. 27–29, 91–92, 95, 97.

Exile:
P Nothoemist Poem. (Misprint for *Neothomist Poem.*) Vol. 1, Spring 1927.

Fact:
D The Spanish War, No. 16, July 15, 1938, pp. 7–72. (The Saving of Madrid, pp. 7–33; The Aragon Front, pp. 34–40; Teruel, pp. 41–51; Franco Advancing, pp. 52–67; and Last Despatches, pp. 68–72, all reprinted from North American Newspaper Alliance despatches, slightly abridged.)

Fortune:
A Bullfighting, Sport and Industry. Vol. 1, March 1930, pp. 83–88, 139–150.

Free World:
A The Sling and the Pebble. Vol. 11, March 1946, pp. 16–17.

Holiday:

A The Great Blue River. Vol. 6, July 1949, pp. 60–63, 95–97.
FABLE The Good Lion. Vol. 9, March 1951, pp. 50–51.
FABLE The Faithful Bull. Vol. 9, March 1951, p. 51.

Ken:

A The Time Now, the Place Spain. Vol. 1, April 7, 1938, pp. 36–37.
A Dying, Well or Badly. Vol. 1, April 21, 1938, p. 68.
A The Cardinal Picks a Winner. Vol. 1, May 5, 1938, p. 38.
SS Old Man at the Bridge. Vol. 1, May 19, 1938, p. 36. *First 49.*
A United We Fall upon Ken. Vol. 1, June 2, 1938, p. 38.
A H.M.'s Loyal State Department. Vol. 1, June 16, 1938, p. 36.
A Treachery in Aragon. Vol. 1, June 30, 1938, p. 26.
A Call for Greatness. Vol. 2, July 14, 1938, p. 23.
A My Pal the Gorilla Gargantua. Vol. 2, July 28, 1938, p. 26.
A A Program for U.S. Realism. Vol. 2, August 11, 1938, p. 26.
A Good Generals Hug the Line. Vol. 2, August 25, 1938, p. 28.
A False News to the President. Vol. 2, September 8, 1938, pp. 17–18.
A Fresh Air on an Inside Story. Vol. 2, September 22, 1938, p. 28.
A The Next Outbreak of Peace. Vol. 3, January 12, 1939, pp. 12–13.

Library Journal:

L Hemingway Pays his Respects to Oak Park Library. Vol. 79, February 15, 1954, p. 292.

Life:

SS The Old Man and the Sea. Vol. 33, September 1, 1952, pp. 35–54.
A The Dangerous Summer. Vol. 49, September 5, 1960, pp. 77–109; September 12, 1960, pp. 60–82; September 19, 1960, pp. 74–96.

Little Review:

SS [Six miniatures]. Vol. 9, Spring 1923, pp. 3–5. *iot,* chapters 1–6.
P They All Made Peace. What Is Peace? Vol. 9, Spring 1923, pp. 20–21.
SS Mr. and Mrs. Elliot. Vol. 10, Autumn and Winter 1924–1925, pp. 9–12. *IOT.*
SS Banal Story. Vol. 12, Spring–Summer 1926, pp. 22–23. *MWW.*
P Valentine. Vol. 12, May 1929, p. 42. There is a short covering letter on p. 41.

Look:

A Safari. Vol. 18, January 26, 1954, pp. 19–34.

A The Christmas Gift. Vol. 18, April 20, 1954, pp. 29–37; May 4, 1954, pp. 79–89.

  Africa: Happy Is the Dream. Vol. 19, November 15, 1955, pp. 38–39.

  (Excerpt from *GHOA*)

A A Visit with Hemingway. Vol. 20, September 4, 1956, pp. 23–31.

  (Hemingway wrote the text and the captions for the photographs.)

New Masses:

A Who Murdered the Vets? Vol. 16, September 17, 1935, pp. 9–10.

A On the American Dead in Spain. Vol. 30, February 14, 1939, p. 3.

New Republic:

ss Italy, 1927. Vol. 50, May 18, 1927, pp. 350–353. *MWW*, with the new title, "Che Ti Dice La Patria."

D Hemingway Reports Spain. Vols. 90, May 5, 1937, pp. 376–379; 93, January 12, 1938, pp. 273–276; 94, April 27, 1938, pp. 350–351; and 95, June 8, 1938, pp. 124–126. These are 18 reprints of Hemingway's original NANA despatches.

New Yorker:

A My Own Life. Vol. 2, February 12, 1927, pp. 23–24.

Poetry: A Magazine of Verse:

P Wanderings [general title for 6 poems]. Vol. 21, January 1923, pp. 193–195. Note: the poem, "They All Made Peace. What Is Peace?" was reprinted in the course of an article in *Poetry*, vol. 37, February 1931. It had originally appeared in *The Little Review* for Spring 1923.

Querschnitt:

P The Soul of Spain with McAlmon and Bird the Publishers, [Part I.] Vol. 4, Autumn 1924, pp. 229–230.

P The Earnest Liberal's Lament. Vol. 4, Autumn 1924, p. 231.

P The Soul of Spain with McAlmon and Bird the Publishers, [Parts II–VI.] Vol. 4, November 1924, p. 278. Note: Part VI is a miniature on the death of a bull.

P The Lady Poets with Foot Notes. Vol. 4, November 1924, p. 317.

P The Age Demanded. Vol. 5, February 1925, p. 111.

ss The Undefeated. Published in two parts, Vol. 5, Summer 1925 and July 1925, and here entitled "Stierkampf." Appeared also as "L'Invincible" in *Le Navire d'Argent,* Vol. 2, March 1926, pp. 161–194. For English version, see below under *This Quarter.*

ss The Man with the Tyrolese Hat. Vol. 16, June 1936, pp. 355–356. Note: This is the extract about Kandisky from *GHOA.*

Saturday Review:
L Letter from Hemingway to Bernard Kalb. Vol. 35, September 6, 1952, p. 11.

Scribner's Magazine:
ss The Killers. Vol. 81, March 1927, pp. 227–233. *MWW.*
ss In Another Country. Vol. 81, April 1927, pp. 355–357. *MWW.*
ss A Canary for One. Vol. 81, April 1927, pp. 357–360. *MWW.*
ss Wine of Wyoming. Vol. 88, August 1930, pp. 195–204. *WTN.*
ss A Clean Well-lighted Place. Vol. 93, March 1933, pp. 149–150. *WTN.*
ss Homage to Switzerland. Vol. 93, April 1933, pp. 204–208. *WTN.*
ss Give Us a Prescription, Doctor. Vol. 93, May 1933, pp. 272–278. Note: Retitled in *WTN:* The Gambler, The Nun, and the Radio.

This Quarter:
ss Big Two Hearted River. Vol. 1, May 1925, pp. 110–128. *IOT.*
A Homage to Ezra [Pound]. Vol. 1, May 1925, pp. 221–225.
ss The Undefeated. Vol. 1, Autumn–Winter 1925–1926, pp. 203–232. *MWW.*
ss The Sea Change. Vol. 4, December 1931, pp. 247–251. *WTN.*

transatlantic review:
ss Work in Progress. Vol. 1, April 1924, pp. 230–234. Note: Entitled in *IOT:* Indian Camp.
L And to the United States. The Quarter. Early Spring. Vol. 1, May–June 1924, pp. 355–357. Note: Hemingway here comments that "Dada is dead" and refers to the boxer Criqui (p. 356) "in the contemplation of whose work I experience a certain ecstasy which is not given me by reading the works of my contemporaries."
A And Out of America. Vol. 2, August 1924, pp. 102–103.
L Pamplona Letter. Vol. 2, October 1924, pp. 300–302.
A Conrad. Vol. 2, October 1924, pp. 341–342.
ss The Doctor and the Doctor's Wife. Vol. 2, December 1924, pp. 497–501. *IOT.*
ss Cross Country Snow. Vol. 2, January 1925, pp. 633–638. *IOT.*

transition:
ss Hills Like White Elephants. Vol. 5, August 1927, pp. 9–14.
   MWW.

True:
A The Shot. Vol. 28, April 1951, pp. 25–28.

Verve:
A The Heat and the Cold. Vol. 1, Spring 1938, p. 46. Note: This
   issue covered the period March–June, and appeared in June.
   The essay was almost immediately reprinted in the published
   version of *The Spanish Earth*. Section 1, item 13.

Vogue:
A The Clark's Fork Valley, Wyoming. Vol. 93, February 1939,
   pp. 68, 157.

IV. INTRODUCTIONS, PREFACES, FOREWORDS, CONTRIBUTIONS

Jerome Bahr, *All Good Americans*. New York, 1937. Preface by
   Hemingway.
James Charters, *This Must Be the Place*. London, 1934. Introduction
   by Hemingway. [The actual author of the book was Morrill Cody.]
S. K. Farrington, Jr., *Atlantic Game Fishing*. New York, 1937. Intro-
   duction by Hemingway.
Henry Goodman, ed., *Creating the Short Story*, New York, 1929.
   Contains "Who Knows How?"—Hemingway on "The Killers," p.
   121.
John Groth, *Studio Europe*. New York, 1945. Introduction by Hem-
   ingway.
Henry Hart, ed., *The Writer in a Changing World*. New York, 1937.
   Contains Hemingway's speech to the Writers' Congress.
Joseph North, *Men in the Ranks*. New York, March 1939. Foreword
   by Hemingway, pp. 3–4.
Samuel Putnam, translator, *Kiki's Memoirs*. Paris, 1930. Preface by
   Hemingway. For interesting bibliographical data see Cohn's Bib-
   liography.
Luis Quintanilla (in collaboration with Elliot Paul and Jay Allen),
   All the Brave. New York, 1939. Preface by Hemingway, p. 7.
Ben Raeburn, ed., *Treasury for the Free World*. New York, February
   1946. Foreword by Hemingway.
Gustav Regler, *The Great Crusade*. New York, 1940. Preface by
   Hemingway.
Charles Ritz, *A Fly Fisher's Life*. New York, 1959. Foreword by
   Hemingway.
Lee Samuels, *A Hemingway Check List*. New York, August 1951.
   Preface by Hemingway.

Georges Schreiber, *Portraits and Self Portraits.* Boston, 1936. Contains self-portrait by Hemingway, p. 57.

Elio Vittorini, *In Sicily.* New York, 1949. Introduction by Hemingway.

V. OBSERVATIONS ON ART AND ARTISTS

Gattorno. Havana, Cuba, April 1935. This publication includes a valuable commentary on the work of Gattorno by Hemingway (pp. 11–16). This article was later reprinted in *Esquire* Vol. 5, May 1936, pp. 111, 141.

Henrietta Hoopes. New York, 1940. Leaflet containing Hemingway's note on her paintings.

Joan Miro. New York, 1934. Leaflet containing first printing of part of an article on Miro which later appeared in *Cahiers d'Art.*

Waldo Peirce. For some humorous observations by Hemingway on his good friend Peirce, see Harry Salpeter, "Rabelais in a Smock," *Esquire,* Vol. 5, July 1936, pp. 101, 118, 121–122.

Quintanilla. Pierre Matisse Gallery Catalogue, *Exhibition of Drawings and Paintings by Luis Quintanilla.* New York, November 20 to December 4, 1934. Contains appraisal of Quintanilla's work by Hemingway. The article was later reprinted in *Esquire,* Vol. 3, February 1935, pp. 26–27.

See also *Quintanilla: An Exhibition of Drawings of the War in Spain.* Museum of Modern Art, New York, March 1938. Contains a preface by Hemingway.

VI. DESPATCHES FROM THE FAR EAST

The newspaper *PM.* Between June 10 and June 18, 1941, this newspaper printed seven despatches from Hemingway on the situation in the Far East six to seven months before Pearl Harbor; preceding these was an interview, edited by Hemingway.

Story of Ernest Hemingway's Far East Trip To See for Himself if War with Japan Is Inevitable. By Ralph Ingersoll. June 9, 1941, pp. 6–10.

Russo-Jap Pact Hasn't Kept Soviet From Sending Aid to China. June 10, 1941, pp. 4–5.

We Can't Let Japan Grab Our Rubber Supplies in Dutch East Indies. June 11, 1941, p. 6.

Japan Must Conquer China or Satisfy USSR Before Moving South. June 13, 1941, p. 6.

Aid to China Gives U.S. Two-Ocean Navy Security For Price of One Battleship. June 15, 1941, p. 6.

After Four Years of War in China Japs Have Conquered Only Flat Lands. June 16, 1941, p. 6.

China Needs Pilots As Well as Planes to Beat Japanese in the Air. June 17, 1941, p. 5.
How 100,000 Chinese Labored Night and Day to Build Huge Landing Field for Bombers. June 18, 1941, pp. 16–17.

VII. CONTRIBUTIONS TO *THE TORONTO STAR WEEKLY*

Although Hemingway distinguished between journalism and serious writing (see his opinion in Captain Cohn's bibliography, p. 112), a few of his stories were first published as journalism in newspapers and magazines. A collection of 73 of his 141 identifiable articles in *The Toronto Star Weekly* and *The Toronto Daily Star* was published as *The Wild Years,* Edited and Introduced by Gene Z. Hanrahan, New York, Dell Publishing Co., Inc., 1962. Those articles listed below which appear in the Hanrahan volume are designated *WY.* (In 58 instances, titles have been changed.)

Circulating Pictures a New High-Art Idea in Toronto. February 14, 1920, p. 7, unsigned.
Taking a Chance for a Free Shave. March 6, 1920, p. 13. *WY.*
Sporting Mayor at Boxing Bouts. March 13, 1920, p. 10. *WY.*
How to Be Popular in Peace Though a Slacker in War. March 13, 1920, p. 11. *WY.*
Store Thieves Use Three Tricks. April 3, 1920, pp. 9, 12. *WY.*
Are You All Set for the Trout? April 10, 1920, p. 11, unsigned.
Toothpulling Not a Cure-for-All. April 10, 1920, p. 12.
Stores in the Wilds Graveyards of Style. April 24, 1920, p. 11. *WY.*
Fishing for Trout in a Sporting Way. April 24, 1920, p. 13. *WY.*
Keeping Up with the Jones the Tragedy of the Other Half. May 1, 1920, p. 12.
Toronto Women Who Went to the Prize Fights Applauded the Rough Stuff. May 15, 1920, p. 13.
Canuck Whiskey Pouring into U. S. June 5, 1920, p. 1. *WY.*
It's Time to Bury the Hamilton Gag, Comedians Have Worked It to Death. June 12, 1920, p. 1.
When You Camp Out Do It Right. June 26, 1920, p. 17. *WY.*
When You Go Camping Take Lots of Skeeter Dope and Don't Ever Lose It. August 7, 1920, p. 11. *WY.*
The Best Rainbow Trout Fishing in the World [Is at the Canadian Soo]. August 28, 1920, p. 24. *WY.*
The Average Yank Divides Canadians into Two Classes—Wild and Tame. October 9, 1920, p. 13.
Carpentier Sure to Give Dempsey Fight Worth While. October 30, 1920, p. 8.
The Wild West Is Now in Chicago. November 6, 1920, pp. 9, 13.

No Danger of Commercial Tie-Up Because Men Carry Too Much Money. November 6, 1920, general and fiction section, p. 11.

A Fight with a 20-Pound Trout. November 20, 1920, pp. 25, 26. *WY.*

Plain and Fancy Killings, $400 Up. December 11, 1920, pp. 25, 26. *WY.*

Why Not Trade Other Public Entertainers Among the Nations as the Big Leagues Do Baseball Players. February 19, 1921, p. 13.

Our Confidential Vacation Guide. May 21, 1921, p. 21. *WY.*

Gun-Men's Wild Political War On in Chicago. May 28, 1921, p. 21. *WY.*

Chicago Never Wetter than It Is To-day. July 2, 1921, p. 21. *WY.*

Condensing the Classics. August 20, 1921, p. 22.

Cheap Nitrates Will Mean Cheaper Bread. November 12, 1921, p. 11.

On Weddynge Gyftes. December 17, 1921, p. 15. Contains a free-verse poem by Hemingway. *WY.*

Tourists Are Scarce at the Swiss Resorts. February 4, 1922, p. 3. *WY.*

At Vigo, in Spain, Is Where You Catch the Silver and Blue Tuna, the King of All Fish. February 18, 1922, p. 15. *WY.*

Exchange Pirates Hit by German Export Tax. February 25, 1922, p. 10.

Behind the Scenes at Papal Elections. March 4, 1922, p. 3.

Queer Mixture of Aristocrats, Profiteers, Sheep and Wolves at the Hotels in Switzerland. March 4, 1922, p. 25. *WY.*

Wives Buy Clothes for French Husbands. March 11, 1922, p. 12. *WY.*

How'd You Like to Tip Postman Every Time? March 11, 1922, p. 13. *WY.*

Sparrow Hat Appears on Paris Boulevards. March 18, 1922, p. 12. *WY.*

Flivver, Canoe, Pram and Taxi Combined Is the Luge, the Joy of Everybody in Switzerland. March 18, 1922, p. 15. *WY.*

Prize-Winning Book Is Centre of Storm. March 25, 1922, p. 3.

American Bohemians in Paris a Weird Lot. March 25, 1922, p. 15. *WY.*

Wild Night Music of Paris Makes Visitor Feel a Man of the World. March 25, 1922, p. 22. *WY.*

French Politeness. April 15, 1922, p. 29. *WY.*

"Pot-Shot Patriots" Unpopular in Italy. June 24, 1922, p. 5. *WY.*

Expecting Too Much in Old London Town. August 5, 1922, p. 17.

Latest Drink Scandal Now Agitates Paris. August 12, 1922, p. 11. *WY.*

Riots Are Frequent Throughout Germany. September 30, 1922, p. 16. *WY.*

King Business in Europe Isn't What It Used to Be. September 15, 1923, p. 15. *WY.*

Cope Denies Hearst Paying Lloyd George. October 6, 1923, p. 1.

Lloyd George Attends Theatre in New York. October 6, 1923, p. 2.

Bull Fighting Is Not a Sport—It Is a Tragedy. October 20, 1923, p. 33. *WY.*

World's Series of Bullfighting a Mad, Whirling Carnival. October 27, 1923, p. 33. *WY.*

More Game to Shoot in Crowded Europe than in Ontario [Forests and Animals Are Really Protected Over There]. November 3, 1923, p. 20. *WY.*

Cheer Up! The Lakes Aren't Going Dry: High Up and Low Down Is Just Their Habit. November 17, 1923, p. 18, John Hadley byline.

Trout Fishing All Across Europe: Spain Has the Best, Then Germany. November 17, 1923, p. 19. *WY.*

Gen. Wolfe's Diaries Saved for Canada. November 24, 1923, p. 19.

Learns to Commune With the Fairies: Now Wins the $40,000 Nobel Prize [W. B. Yeats]. November 24, 1923, p. 35, unsigned.

Fifty-Ton Doors Laugh at Robbers' Tools: Bank Vaults Defy Scientific Cracksmen. December 1, 1923, p. 33. *WY.*

German Marks Make Last Stand as Real Money in Toronto's "Ward." December 8, 1923, p. 18, John Hadley byline. *WY.*

Lots of War Medals for Sale But Nobody Will Buy Them. December 8, 1923, p. 21. *WY.*

Night Life in Europe a Disease: Constantinople's Most Hectic. December 15, 1923, p. 21. *WY.*

Dose Whole City's Water Supply to Cure Goiter by Mass Medication. December 15, 1923, p. 33, John Hadley byline.

Christmas on the Roof of the World. December 22, 1923, p. 19.

Toronto "Red" Children Don't Know Santa Claus. December 22, 1923, p. 33.

W. B. Yeats a Night Hawk: Kept Toronto Host Up. December 22, 1923, p. 35, unsigned.

Toronto Is Biggest Betting Place in North America—10,000 People Bet $100,000 on Horses Every Day. December 29, 1923, p. 17. *WY.*

Wild New Year's Eve Party Gone Forever: Only Ghost of 1914 Party Remains. December 29, 1923, p. 20, John Hadley byline.

Weird, Wild Adventures of Some of Our Modern Amateur Imposters. December 29, 1923, pp. 20–21. *WY.*

Ski-ers Only Escape from Alpine Avalanche Is to Swim! [Snow Slides off Mountain as Fast as off Roof of House]. January 12, 1924, p. 20. *WY.*

So This Is Chicago. January 19, 1924, p. 19.

Must Wear Hats Like Other Folks If You Live in Toronto. January 19, 1924, p. 33.

Tackling a Spanish Bull Is "Just Like Rugby": Hemingway Tells He Surprised the Natives. September 13, 1924, p. 18.

VIII. CONTRIBUTIONS TO *THE TORONTO DAILY STAR*

Builder, Not Fighter, Is What France Wants. February 18, 1922, p. 7.
Influx of Russians to All Parts of Paris. February 25, 1922, p. 29.
Try Bob-Sledding If You Want Thrills. March 4, 1922, p. 9.
Poincaire Making Good on Election Promises. March 11, 1922, p. 13.
The Mecca of Fakers Is French Capital. March 25, 1922, p. 4.
Much Feared Man Is Monsieur Deibler. April 1, 1922, p. 7.
95,000 Now Wearing The Legion of Honour. April 1, 1922, p. 7.
Anti-Alcohol League Is Active in France. April 8, 1922, p. 13.
World Economic Conference Opens in Genoa: Tchitcherin Speaks. April 10, 1922, p. 1. *WY.*
Jap Presence at Genoa Protested by Russia. April 11, 1922, p. 1.
Picked Sharpshooters Patrol Genoa Streets. April 13, 1922, p. 17. *WY.*
Regarded by Allies as German Cunning. April 18, 1922, p. 1. A few lines.
Two Russian Girls the Best Looking at Genoa Parley. April 24, 1922, p. 1. *WY.*
Barthou, Like a Smith Brother, Crosses Hissing Tchitcherin. April 24, 1922, p. 2. *WY.*
Strangest Premier in Parley Is Stamboulski of Bulgaria. April 25, 1922, p. 5.
Schober of Austria, at Genoa Looks Every Inch a Chancellor. April 26, 1922, p. 9.
Russian Delegates at Genoa Appear Not to Be of This World. April 27, 1922, p. 9.
German Delegation at Genoa Keep Stinnes in Background. April 28, 1922, p. 9.
Getting a Hot Bath an Adventure in Genoa. May 2, 1922, p. 5.
Russian Delegation Well Guarded at Genoa. May 4, 1922, p. 10.
German Journalists a Strange Collection. May 8, 1922, p. 3.
All Genoa Goes Crazy Over New Betting Game. May 9, 1922, p. 2.
Lloyd George Gives Magic to the Parley. May 13, 1922, p. 7.
There Are Great Fish in the Rhone Canal. June 10, 1922, p. 5. *WY.*
Fascisti Party Now Half-Million Strong. June 24, 1924, p. 16. *WY.*
A Veteran Visits Old Front, Wishes He Had Stayed Away. July 22, 1922, p. 7.
Did Poincaire Laugh in Verdun Cemetery? August 12, 1922, p. 4.
Rug Vendor Is Fixture in Parisian Life. August 12, 1922, p. 5.
Old Order Changeth in Alsace-Lorraine. August 26, 1922, p. 4.
Takes to the Water: Solves Flat Problem. August 26, 1922, p. 8.

Germans Are Doggedly Sullen or Desperate Over the Mark. September 1, 1922, p. 23. *WY.*

Once Over Permit Obstacle Fishing in Baden Perfect. September 2, 1922, p. 28. *WY.*

German Inn-Keepers Rough Dealing with "Auslanders." September 5, 1922, p. 9. *WY.*

A Paris-to-Strasbourg Flight Shows Living Cubist Picture. September 9, 1922, p. 8. *WY.*

Crossing to Germany Is Way to Make Money. September 19, 1922, p. 4. *WY.*

British Strong Enough to Save Constantinople. September 30, 1922, p. 1. *WY.*

Hubby Dines First: Wifie Gets Crumbs! September 30, 1922, p. 9. *WY.*

Turk Red Crescent Propaganda Agency. October 4, 1922, p. 1.

Hamid Bey Wears Shirt Tucked In When Seen by Star. October 9, 1922, p. 1. *WY.*

Balkans Look Like Ontario: A Picture of Peace, Not War. October 16, 1922, p. 13.

Constantinople, Dirty White, Not Glistening and Sinister. October 18, 1922, p. 17.

Constantinople Cut-Throats Await Chance for an Orgy. October 19, 1922, p. 4.

A Silent, Ghastly Procession Wends Way from Thrace. October 20, 1922, p. 17. *WY.*

Russia to Spoil the French Game with Kemalists. October 23, 1922, p. 13. *WY.*

Turks Beginning to Show Distrust of Kemal Pasha. October 24, 1922, p. 17. *WY.*

Censor Too "Thorough" in the Near East Crisis. October 25, 1922, p. 7. *WY.*

"Old Constan" in True Light; Is Tough Town. October 28, 1922, p. 17. *WY.*

Kemal Has Afgans Ready to Make Trouble for Britain. October 31, 1922, p. 5. *WY.*

Betrayal Preceded Defeat, Then Came Greek Revolt. November 3, 1922, p. 10. *WY.*

Destroyers Were on Lookout for Kemal's One Submarine. November 10, 1922, p. 12.

Refugee Procession Is Scene of Horror. November 14, 1922, p. 7. *WY.*

Mussolini, Europe's Prize Bluffer, More Like Bottomley than Napoleon. January 27, 1923, p. 11. *WY.*

Gaudy Uniform Is Tchitcherin's Weakness: A "Chocolate Soldier" of the Soviet Army. February 10, 1923, p. 2. *WY.*

Will France Have a King Again? April 13, 1923, p. 29, viz. ad for forthcoming series.

A Victory Without Peace Forced the French to Undertake the Occupation of the Ruhr. April 14, 1923, p. 4. *WY.*

French Royalist Party Most Solidly Organized. April 18, 1923, pp. 1, 4. *WY.*

Government Pays for News in French Papers. April 21, 1923, pp. 1, 7. *WY.*

Ruhr Commercial War Question of Bankruptcy. April 25, 1923, pp. 1, 2. *WY.*

A Brave Belgian Lady Shuts up German Hater. April 28, 1923, pp. 1, 2. *WY.*

Getting into Germany Quite a Job, Nowadays. May 2, 1923, pp. 1, 28. *WY.*

Quite Easy to Spend a Million, If in Marks. May 5, 1923, pp. 1, 34. *WY.*

Amateur Starvers Keep Out of View in Germany. May 9, 1923, p. 17. *WY.*

Hate in Occupied Zone a Real, Concrete Thing. May 12, 1923, p. 19. *WY.*

French Register Speed When Movies Are on Job. May 16, 1923, p. 19.

Search for Sudbury Coal a Gamble: Driller Tells of What He Has Found. September 25, 1923, p. 4.

He's a Personality, No Doubt, But a Much Maligned One. October 4, 1923, p. 12, unsigned.

Ll. George up Early as Big Liner Arrives. October 5, 1923, p. 14.

Little Welshman Lands; Anxious to Play Golf. October 6, 1923, p. 3.

Wonderful Voice Is Chief Charm of Lloyd George. October 6, 1923, p. 17.

"A Man of the People, Will Fight for People." October 8, 1923, p. 14.

Index

Made in the USA
Lexington, KY
09 January 2012